MOVIES
INTO FILM

MOVIES
INTO FILM

Film Criticism

1967-1970

JOHN ⌐SIMON

The Dial Press   New York   1971

The author wishes to express his special indebtedness to *The New Leader,* where the bulk of the pieces in this book first appeared, and by whose permission they are here reprinted. He also wishes to thank the *Arts and Leisure* section and *The Book Review* of *The New York Times; Book World* of the *Washington Post* and *Chicago Tribune;* Commonweal Publishing Co., Inc.; *Film Heritage;* and *The Magazine,* for special permission to reprint "The Revolutionary," "The Activist," and *"Joe,"* © by Meredith Corporation, 1970.

Library of Congress Catalog Card Number: 77-144372

Printed in the United States of America

First Printing 1971

For Sharon who shared in the experience
And Karen who cared for the editing

Contents

MOVIES
INTO FILM

Introduction:
Movies into Film

In "A Critical Credo," the introduction to my previous collection of film criticism, *Private Screenings,* I set down the problems, requirements, and functions of film criticism and critics, as I see them. I have no wish to repeat myself here, beyond saying that I continue to believe that a film critic, or any other kind of critic, must be an artist, a teacher, and a philosopher, and that the ideal critique is itself a work of art as well as an explication of and meditation on the work of art it examines. What I want to speak about here is the change of status that both film and film criticism have been undergoing in recent years.

Not so very long ago—do not ask me for exact dates where none can be posited—one went to the movies. Of course, most people still go to the movies. But more than ever before we are aware of something bigger than movies, something that might be called film. Looked at casually, the two words seem synonymous; and so they are in the area of denotations. In the less explored realm of connotations, however, they are not quite the same. When a group that was to become the National Society of Film Critics pondered at its first meetings what name to settle on, some members, and notably Pauline Kael, argued for the term Movie Critics instead of Film Critics. Indeed, when Miss Kael took over as critic of—let's call it, for the moment, cinema—at *The New Republic,* she changed "Film" in the title of the column to "Movies." Returning to the magazine and that job, Stanley Kauffmann changed the heading back to "Film." And so at that first meeting, Kauffmann asked whether, if we called films movies, we would also call books printies?

There is, obviously, no harm in calling films movies, or cinema, or flicks, or anything else. Nevertheless, "movies" is a diminutive of "motion pictures," a somewhat cumbersome term much beloved of the Hollywood industry, which finds in its two-worded, quadrisyllabic sonorities a guarantee of respectabiity and importance. But a diminutive is not what one usually applies to an art. Not only are books not printies, but a non-motion picture is not a paintie, and a work of architecture is not Archie, and so on. To call film movies is, however fondly, to derogate from it; or, more precisely, to view it as an entertainment rather than as an art. The implication is that we go to the movies purely for fun, and to hell with the highbrows, scholars, and other squares who would try to turn a movie into Art, with a long-faced upper-case A, and a joyous experience into a cultural obligation.

This concept is widespread not only among the public, but also among critics. Men as different as Robert Brustein and Richard Schickel tend to think of film as principally fun; thus Schickel wrote about "a holiday feast (which is what the cinema ideally is)" and Hollis Alpert told me not long ago that a film could be artistic, but that he doubted its ever being a true work of art, like a novel. And so, instead of going to something with an international, and therefore fancily un-American, name like "film" (even though this is merely a new meaning for a good old Anglo-Saxon four-letter word), we go to something strictly American, homemade, unpretentious: the movies.

There is nothing wrong with enjoying film as an entertainment, any more than there is anything wrong with enjoying parlor games or conversation as an entertainment. But if film were merely an amusement, if it could not and should not go beyond that, there would be little need or justification for publishing books about it—mine or anyone else's. A book or two have been published about Scrabble, I dare say, but none, I hope, about charades: one enjoys such things without waxing analytical and critical. Books about chess and bridge exist in profusion, yet they seem to me ultimately frivolous, for a game is neither a science nor an art. And, indeed, such books can never be more than anecdotal or how-to-do-it books; criticism has nothing to do with how to win at something or other. And if critics like Pauline Kael and Andrew Sarris really thought of movies as only an entertainment (which, despite ambivalent statements, they don't), I doubt that either would write books about them.

As Miss Kael herself, among others, has pointed out, entertainment and art are not opposites. And, further, whereas not all entertainment—by a long shot—is art, all true art is entertaining. It may, however, be entertaining only for those who by a native endowment of intelligence and sensitivity or by education, training, and experience—and preferably by both—possess the wherewithal for being entertained by it. For example, to enjoy a play in French, you must know French; to enjoy French cooking, you may have to have some experience of food beyond hamburgers and so-called French fries—although here I say "may," not "must," there probably being such a thing as a naturally gifted though untrained palate. And to enjoy a serious debate about the possibility of love's surviving in the modern world—but a debate couched in the form of a work of art, say, a film of Ingmar Bergman's—you must have your mind sufficiently developed to find serious discussion bracing, and sufficient esthetic sensibility to be able to recognize such a debate in its fictional, filmic, artistic rather than dialectical, form. In this sense, I would define art as entertainment of the most far-ranging and penetrating sort; or, conversely, as matters of the most encompassing and profound human concern couched in the most moving or amusing, tragic or comic, form.

For the civilized person, then, art is the supreme type of entertainment, different from others chiefly by its greater human relevance or, more simply, truth. This does not, however, exclude the possibility or even the desirability (and, certainly, the acceptability) of a highly cultivated person's finding various forms of non-art entertaining. Only there need be a sense of distinctions, proportions, values. We must not confuse pleasures with higher pleasures, fleeting with lasting goods, laughter with laughter that taught us something, carefree moments with moments which, by making us face them, might actually free us from our cares.

I think we must accept man as a dual creature: whether we want to call him part angel, part beast; part Jekyll, part Hyde; part superego, part id; or any other kind of bipartite being, is immaterial. What matters is that he can enjoy both Bach and the Beatles, both Kafka and comic strips, both looking at a great dancer perform a perfect arabesque and watching a champion tennis player return an impossible smash. But it is wrong to call the tennis player an artist, wrong to prefer Superman to Joseph K., wrong to equate a popular song with a concerto. Not morally wrong (though, in some cases, that too), but esthetically wrong. A great deal of critical confusion stems from critics' trying to treat the aristocracy and hierarchy of art as a democracy or anarchy; either because they refuse to admit that, along with their high tastes, they have low tastes as well; or that, along with their low tastes, they have no high tastes at all.

Another major problem in the world of film is the movie buff. Not the movie *fan,* a lowly and harmless species of aficionado, who is surely no trouble to anyone except to the stars whose shirts and blouses he (or, more often, she) may rip off. But the movie *buff* is someone who lives in and through the movies, who knows all their obscurest data (the obscurer, the better), and who follows his devouring of movies with much pseudo-learned post-prandial chatter, but with virtually no critical standards. Buffs are made mostly of disaffected middle-class drifters, intellectual failures, neurotics who find movies and movie-talk an ideal form of escape, and seekers after easy types of one-upmanship. Significantly, popular parlance recognizes the existence of movie buffs and, perhaps, opera buffs, but not of theater buffs, museum buffs, concert buffs. For the movies are the cheapest and most accessible playground for the acquisition of meaningless expertise, and the fellow who can rattle off the filmography of a George Cukor or Douglas Sirk is no better than the guy who memorizes baseball batting averages, but usually much more pretentious.

Perhaps the best way to define a movie buff is as a scholar without portfolio; but, often enough, he acquires one. For it happens not infrequently that a movie buff becomes a movie reviewer, and though what he practices has to do with buffery, not criticism, in the generally sad state of film criticism—where some reviewers, in their ignorance, cannot even be called buffs —this type of film critic may prosper and grow famous. Thus, Andrew Sarris, to whom no one can deny a most engaging candor about himself, writes in the foreword to his collected reviews, *Confessions of a Cultist:* ". . . as an undergraduate at Columbia I had drifted, like Jack Kerouac, down from Morningside Heights ever deeper into the darkness of movie houses, not so much in search of a vocation as in flight from the laborious realities of careerism." But, seemingly paradoxically yet quite in keeping with the archetypal buff, Sarris confesses: "There was never a time that [*sic*] I would not have given up being a cultist to be a careerist." In due time, Sarris managed to combine his two "isms" quite successfully, and for this one must have talent— though whether of a critical nature is open to question.

Buffs, of course, prefer movies to films, in the sense in which I, and others before me, have distinguished between them. The reason is obvious: there are not enough films with artistic merit to keep a cultist immersed—or, more properly, submerged—around the clock. But even if there were, the buff is by inclination happier with movies than with film because non-art, being unreal and making few demands, is a much better escape route than art. To be sure, in times past, the film critic virtually had to be a buff, so very few were the films of any artistic value. Thus even James Agee was, in many ways, a buff; and his friend and admirer, Dwight Macdonald, has concisely and sympathetically stated Agee's problem: "Not that his infatuation with the movies didn't have its drawbacks. A lover sees many aspects, mostly interesting ones, of his beloved that more objective observers miss, but he also sees many aspects, mostly interesting ones, that aren't there." Still, things have changed sufficiently by now for the emergence of two distinct groups of critics, small but not uninfluential, with members who are by no means in slavish agreement with one another, but who share distinct family resemblances nevertheless.

One group is concerned chiefly with film as art, or as one of the arts. They are critics who have written extensively on other arts besides film—indeed, one of them, Charles Thomas Samuels, has made a pertinent dictum, "Never trust a film critic who is only a film critic," to which I shall return—and they resist movements, schools, fads, as much as possible. They write with posterity rather than the mere moment in mind, and they are at least as concerned with meanings and implications as with the feel of a film. The main representatives of this persuasion—Sarris calls them "bookish film critics," others call them, contemptuously or not, "highbrow"—are Dwight Macdonald, Stanley Kauffmann, Vernon Young, Charles T. Samuels (who writes, much too infrequently on film, for various journals, is film critic for *The American Scholar,* author of *A Casebook on Film,* and at work on a book about the major filmmakers), Wilfrid Sheed (while he was film critic for *Esquire,* a tenure that proved all too short), and myself (if I may be excused the lack of false and, very possibly, genuine modesty). I would call this group film critics, and add only that they, like the group that follows, have foreign equivalents, but that I concern myself here only with those writing or publishing in the United States.

The other group, much more at odds with one another than the first (so much so that, unlike the former, they would resent being bracketed together), I would call movie critics. They do not, as a rule, write on the other arts; they are not primarily concerned with film as art—or, if so, have a rather demotic or idiosyncratic conception of art; they tend to be buffs *emeriti* (or *emeritae*), and are much more interested in the politics, the social (or, simply, gregarious) aspects of cinema; they are primarily involved with the feel of the film, the immediate impact it produces, its relation to the temper of the times. They are not, however, to be confused with mere reviewers; for their dedication, zeal (sometimes fanaticism), and film scholarship far exceeds that of the reviewers or journalists (of whom Judith Crist can be considered a supreme example). Though I find myself not only in frequent disagreement but also in basic antipathy with their positions, I reckon with their abilities, often enjoy their writings, and like some of them, as people, very much. In this group I would number Pauline Kael and Andrew Sarris, Manny Farber and, with minor differences, Penelope Gilliatt, and also, with important but not all-important differences, Parker Tyler and Susan Sontag.

Andrew Sarris is the main representative in America of a kind of movie criticism called *auteur* criticism, a term perhaps not yet so generally known as not to require some explanation. Under the aegis of the late André Bazin, the French film critic and founder of *La Revue du Cinéma* (1947), which turned into the *Cahiers du Cinéma,* there developed the new breed of so-called *Cahiers* critics. Bazin, himself an editor of *Cahiers,* was a cultivated, extremely well-meaning, Roman Catholic critic—and, essentially, a buff. He clasped movies of every kidney to his bosom, wrote about them thoughtfully but rather convolutedly and inelegantly, and also, alas, quite humorlessly. Nevertheless, he was one of the first scholar-critics—perhaps *the* first—of importance; in France he occupies much the same charismatic, semilegendary position that James Agee occupies here. The critical disciples of Bazin started, under the leadership of François Truffaut and with considerable though not total support from their master, something they called the *politique des auteurs,* or the politics of authorship. According to this view, a truly great director is an auteur (author); whether or not he has written the screenplay, he imposes his personality on every aspect of the film, which then can be said to reveal, rather than anything else, the artistic personality of that director or auteur. But in filmmaking, and especially in American filmmaking, which the *Cahiers* crowd has always idolized, the director is often at the mercy of the producer or studio; hence the auteurists elaborated a theory according to which the brilliance of an auteur, the very quality that distinguishes him from a mere director, shows up in the skill with which he puts his individuality across despite the rigid mold into which his film must be fitted.

From there it was only a short step to admiring films for their quirks, real or imaginary idiosyncrasies that were discovered in this or that corner of a movie. There was a shot here, a bit of technique there, a small twist in the plot yonder that came in for the most ardent and eccentric admiration. The entire output of an auteur had to be scrutinized for almost imperceptible, true or alleged, oddities, which could be traced from film to film in the auteur's *oeuvre*. The obscurer the auteur, the better; the more the auteur critic has the opportunity to impress us with his esoteric knowledge—often so esoteric that it is hardly worth having. Unfortunately, it has never been revealed how someone becomes an auteur; as far as I can ascertain, it is a status conferred upon one by an official or unofficial poll of the *Cahiers* critics, or even by the sufficiently obstreperous approbation of a minority among them. Here is an account of the changing tastes in auteurs at the *Cahiers* as given in 1962 by Robert Benayoun, an unsympathetic critic from the rival, and equally auteurist, publication, *Positif,* but accurate enough for all that: "As generation after generation went its way, the idols were shuffled: those who once worshiped Welles, Huston, and Rossellini were ousted by the champions of Aldrich, Hawks, and Anthony Mann, and then by those of Fuller, Lang, and Losey. Today, all this has been swept away by a new brood of *cinéphiles* who are blithely ignorant of any films that are more than five years old, and new gods have been installed: Ulmer, Walsh, and Cottafavi. The *politique des auteurs* is, as can be seen, a dialectic of hormonal rejuvenation sustained by the criterion of rediscovery on virgin ground."

Benayoun disregards the fact that some of the auteur critics are very up on their film history, having spent years and years of their lives in Henri Langlois's French Cinémathèque, there absorbing, along with films of value, some of the most slime-covered flotsam of both the silent- and sound-film eras. In any case, the judgments of the *Cahiers* critics are scandalous; thus an entire issue of the magazine was dedicated to the work of Edgar G. Ulmer, a prototypical hack if ever there was one. Here is Sarris (*The American Cinema,* p. 143) on Ulmer: "Strictly speaking, most of Ulmer's films are of interest only to unthinking audiences and specialists in mise-en-scène. Yet, anyone who loves the cinema [which a thinking audience, apparently, cannot do] must be moved by *Daughter of Dr. Jekyll,* a film with a scenario so atrocious that it takes forty minutes to establish that the daughter of Dr. Jekyll is indeed the daughter of Dr. Jekyll. Ulmer's camera never falters even when his characters disintegrate . . . his reflexes are still sharp for the meaningful challenges of *The Black Cat, Bluebeard, Ruthless, Murder Is My Beat, Detour,* and *The Naked Dawn.* That a personal style could emerge from the lowest depths of Poverty Row is a tribute to a director without alibis." And Ulmer, for Sarris, is "one of the minor glories of the cinema. Here is a career, more subterranean than most, which be [*sic*] signature of a genuine artist."

Now if you should wonder about which bee [*sic*] might have stung Sarris, you will find that it is the *Cahiers* critics. Thus Fereydoun Hoveyda (I again quote Benayoun) extolled Nicholas Ray's *Party Girl* simply *because* he found the plot particularly "silly," and Luc Moullet admired in the work of that abysmal director, Samuel Fuller, "the gratuitousness, fortunately total, of the camera movements." Similarly, the *Cahiers* critic André S. Labarthe writes about Godard's *A Woman Is a Woman:* "The words are not there to express something, but rather to express the characters. They are reactives, obstacles, and their function is in a certain sense *lateral.* . . . Only *accidents* count here: the accent, intonation, modulation—in short, the *form.*" Labarthe calls the film, among other things, a documentary of Karina, Godard's then wife; Sarris, without acknowledging Labarthe— or, perhaps, taking universal familiarity with *Cahiers* lucubrations for granted—declares: "*Woman* is a documentary not merely of Karina but of the sheer otherness of all women . . . [it] employs all the resources of the cinema to express the exquisite agony of heterosexual love." This about the shenanigans of three comic-strip characters, lacking even the thickness of cardboard, in a film whose direction consists of piling capricious gimmick on gimmick. And, Sarris concludes, "The ultimate paradox of *A Woman Is a Woman* is its genuinely tragic spirit." If there is anything tragic about that manifestly farcical (though unfunny) film, it is the number of viewers and reviewers it has duped.

What has made the auteur critics what they are? Let us remember that the first wave of them were schoolboys during World War II: Chabrol and Godard were born in 1930, Truffaut in 1932, Rivette in 1928. This in itself must have been a disruptive experience, driving the boys into the movies as a haven from reality. After the war, at the Cinémathèque and elsewhere, they were finally able to get at the American films they could not see during the Occupation, and this formerly forbidden fruit must have tasted doubly sweet. We recall that Godard dedicated *Breathless* to Monogram Pictures, the studio that specialized in low-budget abortions. The American cinematic violence, glossiness, and mindlessness must have compensated for the sense of inertia, indigence, and stern philosophical speculation—it was the era of Existentialism on the rise—that characterized the postwar years in Paris. The American movie became both an antidote and an anodyne. Some dozen or fifteen years later, these no longer so very young men found themselves in the situation of having to justify the fact that they did not know much about anything except poor to rotten American movies. The solution, clearly, was to elevate this abstruse and absurd information to the level of high and important erudition and thereby justify one's misspent youth, a process which, by the way, need not be a conscious one.

In all this the French, or, more properly, Cartesian, spirit of cogitation as proof of one's existence plays an important role. For though cogitation is one of the three noblest functions of man (along with love and artistic or scientific creation), it does not come as easy as one might wish; it is certainly much harder than concoction, which it may superficially resemble. The concocting of elaborate theories, systems, structures, categorizations, is a favorite French pastime, and has, on occasion, yielded useful results. It has also, on other and more numerous occasions, produced reckless and sterile theorizing, of which the *politique des auteurs* is a depressing example. Not only is there no critical basis for the canonization of directors into auteurs, but also, empirically, a simple trip to Hollywood and observation of moviemaking under the studio bosses would have taught these Fench critics that the supposed auteur had immeasurably less power than they attributed to him, and that what they took to be his choices were either no choices, or not his.

Though the auteurist accolade usually went to American mediocrities or nonentities, it could go to anyone as long as it ran sufficiently contrary to generally held notions. Thus Rossellini's banal and boring *Voyage to Italy,* made in 1953—well after the neo-realist impulse and inspiration had forsaken the director— was voted top film of, I believe, all time by the *Cahiers* critics years after it was made—an opinion that was duly echoed, much later yet, by Susan Sontag when she introduced the film at its first

New York screening at the Museum of Modern Art. Similarly, at one point, the *Cahiers* critics concurred that *Under Capricorn* was Hitchcock's greatest film, a verdict that must shock any discriminating mind, as it apparently did even Hitchcock's. Years later, in the book-length interview Truffaut conducted with the director, we still find Hitchcock warding off the interviewer's excessive enthusiasm for this failed film. But let us get to the auteur theory's American branch (there is also an English one, represented chiefly by the critics on *Sight and Sound* and *Movie;* and, for all I know, there are others flourishing from Latvia to Lebanon). The American *chef d'école* is, I repeat, Andrew Sarris, who was also the editor of the English-language edition of the *Cahiers* that appeared here between 1965 and 1967.

Apropos the Americanization of the auteur theory, Pauline Kael had some cogent and devastating things to say in her 1963 article, "Circles and Squares." Since then, however, her position —or, more accurately, her way of defining it—has changed drastically, bringing her much closer to Sarris and his band of insiders whom she attacked in that essay, reprinted in *I Lost It at the Movies.* Among other pertinent observations about the auteurists, Miss Kael noted that "their decisions are *beyond* criticism. It's like a woman's telling us that she feels a certain dress *does* something for her: her feeling has about as much to do with critical judgment as the auteur critics' feeling that Minnelli *has* 'it,' but Huston never had 'it.' " In this light, let us survey some examples of the Sarris method at work. Claude Chabrol is not only an auteur critic but also a filmmaker, which almost automatically grants him auteur status. So we find Sarris justifying his unconvincing endorsement of the dreary *Landru* with this concluding statement (which, like all those not otherwise identified, comes from *Confessions of a Cultist*): "What Chabrol proves once again is that stupidity when viewed honestly and sympathetically is the stuff of poetry." By the same argument one could prove that Wordsworth's "The Idiot Boy" is one of the great achievements of English poetry. Even more extraordinary is Sarris's special pleading for Chabrol's pretentiously trashy *Les Biches* (*The Village Voice,* October 17, 1968): "Chabrol's compassionate view of uselessness and stupidity makes every apparently gratuitous camera movement a warm caress." This is marvelously circular reasoning: how do we know that Chabrol is compassionate with stupidity? Because of all those apparently gratuitous but really caressing camera movements. And how do we know that those apparently gratuitous camera movements are really warm caresses? Because of Chabrol's compassion for stupidity. I shall not go into the murky issue of why Chabrol views stupidity with a compassion that looks more like lurid complaisance to me; but I cannot help wondering how camera movement can be anything but apparent, anything but what we see on screen? Thus if a camera movement is a warm caress, it is so because it appears to be so; if it is "apparently" something else, e.g., a gratuitous bit of tomfoolery, then gratuitous tomfoolery it is.

"*Les Biches*," Sarris continues, "is . . . a thing of beauty, a film of subjective feelings rather than objective facts, a film of more style than substance, delirious, decadent, but ultimately delightful to those with a taste for appearances as the purest language of the cinema." One wonders by what hocus-pocus "subjective feelings" (what other kind is there?) can be made, *ipso facto*, into a positive value? And what films can possibly be said to deal in "objective facts" (another redundancy), except perhaps newsreels? Surely it is the nature and application of feelings that matters, not just their existence. And why adduce in a film's defense that it has "more style than substance"? The very fact that the style and substance are not identical, that elements we recognize as necessarily fused should here be not only imperfectly matched but also readily separable, is evidence of artistic failure. And if we can and must make a separation, why should we put style over substance? It all comes out in the wash: because those among whom Sarris proudly numbers himself perceive "appearances as the purest language of cinema." Why should appearances be that? And, in any case, what does Sarris mean by "appearances"—to say nothing of "purest" and "language." As I understand language, it has to do not with appearances but with signs or symbols for meanings. And what is the "purest" language? The one that is farthest from the *mots de la tribu*, most poetic? Or the one that is most accurate, most algebraic? Or the one that is simplest, most universally comprehensible? And why, above all, should appearances have such a positive value? Only a moment ago Sarris warned us against accepting Chabrol's camera movements at their *apparent* value.

It is fairly easy to recognize what lurks behind this hopeless jumbling of words and ideas: a simple desire to justify one's use of movies as an escape from reality. So Pauline Kael writes in her already quoted essay, "These critics work embarrassingly hard trying to give some semblance of intellectual respectability to a

preoccupation with mindless, repetitious commercial products—
the kind of action movies that the restless, rootless men who
wander on Forty-second Street and in the Tenderloin of all our
big cities have always preferred because they could respond to
them without thought. These movies soak up your time . . . they
serve a very different function for Sarris or Bogdanovich . . . even
though they devise elaborate theories to justify taking up their
time." (As we shall see later, they don't serve a very different
function for Miss Kael, either.) *Les Biches,* to be sure, is more of
an inaction movie, but what it lacks in action it more than makes
up for in mindlessness and repetitiousness.

But it is true that action movies are particularly appealing to
this crowd. Take the case of the action-director Samuel Fuller.
Peter Wollen, an English auteurist who admires Sarris as much
as Sarris admires him, lists his favorite auteurs, the absolute
greats, under Sarris's term of "Pantheon Directors"; among
them, we find the usual competent technicians (Ford, Hawks,
Hitchcock) and more or less clever entertainers (Lubitsch, Sternberg, Ophüls) who appear also in Sarris's Pantheon and many
other auteurist hit parades. But there, too, is Samuel Fuller,
whom even Sarris relegates to the second circle of greats, "The
Far Side of Paradise," as he calls it. Nevertheless, here is Sarris
on Fuller's *Shock Corridor,* to which he concedes "the earmarks
of transparent trashiness," and goes on to say, "The dialogue is
so intense, so compressed, so lacking in all the shadings of wit and
verisimilitude, that it is impossible to escape the impression of a
primitive artist at work." And "*Shock Corridor* emerges as a distinguished addition to the art form in which Hollywood has
always excelled—the baroque B-picture." In 1963, when Sarris
wrote this, you were lucky to find among Hollywood's preceding fifty years' worth of A-pictures a handful of works of art; even
to call the B-pictures an art form is laughable or pitiful, or both
at once.

Sarris will stop at no desperate stratagem to make his baggy-
pants theory appear iron-clad. Thus Hitchcock's tawdry *The
Birds* is praised as "a joy," because it "does not feed parasitically
on outside cultural references—Chekhov, Synge, O'Neill,
Genet, Behan, Melville, or what have you." On that basis, you
could rejoice in every skinflick along 42nd Street from *Olga's
Girls* to *Tales for Males*—unless, of course, Sarris should be able
to prove that they feed on "what have you." And, by way of a
final example, who would not cherish Sarris's last-ditch maneu-

vers to save Hitchcock's senile *Topaz,* which Vincent Canby of
the *New York Times,* an auteurish reviewer (his colleague, Roger
Greenspun, is a dyed-in-the-wool auteurist) also raved about and
placed on his ten-best list. Sarris is reduced to praising a fagged-
out Hitchcock for having "improvised to the extent of exploiting
John Vernon's expressively blue eyes in a morally ambivalent
situation." (*The Village Voice,* December 25, 1969.) Just how a
pair of eyes, even if it were something more remarkable than
blue, say, yellow, can be exploited in a morally ambivalent situation, to say nothing of how one improvises with this—by not
allowing Vernon to blink, lest we lose some of that azure elo-
quence?—Sarris, of course, neglects to tell us. But he does affirm
that *Topaz* affords us "unexpected glimpses of the most saving of
all human graces: perversity and humor." Why perversity should
be a most saving human grace I cannot imagine, unless it be that
Sarris is dimly aware that one most saving (or Pantheon) grace
is insufficient to save a film as wretched as *Topaz,* so another one
has to be recruited from among the vices.

Perversity, however, is certainly the most saving grace of Sarris's criticism, as well as the only deliberate one, the humor being
mostly unintentional. Writing of Sarris's (and, by implication,
any other auteur critic's) struggles to force directors into categories more suited for the grading of eggs, Dwight Macdonald remarks, "One can't deny [Sarris's] labors have been heroic, but
Procrustes rather than the fire-giving Prometheus is the hero."

Pauline Kael's case is rather more complicated. Miss Kael's
critical activities fall, as of now, into three periods, each represented by a volume of collected criticism. There was, first, the
period of near-obscurity in San Francisco, where Miss Kael, with
her then husband, ran a couple of art-film theaters and wrote the
program notes, afterward doing movie reviews for a local FM
station. She was being published in film magazines and, occasionally, in *Partisan Review* and the *Atlantic;* but her reputation was
an underground one, among movie buffs, academics, the more
literate members of the film business (if any). Let me call this her
Voice in the Wilderness period, when she was trying to spread
her gospel by crying in the desert. *I Lost It at the Movies* collects
most of the output of this phase except for the program notes,
which had to wait for the next collection. The tone here is largely
argumentative and querulous, often self-servingly autobiographical, and flagrantly self-righteous. The attacks on other reviewers
become unendurable, not because one may think them unjus-

tified, but because most of those reviewers are fly-weights, and the frequency and similarity of the lambastings make them, finally, predictable and boring. They did, none the less, serve a purpose by showing us the uses of ungentlemanly, or ungentle-womanly, criticism in calling attention to how inept and irresponsible most movie reviews were. More tiresome even than this shrillness was the omnipresent anecdotal information, gratuitous but self-gratifying, about Miss Kael's private life: about how she ingenuously wore her one good dress to meet Hollywood's smart set who turned out to be all in poolside deshabillé; about the persistent young academic who would not leave at party's end, apparently wishing to spend the night and having to be pushed out the door; about her early days on the farm and accompanying her father on his womanizing forays; about her unsuccessful attempts at being a private tutor; about seeing a movie after a lovers' quarrel simultaneously with her lover, each unaware of the other's presence, until they bumped into each other at the exit, both shedding tears by the bucket; and so on and on.

In reviewing the book, I was tempted to describe it as a rather interesting autobiography, periodically interrupted by irrelevant movie reviews. This would have been unfair, for the reviews are often very good: scrappy, clever, socially alert, unwilling to put up with pretensions of any kind. Unfortunately, Miss Kael was always a little too eager to deride genuine art along with the fake —thus Antonioni and Bergman were, in *The Eclipse* and *The Silence,* allegedly stripping movies of such essentials as light and sound—but, on the whole, her concern was still to differentiate between trash and art and uphold the latter, or what she thought was worthy, against Bosley Crowther, *Time, The Saturday Review,* and, ironically, the *New Yorker.* But she was no less vehement in her arguments with Kauffmann and Macdonald, and I often had the feeling that she liked the "highbrows" even less—if, indeed, she distinguished between the two groups at all.

The next phase might be described as Miss Kael's *Wanderjahre* or, more precisely, her *gradus ad Parnassum;* the pieces in her second collection, *Kiss Kiss Bang Bang,* come from the *Atlantic, Holiday, Life, Mademoiselle, McCall's* (whose movie critic she briefly was), *Vogue, The New Republic,* where she succeeded Stanley Kauffmann, who had gone over to the *Times.* This truly became Miss Kael's period of glory, for from the high but not too high or exalted platform of *The New Republic*—Parnassus but not Olympus—she was able to reach readers from middlebrow to highbrow, and regale them with her folksily judicious, socially hip, fellow-conspiratorial and no-nonsense approach, equally appealing to the middlebrow's yearning to be elevated and the highbrow's penchant for slumming. As Dwight Macdonald noted at this time (*Esquire,* July 1969): "In admirable contrast to Mr. Crowther, the eternal philistine, forever insecure and so a pushover for whatever 'trends' are pushing hardest, Miss Kael refuses to be bullied by highbrow fashion, reacting against the European 'art' film and in favor of our domestic commercial product; okay but she overdoes it; and she forgets that sometimes a fashionable trend is justified."

The key to Miss Kael's critical persona seems to be this: she is an intelligent, gifted lowbrow, who does not really fit in anywhere along the cultural scale. She despises the middlebrows, does not feel comfortable with the highbrows (not sharing their background, tastes, and erudition), and is clearly too good for the lowbrows. This throws her back on her own resources, her own alleged superiority to all categories and, by extension, all members of all categories except the occasional younger reviewer who fawningly declares his fealty to her (in this way she has been known to be patroness—and patronizing—to reviewers as different as Joseph Morgenstern, Richard Schickel, and Roger Ebert). But the attitudes of the lowbrow will out. Ingmar Bergman's masterly *The Naked Night* she calls "powerfully awful," because it is "heavy, mawkish expressionism circa 1920" in which "no one is saved from total damnation." Yet she admits that it "has upsetting qualities all its own," and overlooks the fact that its final vision of the unhappy couple sticking it out together is typical Bergman, not total damnation, and certainly not expressionism, where the individual is always damned and there is only socialist salvation. But the film *is* gloomy, and the lowbrow does not like gloom.

In much the same way *Viridiana* struck Miss Kael as "incomprehensible," *Blow-Up* "becomes ah-sweet-mystery-of-life we-are-all-fools, which, pitched too high for human ears, might seem like great music beyond our grasp"—perish the thought that anything might not be immediately comprehensible: what would Miss Kael do with a sonnet of Mallarmé? Hecht and MacArthur's "light satirical comedies about shallow people living venal lives . . . said most of what Antonioni does and more, and were entertaining besides" or Who Needs *L'Avventura* When He Can

Have *His Girl Friday? Masculine-Feminine,* Godard's exercise in self-indulgence, is "a work of grace and beauty," but in Bergman's *Persona* there is no "structure of meanings," whatever that might be, and "If there is, it is so buried that,it does not function in the work." Miss Kael is, however, quite indulgent with lack of clarity ("not the worst crime") when the film is Bertolucci's Godardian *Before the Revolution,* from which she emerges "elated"—presumably by its puerile attitudinizing. The "goddamn good taste" of David Lean's *Lawrence of Arabia* is inferior to John Huston's *The Bible* (an artistic, critical, and box-office fiasco) because "Huston (like Mailer) plays the crazy game crazy —to beat it, to win," where we note the crowd-pleasing bad grammar, and wonder whether, if you're going to lose, you had not better play the crazy game sane. There is no good at all, however, in *The Gospel According to St. Matthew,* and Miss Kael "could hardly wait for that loathsome prissy young man to get crucified," but her pity for Bonnie and Clyde knows no bounds. In fact, her panegyric about *Bonnie and Clyde* runs sixteen and one-half tall octavo pages in rather fine print, and her enthusiasm for this American imitation–New Wave film epitomizes a sensibility that prefers trash to art, and plays, albeit more cleverly and guardedly, the same kind of games as the auteur critics to justify low-down cravings.

It is interesting to note that Miss Kael, unlike the auteurists, and especially the French ones, introduces few outside references into her writing. Even Sarris will dutifully trot out some mention of Dos Passos, Huxley, or Stravinsky, but Miss Kael appears to disdain such ostentation. Still, she can do it: *Miracle in Milan* conjures up Dostoevsky, and *The Italian Straw Hat,* Bergson; but Miss Kael is certainly not one of your (or Sarris's) bookish film critics. This must be either because she keeps her shamefully highbrow traffic with books well hidden, or because they, like the other nonfilmic arts, don't matter to her. I find the essential Kael in remarks like this one about *The Big Knife:* "But with all these faults of taste, perhaps because of them, who can take his eyes off the screen?" The answer, of course, is: anyone who would rather go to a concert, visit a picture gallery, or read a book.

But the Pauline Kael of the Parnassian period was, at least on the surface, already quite different from the Kael of the Wilderness period. She was now a part of the critical establishment, which meant that she could (*a*) assert herself more freely, even reprint her old program notes in all their headlong breeziness; and (*b*) become more outrageous, lest she be mistaken for one of those old-timers, pundits, squares—in short, Establishment figures. Consequently, the taste for trash was to be trumpeted more brazenly, as in the *Bonnie and Clyde* encomium, which marked her triumphal entry into the halls of the *New Yorker.* Becoming its film critic guaranteed her a much bigger readership than ever before—to be sure, almost exclusively middlebrow, but her faithful fans would follow her even into DeVriesland— and much more space than *The New Republic* could give her, and rather more than subjects like *Bonnie and Clyde* deserve. With this began her third phase, what might be called her Gilded Cage period, for though the *New Yorker* treats its writers with prodigal lavishness, it does not permit the kind of acrimony that spiked Miss Kael's earlier writings; and so attacks on fellow critics, except occasionally in milder form and under the name of their magazines only, were dropped, along with other more savage traits. But the Gilded Cage image does not suit Miss Kael: she is neither the kind of girl nor the species of bird one would keep as a pet. Perhaps, then, we had better call it her Mausoleum period, bearing in mind that it is a mausoleum onto whose walls she is still sneaking hasty graffiti whenever the watchful eye of the editor, Mr. Shawn, happens to be blinking.

The Mausoleum period is represented by Miss Kael's third critical collection, whose very title, *Going Steady,* is much more sedate and genteel than her previous ones: it is the kind of title one wears at the Taj Mahal rather than while fulminating in the Waste Land or climbing Parnassus. (Originally, the book was to have been called *The Great Bastard Cross-Fertilized Super-Art,* but the Wolfe was kept from the door.) Here Miss Kael is, on the whole, writing nice, chatty *New Yorker*ish pieces, say, on Omar Sharif's star quality, or on Barbra Streisand's much greater beauty than that of "pretty" people. Miss Kael's talent for demolishing stupid ineptitude and dismantling pretentiousness continues here; indeed, by way of a pleasant surprise, Bergman gets a reprieve and *Shame* is termed a masterpiece—though calling it "Bergman's equivalent of Godard's *Weekend*" is rather like praising *Cities of the Plain* as Proust's equivalent of Robbe-Grillet's *La Maison des rendez-vous.* But, at the same time, that quintessential sentimental hack, Jacques Demy, is "an artist for whose work I have the deepest affection," the trendily flashy John Boorman has "directorial flair," and, in a largely favorable review of the feeble *The Night They Raided Minsky's*, we are reminded that "Movies are not built on talent alone."

Going Steady also contains the crucial essay, originally published in *Harper's*, "Trash, Art, and the Movies," which, for the sake of brevity and accuracy (art is barely mentioned in it), I shall call "Trash." In this forty-three-page piece Miss Kael picks up her leitmotiv, first sounded in the introduction to *I Lost It at the Movies*. There, in a passage mocking Macdonald, she had stated that "There is more energy, more originality, more excitement, more *art* in American kitsch like *Gunga Din*, *Easy Living*, the Rogers and Astaire pictures like *Swingtime* and *Top Hat*, in *Strangers on a Train*, *His Girl Friday*, *The Crimson Pirate*, *Citizen Kane*, *The Lady Eve*, *To Have and Have Not*, *The African Queen*, *Singin' in the Rain*, *Sweet Smell of Success*, or more recently, *The Hustler*, *Lolita*, *The Manchurian Candidate*, *Hud*, *Charade*, than in the presumed 'High Culture' of *Hiroshima Mon Amour*, *Marienbad*, *La Notte*, *The Eclipse*, and the Torre Nilsson pictures. As Nabokov remarked, 'Nothing is more exhilarating than Philistine vulgarity.' " This paragraph is a perfect mirror not only of Miss Kael's esthetics, but also of that strategy of hers of which it is hard to say whether it is actually dishonest or merely insensitive. One wonders, first, how, even by her definition, there can be more art in kitsch than in non-kitsch, unless, of course, by *art* (her italics) one does not mean art at all. Again, "excitement" and "energy" are unfair criteria to invoke when dealing with films like Antonioni's, where, superficially, there can be no energy, the subject being precisely its absence. There is, however, the energy of artistic vision, the excitement of innovation—as in the final sequence of *Eclipse*, which in itself contains more "originality" than most of the films on Miss Kael's honor roll rolled together. But what a dishonest list it is! How can one casually introduce a true and remarkable work of art like *Citizen Kane* into the category of "American kitsch," except as a scented disinfectant meant to throw us off the real odors involved? In its more modest way, *The African Queen* is also a work of art; other items, like *Strangers on a Train*, *The Lady Eve*, *Singin' in the Rain* are sound, skillful entertainments, not to be sneeezed at, but neither to be uncritically bracketed with failed attempts at art, whether still quite powerful, like *Hud* and *Sweet Smell of Success*, or mostly irritating, like *The Hustler* and *Lolita*. As for *The Crimson Pirate*, it is camp, presumably thrown in to allow the outrageous a place in the temple, just as *Charade* is there to legitimize a certain slick commercialism, which indeed has energy, but very little else. *His Girl Friday* comes across as something rather sleazy today, its jokes leaving a sour rather than peppery taste in the mouth; as for *Gunga Din,* another Hecht-MacArthur opus, I have, frankly, forgotten it. For Mitchell Leisen's *Easy Living,* which is presumably what Miss Kael has in mind here, I can at least say that it is better than Jacques Tourneur's film of the same name.

Take now the despised "High Culture" items. *Hiroshima Mon Amour* is a work of art, which for all its considerable unevenness has enormously enriched the grammar of film, introducing a whole new way of telling a story that has become as much a part of modern filmmaking as anything Miss Kael's beloved D. W. Griffith ever devised. *Marienbad,* I wholeheartedly agree, is a failure; but as for Torre Nilsson, what is he doing there at all? He has been smuggled in by Miss Kael as a Judas ram, to lead the other sheep to slaughter. But *La Notte* and, especially, *Eclipse* cannot be disposed of so easily. Least of all with a quotation from Nabokov that Miss Kael, guilefully or gullibly, takes at face value. The author of *Lolita* and *Pnin* finds the vulgar Philistines exhilarating only to the extent that he can skewer them to devastating satiric effect. Whoever reads Nabokov's utterance as Miss Kael does, can read (to quote one of her tropes back at her) Swift's "A Modest Proposal" as a gourmet.

But in "Trash" Miss Kael goes well beyond that initial statement of her chosen theme, and the so-called art of kitsch becomes the essence of film art. "An actor's scowl, a small subversive gesture, a dirty remark that someone tosses off with a mock-innocent face, and the world makes a little bit of sense," Miss Kael writes. This, to elaborate my previous image, is precisely the notion that film—or art—consists of making the world endurable by scrawling graffiti on it, giving it the finger, shouting "Up yours!"—all impotent and infantile gestures by means of which a child tries to get even with reality. Again we read: "The romance of movies is not just in those stories and those people on the screen, but in the adolescent dream of meeting others who feel as you do about what you've seen. You do meet them, of course, and you know each other at once because you talk less about good movies than about what you love in bad movies." This tells us two things about its author: first, that movies for her are a way of belonging to a club—perhaps a lonely-hearts club —through which you meet other like-minded persons for the exchange of adolescent enthusiasms; and, secondly, that however much she may pay lip service to works of art, where she really feels at home is in the world of trash. This is very much the auteurist position, only Miss Kael is too shrewd to turn auteurism into an obvious *politique,* into a chart with labels and classifications. She prefers to be more gustatory and improvisatory where the auteurists are pseudo-systematic and doctrinairely organizational.

And now hear this: "From *I Was a Teen-Age Werewolf* through the beach parties to *Wild in the Streets* and *The Savage Seven,* American International Pictures has sold a cheap commodity, which by its lack of artistry and in its blatant and sometimes funny way of delivering action serves to remind us that one of the great appeals of movies is that we don't have to take them too seriously." Which makes one wonder on what authority the critic manages to take herself so much more seriously than her subject? But to cite only one more gem from "Trash" (which is full of them), Miss Kael commends a script by the hack George Axelrod out of a novel by Richard Condon, another hack, as having been "ambivalent and funny in a way that was trashy yet liberating." "Liberating" is one of her favorite terms of praise, as dear to her as the concept of *mise en scène* is to Sarris and the auteurists. Now *mise en scène* means simply putting on stage or screen, i.e., direction; but the auteurists have elaborated and bloated it into a mystical essence, a fictitious quiddity always good for a synthetic disquisition. And this "liberating"—what exactly is it that Miss Kael wants to, needs to, be liberated from? Clearly, reality: some kind of psychological, philosophical, metaphysical, or sensual view of reality, which art insists on, whether in terms that are naturalistic or symbolic, intensely personal or mythic. The result may be disturbing or exhilarating, enlightening and just possibly ennobling. But only rarely is it instantly liberating. Trash, I dare say, is; the way at the end of a solemn and boring reception in London Sarah Bernhardt pounced on a familiar French face and said something like "For God's sake, let's get out of here" and *"allons nous encanailler"*—let's go make pigs of ourselves. But to confuse *encanaillement* with art, to become a critic in order to justify one's love and need for slumming because life and art strike one as oppressive—that is a very different, and considerably fishier, kettle of fish.

Yet even granting Miss Kael her espousal of movies as "fun," I would still have to question her recurrent failure to convey that fun in her reviews, to articulate her approbation compellingly. And I could go further and point to her frequent inability to write *about* a film at all, preferring to write *around* it instead. A good example in *Going Steady* is her lengthy review of Buñuel's splendid *Simon of the Desert,* which she greatly likes, but uses almost exclusively as a pretext for attacking fuzzy liberals and so not talking about the film. Another favorite trick for avoiding film criticism is to set up a straw man—some harmless cocktail-party chatterbox or somewhat less harmless academic pontificator—whose inanities she quotes at great length in support of a film she dislikes (*Blow-Up,* for example), only to knock them down with triumphant but unearned glee.

Charles T. Samuels in his review of *Going Steady* (*New York Times Book Review,* February 22, 1970) points to another interesting contradiction in Miss Kael's stance, her styling herself "the apostle of common feelings" while indulging in "élitist yearning and suspicion of the audience." He proceeds to cite a number of instances in which Miss Kael strikes either a We-the-People-Won't-Be-Fooled attitude; or, on the contrary, laments, with appropriate quotations, the foolishness of individuals, groups, entire audiences, or the public itself. Clearly, either position is perfectly possible, but not blithely inconsistent shuttling between the two—although this seems to pay off by allowing both low-brows and highbrows to find in her at least a part-time ally, which seems to them better than nothing. She reaches for the opium of the people, movies, and for the people in the opium den; and she is indignant when the screen does not reflect her image of opium, and the people do not reflect her image of herself.

Yet the upshot is that the Kael who wrote an attack on auteurism subtitled "Joys and Sarris," and the Sarris who responded with a piece called "The Perils of Pauline," have, without acknowledging it, come to occupy neighboring positions. Whether in the name of the politics of authorship or of the delights of trash, each is peddling inferior goods. That their trash is not always the same trash—indeed, it often differs—matters less than that it is trash; and that movie criticism, united in all but name, rules the roost and makes it hard for the voice of film criticism to be heard in the land. What accounts for the many Sarrisites and Kaelists among critics and reviewers? Auteurism appeals to all quasi- and para-intellectual game-players—its tie-in with the voguish disciplines of structuralism and semiology is evident—while trashism, especially when backed up by intimacy with film history and an amusingly authoritative tone, has great appeal as a culture-surrogate. By a curious paradox, Sarris writes his quasi-mystical criticism in a thumpingly earthbound style; whereas Kael couches her often trivial mash notes and grumblings in a worldly and tripping prose. Thus each critic can captivate students and faculty-members alike, and nowadays they constitute the chief audience for movies and movie criticism. Moreover, since movie critics are much easier to emulate than film critics, Kael or Sarris disciples spring up everywhere, starting with college movie magazines and ending with the *New York Times*. It is worth pondering that the tremendously influential film criticism of the *Times* should have become thoroughly auteurized.

I am not suggesting that there is a conspiracy afoot, only that movie critics, while overtly in disagreement with their fellow practitioners, manage to come out as a much more solid block than the film critics, who, while in general sympathy with one another, are too individualistic to present a united front. Yet a front, a battlefield, there is, and, as Stanley Kauffmann was perhaps first to note, the line along which the hostile troops confront each other is called the Godard line. The movie critics, though not always and not equally, tend to favor Godard and his cinematic followers; the film critics, again with considerable difference in degree, tend to be dubious or antipathetic. As Kauffmann observed, an anti-Godardian will never get a favorable review from a Godardian, and vice versa. But there are signs that film criticism, too, is coming into its own. The reasons are near at hand. As the old Hollywood studio empires are crumbling and independents are taking over; as the art of film rather than just moviegoing fascinates a growing number of bright young and older minds; as the advent of the more vulgar medium of television syphons off the dregs of the film world; as film study and filmmaking become daily more available in our schools; film prospers and gradually improves. As one result, mere movie criticism can no longer cope with what is on screen and with what the public wants to have interpreted and evaluated. As another, better minds are being drawn to film criticism as an honorable and rewarding activity. Let there be movies and movie critics, by all means; but let there also be film and film criticism.

The pieces in this book are my film criticism for the last three or four years, taking off from where my previous collection, *Private Screenings,* ended. A few pieces have been expanded, and minor corrections, mostly stylistic, have been made in many of them. This time, however, the essays—mostly reviews from *The New Leader,* where I publish a three-page column in every issue —are not arranged chronologically. Instead, they are divided into categories, which represent some of the main types of current movie- and filmmaking. Within each category or subcategory, however, the pieces are ordered chronologically. This arrangement seems to me useful in several ways. It calls attention to major trends in filmmaking and how they evolve; it stresses themes or salient characteristics of films and how they relate to similar themes and characteristics in other films, thereby informing us about the changing attitudes and preoccupations of our society; it enables the reader to see more clearly the achievement of a given film with respect to its peers, both immediately preceding and following it; and it brings specific films into sharper focus by giving the reader a frame of reference, an avenue of access to the central problem involved. Yet these categories should not be viewed as straitjackets, and one should be prepared for cross-references and cross-fertilization almost anywhere. Although more often than not I will be found to use the terms "film" and "movies" in the senses I give them in this introduction, there will doubtless be times when I fail to do so. Sometimes, for the sake of variety or prose rhythm, near-synonyms become irresistible, and the reader is advised not to jump to hasty conclusions. But the distinction becomes important and immediate again in the last section of the book, where other film and movie critics are discussed, and which, in a sense, should be read as an extension of the introduction, reinforcing and reinforced by it.

Lastly, there is one point raised in the foregoing pages whose elaboration I have purposely withheld till the end of this essay: my reasons for agreement with Charles Samuels's remark about not trusting a film critic who writes only about film. There is very possibly nothing wrong with a music critic who writes only about music, or an architecture critic who writes only about architecture. But film is both a much newer art than any of the others, and one which, as a true *Gesamtkunstwerk,* subsumes all the others. (For a fuller discussion of this, see "A Critical Credo" in *Private Screenings.*) The newness means that there is an insufficient body of film criticism, scholarship, and theory available to the aspiring critic, and that he had therefore best draw in part on the esthetics and methodology of the other arts and their criticism— all the more so since every one of those arts has to some degree been utilized by the cinema. Again, because film is still relatively unexplored and undervalued critically, it has the same fascination for critics that a barely discovered resort has for tourists: it becomes a fad and invites fanatical partisanship. So out of both ignorance and overenthusiasm it is horribly easy for the film critic to be or become one-sided, overzealous, derailed to the point of not making, or ceasing to make, sense on his own subject. To prevent this from happening, the film critic must be something else as well. His experience in other arts and critical disciplines will give him that lever and fulcrum with which Archimedes offered to lift the earth. Certainly film criticism could do with some heightening.

On the other hand, I hope that I am not guilty of the charge Andrew Sarris leveled at "too many bookish film critics," who, he claims, "have perverted the notion of ecumenical erudition by snobbishly subordinating film to every other art." I consider film inferior to no art, but neither do I make the dangerous assumption widely held by illiterate film critics (or whatever the opposite of "bookish" ones may be) that film is superior to all the other arts. A critic may be a lover; he must not become an idolater.

August, 1970

1

Adaptations

SOME YEARS ago, writing about stage adaptations of fiction, I noted: "There is a simple law governing the dramatization of novels: if it is worth doing, it can't be done; if it can be done, it wasn't worth it." Certain reviewers did me the honor of calling this Simon's Law, and I might as well state it now that as far as the screen is concerned, "Simon's Law" may still serve as a useful warning, but has no legality. For two reasons. First, because, unlike the stage, the screen possesses as many resources as fiction, so that, for example, extended narration is possible on screen, backed up by an extensive visual scenario, but not on the stage, where it must become monotonous; similarly, stream of consciousness has its filmic equivalents in montage, voice-over dialogue, closeups and extreme closeups, dissolves, etc., whereas on stage, as mere verbiage, it cannot fail to bore. Secondly, because the screen can fully illustrate what the novel can often only name or describe. Of course, this is a mixed blessing, because such illustration can make things overexplicit and oppressive; still, it is there as a resource for those who can effectively handle it.

Nonetheless, it remains true that great novels and stories make such sovereign use of their form—indeed, to a large extent, are their form—that any kind of transposition becomes a diminishment. It follows, then, that the greater the fiction, i.e., the more its form and content are indissoluble, the greater the loss incurred by transposition. Here, however, film comes through with another possibility: it can turn a mediocre novel or story into a fine movie, precisely because what the writer may have been able to outline and adumbrate only in his prose, the filmmaker can flesh out and make filmically exciting by finding cinematic equivalents or better-than-equivalents without leaving us frustrated or indignant over the verbal beauties that have been jettisoned.

It should not, however, be assumed that the worse the book, the better will be the film version: a sow's ear cannot be adapted into any medium, silk purse or silver screen. And there remains a residual notion in my mind that the great filmmaker will not want to adapt anything preexistent: that he will want to create in and with the medium, unhampered by any considerations of fidelity to anything but his own cinematic genius.

MARAT/SADE

The film of *Marat/Sade* begins inauspiciously with a misspelling of Peter Brook's name in the credits (unless they have corrected it since). But it turns out to be the most effective transfer yet of a stage production to the screen. I say transfer as distinct from adaptation, because, except for two features, we have here a faithful filmic record of a memorable stage event: the clever but mediocre play by Peter Weiss that provided Peter Brook with a pretext for a rousing piece of theatrical prestidigitation.

The first of the two main departures from the stage presentation is a curtain of iron bars that separates the lunatics on stage from the sane spectators who have come to gape at them. These theatergoers are included by Brook in the film; they are dressed according to today's fashions and behave with interesting unruliness. The idea has its merits, in that it adds another dimension to a film limited by its recording function, and the bars, too, come in for good use from time to time. Still, that filmed theater audience is present often enough to begin to be distracting, yet not quite enough to make a significant contribution by its presence.

The second major alteration is both more beautiful and more worrisome. It eliminates episode twenty-six of the play, which the translators mistranslate as "The Faces of Marat." (The German reads *Gesichte*, visions, not *Gesichter*, faces. Such lapses are not infrequent in this prize-winning English version.) Here Marat sees figures from his past in a hallucination that serves, among other things, to introduce Marat's life story. Instead of this lengthy episode, Brook now gives us a surrealist phantasmagoria of blurry images, polychrome bats emerging from and dissolving into opalescent mists. Besides cutting down on the running time, this must have struck Brook as being "purely filmic."

But it not only subtracts something from an already deficient script, it also weakens the film's validity as a record of the stage production. And it is no use arguing that the play isn't worth much, anyhow; in that case, why bother with it at all? Furthermore, characters from this episode (originally filmed, then cut out) are seen trailing about in what remains like so many red, or varicolored, herrings.

Aside from this, the film is thoroughly lovely to watch. The camera-man, David Watkin, has captured, under Brook's guidance, a double world: characters in the foreground emerge in cruelly detailed focus, while those in the background mill about in a state of hazy deliquescence, semiabstract mirages that might be people or just the delusions of madness. Artists as different as Odilon Redon and Nicolas de Staël would have been thrilled and tickled by this spectacle, no less fascinating to the layman's eye. Against the whites and grays of the asylum's bathhouse and the inmates' garb, the splashes of color from costumes, warders' uniforms, and props function in a similarly dual way as do focus and nonfocus: color solos performed dazzlingly to an accompaniment of amorphous drabness. The handheld camera, in harmony or discord, whirls around with or against the swirls of the spectacle. It is a split world, frightening yet not without its terrible beauty.

Compared with the play, the film version has, as might be expected, both advantages and disadvantages, though they do not always come where we expect them. So we are not surprised to find the film unable to convey the crazy simultaneity of the stage madhouse, the sense of a thirty-three-ring circus summarizing the entire world in caricature. The selective eye of the camera forces us to concentrate on this or that panel of the polyptych. But, to our astonishment, the work thus emerges more playlike. For the duologue-duel of Sade and Marat becomes unexpectedly clearer than it was on the stage, where it tended to get submerged in the perpetual peripheral upheavals. To be sure, this is a dubious gain, for it reveals more clearly the unfreshness and exiguity of the ideas and their verbalization. Still, it does give us a little more the sense of an agon. It also drives home the superficiality of Patrick Magee's Sade, the splendidly contained doggedness of Ian Richardson's Marat, and the marvelous ambiguity of Glenda Jackson's Corday.

Again, where we might have supposed the madmen less awesome when seen close enough for the makeup to show, they turn out to be actually more alarming, partly because they are such superb actors, partly because, with Brook's help, they have developed such meticulous scenarios of tics, spasms, and eccentricities. These twitches and grimaces are, however, more than just horrible; they are profoundly unsettling and haunting. There seems to be no such thing as an untalented bit player in the Royal Shakespeare Company.

On the other hand, the fine music and English lyrics by Richard Peaslee and Adrian Mitchell can, oddly enough, be less well heard on screen. Brook has also added some superviolence that would have been unsafe on stage. Some of these effects are good, though Brook cannot resist occasional excesses, such as a closeup of the erotomaniac Duperret's semen-stained trousers. All in all, there is something in this film version both for those who have seen the play and those who haven't, which cannot be said of many such undertakings. I just wish now that they would also bring back another, unduly neglected, Brook film version of a play, *The Beggars' Opera,* which seems to have failed only for the insufficient reason of not being *The Threepenny Opera.*

March, 1967

THE TAMING OF THE SHREW

Commenting on Beerbohm-Tree's defense of Garrick's version of *The Taming of the Shrew,* Bernard Shaw observed that it was "either an artistic misdemeanor or a profession of Philistinism." Franco Zeffirelli's and the Burtons' (or is it the Taylors'?) film of the *Shrew* manages to be both: Zeffirelli's misdemeanor and the Burtons' philistinism. *The Taming of the Shrew* is one of Shakespeare's least interesting plays, but given a good production such as Peter Hall's at the English or Michael Langham's at the Canadian Stratford, it can still divert us in its simpleminded way. It has only one point to make: the elementary psychology —or is it sheer bullying?—by which a tough nut of a girl is cracked by a fellow who is even tougher and nuttier. One can be revolted by its antifeminism, or wax nostalgic about the good old days when men were men and women slaves, but one must, in either case, get some sense of the parabola of the rough-and-ready plot, of the unclassic but sharp profile of the action.

Zeffirelli, with his usual preference for re-creating "the Renaissance atmosphere" at the expense of everything else, has chosen to give us lavishly animated canvases by Veronese, that champion of pictorial license and spiritual ancestor of Zeffirelli. These bustling tableaus are occasionally interrupted by plot, but even then only by the plot as accommodated to Zeffirelli's or the Burtons' idiosyncrasies. The rather amusing Sly the Tinker framework was first to go in the general tinkering; most of the Bianca subplot went next; and, finally, a good deal of the main plot. Now, it's no use saying the plot of the *Shrew* is not much anyway; plot and a few good lines are almost all there is, and you had best stick to that unless you can come up with something better. And, I submit, a session of the University of Padua, a fat Paduan courtesan disporting herself, and a bedeviled priest at the wedding camping it up are not something better. Neither is Burton's levee, in all its blustering detail.

If Zeffirelli's idiosyncrasy is fancy production values and disrespect for the work of art, Elizabeth Taylor's is godawful acting. I nominate her Katharina for a place of honor in the Hall of Histrionic Infamy. Miss Taylor has a hard enough time of it with contemporary speech; with Shakespeare's language, even somewhat modernized as it is here, she is at a total loss—we actually hear her say "Whom dost thou lovest best?" But just how garish her commonplace accent, squeakily shrill voice, and the childish petulance with which she delivers her lines are, my pen is neither scratchy nor leaky enough to convey. The once pretty face has become coarse, though from a distance it can still look good —but only if it avoids any attempt at expression, as, to be sure, it not infrequently does. Only the bosom keeps implacably marching on—or down, as the case may be—but I do not feel qualified to be the Xenophon of this reverse anabasis.

Richard Burton tends to give cleverly externalized performances in which a nice overlay of melancholy is shot through by flashes of something or other. Here we are treated to the obverse: instead of the customarily weary and sullen Burton, we get an infantile, bellowing, guffawing boor, a cross between Jack the Ripper and Jack the Giant Killer. Aside from a red beard that fits in with the predominantly reddish-tawny set and costume design, Burton's chief dramatic contribution is a somewhat manic laugh, really a sort of tic halfway between a giggle and a snarl. This bit of rough-hewn bonhomie is worked so heavily by Burton (and later by other members of the cast to whom it apparently spread) that were all specimens of it cut from the film, this *Shrew* might be a good—no, a bad—quarter of an hour shorter.

Typical of the film is the wanton cutting of one of the two or three most famous lines of the play, "And for your love to her, lead apes in hell." But a line is left in that, as delivered by Burton, takes on new significance. Petruchio announces that, as long as she is rich, he will marry this Kate: "Be she as foul as was Florentius' love,/ As old as Sibyl, and as curst and shrewd . . . " Burton's embarrassment as he scooted over that line (why was *it* kept in, when better ones bit the dust?) was the one unmistakably genuine moment in the entire film.

Granted, there is some visual excitement in the cleverly designed sets, in Danilo Donati's gaily turbulent costumes (though not in Irene Sharaf's overwrought ones for the two principals) and, above all, in Oswald Morris's distinctive color photography. Morris is one of the best cinematographers at work in Europe today, albeit much less highly touted than some of his continental confreres. What he has done here is not only delicious in itself but also remarkable in its faithful re-creation of Veronese's palette.

Nino Rota's score is a disappointment. Besides writing all those superb Fellini scores, Rota has composed some splendid ones for Clément (*This Angry Age*) and Visconti (*Rocco and His Brothers*); with the Renaissance, however, he is clearly not in tune. Disappointing, too, is a supporting cast full of good actors either miscast like Cyril Cusack, or shamelessly overacting like Victor Spinetti. Most disconcerting is Natasha Pyne in the crucial role of Bianca, which must not be done uncharmingly and ineptly, but for which Miss Pyne seems to have been chosen expressly to provide Miss Taylor with the least competition, thespian or visual.

April, 1967

FALSTAFF

Orson Welles in *Falstaff* (or *Chimes at Midnight*), has tried to surround himself with nothing but dazzlers—regardless of whether Marina Vlady, as a dubbed Kate Percy, and Jeanne Moreau, as an undubbed Doll Tearsheet, are dragged in by their lovely hair and made to look misplaced, insignificant, and ridiculous. But ridiculous is the word for the whole enterprise—not funny, and certainly not moving.

There is probably no harm in fusing the Falstaff material from three Shakespearean plays (not five, as Judith Crist would have it) into a film where the fat knight becomes the foreground and English history the background—the two are equally colossal and equally absurd. What is required, though, is a better actor and director than Welles is now, and less of a shoestring production. Never mind the flagrantly Spanish backgrounds, never mind the glaringly clumsy lip synchronization (almost every speech seems to be delivered by offscreen voices), never mind even the synthetic, routine performance given by so distinguished an actor as John Gielgud, who, moreover, plays the aging warrior-king as a flabby, aging queen.

What I truly do mind is Welles's self-indulgent Falstaff—mumbling, showily underplayed, sliding along surfaces, reveling in coyness, and speaking with an unattractive Midwestern accent into which he introduces, when he remembers, an occasional broad "a." Whenever possible, both he and Keith Baxter, the extremely plebeian Prince Hal, go into whispers, which they think highly cinematic, but which are only inverse hamminess. And what awful direction! The camera seems to have been entrusted only to operators who are Shakers, Holy Rollers, or, preferably, whirling dervishes, and what with the cast running off simultaneously in all directions and the camera in several others—well, it beats the roller coaster any time.

The camera work of Edmond Richard is arty to a fault, though the fault may as easily be Welles's. Thus there is a battle scene (effective but quite extraneous) that takes place in three different kinds of weather at once—sunny, overcast, and foggy—and with two kinds of ground—hard and dry for cavalry charges, and deeply muddy for footsoldiers to wallow and croak in. Fritz Mueller's editing is frenetic, with the ends and even beginnings of speeches often neatly apocopated. As for Alberto Lavagnino's music (a thoroughly international production, this!), it is comparable only to Giovanni Fusco's for *La Guerre est finie* in its unattractiveness and inappositeness.

Alan Webb's Shallow is just as schematic as was his Gremio in the *Shrew;* Walter Chiari's Silence is turned here, inappropriately and diminishingly, into a near-cretinous stutterer; Norman Rodway is a lumpish Hotspur and Keith Baxter a *lumpen* Hal—but why go on? Only Margaret Rutherford as Mistress Quickly and Ralph Richardson as the narrator come out ahead of the game, but she is barely on screen, and he entirely off.

The direction, I repeat, is much to blame. Thus the Boar's Head Inn is turned into a whorehouse, with numerous scantily clad bawds forming a kind of Aristophanic chorus to whatever goes on; and there are more bed and toilet scenes (the shooting, happily, is over the privy door, not under) than you can shake a brush at. Hotspur's farewell to his wife, a movingly restrained scene, is completely ruined by repeated crosscutting to a bunch of bleating trumpeters on the ramparts; by having Harry take a bath through much of it and even running to the door, losing his towel, and being caught bare-arsed; and by playing the end of it in a whirl of men galloping away, with Harry's voice coming from between the hind parts of rampaging horses.

April, 1967

ULYSSES

Joseph Strick's film adaptation of *Ulysses* is earnest, deferential, old-fashioned, and plodding. It is rather like a highminded comic-strip version of *Stephen Hero* or *Dubliners,* and on the few occasions when a bit of genuine Joycean complexity is allowed to survive in the midst of all that jolly, naturalistic Irishry, it strikes one as self-conscious and out of place. To make the film less expensive to produce, it has been updated, so that all the Celtic Twilight and Irish revolutionism had to be dropped, and much that is left (like the references to England's being taken over by the Jews) is out of keeping. To make the film more accessible, almost every "difficult" reference has been omitted. To make it conform to present tastes, the sex angle has been broadened (*e.g.,* the masturbation in the Nausicaa sequence) but the anti-Catholicism discreetly soft-pedaled (though one or two token blasphemies have been preserved for prestige purposes).

The photography is consistently second-rate, the music dull, the direction unimaginative. Not even the topography of Dublin, so vivid in the book, survives, and the movements and crisscrossings of the characters, so scrupulously worked out by Joyce, become jerky, arbitrary, incomprehensible. Stephen, who in the novel is all intellectual stream of consciousness, is here reduced to being hardly more than a bit part; even Bloom is translated into basic English, and Molly's monologue loses a good deal by being fully acted out rather than a luscious verbal tapestry for the eye and inner ear. Bloom's and Stephen's father-son relationship is almost entirely lost; the Homeric parallels, entirely, and with them the mythic, universal quality of the work. The secondary characters are thinned out to shadows, and even an episode that is relatively uncut, such as the nighttown sequence, is vulgarized down from a surrealist *Walpurgisnacht* to a series of burlesque skits reminiscent of Strick's appalling movie of *The Balcony.*

If ever a novel demanded to be left alone by the adapters, *Ulysses* is it. Its beauties and meaning lie almost exclusively in its form: in its musical interweaving of themes, in its cerebral texture of allusions and parallels, in its linguistic constructs, and, not the least, in its typographical appearance. The filmmaker can either pedestrianly transpose whatever is literally transposable or invent daring cinematic equivalents. Either way, the particular grandeur of the novel is betrayed. It may be that Strick, through sheer lack of imagination, betrayed and raped it less completely. But rape, like virginity, is not easily divisible—it is, in fact, quite Kierkegaardian in its either/or.

In any case, only a very crude sensibility could conceive of taking bits and pieces out of this enormous and difficult book, stringing them together *talis qualis,* and calling the whole thing either an illumination of the original or a tribute to its author. Shoddy as it is, even the generally acceptable performances cannot make it much of a film in its own right. Its chief purpose, I imagine, is to give those who haven't read the book (whether or not they can follow the film) an excuse for never reading it; and those who have, an occasional pleasant reminder of something in the novel. But to have to pay $5.50 for an *aide-mémoire* is an outrage. No amount of pious invoking of Joyce's name can disguise the fact that a cheaply produced film is being sold at exorbitant prices so that someone can make his boodle off "culture."

April, 1967

FAR FROM THE MADDING CROWD; REFLECTIONS IN A GOLDEN EYE

Two films of a rather ambitious nature, *Far from the Madding Crowd* and *Reflections in a Golden Eye* illustrate complementary failures: one derived from an important novel, the other from a supremely unimportant one. In the case of the Hardy novel, Frederick Raphael (rapidly becoming the most overrated scriptwriter of our time—see *Darling* and *Two for the Road*), I suppose, had to cut much of the bucolic-philosophic chorus of the rustics, but what justification is there for updating some of the main characters' utterances? Whatever was done or not done in the film, a great deal of its intensity and flavor was lost, along with the brooding, poetic nature descriptions for which John Schlesinger, the director, has found some, but not enough, filmic equivalents. Still, he and his cinematographer, Nick Roeg, have captured several seductive landscapes and townscapes that exude the past. Schlesinger's camera placements and movements are, as always, effective, and Roeg obtains images with the fluency and subtlety of watercolors from which Sergeant Troy's scarlet coat and the bustle of Casterbridge Fair stand out with heightened swagger.

But in the midst of this sense of period and locale, Julie Christie, Terence Stamp, and Alan Bates emerge merely as strayed revelers from a resplendent costume party: their very countenances modern and out of place. Only Peter Finch as Boldwood, an anachronism even in his own age and doubly so in ours, achieves authenticity and pathos well beyond what the script provided him with. The weakest link of all is Stamp's Sergeant Troy, perhaps from an excessive effort to make him attractive to audiences a century after the fiction. Yet in this rather plodding film the insufficiency of the foreground is partly offset by the winsomeness of the backgrounds. The very sheep are so engaging as to entice our gaze into some extremely amiable woolgathering.

A much more disheartening, in fact distasteful, movie is *Reflections in a Golden Eye*. Carson McCullers's vision was that of a world where aberration is the norm, where perversion is worn as a badge of genuineness if not of honor. But her quaint style—a kind of schoolgirl baroque laced with inversions (verbal as well as sexual), an innnocent relish of unhealthiness couched in wobbly poeticisms—creates an atmosphere redolent with morbid fascination. Yet for all its superficial fidelity to the original, John Huston's film, with a script by Chapman Mortimer and Gladys Hill, is pedestrian, crass, and uninvolving to the point of repellence. Things are clumsily spelled out here. If, in the novel, Leonora threatens to horsewhip her officer husband, in the film she actually does it, and publicly, too. If, in the novel, the husband, consumed with love-hate for Private Williams, picks up the candy wrapper the soldier discards, in the film he is seen droolingly smoothing it out in the guilty privacy of his study.

Thus we are left here with a somewhat feebleminded sexpot (Liz Taylor) married to a sadomasochistic crypto-homosexual afflicted also with impotence and fetishism (Marlon Brando). He is obsessed by a mentally retarded soldier, another fetishist who rides about in the nude and suffers from advanced voyeurism and possible zooerastia (Richard Forster); she is the mistress of her husband's fellow officer, a crude ox of a man (Brian Keith). The latter is married to a refined psychopath (Julie Harris) who cuts her nipples off with the garden shears, and dotes on as she is doted upon by a semidemented, wholly effete Filipino houseboy—a character preposterous enough as written, but at least not quite the screaming queen Zorro David makes of him in the movie.

Huston's direction is as literal-minded as can be, except for one far-fetched but abhorrent device. By some photographic process, the film emerges in one color, a kind of burnished gold (a top-heavy allusion to the already pretentious and meaningless title), but with one other color allowed to peep through: red, which comes out as a sickly rose madder in a piece of clothing or upholstery, and even more grotesquely in a woman's cheek. This envelops a painfully artless film in a painfully arty shell, and one feels trapped in a huge, overheated hothouse containing nothing but common snapdragons.

Plastic snapdragons, at that. Miss Taylor makes Leonora beefy down to her very playfulness, with never a hint of the pathos inherent in slowwittedness; while Brian Keith, as her lover, reproduces bovineness all too faithfully. Marlon Brando makes the husband not just sick but disgusting, the perversions daubed on as thickly as the triple-dyed Southern accent. Julie Harris, for once, is quite restrained, but the invalid Alison is not much of a part, and having to lavish her affection on the monstrous houseboy of Zorro David alienates her almost completely from us. As the barebacksided rider, Richard Forster does nothing for a part even more denuded in the film than in the book. And over all this presides the once considerable talent of John Huston, contributing nothing except a final crazed panning shot in which the camera shuttles schizophrenically back and forth, as out of control as this whole unhappy venture.

December, 1967

THE STRANGER

By far the most absorbing film of the year's end is Luchino Visconti's version of Camus's *The Stranger*. Not since Bresson's *Diary of a Country Priest* has there been such a reverent, doggedly faithful filmization of a fine novel; and if Bresson was, perhaps, a little more daring (or fanatical) in his work, Visconti has a more important book and some abler teammates in his favor. It is true that the film of *The Stranger* cannot begin to equal its source as a work of art, and it may well be that people who have not read the book will not see what all the fuss in the film is about.

Visconti's picture is primarily for those who know the novel—and I think that knowledge of so philosophically influential and artistically seminal a work can be demanded by the filmmaker—and for them this will be a devoted and beautiful visualization. I say visualization—not a mere set of illustrations for Camus's novel, but a respectful translation into another medium, which, while gathering radiance from the original also reflects renewed luster upon it. I am reminded of the aged Goethe saying that he was bored with his *Faust* and could bear to read it only in Nerval's French translation. Camus, were he alive, might have felt the same way about Visconti's transposition.

The great accomplishment of the novel, of course, was its presentation of the concept of the Absurd, and of an exemplar of a life lived and thrown away for its sake. The hero, Meursault, thus becomes the patron saint of Absurdism. But as Camus insisted, "a novel is never just a philosophy couched in images," and so the very style of the book is a triumph of the Absurd. This was managed, as Sartre points out in his famous explication of *The Stranger,* by presenting the events of the story as happening behind plate glass; that glass "will be the consciousness of the Stranger. It is, certainly, a transparency: we see everything that it sees. Only it has been constructed in such a way that it is transparent for things and opaque for meanings." Sartre shows how this is achieved: by the shortness and disconnectedness of the sentences, each of them seeming to be a fresh start; by the preponderance of indirect discourse, reducing everything to a kind of outline; by the steady use of the French *passé composé* tense (instead of the customary narrative *passé simple*) which, in fiction, not only falls offputtingly on French ears, but also, in minimizing the active ingredient of the verbs, gives events a viscous, inert quality.

How is the cinema to convey all this? A boldly modernistic director might have found equivalents, although, I fear, only at the cost of the luminous simplicity of the novel—an artful simplicity, if you like, yet one that hides its art. By his absolute straightforwardness, Visconti makes up to a large extent for the three failings of the film: the inability quite to convey the oppressive, brutalizing, maddening Algerian sun; the attempt to render the absurdity of Meursault's trial by resorting to conventional caricature (the wrong equivalent: the grotesque is not the same as the senseless); and a lack of humor in the basic approach—though some of Camus's and Mastroianni's humor gets in anyway. Still, in the main, the *mise en scène* is stunningly right—with two minor exceptions. It is too bad that in the beach scene money could not be found to equip others besides the principals with period bathing suits; and it is unfortunate that Visconti could not restrain his propensity for casting pretty boys in the cases of the avenging Arabs.

The director gets his greatest help from his cinematographer, the incomparable Giuseppe Rotunno. No one who has seen *Family Diary, The Leopard, The Organizer, The Bible* (to name only a few of his triumphs), can be unaware of what this genuine artist can do with his —is it camera? In black and white, it would seem to be etchings rather, or delicate washes; in color, the most comprehensive palette of oils. Rotunno is the master of what might be called flexible color: color that you notice when necessary, but that can as easily fade into—or out of

—the background when required. This is achieved only to a slight extent by controlling the costume and set design or manipulating backgrounds; it is done mostly with one of the subtlest uses of light values since Impressionist painting.

And, at the risk of sounding fanciful, I must pay homage to Rotunno's yellows. Or, more particularly, a special shade of yellow. You find it in *Family Diary,* and again here in a wall of Meursault's prison. That yellow is worthy of Vermeer, and of the little patch of Vermeerian yellow that Proust's Bergotte must get up from his deathbed to study. In a modest but undeniable way, Rotunno's use of yellow constitutes a stroke of genius time will not etiolate.

The screenplay by Suso Cechi d'Amico, Georges Conchon, and Emmanuel Robles consists mostly of translating Camus's indirect discourse into direct, which, unfortunately, sounds sometimes more ludicrous, sometimes less, and either way lessens the sense of alienation. Otherwise, the scenarists are true to the original in a way that the execrable subtitles are not. The all-important *"Plutôt que du regret j'éprouve un certain ennui,"* dwindles to "What I feel isn't so much regret"; *"Elle m'a dit que j'étais bizarre"* comes out backward as "I told her she was a strange one." There is, I suppose, a slight soft-pedaling even in the script. Thus the chaplain in the book asks the condemned Meursault how he will face death, *"cette terrible épreuve,"* which is pretty grandiose language. The priest in the movie has more cool and speaks of *"cette pénible épreuve."*

In Marcello Mastroianni—even dubbed into French—Visconti has a superb Meursault. Though the actor is much too glamorous for the part, he manages to shrink himself into the disaffected, slightly dazed, but intelligent nonentity Camus had in mind. And Mastroianni is one of the few actors who can convey thinking on camera, communicate the effort or excitement of it, and make it exhilarating to watch. This is not an easy thing to do: Yves Montand has been trying for years and still has only scratched the surface. Paul Scofield and Dirk Bogarde are marvelous at it, and so were once Trevor Howard and John Mills. But Mastroianni is probably the only great screen lover—and only Latin— who can do it, and that combination is particularly piquant. The aura of a damnably logical brain chewing away dumbfounded and slightly amused on the illogic of the world is portrayed by Mastroianni with exquisite fastidiousness as well as a shy, courteous modesty.

The supporting cast performs remarkably down to the very extras; only Pierre Bertin as the judge and Alfred Adam as the prosecutor are guilty of virtuoso histrionics. Most surprising is the warm and touching portrayal of Marie that Visconti has elicited from Anna Karina, an actress whose talent Godard succeeded in keeping under wraps throughout the many films he made with her. Her talent was not the only thing he kept swathed: her body, too, remained hidden until now, when a delightful physique emerges. Andrew Sarris has commented on this unveiling, complaining that the actual bosom can be no match for what we imagined. Sarris is undoubtedly more learned than I am in matters of filmography, but when it comes to appreciating bathycolpian endowments, I yield to no man. Karina's bosom is a joy, and so, in many ways, is *The Stranger.* Pauline Kael complains, not without justice, that it was filmed too late; I am pleased that it has been filmed at all.

January, 1968

WAR AND PEACE

Bulk has never particularly appealed to me. I do not mean merely the elephantine variety, which, except on elephants, I thoroughly deplore. Even powerful, all-embracing, sublime bulk—Rubensian, Wagnerian, Dostoevskian—is nothing I would preconize. But I am willing to make exceptions for what might oxymoronically be called subtle or graceful bulk, as in Proust or Gaston Lachaise, "The Massacre of Chios" or "Das Lied von der Erde," *The Faerie Queene* or *Don Quixote.* Miltonic or Dickensian bulk, however, the bloatedness of Beethoven's Ninth or the chunkiness of a Henry Moore family group, I can leave rather more easily than take. The same with *War and Peace,* a novel I have not been able to get through—a fact I record neither proudly nor apologetically, only to indicate that I come to Sergei Bondarchuk's enormous film version of the novel unprejudiced, except for memories of Audrey Hepburn and Mel Ferrer, which is to say a prejudice in its favor.

By the time some future, though not so very future, Ph.D. candidate writes his dissertation on "The Comparative Esthetics of the Russian and American Cinemas," he will discover many more similarities than differences. Both the Soviets and Hollywood go in for gigantism, obviousness, sentimentality, and mythologizing, with only the natures of the myths being somewhat different. I say "somewhat" because the official idea of fulfillment is just as naïve on fabled Nevsky Prospect as on fabulous Hollywood Boulevard; it is simply the trappings and the way of achieving it that differ—and even that gap is decreasing. I am speaking, of course, of the typical product, not of the exception; and, save for its length and some action footage, *War and Peace* is no exception.

There is, to be sure, Leo Tolstoy. But after the adapters, dubbers, and American cutters have taken their toll, only stoy is left. The very idea of dubbing a film with serious artistic intentions is profoundly misguided; in this case, though the dubbing is technically fair, the Babel of tongues ranges all the way from the Royal Academy of Dramatic Art to the Neighborhood Playhouse, without a distinguished vocal performance in the lot of them. The translation, whether an already existing one or made up to match the lip movements, is not memorable prose. And the film was cut down to six hours and thirteen minutes, about an hour shorter than the Russian version—itself a boiling down of the novel.

What remains is still monumental—including, unfortunately, the most intimate, personal details. The actors, or, at any rate, those uneasy centaurs with Russian exteriors and Anglo-American insides, come across as horrendous bores. I suspect that even in Russian most of these performances are wooden; in the dubbed version, they are positively stony. Though "War," where there is a minimum of dialogue, has life to it, "Peace" emerges marmoreal and ponderous, with actors sitting like so many patiences on a monument. There are exceptions: Though the part of Princess Maria has the rather limited range from tearfulness to uncontrollable sobbing, Antonina Shuranova brings to it a magnificently eloquent face and great dignity. Some other smaller parts are well handled: Kutuzov, Captain Tushin, and, at least in looks and deportment, Napoleon.

The leads, however, fall short of expectation. Bondarchuk, the director and co-adapter, is a middle-aged, inflexible, uncharming Pierre; I much preferred Henry Fonda in the King Vidor version. Vyacheslav Tihonov, as Andrei, has an extremely suggestive face, but he likes to keep it looking dashingly morose, except when he has it look morosely dashing. As Natasha, Ludmila Savelyeva looks agreeable from some angles and pudgily babyish from others; her acting seems to consist mostly of beams of bliss, pretty pouts, and, in moments of extreme tension, a palsied trembling of the head. She does her little dance rather well, but then she is a professional ballet dancer. The worst acting comes from Anatoly Ktorov, who makes old Prince Bolkonsky into a petty tyrant, and Irina Skobtseva, who turns Helene into a large cow.

The color photography is extremely workmanlike, but no more than that. Still, inasmuch as what it gets to shoot is spectacular—imperial battlefields and ballrooms, wolf hunts, the burning of Moscow—it has its stretches of magnificence. The editing, costume and set design are all conscientious, albeit without particular brilliance. (Exactly how much has been lost by the cutting of the American version I cannot say, though such incidents as Pierre's divorce and his liberation from French captivity did not sufficiently register on me.) The music by Vyacheslav Ovchinnikov is hopelessly banal, on a par with what Hollywood lavishes on *its* spectaculars, give or take a demiquaver. This is shocking when you consider that Prokofiev's opera *War and Peace* could have surely been converted into a worthy score; failing that, there was always Shostakovich.

As a director, Bondarchuk is, with one or two exceptions, unable to make the "Peace" scenes come alive, despite his use of almost every available cinematic technique. Indeed, these techniques become *idées fixes* with him: during the many ballroom sequences, there are always bits of colored muslin (ostensibly parts of the ladies' gowns) whooshing past the lens; with great frequency and doggedness, the camera goes poking around the sky as if stalking the Almighty; and there is an often repeated, protracted shot of a river from a fast, low-flying plane that follows its course. This last is particularly distracting: by calling our attention to modern technology, it wrenches us out of Tolstoy's world. Only occasionally does the resultant beauty justify such extravagance; thus there is a shot of an Imperial Ball from what must be the highest crane ever built—almost a helicopter—that gives you the feeling that the very stars are looking in on the dance.

Even the "War" sequences, the best thing in the film, are frequently marred by Bondarchuk's passion for superimposition. A veritable legion of process shots obtrudes on the battle action: Sometimes it is one army advancing in one direction superimposed on another advancing in the opposite; sometimes it is superimposed memories, flashbacks, slow dissolves. The effect is to make the fighting unreal, not by legitimately increasing its fierceness, but rather by imposing a schematic, poeticizing orderliness on it, a discernible would-be lyrical methodology that actually kills the poetry of horror.

Nevertheless, the many battle sequences offer numerous moments that are—there is no other word for it—epic. They may be too beautiful, they may err by overemphasizing the totality at the expense of the individual's share, they may produce an unintended detachment in the viewer. But there is no getting away from the fact that they make the eye gape, that they give a sense of vastness and dazzlement if not awe, that they come as close to the Homeric as anything on film ever has.

There are giant swirls of movement, maelstroms of color, antiphonal barrages of hoofbeats and cannon: a sense of ourselves being projected onto a screen larger than the canvas of our daily lives—something that demands to be experienced. This is where literalness pays off: if the Battle of Borodino was fought by 120,000 men, the film employs exactly that many; if there was reckless stupidity in contemporary tactics and extravagant throwing away of life, that, too, is recorded with fanatical fidelity. Gigantism finally reaps its hard-earned, exhausting, yet undeniable rewards.

June, 1968

THE HEART IS A LONELY HUNTER

One of the prerequisites for a well-made film is texture: a certain density in the relations among the characters, a certain solidity of the setting, a topography you can feel in the soles of your feet. Houses, for instance, must seem lived in, and their rooms must have a recognizable spatial relationship to one another. A town must hang together, so that you can sense how people get from one point to another. That is what I mean by texture, and that is what *The Heart Is a Lonely Hunter* hasn't got.

Carson McCullers's novel is episodic, somewhat lopsided, and too fragile. It is also rather dated in its social reportage about Negroes and poor whites, and it is the victim of sexual reticences that today make it seem even more of a period piece. Yet it has the slightly demented authoritativeness of dreams brooking no argument.

Thomas C. Ryan, who both coproduced and wrote the script, has updated the events and retarded the psychology and dialogue, so that we are served an unconvincing Southern society of the sixties blithely mouthing early Hollywoodese. It is perhaps possible to streamline some novels into acceptable movies, though not by Ryan's methods; this novel, devious and elusive, would most likely resist any adaptation.

Ryan, for example, has Mick say to her sheepish boy friend, "I want you to kiss me the way a husband kisses his wife," or some such endearing garbage, which is just the wrong kind of baby talk for her, especially as her age has been upped in the movie. Or he has the film ending with Mick sobbing on Mr. Singer's grave, "I loved you, Mr. Singer, I loved you"—the kind of obviousness the novel scrupulously avoids.

The Negro question doesn't work at all in the film; clearly it should have been left in the novel's period without half-baked changes that place it squarely in no period at all. But where the film could have gone beyond the book is in the treatment of the homosexual motifs. Joseph Strick, the original director, wanted to make more of these, and was promptly fired for his pains. Strick is not much of a director, except perhaps by comparison to his successor, Robert Ellis Miller. What with Ryan's screenplay (from the same hand that gave us such bloopers as *Bunny Lake is Missing* and *The Pad*—a bastardization of *The Private Ear*) and Miller's direction, we are treated to something less than a slick commercial product with some unusual saving graces.

Foremost among these, aside from some fetching remnants of the original, is Alan Arkin's performance as Mr. Singer. Arkin has lately been used as an accent comedian, though some of his accents are rather poor. His Inspector Clouzeau was strictly from Brouqueline; his Russian submarine officer, from Brukljin. But his deaf mute is a genuine deaf mute coming from a spiritual isolation ward out of which only his brightness and decency have partly sprung him. While he does not look a bit Southern, what he does convey is more difficult and important—humanity and attractiveness, against the grain of the script, which would make Singer into a conventional do-gooder. His robotlike minuet of despair at his friend's grave is a memorable invention—as, indeed, are all his moments of muzzled grief. And he invests the part with a wonderfully unself-pitying, bittersweet humor.

Another asset of the film is James Wong Howe's color photography. In one scene, perhaps the best in the film, the veteran cinematographer surpasses himself: Singer has taken Antonapoulos out to dinner on the terrace of a hotel in fake Venetian style; the way a neighboring church tower peers in between the arches is a triumph of the camera. The character of Antonapoulos has been much flattened out; still, the mixture of comedy and pathos in this sequence is persuasive and affecting. Chuck McCann is adequate as the infantilized Antonapoulos; Sondra Locke just barely squeezes by as the adultified Mick. Some of the juveniles are quite good, but most of the supporting roles are routinely handled, and Stacy Keach is surprisingly ineffectual as a tramp—a character, to be sure, rather more complex in the novel.

September, 1968

THE KILLING OF SISTER GEORGE

A far from happy adaptation is *The Killing of Sister George*. Frank Marcus had written a blackish comedy about a foul-mouthed, gin-swilling, middle-aged actress, June Buckridge, who portrays a jolly country nurse, Sister George, on a TV serial, and is the darling of British television viewers; and "Childie," a superior shopgirl and bal-letomane, who plays with dolls and is June's mistress-slave, although she herself has an adolescent daughter somewhere. The two have a sadomasochistic lesbian ménage, which contrasts acridly with their outward lives, and particulary with the genteel Machiavellianism of the BBC potentates and the pathetic benightedness of the fans, whose mail and gifts keep pouring in. From the world invented in the BBC studio at Shepherd's Bush to the June-Childie flat in Hampstead, the distance is measurable only in light years. The play ends with the double undo-ing of Sister George at the hands of an icily suave female BBC execu-tive, who is instrumental in losing June her serial and ends up by stealing Childie as well.

The play was second-rate, but with its nice blend of the homey and the chilling, the absurdist and the perverse, it had the quality of a Krafft-Ebing comicbook. Robert Aldrich and his scenarist, Lukas Heller, have turned this material into a crawling tear-jerker, the lines spoken at a speed adjusted to non-English or non-language-speaking audiences. The sadism is omitted or turned into a joke, the "cultural" references are cut, the idiocy of the vast audience excised (for obvious reasons), the sauciness so reduced you can't tell whether it was béar-naise or hollandaise, and "humanizing" touches are added everywhere with thoroughly dehumanizing results. Thus when the sacked Sister George drunkenly smashes the studio equipment, instead of sympathiz-ing with her, we find her mawkish and stupid, something she never was in the play.

Beryl Reid's performance as George has become much more schematized than it was on stage; Susannah York is unconvincing at everything: lesbianism, childishness, acting; but Coral Browne does make something impressive out of the sensible, steely, patronizing BBC crypto-tribade. The film also boasts the most unnecessary obliga-tory scene in film history: a bedroom bit between the Misses Browne and York in which the former, looking as if she were mentally reciting the Second Catilinian Oration, probes the latter's breast as though testing a particularly inscrutable cantaloupe for its ripeness. Had Ger-trude Stein and Alice B. Toklas been shown this sequence, it might have driven them screaming into heterosexuality. For the record, Miss York possesses a lovely bosom that stands up remarkably even lying down and deserves to be bared in a less barren film than *The Killing of Sister George.*

December, 1968

THE SEA GULL

Chekhov was the musician of boredom. No one, not even Beckett, has drawn such recondite harmonies and such subtle discords from the motions, utterances, and silences of boredom. Frustrated lives palpitating in concert, hurling unsolicited gifts and demands at one another, misunderstanding or understanding one another too well, and hurting either way, they talk and live right past one another. Dialogues are not so much conversations as reciprocally embarrassing confessions colliding in mid-air, and the atmosphere is so smoky with frustration that joy cannot grow in it. Yet sapling joys do shoot up from time to time, only to wither swiftly and sheepishly.

That is the basic quality of *The Sea Gull,* and even if Sidney Lumet had captured it in his film version, it would probably have made for a cumbrous, oppressive film. But he captures nothing of the sort. Lumet's boredom is one that settles viscously on the viewer who cares not a straw for Lumet's straw men; whereas Chekhov's people, properly interpreted on the stage are as fascinating as a juggling act in which the balls are continually dropped until one hangs on every move of the bizarre, unhappy prestidigitators in the hope that one of their tricks might succeed.

Part of the trouble is the medium itself. The stage always affords full view of the arena of fumbles; every unsuccessful move can be seen in all its ramifications. Or, more precisely, the stage always shows you the space between the actors, the small but sufficient abyss into which their enterprises hurtle. The camera—except as handled by a master, which Lumet categorically is not—cannot capture the hollowness of space, the oppressive immovableness of a seemingly harmless enclosure, stasis settling on everything like a fine, corrosive dust. Then, again, a filmed play requires inventiveness in camera setups, a sharp feeling for montage, and self-effacing camera movements, lest, given the sparseness of action, one become aware of technical overcompensation. But Lumet is either too dazzled or too crudely confident to be at home in art.

And, of course, there must be performances. Performances that can make demanding stage roles survive this transplanting into alien ground. Even from good actors, though, Lumet can extract glutinous or shrill, colorless or desperate, performances. Least excusable here is the casting of Simone Signoret as Arkadina. While most of the actors speak in well-tailored English accents, Miss Signoret putters or sloshes about in a *débraillé* French one (not a stylish one *à la* Charles Boyer) that is often incomprehensible. Her appearance has also become hard to take, especially when the text has her remark on how well she has kept her figure, and her acting is unsubtle—in part, I suppose, from exhaustion from her bouts with English.

As Trigorin, James Mason acts dazed, uncomfortable, constrained. Yet that is the opposite of what characterizes this successful second-rate writer: postures of existential despair, affectations of bluff simplicity, and, underneath, complacency; if the actor is very great, he may be able also to show the genuine sense of emptiness at the core. Mason maintains an all-purpose remoteness, relieved only by faint but rather too genuine yearning, and makes Trigorin uninteresting.

Vanessa Redgrave is—by now, at any rate—too much of a raw-boned, thirtyish, English governess to pass for the vulnerably young, sweetly tremulous Nina. A jaw like hers could take all of fate's punches; and how could poetry, except perhaps Edwin Markham's, live under that backward-sloping brow? Her innocence comes across studied, and she pathetically lacks pathos. Her fourth-act scene (which loses much by being shot outdoors) remains wholly unmoving. Even if Lumet was trying to adhere to Chekhov's designation of the play as a "comedy," that surely means a sad comedy of absurd waste, and it is better for Nina to err on the side of Ophelia than on that of a budding Madwoman of Chaillot. As Konstantin, David Warner tries hard to compensate for his lack of sensitive looks and personal charm; what comes out is not a young Aleksandr Blok but a young blockhead with pretensions.

Harry Andrews is an unshaded, frenetic Sorin; Eileen Herlie, a flat Paulina. While Kathleen Widdoes acts Masha well enough, the aura of smugness and prissiness that always surrounds this actress erects a sympathy barrier. Alfred Lynch is a believable Medvedenko, but Ronald Radd a noisy cliché of a Shamrayev. Perhaps the worst performance (after Signoret's) is Denholm Elliott's Dorn. Elliott, who can be brilliant as a roué, weakling, or bounder, simply cannot cope with the decent, weary doctor—a sympathetic and perceptive man gone stale with age and provincial drudgery. His wig, moreover, makes him look like some villainous marquis at the court of Louis XV, or, equally inappropriately, a diabolical Mark Twain. It is not so much a question of individual shortcomings, however, as of what these actors jointly undo.

Here Lumet is most to blame, And what preposterous directorial ideas he has! At the beginning, Masha and Medvedenko, totally out of period and character, are shown rolling around in the tall grass; as Masha adjusts her disarrayed undergarments, she declares that she wears black out of mourning for her life. Or, at the end, how stupid to cut that great line, "The fact is, Konstantin has shot himself," and substitute a view of Treplev's bloody body—just like the sea gull's!—floating in the lake, then have Dorn enter the drawing room ominous and silent, and have a slow circular panning shot (a favorite Lumetian device) around the lotto table, where each face registers a different yet obvious expression. A long hammy silence, then blackout. No! It is that awkward, whispered last line—with its "the fact is" and to Trigorin, of all people—that is needed; and the lotto players playing on as if nothing had happened.

Gerry Fisher's color photography, at least in the print on display at the Plaza Theater, is rather poor: it looks like hand-tinted film, the faces mostly heliotrope, and nature a washed-out bluish green or greenish blue. The interiors are better. The Swedish house and lake used work in quite nicely, although one never gets a sense of exactly who lives in that house and exactly where. The translation by Moura Budberg is all right, but it has been carefully pruned of literary or cultural references that might puzzle the customers of less privileged neighborhood theaters. As I myself was leaving the Plaza, a woman was explaining portentously: "Unrequited love!" That may have been her own, unabetted cloddishness, but I cannot help feeling that Lumet's unrequited love for "Art" encourages such vulgar errors.

February, 1969

THE PRIME OF MISS JEAN BRODIE

The Prime of Miss Jean Brodie lost a good deal in its stage simplification by Jay Presson Allen, and loses still more in its movie reduction of that stage version. Not that Muriel Spark's novella is so very complex a work, but its subtleties of narrative technique, its ambiguities of character, and its moral dilemma have all been twice subjected to Mrs. Allen's flatiron. This is, of course, as much the fault of the industry, which wrongly or (alas!) rightly assumes that the audience cannot make out an undotted "i" or an uncrossed "t."

Ronald Neame's old-hat direction assists the process of vulgarization. When people are dancing, we always begin with closeups of their feet; when two pubescent girls speculate about sexual intercourse— "they're bound to be put off their passion with their clothes off"—a phonograph record suggestively runs down; after Miss Brodie has hurled her despairing (and echo-reinforced) cry of "Assassin!" at young Sandy for getting her dismissed, we cut to Chapel and all the girls singing "Lord, dismiss us . . ." I uttered my *nunc dimittis* well before that.

Maggie Smith is fine in the quieter moments of the part, but much of the time she does a grossly mannered, female-impersonatorish camping around—which undoubtedly earned her the praises of our most masculine female and feminine male reviewers. Robert Stephens, Miss Smith's equally gifted husband, plays her one-armed lover with his missing arm restored for the movie version. But I would have given his right arm for a better performance. Celia Johnson, inevitably yet heartbreakingly aged, does a beautifully restrained job as the headmistress, and among the girls, Pamela Franklin and Jane Carr were especially impressive. But minor parts get caricatured, Edinburgh is wasted, and Ted Moore's color photography seems uneven, though the trouble may lie in the print: with every change of reel there was about as much change in color values as between the palettes of Bonnard and Puvis de Chavannes.

March, 1969

LAUGHTER IN THE DARK

There is nothing to shout about in Tony Richardson's mistreatment of Vladimir Nabokov's dazzling and poisonous display piece of human folly and cruelty, *Laughter in the Dark*. This short novel is inconceivable outside its 1930-ish Central European setting. Transposed in Edward Bond's unsubtle screenplay to contemporary London, it has little meaning and less place and period flavor. Richardson has omitted almost all the intellectual content and mental cruelty of the tale, concentrating instead on the sheer physical nastiness and on sweltering sexuality, which he manages to make thoroughly repugnant. Instead of showing the faintly repellent pitiableness of sexual dependency, and the horror of sexual domination and exploitation, the film turns the very heterosexual sex act into the clumsy villain of the piece.

Though the color photography by Dick Burns is adequate, and Peter Bowles's performance as the rejected wife's prissy but decent brother is accurate and touching, little else works. (There are, to be sure, two or three striking visual effects.) Nicol Williamson is much too young and lower class to get the degradation and pathos out of Sir Edward More, as the hero is now called, but at least his performance has moments of intensity. Jean-Claude Drouot, as his sneakily cruel rival, is beefy and stodgy. Anna Karina, as the amoral heroine, besides being too old for the part, reverts to her sleazy and vacuous nonperformances in Godard's films. Peculiarly infelicitous is the trio of accents: Williamson's stridulant, nasal and provincial; Karina's an olio of—Danish, French, and cockney; Drouot's throat-bound, uninflected—perhaps Martian. Under Richardson's direction, this devastatingly sadistic but believable reverse *Taming of the Shrew* emerges as a preposterous shaming of the true.

June, 1969

JUSTINE

And now we have *Justine* on film. Actually it is not so much *Justine* as *The Alexandria Quartet* without Alexandria and without any quartet. How far can you go on a *The?*

Durrell's tetralogy is not a work of genius, but it is imbued with the *genius loci.* The four books have a single protagonist whose name is not Justine or Clea or Darley but Alexandria, the loved and hated city, which alone pervades the pages of the work with its ruthless amorality and immutable variousness. This is the Alexandria about which the poet Cavafy (himself a shadowy presence in the novel) warned: "You will find no new lands, you will find no other seas./ The city will follow you." But not, it would seem, as far as Hollywood. Yet it is not so much the fact that the film was shot largely in Hollywood (and slightly in Tunisia) that syphons Alexandria out of the screenplay; it is the scriptwriter, the director, and, behind them, the studio that see to that. Of course, it is devilishly hard to get the atmosphere of a place on film when that place is to take precedence over its people.

Consider this passage from the novel *Justine:* "Place Zagloul—silverware and caged doves. A vaulted cave lined with black barrels and choking with the smoke from flying whitebait and the smell of *retzin-nato*. A message scribbled on the edge of a newspaper. Here I spilt wine on her cloak, and while attempting to help her repair the damage, accidentally touched her breasts. No word was spoken. While Purse-warden spoke so brilliantly of Alexandria and the burning library. In the room above a poor wretch screaming with meningitis. . . ." Notice how plot is encroached on by locale, and how the latter preponderates. This is the sort of thing that our film dare not, will not, cannot, do. But what it could have easily and impressively done is to convey Durrell's neo-Proustian perspective: the changing point of view, which redefines and refines people and events as it adds to them new dimensions, further understanding, or just a more hermetic mystery. Such third and fourth dimensions, however, were stripped off the story and it now unfolds in linear conventionality.

What George Cukor, the director, and Lawrence B. Marcus, the scenarist, have left us with is the slick portrait of a fascinating woman of Alexandria, Justine Hosnani. In the interest of concentrating on this sinner and saint, the novel has been cut, simplified, and changed—to the extent that it would be idle even to begin to list the departures and simplifications of the screenplay. The ambiguities of woman—or of the concept of woman as imagined and depicted by men—are not new to either Durrell's or Hollywood's Alexandria. Some sixteen centuries ago, the poet-grammarian Palladas of Alexandria wrote of woman: "Be she chaste or a whore, either way she is perdition. . . . All the woes of the *Iliad* were for the sake of one woman, and Penelope was the cause of the *Odyssey*." Justine is both faithful and whorish, both Helen and Penelope, and the cause of the film we are discussing.

If only George Cukor were more than a commercial director! Joseph Strick, who began work on the film and was fired (or quit), is more intellectually inclined, but lacks even Cukor's slick competence. Cukor, declared "a genuine artist" by Andrew Sarris, is, in my opinion, a paradigmatic hack. This becomes evident when you consider that the complexities and contradictions of Justine are no more brought out by him than are the anfractuosities of Alexandria. It is true that the marvel-ous Anouk Aimée has progressively ceased being an actress in order to turn more and more into a star. As one of her recent directors told me, her head is now so swelled that she can hardly walk through an ordinary door. It shows in her work: where is the actress who en-chanted us first in *The Golden Salamander* and *The Lovers of Verona*, later in *La dolce vita* and *8½*, and last in *A Man and a Woman*? In *Justine* we still get a beautiful woman when her hair is down; a less beautiful one when her hair is up; a double when there is a nude bathing scene; a Gioconda smile when mystery is to be suggested; but an actress, never. In all fairness, we must admit that English is not Miss Aimée's strong suit (not so long ago, coming out of *Fiddler on the Roof,* she ran into me and asked, *"Qu' est-ce que ça veut dire,* 'fidelère'?"), and there were moments when her mere accent is a burden on her characterization. But what is ultimately amiss is not what hits our eyes and ears; it is what does not strike our hearts.

The movie *Justine,* despite leaden forays into homosexuality, transvestitism, incest, and child prostitution, remains as naïvely old-fashioned in its emotional and intellectual vocabulary as in its actual verbiage and cinematic technique. Pursewarden, for example, is described as the wittiest man in Alexandria, yet the film shies away from letting him deploy his erudite and dissecting wit. The scene in which he confesses his incest to Melissa, who lies in bed next to him, unsatisfied, is so dramatically unprepared for, sketchy, and dully staged and photographed that it affects us, if at all, comically. Michael York, as Darley, does not succeed in suggesting a struggling artist, and Pursewarden's novelistic activities are eliminated altogether. The transvestites seem to shriek their maleness, whereas the meaty Melissa scarcely conveys consumption. Even the many-faced Justine is not so different from other Hollywood North-Africana—say, Gene Tierney in *Sundown.*

Details are carelessly mismanaged or glossed over. The dictionary at the British embassy is not the *Shorter Oxford,* but, inappropriately, *Webster's Second;* the child brothel looks much less sordid than Durrell (and, I suppose, truth) would have it. Even the final editing is faulty; thus a scene in which Pursewarden's blind sister, Lisa, has a letter from her brother read to her—this establishes the incest motif and makes clear her blindness, as her one previous scene does not—is cut from the film, though it is still listed in the official synopsis. In fact, this could be a perfect late thirties–early forties movie; all that is missing is Norma Shearer or Barbara Stanwyck swishing about.

The acting tends to be uninspired and conventional—so the Nessim of John Vernon and the Pursewarden of Dirk Bogarde (that remarkable actor is here crippled by the script); or obvious and embarrassing —thus Robert Forster's Narouz and Jack Albertson's Cohen. Cliff Gorman and Elaine Church (Toto and Liza) make nothing of their small parts, and George Baker and Severn Darden (Mountolive and Balthazar) get wholly lost in the shuffle. But Michael Dunn is drippingly effective as Mnemjian the barber, shorn though his part may be; Anna Karina is passable as Melissa; and the irrepressible Philippe Noiret is splendid as Pombal. Saddest of all is the pitiful showing of the great Marcel Dalio in an almost subliminal part. Leon Shamroy's color photography is, once again, workmanlike but unlovely (compare his desert with Frederick Young's in *Lawrence of Arabia*); Irene Sharaff's costumes lack brio; and Jerry Goldsmith's music is a disaster.

For all this, the film is watchable, especially if one has not read the book or forgotten it, which is easy to do. But that City, whose situation E. M. Forster called "most curious," is curiously and grievously absent from the film. This Cavafian Alexandria is as vanished as the Pharos and the Library, if indeed it ever existed. But writers' Alexandrias remain; though Durrell's City may be as imaginary as Pierre Louÿs's or Anatole France's, the film must re-create it. Yet what can we expect from a movie that omits the novel's most delightful character, Scobie?

September, 1969

THE MADWOMAN OF CHAILLOT

Shaking the dust of the Seventh Festival off my mind, let me turn to some other recent films, permitting me to put the dust right back on. Without doubt the most execrable of these is *The Madwoman of Chaillot,* screenplay by Edward Anhalt (Hollywood's resident saboteur of French drama—remember his version of Anouilh's *Becket?*) and direction by Bryan Forbes, a slick and arty director, who here does not even manage slickness. One of Giraudoux's less good and most fragile plays has been rewritten, bloated with inept contemporary references, drawn out to gigantic proportions of humorless vacuity, peopled with a barrelful of nonacting stars (Yul Brynner, Paul Henreid, John Gavin, Richard Chamberlain) and others who are miscast or not given a chance. The level of the invention is best conveyed by the fact that members of the Communist party are usually shown wearing a red garment.

Three particular horrors must be noted. First, the casting of Katharine Hepburn as Aurelia, the Madwoman. Miss Hepburn's quality was and will be that of an offbeat, madcap debutante, and she has now simply entered the *emerita* division of the same category. Her Aurelia is all huskily doddering sexiness and girlish flutters, senior division. When you think of the great Marguerite Moreno, who created the role, and then look at this performance, exact replicas of which have already earned Miss Hepburn two ill-deserved Oscars, you may wish to forsake the auditorium for the vomitorium.

Then there is Danny Kaye as the Ragpicker, a part created by Louis Jouvet. The comedian reads his lines by Anhalt out of Maurice Valency's adaptation of Giraudoux, and what the Kaye-Anhalt-Valency trio does to the late playwright can be described only as a necrophilic gang bang. Kaye's delivery is slow, heavy, oily; the accent, some ghastly culture-surrogate belonging to no class; the face, smug and expressionless, fitting this film to dismal perfection. The third horror is Forbes's unattractive and untalented wife, Nanette Newman, in the ingenue role that she is, moreover, far too old for—especially opposite Richard Chamberlain, whose pretty face is as unblemished as a newborn calf's.

November, 1969

END OF THE ROAD;
TROPIC OF CANCER

Two films based on notable novels have recently opened: *End of the Road,* derived from John Barth's second, and probably best, novel, *The End of the Road;* and *Tropic of Cancer,* adapted from Henry Miller's fictionalized autobiography, possibly the favorite forbidden book of yesteryear.

End of the Road, from which a great deal more of Barth than the initial article has been slashed, is based on a novel that ends with a harrowing abortion. The film goes the book one better, by being an abortion from beginning to end. I don't know who the main culprit is: Aram Avakian, the former film editor newly turned director, or one or all of the scenarists, Dennis McGuire, Terry Southern and Avakian himself.

The name that sticks out sinisterly from this lineup is that of Terry Southern, the novelist-scenarist who, considering his slender and unwholesome talent, has been able to make a mountain out of a dunghill. Though his earliest fiction contained some promisingly rampaging rowdiness, this vest-pocket Rabelais never laid open vistas wider than an unzipped fly. His most successful book, *Candy,* was, in fact, a collaboration, and revealed, on closer inspection, small control of humor, style, or even English grammar.

It was again a collaboration, the sort of thing for which the least silent partner ends up getting most of the credit, that brought Southern into the scriptwriting limelight. This was the delightful *Dr. Strangelove,* a tripartite screenwriting credit for which Southern managed to corral almost as much praise as Stanley Kubrick, the principal writer as well as director of the film. From there, Southern went on to butcher, with admirable impartiality, whatever came his way to be adapted: the good, like Evelyn Waugh's novella, *The Loved One;* the bad, like the comic strip, *Barbarella;* or the in-between, like his own early novelette, *The Magic Christian.* (This last, which just arrived here, is as inept and piggish a film as *Futz,* of unlamented memory.) Southern keeps frantically stretching his minuscle means, only making the same thing bigger, weirder, cruder, and, above all, more scatological.

The End of the Road, the novel, was a comedy of college life in the fifties, a satire on psychotherapy, and a personal tragedy. The film sets out to be absurdist farce, gobs of black humor, and, most of all, as "now" as all get-out. It begins, accordingly, with a montage of stock shots, including, among other things, Hitler, concentration camps, Mussolini and mistress hanged upside down, atom-bomb explosions, Harry Truman, launchings at Cape Kennedy, the assassination of JFK, LBJ and the beagle, Dr. King's funeral, the Saigon police chief executing at point-blank range, other Vietnam executions, Nixon, Jasper Johnsish closeups of the Stars and Stripes, the Chicago riots—all this interspersed with sweet, burbling babies. It is flanked by shots of a college graduation that turns into a violent demonstration. On the sound track, as Jacob Horner, the disaffected hero, walks directly from graduation into catatonia, we hear Billie Holiday singing "Don't Worry 'Bout Me," for a bit of easy irony. This is supposed to provide, in a nutshell, justification for the problems of Horner, America, humanity, and the scriptwriters. For every outlandish, demented, and, yes, swinish spectacle on the screen is to be taken as sufficiently justified by these references.

There is hardly a love scene, a psychiatric session, a daydream, without these portentous allusions being reintroduced in a fashionable, facile, and fatuous Dance of Death. (Rule of thumb: a film containing library shots of either concentration camps or atomic explosions will be almost certainly bad; a film containing both, certainly.) But every kind of grossness proliferates in the film. In the book, Jake Horner is treated by a preposterous psychiatrist. In the film, the doctor becomes a menacing black man, by turns a militant, a buffoon, a guru, an Uncle Tom, a primitive Bushman, an image of stern or cackling omniscience and invincibility. As James Earl Jones plays him (horribly, in both senses of the world), he keeps shifting accents—as, indeed, does almost everyone else in the movie, the scenarists evidently considering this a capital jest—sometimes turning his mouth into an obscene snout, and squealing, grunting, trumpeting his lines.

The doctor's sanatorium is, for the outdoorsy patients, a nonstop orgy on the front lawn and in the surrounding bushes; for indoor lunatics, it is the fulfillment of fantasies in which they can enact punished schoolboys, dogs, snipers, or, in the case of one particularly imaginative male patient, a masked, gagged, and crucified ballerina. A nurse, described by Barth as "a large, masculine woman," becomes here a scowling, hirsute man in drag, outfitted with an untidy gray wig. A reference in the book to the possible passes the male patients might make at Horner, becomes in the film a lightning homosexual rape performed on him as he is following the doctor down a staircase, while the latter continues his insouciant descent, spouting metaphysical, or metapsychiatric, cant. A particularly jolly scene has one naked patient, by way of "mythotherapy," copulating with a chicken (Leda and the hen?), raising once again the age-old question of which comes first, the chicken or the ech?

If, in such matters, the hand of Terry Southern is stranglingly recognizable, there are other offenses for which the director must be blamed. Avakian has gotten from the skillful Gordon Willis color cinematography that is exceedingly artful and thoroughly cloying. A forest into which ride Jacob and Rennie, the wife of his teacher-friend soon to become his mistress, is made into an enormous goo of turquoise and pistachio, from which the strongest eye gets indigestion. A sanatorium room is all white, with only snatches of brown and black obtruding on it, so that the color film is artily aping black-and-white photography. A body of water deliquesces into tiny, fragmented, silvery wavelets, which, in turn, change into bubbles bursting into a pristine blank screen. Two people descending a winding outdoor staircase are not only burnished by the sunset to every shade from amber to terra cotta, but also shown both approaching and moving away from the camera in a long, schizoid superimposition. A pair of horsemen, riding from left to right, meet themselves, superimposed and doppelgängerlike, riding from right to left, the whole thing superimposed yet again, in an achingly slow dissolve, over sparkling waves of a lake that gradually inundate the riders.

For no reason at all, everything stops while we watch flies in extreme closeup climbing up a window pane or disporting themselves on a light fixture. Out of nowhere, distorting lenses are conjured up to knead the image into funhouse-mirror distentions. When the film is not projected in triplicate, the actors turn into plasticene. The camera angles and movements are often as bizarre as if the camera were mounted on a drunken pogo stick.

The musical score, arranged by the director's brother, George, is condignly turgid and pretentious. It totters from Teo Macero's banal symphonic jazz into Bach played (I think) on a Moog synthesizer; thence it backtracks into jazz, or, for the crucified transvestite ballerina, leaps into *Swan Lake*. But another relative of the director's, his wife, Dorothy Tristan, turns nepotism into inspiration. The actress can make her pleasant but unremarkable face into a dozen different faces: beautiful, pain-riddled, childlike, wizened, otherwordly, furibund, ethereal, earth-motherish—you name it—and even unnameable. Now she is the prototypical dowdy faculty wife, now a blazing maenad unleashed on our libido, now a china shepherdess so fragile her own breathing might shatter her, now a goddess shooting up high above any mere man in the immensity of her love or wrath. Aram Avakian's dreadful *End of the Road* should perhaps be seen, after all, just for that shiningly irrefutable performance that triumphs over sabotaging script and fracturing photography.

The director of *Tropic of Cancer*, Joseph Strick, has a distinguished record of turning his attention only to genuine works of art and consistently botching them. Genet's *The Balcony* and Joyce's *Ulysses* had to bear the brunt of his highminded amateurishness, and emerged from his hands as Stricken deer. Though a lesser work, *Tropic of Cancer* is an important novel in two ways: as a torrentially lyrical outpouring of Miller's sometimes inspired, sometimes merely garrulous, lust for life, lust for art, lust for lust; and as a documentary of the American "lost generation" in Paris in the twenties and thirties—their scrounging, hustling, loafing, and strangely symbiotic kind of parasitism. As George Orwell correctly noted, the book's importance is "symptomatic."

Strick has managed to lose the second characteristic completely. By updating the film—not so much to make it "now" as simply to save money—he has cast his characters into a flabby limbo, lacking even the firm unreality of Ruritania. For this is a recognizable 1969 Paris in which overage American expatriates rhapsodize schoolboyishly about sexual experiences, people catch boat trains to get back to the States, and Henry Miller himself, played by Rip Torn, barely knows three words of French and speaks them as if the phrasebook had not yet turned cold in his pocket. Moreover, Miller and his motley moochers were all as passionately enamored of literature and art as they were of sex, or of talking about sex (which, better yet, combined sex and literature!); but the people in the film might as well be in the meatpacking or undertaking business for all they seem to know or care about the arts.

As for the crazy, lopsided poetry, Strick, co-scenarist as well as director, tries to hang on to some of it by preserving chunks of Miller's mammoth monologues as offscreen narration. But, alas, the simplified onscreen dialogue painfully clashes with the flights of voice-over fancy —as if the film were shot simultaneously in two languages: English and basic (or even baser) English. Nor does the narration profit from Rip Torn's delivery, as Texanly monotonous as if the flat side of a cleaver had mercilessly reduced it to its own image. But at least Torn is of a piece, playing Miller equally monotonously as a beaming, bedazzled goat, leaping about in ecstasy for having discovered some simple arithmetical fact, such as one plus one equals two, or yin plus yang equals BANG!

Nevertheless, the film does, almost accidentally, preserve some of Miller's existential ecstasy, sense of humor and smiling amorality. Never before have four-letter words so deluged us from the screen, never has sex been made more blatant, obsessive, and at the same time, as naïvely innocent as stamp-collecting, as amiably competitive as autograph hunters comparing their albums. Moreover, Strick's device of having the narration wallow in mendacious accounts of gigantic sexual feats while the camera tells the sober and pitiful truth, creates some smartly comic effects—until the joke dies from overuse. Even a lesser conceit, the quickly shifting closeups of different parts of feminine anatomy marching, bounding, hurtling, at you, proves a nice objective correlative for a sexual greed starving, like Buridan's ass, amid breasts, bellies, behinds, among which it cannot choose. In all this, Strick is greatly aided by the excellent editing of the late Sidney Meyers and Sylvia Sarner.

The acting, by a cast of relative unknowns, is largely unnoteworthy. There are exceptions: James Callahan, as Fillmore, captures much of Miller's zany pathos; the dependable Magali Noël makes a dubious Princess indubitable fun; and Françoise Lugagne is quietly touching as a woman whose age is a deterrent even to dedicated satyrs. The passing parade of adulterous wives, dishonest whores, fun-loving nymphomaniacs, and other miscellaneous doxies is suitably unglamorous, avid, desperate, or indifferent—their clothing as deciduous as autumn leaves, their faces as nakedly weatherbeaten as a winter tree. Two of them are even beautiful: Sabine Sun as a buxomly toothsome Teuton, and Ellen Burstyn as Miller's errant wife, bursting out of her dresses or frontally nude enough to reveal that she is no natural redhead.

End of the Road is a pretentious, unappetizing disaster. *Tropic of*

Cancer, disoriented, diminished, and (figuratively even more than literally) denuded as it is, still exhibits a skittering vitality, as likable as it is laughable.

February, 1970

WOMEN IN LOVE

D. H. Lawrence used to remind me of a collier who, refusing to leave the hated mine by the elevator, insists on burrowing his way single-handed to the antipodes. No wonder he got shafted. But that view was less than fair. For one thing, most real writers prefer to dig for China; for another, Lawrence's England was still a hot (or cold) bed of doddering but tenacious Victorianism. So Lawrence's fight was a brave and good one.

But when I look more closely at Lawrence's novels after *Sons and Lovers,* even at the masterpiece *Women in Love* is alleged to be, my discomfiture reasserts itself. There is something faintly repulsive about this novel: in its language, with its fumblings and repetitions; in its ideas, with their contradictions; in its obsessiveness, without our quite knowing by what it is obsessed. "A beautiful enigmatic book," Yeats called it; but Yeats was equally aware that "Lawrence romanticises his material, with such words as 'essential fire,' 'darkness,' etc." and felt that "happiness is not where he seems to place it." And Thomas Mann wrote to Karl Kerényi: "I prefer [Aldous Huxley] to D. H. Lawrence, who is undoubtedly a significant manifestation and characteristic of his time, but whose hectic sensuality has little appeal for me." He went on to stigmatize the anti-intellectualism of the literature of the day. And it was only 1934!

Yet on the subject of the intellect, as on so much else, Lawrence was less outright hostile than hopelessly self-contradictory. This, no less than his febrility, may have spurred on the always loosely reined malice of Dame Edith Sitwell: "Lecturing at Liverpool, [I] said that Lawrence was the head of the Jaeger school of literature, since he was hot, soft, and woolly. Messrs. Jaeger protested mildly. 'We *are* soft,' they wrote to me, 'and we *are* woolly. But we are *never* hot, owing to our system of slow conductivity.' I replied, begging them to invent a system of slow conductivity for Lawrence, adding that I regretted having made the comparison, since their works are unshrinkable by Time, whereas the works of Mr. Lawrence, in my opinion, are not." But E. M. Forster saw in Lawrence "the only prophetic novelist writing today [1927] . . . the only living novelist in whom the song predominates . . ."

I could go on forever adducing contradictory judgments on Lawrence, but for my purpose, which is to show why a film version of *Women in Love* must fail, it is more relevant to point out where friendly criticisms agree, or at least converge. Thus Elizabeth Bowen noted that in *Women in Love* "individual characters may seem to split apart under a too great pressure"; and Lady Ottoline Morrell (whom Lawrence was unkindly to turn into the Hermione Roddice of the novel) wrote in her memoirs: "His insight was indeed very intense, but sometimes so bright that it distorted those it focused." What these basically sympathetic demurrers mean can best be understood when collocated with some critical raves. Thus F. R. Leavis commends "Lawrence's preoccupation with relating the overt expressions of personal life to the impersonal depths . . . his power of presenting in the individual psyche the large movement of civilization."

That Lawrence was attempting something of this sort is beyond dispute; that he succeeded is open to question. For it is very hard to reach such new goals by the older methods of storytelling he generally adhered to. Kafka, Proust, Joyce, even Mann to some extent, had to resort to new novelistic structures. They also were more at ease with language than the often laboriously groping Lawrence. One more "loins" or "darkness" or "electricity" we say, and we've had it; and it comes, frequently in some clattering compound, screaming out against its hyphenation.

As J. I. M. Stewart puts it for the defense, "Lawrence's representative people live at the end of abnormally open channels of communication with infrapersonal worlds, and through these channels their conscious minds are constantly inundated by potent and mysterious floods." So far, so good. But Professor Stewart continues: "Of this violence of Lawrence's language is the necessary and effective instrument." If, as I believe, that second "of" was accidentally dropped in by the compositor (*Eight Modern Writers,* p. 518), Stewart seems to me dead wrong; if, however, this is not a typo, it is a useless truism. I would say that in his stories and novellas, where Lawrence could not let himself go on at inundating length, either in linguistic cataracts or narrative meanders, he is a master indeed. There Professor Stewart's channels of communication have been subjected to Dame Edith's (or Messrs. Jaeger's) system of slow conductivity, and we can get both the Lawrentian depth perception and the Lawrentian ineffable mystery without being flooded or burnt to a crisp.

When a character in *Women in Love* is not only steeped in prophecy and song (to use Forster's terms); when he is also a burstingly open conduit to layers of depth psychology, preindividuality and prehistory; when he becomes both a sketch from life and a larger-than-lifesize principle in action; when he must give voice to dark, electric forces engendered in the loins and best left voiceless—then Lady Ottoline's distortions and Miss Bowen's splitting apart are almost inevitable. The novelist faces pitfalls; his film adapters, one large unfordable morass.

Unfortunately, neither pruning nor complete omission is a satisfactory solution for the filmmaker. What would Joyce be without his puns, or Quasimodo without his hump? A great writer or a great literary creation depends on his characteristics, whether they be eccentricities, foibles, downright flaws, or indeed troublesome strokes of genius. As Graham Hough observes about Lawrence, "because his darker and more vatic utterances contain statements that are literally nonsense, it has often been found easy to reject the whole as nonsense. The whole may very well be untrue, but it certainly makes a kind of sense . . ."

Although it is often rather hard to separate the "kind of sense" from the nonsense, presented with the entire novel, the reader himself can judge which is which, according to his own lights. It is unsatisfactory to have to take someone else's blue pencil or scissors for the sword of absolute justice. Ever since Richard Aldington, critics have tended to boggle at the rabbit episode, and this is—probably just as well—omitted from the film. Almost equally unanimously, even enthusiastic pro-Lawrence critics tend to be unhappy about some of the sexual descriptions—not because they offend as sex, but because they fail as description. Yet most of these scenes are in the new film version, in rather dubious equivalents.

All critics, though, admire the episode where Ursula watches Birkin shatter the reflection of the moon in the water by throwing pebbles at it—"a scene that always stays in the memory," Forster called it—but this, too, is missing from the film. What is definitely and consistently decimated is the artistic-cultural-historic philosophizing which, however hard to swallow it may be, is the essential Lawrence. Take, for example, Birkin's (the Lawrence alter ego's) reply to Hermione about why he is copying an ancient Chinese drawing of geese: "I know what centres they live from—what they perceive and feel—the hot, stinging centrality of a goose in the flux of cold water and mud—the curious bitter stinging heat of a goose's blood, entering their own blood like an inoculation of corruptive fire—fire of the cold-burning mud—the lotus mystery." It may be farrago, but it is what makes Lawrence Lawrence.

The film version of *Women in Love*—produced and written by Larry Kramer, a young American, and directed by Ken Russell, a young Briton—is, for all its superficial fidelity to the novel, a profound betrayal of it. It is also an uneasy compromise between art and entertainment (as if the two were contradictory) and a resultant failure as both. To be sure, Kramer and Russell have been quite faithful to Lawrence in their fashion; moreover, greater faithfulness would not necessarily have been an improvement, very possibly the opposite. The only safe and wise thing to do with a novel like *Women in Love* is not to make a film of it at all.

Even the faithfulnesses, then, are questionable here. For instance, the naked wrestling bout between Gerald and Birkin, which in the novel recedes into the fabric of the whole—an important strand, yes, but nothing particularly sensational—here, what with male genitalia dangled across the screen, takes on the kind of homosexual coloration that Lawrence (whatever might have been latent in his psyche) would certainly have abhorred. Again, Lawrence's enthusiastic nature descriptions are evoked cinematically by making a forest scene as green as roach poison, and the following wheatfield sequence more golden than the bowels of Fort Knox. A love scene presents vertical images in horizontal position, so that a naked Ursula rises in slow motion toward a nude Birkin floating down upon her, the pair of them surrounded by enough pink and gold flora to make it look like two stripped dress-shop dummies accidentally dumped in the middle of a florist's window. This is presumably meant to convey Lawrence's purple prose of physical fulfillment, and, in the most horrible way conceivable, it does just that.

But there are times when small liberties are being taken and prove quite sufficient to oversimplify, distort, and cheapen a scene. Thus the entire figure of Loerke is completely vulgarized and wrong. In Lawrence he is, like Gudrun, an incomplete artist whom the girl gravitates to as Gerald's opposite, but who is no more the solution for her than Gerald was. The movie turns him into a homosexual and precursor of the Fascists who behaves like a pig: he puts on his socks and boots on the dining table and shakes his cigar ashes into Ursula's dessert. Far slimier than in the book, he makes real Nazi sculptures: a delicate, pubescent girl on horseback, as Lawrence describes her, is shown as a ponderous monument to the heavy-limbed Hitler Youth maiden.

Again, the semianonymous couple whose wedding starts the book off become minor characters in the film and then turn into drowned young lovers; in the book, it is a shadowy, half-grown Crich sister and a nameless would-be rescuer who drown. All this so that the director can crosscut from Ursula and Birkin in their first sexual aftermath to these drowned newlyweds at the bottom of the drained lake and reveal —the two couples intertwined in exactly the same way!

Now this is sinister nonsense. First, because Lawrence avoids such obvious symbolism. Second, because it is misleading: Lawrence would never have intended a parallel between the embrace of love and the clasp of death, or between a drowning girl dragging her rescuer down with her and Ursula dragging Birkin into—what? Marriage? Domesticity? She does not, or only to the slightest degree. Third and most important, by introducing a third couple of some importance but uncertain significance the script obfuscates Lawrence's basic design: two clearly antithetical couples working out their exemplary destinies.

Another typically facile symbol is the image of Gerald and his father being driven home in their snow-white Rolls-Royce while pit-blackened colliers trudge wearily homeward all around them. Similarly, the improvised pseudo-Russian ballet is performed in the novel *for* Hermione; in the film, it is danced chiefly by herself, and turned into a crude travesty geared at easy laughs. Indeed, Lawrence's already rather cruel portrait of Lady Ottoline is reduced to caricature by Russell's direction and Eleanor Bron's cabaret-style performance.

Kramer and Russell use a number of little cinematic tricks, intended to liven up things, but actually deadening them with the withering breath of artiness. Particularly damaged are the love scenes, two of which I have already described. But there is also that series of self-conscious quick dissolves that verge on being jump cuts during Gerald's declaration of love after he has seen Gudrun dancing before the cattle; or the pulsation effect (little zoomings in and out) when Gerald makes brutal love to the provoking Gudrun for the last time.

Worse yet is the cross-cutting during Gerald and Gudrun's first mating in her room, when we keep cutting from the thrashing lovers to Gerald's mother insanely laughing at her husband's funeral. Not only is the device obvious, but the laughter at the funeral does not exist in the novel. Kramer may have gotten the idea from Lawrence's beautiful story "Smile," where a somewhat similar incident is treated with infinite finesse. And in that Alpine sex scene between Gerald and Gudrun we get the same kind of cross-cutting—this time to Gudrun's happy or mocking laughter under the Matterhorn, a laughter that similarly infuriates Gerald. Yet if a parallel between Mrs. Crich and Gudrun is intended, it is not developed.

It might be argued that these flaws are at least partly offset by some of the film's virtues. The camera work of Billy Williams is, in its less obstreperous moments, by no means unimpressive; the set and costume design and general period atmosphere are accurate and suggestive; and some of the scenes convey certain Lawrentian points with economy and efficiency. But against this I must set the overriding flaw of a largely social novel's being so pared down that there is hardly any social fabric left in the film. Gone are all sorts of minor characters and social milieus that explain how the main characters live and why, ambiences into which they fit or against which they rebel. As it is, the Brangwen girls and Rupert Birkin float mysteriously and arbitrarily through the movie, and the uninitiated filmgoer can hardly figure out their class or their occupations, if any. What philosophizing the script still allows them, seems, therefore, idle and gratuitous.

The casting, too, leaves much to be desired. I have already mentioned the simplistically conceived and executed Hermione, Loerke, and Mrs. Crich. But the leads are also problematic. Alan Bates is a breezy iconoclast of a Birkin, without the character's disturbing ambiguities. Jennie Linden's Ursula is a typical soubrette with little of the New Woman about her. And Oliver Reed is miscast as Gerald: the icy, blond, open Nordic god becomes a blackhaired, pear-faced, sinisterly mustachioed skulker. Reed, moreover, likes to pad out his dialogue with a breathing scenario, so that many speeches are prefaced by a stertorously melodramatic intake of breath.

As Gudrun, Glenda Jackson gives the most interesting performance of the film, but is, alas, almost frighteningly plain. Her features are heavy and somehow malevolent in their irregularity; her body is like a block of uncarved stone except for her much-revealed breasts, shaped like collapsing gourds; and her thick arms and legs might as well be those of the West African fetish that figures so prominently in the novel but is cut from the film. Even her line-reading is rather too slow and mannered, but at least it is intelligent and arresting.

April, 1970

THE VIRGIN AND THE GYPSY

Why does *The Virgin and the Gypsy* work for me as a film, whereas *Women in Love* did not? The main reason, I suppose, is that *Virgin* is a novella of some hundred pages; *Women,* on the other hand, is a novel of well over five hundred. The novella may be just about the only form of fiction that readily lends itself to cinematic adaptation: it is long enough to offer the filmmaker a sufficiency of material to use, expand, or drop; but it is not so long as to oblige him to cut ruthlessly and disfiguringly, nor so short as to force him into wholesale inventions and additions. In any case, this film version, written by Alan Plater, a Yorkshire playwright (the novella takes place in a vague North Country setting), and directed by twenty-nine-year-old Christopher Miles (his first feature film), emerges as a minor but lively pleasure.

The Virgin and the Gypsy (Lawrence's spelling, gipsy, is not preserved) concerns two young sisters who return to their father's gloomy rectory after school days in France (Lausanne, in the story). Lucille is gradually submerged in the life-denying puritanism of the rectory, while Yvette, partly through her own healthiness, partly through a fleeting involvement with a gypsy, and partly through her friendship with a more enlightened couple who spend a holiday in the neighborhood, manages to emancipate herself. In the film, she actually leaves for London with the pair (Major Eastwood and Mrs. Fawcett, not yet married pending her divorce, but living together and ostracized); in the book, she stays on, having just a slight chance of full self-realization.

The film spells things out more than the story, adds illustrative incidents or details that are a trifle obvious, but does not, on the whole, take liberties of a distracting nature. Even such an added episode as Uncle Fred's risqué contribution to the Church Benefit is handled tactfully enough and remains in character. As for Yvette's departure with her new friends, it is both more contemporary (a dubious motivation) and more cinematic (a justifiable motivation) than Lawrence's minor-key ending. Plater and Miles treat this closing scene wistfully rather than triumphantly; the mood is not one of easy victory but of guarded hope.

The filmmakers rightly chose to shoot the picture in "Lawrence country" instead of farther north, for the descriptions in the tale are pure Derbyshire. And how beautifully Miles has re-created the look and feel of both the exteriors and interiors of the place and time (the twenties), avoiding the flashiness from which Ken Russell's *Women in Love* is never quite free. True, the local rich boy who is Yvette's swain is made a bit unduly bumpkinish, and the atmosphere at the rectory seems a shade more unrelievedly dank than in the book—perhaps because Maurice Denham lacks the handsomeness and boyishness Lawrence accords the Rector. But the film exudes atmosphere without, somehow, acting smug about it.

Compare, for instance, the way nature looks in this film and in *Women in Love.* There the colors are exaggerated to the point where England seems to be Italy if not Brazil, and you wonder why a trip to Switzerland should have had such an effect on the principals: the Matterhorn, after all that green and gold and pink, looks rather sober and puritanical. Here, with Bob Huke's much more controlled color photography, the landscape looks sheerly English: the sunlight seems spread about thinly and frangibly, an infinitely precious commodity; the greens seem to have been obliged to fight brown and gray to arrive at their greenness; and the flowers have that doomed look of precociously gifted people who will die young. There is an aura of impermanence here and of exultation in summer while it lasts, very much as in the still more Nordic films of Bergman and the Scandinavians.

Superior, too, in this film are the minor characters: the dread matriarch, Mater, chillingly disembodied by Fay Compton; Aunt Cissy, played with self-pity always abutting on hatefulness by Kay Walsh; Uncle Fred, whom Norman Bird keeps an almost invisible speck; the bustily brooding gypsy wife of Imogen Hassell. Particularly fine is the Eastwood-Fawcett couple: devoted, genial yet vaguely corroded by their ostracism. Nothing is made in the film of her Jewishness, but Honor Blackman's Mrs. Fawcett perfectly personifies a certain Semitic intensity and slightly overrouged vitality. And Mark Burns capably conveys a solidity that stops short of stolidity, a calmness not without heat below.

The great lacuna of the film—aside from Maurice Denham, who, able actor though he is, makes the Rector too rigidly pressed and dried between the pages of a hymnal—is Franco Nero's Gypsy. Nero may be the reason for spelling the word with a "y"—so gypped do we feel by his nonperformance. Unlike the Major, this Gypsy suggests nothing with his empty blue-eyed stare; yet desire, the Gypsy's absurd but absolutely natural craving for Yvette, and the salutary response it kindles, are the subject of the story. In the film, the Major's repressed stirrings toward Yvette register more strongly than the Gypsy's undivided desire. Nero fiddles while Mark burns.

Though the *Gypsy* half of the title is a failure, the *Virgin* is a success. Joanna Shimkus is one of the most captivating actresses of the international screen, a member of an all too select group including her fellow bilingual Canadian, Geneviève Bujold; Lisa Gastoni and Jacqueline Bisset (both shamefully denied the chances they deserve); Vanessa Redgrave and Jane Fonda; Susannah York and Julie Christie (when the spirit happens to move them); and probably one or two others who do not occur to me at the moment. A fashion model, Joanna Shimkus left Canada for Paris on a brief modeling assignment and landed a part in *Paris vu par . . .*—the Godard episode in which she sported a delightful little English accent in her French, a youthfully impudent face fluctuating between blasé sulkiness and bursts of naïve enthusiasm, and a perfect figure: girlish where girlishness is best, womanly where womanliness is better.

Her acting was not yet much, but by the time she appeared in Robert Enrico's *Les Aventuriers* (released here by Universal in mangled form as *The Last Adventure*), she was reborn. Her French was greatly improved; a hairdo was found to give her face the needed softness—there is that large bony nose, which Miss Skimkus stands by as courageously as by her unprepossessing Lithuanian last name; and, under a bright young director, she was undeniably acting. Beneath the muted, velvety surface, there was incandescence; the *gamine* could turn inside out, like a glove, into a *femme fatale;* the *jolie laide,* at a slight turn of the face, became irreproachably lovely. Next, in Enrico's fine little film, *Zita,* her centripetal intensity hovering between childishness and womanhood, Miss Shimkus gave a definitive portrait of a girl's coming of age. There followed *Ho!,* a potboiler I have not seen, with Belmondo; then Joseph Losey's *Boom!,* where the actress was badly photographed and directed, and emerged insignificant and whiny. Things went no better for her in her first fully American movie, *The Lost Man,* Robert Alan Aurthur's dreary updating of *Odd Man Out.*

But now she is Yvette, and, once again, all is well. Lawrence in one place speaks of the girl's "young, clear, baffled" eyes, and that is what Miss Shimkus epitomizes: a baffled clarity. Sometimes it is as if she were fashioned entirely of the finest suede, with only the eyes made of moiré silk. Though many of her actions are performed in a dreamy slow motion, something bristles behind the bars of her gaze and her voice, something spoiling to dart out of its cage. Her entire performance is a quiet fulmination. And Christopher Miles is to be complimented for the most intelligent use of nudity in recent films: it is sparse and artfully scattered through the picture, tasteful and also genuinely erotic. Though held back, sex is alive in this film; in several others currently playing, it is laid on thick and takes a terrible beating.

August, 1970

2

Politics and Society

IT IS extremely difficult to make a good political or social film because the issues are complex and, to some extent, abstract, and have to be embodied in human antagonists to make them come alive. But then in order to make the characters both dramatic and human in a 90- or 100-minute context, the issues usually have to be foreshortened and oversimplified. In effect, the filmmaker is caught between the Scylla of depersonalization and the Charybdis of oversimplification. Even such an almost exemplary film about workers in revolt as *The Organizer* was forced to reduce the employers to cartoons. It is much easier to make a film with political overtones or social implications, like *Citizen Kane,* and not confront the problems head-on. Nevertheless, such important subjects as social and political conflict must not go by unnoticed, even though Hollywood still prefers to ignore them as unsafe at the box office. Thus *Medium Cool,* a deserving pioneer film about our sociopolitical unrest, was coolly ignored by the Oscars. Yet the ability to deal with such crucial problems is indispensable to a mature art form, and it is, therefore, gratifying that this area, hitherto explored only by foreign films, is beginning to be examined by ours as well.

This category, in a certain sense, overlaps with "The Youth Film," and should be considered in conjunction with that. Two of the films included here, *The Activist* and *The Revolutionary,* would have fitted into the latter almost as well; I have placed them at the end of this one, to form, as it were, an appropriate transition to the latter.

LA GUERRE EST FINIE

Can one make films about politics? Not about the rise and fall of a popular leader such as Zapata, which is another matter, nor about war or the villainies of Nazis and Communists, something else again. But about ordinary people embroiled in fairly ordinary politics, so that their private lives become submerged in, overshadowed by political issues? Well, we have had things like *The Best Man* and *Advise and Consent,* which, quite aside from being trashy, deal almost exclusively with spectacular and sinister machinations; on fundamental or everyday matters they are grandiosely simpleminded, if not downright blind. Even novelists, including the best, have difficulties with plain politics: I find much of *The Red and the Black* and *A Sentimental Education* heavy going.

For trying to bring politics—not quite ordinary politics, but not the most sensational kind, either—to the screen, Alain Resnais's *La Guerre est finie* is to be commended. The film concerns Diego, a Spanish refugee living in Paris, who is a full-time agitator. As a member of the Spanish Communist underground, he keeps crossing over into Spain to smuggle propaganda in or people out, and stir up discontent. But it is 1965: the war has been over for twenty-six years, and his youth too has gone by. Yet early middle age is not without its harvest of autumnal pleasures. He has a lovely foreign mistress, Marianne, who is rich (the CP pays him a small fraction of what she earns as a book designer—I had no idea they rewarded such things so well in France!) and in love with him.

In consequence of a close shave at the border, he meets the daughter of the man whose passport he uses, Nadine, and instant consummation results. The young girl, herself a member of a militant Communist underground group, is bowled over by the fact that Diego is "a regular"; Diego, by the fact that she is so very young. Though Diego is still deeply devoted to Spain, he is tired of revolution and the whole Spanish mystique: he hates Lorca's plays and has never gone to the banks of the Ebro, as he blurts out in a rare moment of passion—characteristically negative.

The film examines simultaneously, then, the aging of a cause and the aging of a man. Diego watches the anti-Franco efforts becoming more and more quixotic, his friends landing in prison, his beautiful mistress losing her youthfulness, younger and more militant Communists attacking his "antiquated" methods while his own group rebukes him for excess of caution. A young girl hurls herself at him, and he takes her, both for the wrong reason; age and adiposity are overtaking him. It is all, as the French text says, so *sad;* or, as the American subtitles, more psychiatrically oriented, would have it, so *depressing.* And it could make a magnificent movie, but it doesn't.

Why not? Because the people are clichés, the dialogue undistinguished (alternating between rather high-flown narration by Diego and deliberately low-flown conversation the rest of the time; neither of these is bad, but all of it has been here before), and the filmmaking, though surely better than in *Muriel,* fluctuates between the radical and the conventional, without making much of an impact with either. The chief "modern" device is showing what is in the hero's mind at certain times; this can be relevant, as when Diego is apprehensive about the fate of Juan, a fellow-conspirator, and we see several sequences in which Juan is arrested in different places and in different ways. That has dramatic validity because it introduces an element of anxiety, if not suspense, into a film in which nothing very startling happens; and because it evokes the background of uncertainty and danger against which the hero moves.

But frequently the device is meaningless. When Diego is trying to imagine what Nadine, whom he has met and admired only over the telephone, looks like, we see a girl walk down a staircase, turn into another girl, and so, by jump cuts, into a whole series of girls. I don't think that Diego would be that curious; I don't think the mind works that way; I don't think this tells us anything helpful or important; and I am quite sure that viewers are needlessly confused by it. Or, while Diego still tarries with Nadine after their dalliance, a shot of a staircase suddenly flashes across the screen. Later, one may realize that it is Diego's and Marianne's staircase, and means, presumably, that Diego would like to be getting home. But at that point one has no way of identifying these stairs, and they are merely baffling; besides, there are simpler ways of indicating that Diego wants to get out. And if that is all Diego's thinking consists of—a view of a staircase—why bother?

There are nice touches, though: the effective bit of symbolism that, for the first few shots of him, keeps Diego in the shadow; the sinuous ballet of lights that the nocturnal traffic outside throws on the walls and ceiling of Diego's and Marianne's apartment, a ballet that serves both as an obbligato for some passionate scenes and as a transition between them. There is the Hartung painting (or lithograph) on the wall, its harshly crisscrossing lines appearing behind Diego's head to progressively greater significance; there is that touching little sensual-sentimental insight: Marianne's bra is held together by only one hook, the other one missing altogether. But over against this, there is the familiarity and banality of incidents and utterances, the standard tiredness of this hero (Montand himself has played him a few times before), and, mostly, there is the politics. All but one of the political scenes and all of the political statements are hackneyed—which may serve to stress the theme of creeping boredom with the political issues, but does not make for absorption in the action.

In the last analysis, Resnais and his scenarist, Jorge Semprun, are aware of the fact that politics alone will not carry their film, and they reach over into three other genres. There is the documentary about a strange profession, in this case illegal political agitation, and we are shown sundry minutiae of how leaflets and reports are smuggled in and out of a country. There is the spy intrigue-debunking genre, in which we are exposed to the sordidness of the friendless and underpaid life of an agent. And there is even the sex film, with two fairly elaborately spelled-out sexual encounters. These scenes are supposed to be vastly different: one meant to have a Godardian detachment in its surveying of intercourse that is more experimentation than emotion; the other meant to be involving, the real thing. They both emerge as cerebral, studied, and unmoving.

Studied, and rather pretentious too, is Giovanni Fusco's music, which for Antonioni, especially in *L'Avventura,* has worked splendors if not wonders. Sacha Vierny's photography tries hard to be subdued, which, on the whole, is appropriate and effective, though, at times, wearying. The film is full of little red herrings, false alarms, minor improbabilities (it is unimaginable that our Spaniards would not have a code whereby they could telephonically or telegraphically recall an agent to Paris *before* he has crossed over into Spain), and, as I have mentioned, there is too much talk like "It doesn't do any good to cry or shout, reality doesn't change a bit for all that."

There is, however, one scene that is so successful that is almost makes me believe in the possibilities of the political film. In it, Diego is confronting the young Communists and, incensed by their intemperateness and cocksureness and their implicit slight of him, finds himself obliged to defend the "regulars," even though he has just been criticizing and criticized by them himself. Here the dialogue, staging, acting, and photography (especially an oblique fairly long shot from above, that isolates Diego from everyone and everything—except, perhaps, the cemetery seen through the windows behind him) combine to produce the one undeniably affecting moment of the film.

The acting is consistently convincing, though Yves Montand dredges up his favorite tricks a little too routinely for Diego: we can usually predict a second or two ahead which one of the three dependably irresistible Montand faces will be flashed at us next. But Ingrid Thulin and Geneviève Bujold do just right by the two main supporting parts, though, like all the women in the film, they are stock characters. In lesser roles, Marie Mergey as a regular's wife informed of her husband's disappearance, Jean Bouise as a childlike revolutionary whose heart cracks at the thrill of his first serious assignment, and Annie Farge as a nosy busybody, excel. But *La Guerre est finie* lacks either the intensity of characterization or the consistent freshness of detail that would make these politics assume flesh and urgency.

February, 1967

DUTCHMAN

One kind of play that need not be put on screen is the kind that was already rotten on stage. Such a one is LeRoi Jones's *Dutchman.* It is a work that tries to be both naturalistic and symbolistic, but fails in both modes, individually and in concert. Such behavior on a subway, certain actual cases notwithstanding, is unthinkable: the passengers, as long as they were threatened by nothing more powerful than a crazy blonde, would not put up with any of it. At the very least, they would move to another car. Equally preposterous is the notion that these passengers, many of them Negroes, having patiently tolerated vicious molestation by the girl, would side with her to a man in the murder of the young Negro, even becoming her accomplices. And the idea that this rampant psychopath can go on killing indefinitely (the concept, along with several others in the play, is stolen from Ionesco) is absurd in this nonabsurdist context. But that, of course, is supposed to be the symbolism.

Well, what of the symbolism? Who, first of all, is the presumably Flying Dutchman of the title? An advertisement for Dutch Masters cigars is no help at all, but neither is anything else. The girl, Lula, who travels restlessly up and down the subway lines? But she is not looking for the unselfish love that would redeem her. Besides, with her continuous apple eating and sharing, she is more of a travesty of Eve. But how could Clay, her young Negro victim, be the Dutchman? He, certainly, is not looking for redemption through this white woman's love. No go.

Let's try another symbolic level, then. Lula is the white American woman preying on Negroes. However neurotic American women may be—with black or white men—they are not psychotic murderesses, and, in any case, they are by now indulging fairly freely in interracial intercourse—at any rate on the social level and in the urban milieu here depicted. No go again.

Let's try still another level. Lula is the white society tempting and luring the Negro to his destruction. Now, the oppressor's wrong is wrong indeed, but it is a brutal, blanket subjugation; and though, as Sartre has shown, it may have its sexual implications, it is both more and less sinister than what happens in *Dutchman*. The careful, insane sexual provocation, with the lethal knife awaiting the victim who cannot but respond, is not the way the white society treats the Negro, no matter how unjust the treatment has been until recently and, to a large extent, still is. To substitute titillating perversion for simple brutality is not to shed light on either the social or sexual relations between the races.

Anthony Harvey, the British director, has gone the play's exaggerations one better, wherever possible or impossible. If in Jones's stage directions Lula eats an apple daintily, here it becomes a piece of orgiastic oral sex. If the fellow-passengers in the play are insulted, here they are manhandled. If, in the play, the dead youth slumps across Lula's knees, in the film, he sprawls over her on the subway floor in a kind of necrophilic rape.

Though Al Freeman Jr. gives a nicely tempered performance as Clay, making much of what humor can be extracted from the part and sensibly restraining the violence, Shirley Knight's Lula is another matter. Miss Knight, always a walking compendium of the worst Actors Studio inanities, is here allowed, not to act insane, but to be insane—something that, by Diderot's well-known paradox of the actor, does not work. Whereas the madmen of *Marat/Sade* convince with their controlled patterns, Miss Knight's Lula, who is supposed to be sane enough to ride the subways, is not only a hideous heap of histrionic self-indulgences, she even lacks that smidgen of credibility with which the author has provided her.

And that brings us to the paradox of the author. That LeRoi Jones should be steadily published, produced, awarded grants and applauded would, in view of his unceasing let's-massacre-the-whites tantrums and rabble rousing, be grotesque. In view of his almost total lack of talent, it is, like the rest of white liberal masochism, disgusting. It is the display of a stupidity that, like all extremes, merges with its diehard opposite.

March, 1967

COOL HAND LUKE

Circumstances have prevented my writing about *Cool Hand Luke* until now, and by this time Luke's hand must be positively gelid. Yet a few words are necessary about what may have been the best American film of 1967. Ostensibly a comedy-drama about a Southern prison and chain gangs, it is actually the story of a variously gifted man with no major aptitude other than a superb hate of regimentation. Luke has done poorly in the Army after a brilliant start; now he has been sentenced to two years of hard labor for drunkenly dismantling as menacing a phalanx of parking meters as could have sprouted from the sowing of a dragon's teeth.

What happens to Luke in the prison and chain gang—among guards who span the usual range of sadism, latent homosexuality, and petty meanness; and prisoners who are not all that unlike the jolly GI's of *Stalag 17*—is saved from plummeting into cliché by freshly observed and overheard detail. It is a hairbreadth rescue, but it works in this sympathetic and, for the most part, unsentimental film. To the rescue comes, above all, an offbeat, ironic understatement laced with little jolts of eccentricity in both protagonist and plot. For Luke is a bit of a fantastic, a Jack Armstrong turned Till Eulenspiegel, and the film goes wistful, sardonic, cruel, and uproarious not quite when and not quite as you expect it.

The script is, on the whole, intelligent, and makes only a few concessions to salable obviousness; of these only a conversation with God in an abandoned church and a series of tendentious dissolves at the end can be pronounced indigestible. Stuart Rosenberg, the most recent refugee from television, has directed his first film with what I can best call a very nice kind of slickness. It is not great direction, because one does not feel that anything about it is unique; yet every camera set-up or trick shot, low-angle or overhead shot, slow dissolve or fast cut somehow works. There is a good underlying sense of rhythm, and perky acting from an able, largely New York-based cast whom it is invigorating to watch.

Paul Newman makes Luke into one of his flawless creations; these are fairly infrequent but, when they come, can match anything in films. He is winning without being cute, defeated and groveling without invoking undue pathos, and his muted sadnesses blend seamlessly and manfully with his engagingly muted joys. The quaint, slightly inappropriate ballad he sings and plays on the banjo when he learns of his mother's death—with wryness, defiance, almost a touch of black humor, yet also genuine grief—epitomizes the tart mixture of flavors in this performance and this character. It leaves the memory prickling. Add to this handsome though understated color photography by Conrad Hall and a pawky score by Lalo Schifrin, and you have, in *Cool Hand Luke*, a film that presses ahead with bouncy determination past —even through—various pitfalls.

January, 1968

THE QUEEN

An hour-long documentary, *The Queen*, is not without interest. It shows the on-stage action during the 1967 Miss All-American (a dragqueen) contest at Town Hall as well as the behind-the-scenes preparations, titivations, flirtations, and tantrums. The film would have been better if the backgrounds of these men (some very close to girlishness, others squat and balding) had been examined in greater detail, and if the quality of the photography were better—though there are fairly cogent explanations for both these lacks.

What makes the film fascinating is *(a)* how much like women these persons are, *(b)* how much like men these persons are, and *(c)* how much like neither they really are. There is enough interplay of real and unreal in this slice of imitation-life to equip a couple of plays by Pirandello—though, of course, without their art. But one does get quite a sense of the precariousness, factitiousness, illusoriness, of the world one lives in—so much so that emerging into the street one eyes every passing female with a shiver of suspicion. Among the judges of the beauty contest, by the way, one recognizes such eminent connoisseurs of transvestitedom as Larry Rivers and Terry Southern.

July, 1968

SALESMAN

The Maysles Brothers' new documentary, *Salesman*, follows four Catholic Bible salesmen as they push the Good Book from door to door, attend sales conferences, get pep talks and threats from their sales manager, exchange satisfied or dissatisfied accounts of the day's activities in their motel bedrooms, immerse themselves in TV or the swimming pool, sleep and set out again to badger and bamboozle and, sometimes, sell. Already much discussion has been stirred up by the film: is it an invasion of the privacy of those unhappy people whose living rooms and kitchens are assaulted by worse than salesmen— *cinéma-vérité* cameras? Is it unfair to the poor, decent fellows who happen to be selling Bibles instead of Fuller brushes, and are therefore pilloried as Pharisees? Is it possible to capture the truth of these encounters and lives when cameras and tape recorders are present, or do distortions grow like tumors? Does the editing of the film disingenuously introduce editorial comment where none is alleged to be?

All these questions, I think, have their relevance, but beg the most important question. How does the filmmaker, in a situation like this, avoid having a pronounced view on the subject, and how, having such a view, can he still appear impartial? And if he succeeds in *looking* impartial, how can he avoid being either wishy-washy or a hypocrite? It seems inconceivable to me that he could simply say: "This just happens; it's just there."

Poor people are beleaguered by conniving men who tell them, truthfully, that they got their names through the local church. Their Catholicism is appealed to, questioned, played upon. Often they commit themselves to buying one of those hideous, expensive, gilt-edged Du Pont fabricoid plastic-and-nylon-bound Bibles that look like a cross between *American Heritage* and the *Reader's Digest;* usually they have to pay on the installment plan, although besides a few slick reproductions of famous Biblical paintings, it offers nothing that these folks' old Bibles don't provide just as well.

The neuroses and even psychoses that the salesmen and their dog, the camera, uncover are sometimes alarming; but the placid benightedness in other houses is scarcely more comforting. The way religion is bandied about, merchandised, paid unctuous lip service to, makes the notorious dance around the Golden Calf seem, by comparison, the Spring Frolic at Miss Porter's School. I believe that any religious man, whether devout Catholic or atheist, would have to be disgusted by this.

Nevertheless, it is possible to argue, I imagine, that even this horrible method spreads the word of God and serves a purpose. In that case, the film would have to be more committed to what it shows, just as in the opposite case it would have to be much more severe. But why, someone will ask, can't the film remain neutral? Why can't it present its data as a journalistic report does on poverty, a war, or a riot— without taking sides, but not, presumably, without private opinions? The answer is that a 90-minute film involves much more planning,

organizing, arranging, selecting, editing—contains much more pattern-
ing and good or bad artifice—than any straight, direct newspaper
account. It therefore imposes on us the need to judge it as a construct,
a work of art, and forthwith a new set of esthetic and moral expectations must be reckoned with.

Both from watching the film and from hearing the Maysles talk
about it, a certain moral ambiguity, a slipperiness based as much on
fuzzy thinking as on wanting to have it both ways, comes to light. The
film tries to be at once tough and sentimental, mocking and sympathetic, all of which is epitomized, perhaps inadvertently, in its advertisement. This shows Jesus Christ, complete with halo, carrying two
salesman's suitcases. What is the symbology of this ad: has Jesus become Willy Loman, or has Willy assumed the role of Christ? Are we
debunking religion or apotheosizing that quintessential American, the
salesman? Or are we laughing at both Savior and Salesman? The issues
involved are too grave to permit the Maysles Brothers to get away with
statements about how they really "like" these salesmen while the
advertising copy they release suggests an exposé of dark doings.

And now the other criticisms become meaningful. Wilfrid Sheed has
rightly objected that the film does not show how the Church is involved
with this activity. Nat Hentoff, while professing boundless admiration
for the filmmakers, expressed his conviction that the salesmen are
shown here at their worst, that their essential humanity is sacrificed for
dramatic effect. I myself am inclined to believe that they are even less
sympathetic than the film shows or could show—*vide* e. e. cummings:
"a salesman is an it that stinks . . ./ whether it's in lonjewray/ or
shrouds is immaterial it stinks/ a salesman is an it that stinks to
please . . ." If the salesmen were shown not only on the road but also
at home, I suspect that sorer truths would be revealed.

Still, almost despite itself, the film does achieve some impressively
depressing revelations. There are the Sales Manager and his wife, two
figures so crude and complacent and, in his case, menacing, as to sum
up in themselves the sociopolitical nightmare we live in. There is the
Theological Consultant for the Bible company who, at a testimonial
dinner, makes a speech that is worthy of the pen of Günter Grass.
There are the salesmen themselves who, with the exception of the
film's quasi-hero (who has since switched to the more secular selling
of roofing and siding), show no qualms about the oily or jocular, butch
or sanctimonious chicanery they practice. And, above all, there are the
victims, the people. Their witlessness, especially when trying to be
witty; their boredom and boringness; their oafishness and pathos; their
callousness and hauntedness; the perhaps inevitable degradation of

ignorance they live in, which is nevertheless an accusation and a challenge.

Andrew Sarris has criticized the film (like Hentoff, from a liberal standpoint) for generating an easy sense of superiority in the viewer. This is a correct indictment, considering how superficial and unearned is the superiority of the average middle-class moviegoer. But at the same time, it avoids the issue: that anyone with genuine aspirations to independent thought, esthetic sensibility, the life of the spirit, must feel profoundly shocked and revolted by the lives of these his fellow men, with or without benefit of Bible salesmen.

The Maysles have gone out with their equipment to capture something quaintly unwholesome yet typical; or something typically human and thus, supposedly, forgivable; or something—anything—that presented itself to their mechanically reinforced sensibilities. Instead, they have come back with something Swiftian, scandalous, frightening, and heartbreaking. They have stumbled onto something much bigger than they realize: a condemnation—however fragmented, fortuitous, and even inept—of the human condition, of man himself; but also of a society plagued by superstition, idiotic competitiveness, and stultifying materialism.

April, 1969

MEDIUM COOL

Medium Cool impresses me as a landmark in the new American cinema —more for its intentions than for its achievement, yet in a field so technically hypertrophied and artistically backward as the American film, *Medium Cool* deserves credit for striking out, at long last, in the right direction. Of course, in art as in life, good intentions are only good for paving stones on the most ominous of speedways, but Haskell Wexler's film has much more than that to recommend it. For *Medium Cool* is not just one of your thirties politically oriented dramas, which meant your politics Left and your esthetics left behind. Wexler, who has done very fine cinematography for several otherwise inconsiderable films, functioned here as scriptwriter, director, cinematographer, coproducer, and almost brought off this minor miracle—major, when you add that he also had to contend with the powers at Paramount Pictures.

The plot concerns the awakening of a hardboiled, monomaniacal TV camerman to the facts, rather than the photographs, of life. The scene is Chicago, just before and during the 1968 Democratic convention. Wexler, anticipating trouble, wrote a loose story outline that he then adapted to and fused with his documentary footage. The blending does not jell so smoothly as in *I Am Curious,* and the plot sometimes looks like a slightly smudgy glass case for the display of the *cinéma-vérité.* But the basic idea is sound, and individual scenes work very well, one or two of them brilliantly.

The three major mistakes are the beginning, in which the callousness of a TV cameraman and sound recorder team on the site of a fatal auto accident is exaggerated; the end, where another such accident, this time involving the film's principals, is dragged in by that hyphen linking *cinéma* to *vérité,* so as to round off the film and all too neatly match the national tragedy with a personal one; and, near the end, the heroine's search for her missing son.

That last scene is crucial and necessary: it provides the unifying thread on which all the documentary shots are strung. Yet there is something uncomfortably arbitrary about a young mother in a canary yellow dress wandering in and out of gray-green melees and mayhem looking for a boy whose disappearance whispers "Device!" into your ear. Still, the photography is, under adverse conditions, so powerful, and the sights so grippingly grisly, that we cannot but show some indulgence even here. The fact that Wexler is an artist more than a polemist is demonstrated by his having shot hours and hours' worth of riot footage, but included only a chaste minimum, as severely pared down as if Aristotle had been looking over his shoulder at the movieola.

Two further flaws trouble me in *Medium Cool.* One is the vestigial Pirandellianism that crops up here and there, a remnant of an earlier layer of the film's development. Thus during a tense confrontation at the 1968 Democratic Convention between demonstrators and the National Guard, an off-screen voice yells, "Look out, Haskell, it's real!" referring, presumably, to mace or some such nonlaughing gaseous matter. Again, we see Haskell Wexler and his camera shooting the fatal accident with which the film closes. And in an early sequence, there is a cocktail party attended by John, the TV cameraman hero, and his group. Seen wandering forlornly through the room, in the same yellow dress and dazed manner as at the end of the picture, is Eileen, the heroine. But she could be here only as John's date, and at this point the two haven't even met. Those, and a proleptic announcement of their crash, which John and Eileen hear over their car radio, are the only instances where the device is used, and they are too much or not enough: drink deep or not at all from the Pirandellian spring! The film also uses another device: the *hommage*—a built-in tribute to a film, filmmaker, or actor—much beloved by the *nouvelle vague* crowd. Because Robert Forster, who plays John, looks rather like a young Jack Palance, John is made into an ex-boxer—as Palance is in real life. A film is announced as about to be shown on the TV channel Eileen and John are watching; it is Godard's *Contempt* (an abomination, by the way), in which Palance and Brigitte Bardot are killed in a concluding car accident. So we get Forster and Verna Bloom (Eileen) in a similar accident at the end of *Medium Cool.* In John's apartment there is a large poster of Belmondo. I doubt that *hommages* ever contribute much to a film; often they are a distinct nuisance. Here they are mildly irritating because they suggest a certain in-group, *cinéaste* snobbery that clashes with the broad political and humanitarian values Wexler is after.

But the virtues of the film are many and considerable, and I shall insist on them even though the critic I most respect despises *Medium Cool,* and the reviewers I reprehend most adore it. There is, first of all, the photography. At least two shots will linger in my mind like favorite lines of poetry. One occurs when John and his earlier girlfriend, Ruth (the exceedingly sexy Marianna Hill) walk through a hospital door. The camera shoots through a semi-opaque glass pane, on which the two approaching figures first look like spermatozoa or amoebas, then swiftly recapitulate both ontogeny and phylogeny until, close against the glass, they become reconigizable human beings. And it is during the scene that follows—a date that ends with lovemaking—that John and Ruth become identifiable as a specific man and woman.

Later, there is a shot of John racing along the deserted corridors of his TV station trying to find the boss who just fired him (for protesting against turning over footage of demonstrations to the FBI and CIA). It is a low-angle shot and shows John zooming by in weird, distorting perspective while, in the background, someone is mopping the already spic-and-span floors. You wonder which is drearier: a man fighting for a quasi-worthy, dishonest job; or another having to slave away at an honest but worthless one? I may, of course, be reading more into that shot than it meant to convey, but it surely is, and was meant to be, a haunting image of desolation, active and passive.

There are dazzling episodes in *Medium Cool.* A visit by John and his sound man, Gus, to a group of Negro militants congregated in a small ghetto apartment is perhaps the only instance in the American commercial film of racial tension caught root and branch. These blacks are intelligent and confused, decent yet terrifying, sequestered in their righteous indignation. The whites are nervously apologetic or defiantly logical, and neither attitude works. No one in this room is to blame, but an agony, sometimes masquerading as humor, is imposed on all, and merely to speak means to tread on someone's festering feelings.

The nearest thing to this was a scene in *Nothing But a Man,* when a couple of rednecks threatened a young Negro couple; but *this* scene is more disturbing because it is of more widespread application, there is no villain, no suggestion of obvious melodrama like rape, no pathos —only pathology, the pathology of an entire society in an untenable yet not readily remediable situation. The utmost we see is glittering sarcasm, unreachable doggedness, a leering or lowering fanaticism— closeness preceding a storm. It is truly frightening.

The obverse of the coin is a no less effective scene in which John and Gus (excellently played by Peter Bonerz) interview a socialite by the pool of her club. This is staged *cinéma-vérité,* but it has all the earmarks and smudgy fingerprints of reality. It displays the pathetic stratagems of self-delusion with which white ostriches evade Black Panthers. The matron (a splendid cameo by Beverly Younger) talks about the house the family has acquired in Canada for the long hot summer: "It's good for the soul to get away from civilization sometimes, don't you think so?" And the word "soul" sounds just as unconvincing here as in the opposite camp.

Or take the scene where the National Guard is getting riot training. Some of the men are dressed up as hippies—or their idea of hippies— and they are marching on the improvised city hall of an imaginary city, from which a mock mayor tries to con them: didn't he let them use his swimming pool every Fourth of July? I dare say credit must go chiefly to the situation, a cinematic *objet trouvé* if ever there was one, but Wexler found it and shot it superbly. The relish with which the Guard enacts its adversaries, the brio with which it hurls insults at itself, the abandon with which it wears its bizarre gear, the comic-strip absurdity the "mayor" arrogates to himself—all this raises absurdist comedy to new heights. What makes men who can fight equally well on either side of the fence pick their particular side? Can one change the man just by changing his uniform? Or does he merely have a secret yearning to be his own antithesis—or why else does he put so much conviction into being what he isn't?

There are scenes that do not work. An interview with young pro-Kennedy students is too obviously staged; a scene in the kitchen of the Ambassador Hotel, recreating its languid, vaporous life up to and including the moment when dreadful reality, with its first chaotic outriders, irrupts on it, is cleverly done and effectively cut off before it goes too far, yet one wonders whether it is in good taste. A roller derby scene, showing the full brutality and sordidness of a sport that the uninformed might presume to be more harmless than several others, is highly impressive while it remains documentary; but when its violence is made to serve as an aphrodisiac for Ruth and John, it begins to look didactic. A scene in a gun clinic, where typical little housewives work out bloodlustily at the pistol range (these are parlous times, folks!) is quite good, yet here, again, a faint aroma of writers and actors obtrudes, although straight reportage might have been even more on target.

But these are all documentary or quasi-documentary scenes; what about the plot sequences? They, too, vary greatly in quality. When Verna Bloom, that totally natural and winning actress, is dispensing Eileen's earthy, sensible, yet not unpoignant femininity, the scenes move forward with assurance. As her pigeon-fancying son, Harold Blankenship, an authentic Appalachian-ghetto ragamuffin, contributes almost as much: he is neither attractive nor winsome, only a bright, scrappy, scheming, believable, and finally likable kid. Three scenes back in Kentucky, involving Harold's father, who may have simply walked out on his family but about whom we variously hear that he is "at Vietnam" or a casualty of that war, are brilliant in their succinct, unsentimentalized yet touching evocation of a crude but not undignified way of life. They tell a prodigious amount with the sparsest means.

Even so, these scenes exhibit the fatal flaw of the movie: trying to tell us too much, and more than that, everything. This forces Wexler into miniscenes that are to do the work of giants. Often they cannot; thus the bedroom sequence between Ruth and John has to carry too great a burden of characterization. Even when such scenes succeed, they are often left painfully dangling, without another plot scene to latch on to until several *cinéma-vérité* ones have gone by. And sometimes, to compensate for plot ellipses, overemphasis is hauled in, as when John watches a TV documentary on the just murdered Dr. King and exclaims, "Jesus, I love to shoot film!" Clearly, a sort of pun is intended: the TV documentarist's passion is meant to be bracketed with a more lethal frenzy. But how, then, is *Medium Cool* exempt from the same charge? This shorthand, though writ large, does not abide our question.

At other times, Wexler's wit saves the day. A scene with John's smugly self-pitying boss, who, buzzed by his own superior, can switch to instant groveling, is neat, concise satire, fiendishly well played by William Sickinger. Wexler can do equally well with bubbly Truffaut-like sight gags, as when during a car ride through Washington someone notes that "for every man there are four and a half women," and the camera cuts away to four brief consecutive shots of pretty female strollers, and a fifth, of a girl shot from the hips down.

The acting is generally outstanding even in bit parts; in the lead, Robert Forster, owing probably more to good typecasting than to acting skill, comes across credibly as a stolid but awakening consciousness. Perhaps the best performances come from real people, as when a gumchewing, very young Guardsman and an equally young demonstrator who tries to win him over seem, for a second, to hover on the verge of contact. Here, as in many other scenes, a Hollywood film for the first time faces up to the wretchednesses beneath our prosperity; dares to give us a political America, and one whose politics are not suffused with health. I wish I could like *Medium Cool* completely. But intermittently, at least, I can love it.

September, 1969

THEY SHOOT HORSES, DON'T THEY?

They Shoot Horses, Don't They?, made from Horace McCoy's underground "classic" of 1935, is as impressive as it is flawed. The reel McCoy is, unfortunately, not quite the real McCoy, which itself fell short of a true work of art. Edmund Wilson, while conceding that it was "a subject with possibilities" and "worth reading," also noted the lack of characterization and motivation in the novel. But, in a sense, it was just this spare, straightforward, journalistic account of a monstrous Depression phenomenon, the dance marathon, that made the short book so unsettling: wholesale human degradation as the most matter-of-fact thing in the world. What weighs on this film is the passage of time: McCoy wrote his novel without the knowledge that he was creating a symbolic microcosm embodying universal hopelessness. The French existentialists were not hovering over his shoulders as they are over those of the filmmakers.

Nevertheless, the chief weaknesses of the film are like two or three bad sections of a tangerine, and can easily be spotted and mentally removed. They include a slow-motion prologue, or prelude, reminiscent of Sidney Lumet at his *Pawnbroker*ish worst, in which a boy witnesses the shooting of a glorious white stallion for no very convincing reason; some flash-forwards of Robert Syverton's trial for the shooting of his dancing partner Gloria—scenes shot in spooky ocean green and easily mistakable for flashbacks; and a bit of montage whereby the dying Gloria is seen collapsing no longer on a shabby pier but, in slow motion, in that meadow where the proud steed was killed. The sad thing about these blemishes is that the director, Sydney Pollack, is fully aware of their faultiness, and first made the film without these fatal embellishments. The original version of the film, without any of these elements, was screened for audiences in Palo Alto and San Francisco and elicited so much laughter in the wrong places—notably when Gloria produces a gun from her pocketbook in the last scene—that the additional material was put in to foretell disaster and forestall guffaws.

But, alas, the guffaws are not entirely the fault of cloddish spectators; both in the book and in the film there is something incredible about this ending. In the movie, Gloria is so dynamic, resourceful, and clever that we cannot see her as the loser Rocky, the marathon's shady entrepreneur, recognizes in her. And though Pollack and his screenwriter, Robert E. Thompson, have labored to stick in grim little details to justify this suicide, to me the dosage does not seem lethal enough. I am not even persuaded that the strong-willed Gloria would need the bland Robert to act as her executioner.

Here the fault lies partly in the movie Gloria's greater attractiveness and less pronounced death-wish than her fictional prototype's, and partly in Michael Sarrazin's not being a good enough actor to convey how one may be swept into this deathly compact at the cost of one's own life. I think of an actor like Gérard Philipe in this part, of the Mishkin-like quality he would have brought to it; this might easily have compensated for the insufficiency of characterization which the film in part inherits from the book.

To be sure, the movie does supply Gloria with a reasonably adequate background, as it also provides Rocky, a character largely created by the filmmakers, with a plausible past and interestingly complex personality springing from it. The other figures have to be taken at face value, which in all but Robert's case is not a serious loss. Rather more disturbing is the fact that in the film, as already implied, the marathon tries too hard to be emblematic of the world without quite being able to carry off the allegory. Thus the film makes the marathon's management corrupt in several additional and unconvincing ways, but even this is less of a problem than the sometimes topheavy dialogue, as in the case of that line McCoy relished enough to make it the title of his book. It makes a good title, but it is a poor line.

Yet, for me, these faults fade beside the solid achievements of the film. There is, first of all, the dazzlingly authentic atmosphere: the mendaciously optimistic music nudging on a dance that looks progressively less like dancing and more like chronic somnambulism, as if some sinister narcosis from another planet were infecting our world. And there is the hideous parasitic life that swirls around these staggering corpses: the management, the employees, the audiences. And the garish, pathetic, hysterical backstage activity—or merely leaden inactivity—during the brief rest periods of which many dare not avail themselves lest they never rise again to shuffle on. The sleazy dance emporium is recreated in all its tawdriness, the costumes are painfully accurate, the false gaiety enough to make a tin angel weep. Yet through this jiggling morass there runs a thread of life, of gallows humor, of sheer defiant tenacity, toward a paltry but touching heroism.

Not the least remarkable thing about *They Shoot Horses, Don't They?* is the photography by Philip A. Lathrop. There were considerable problems to contend with. Though shot in color, the film had to have the shoddy look of a godforsaken ballroom jutting out into the Pacific, and Lathrop accordingly underexposed and overdeveloped the film, getting a grainy texture and somber coloration—predominantly purplish brown of an unwholesome, almost macabre quality. And because the camera had to keep whirling along with the dancers, no ground-level lights, only overhead ones, could be used. It all works very well, despite the difficulties, and when Lathrop's camera seems to collide head-on with some of those overhead light beams, the result is not only glaringly realistic, it is almost hallucinatory.

Pollack and Lathrop keep the camera chasing after the dancers to good effect, particularly in the brutal elimination sprints. These grueling footraces around the ballroom, with the couples holding hands while the band plays rousing music, automatically eliminate the last three pairs to cross the finish line. Even during the regular dancing one partner has to support the other while he or she sleeps; here one or the other virtually has to carry the partner through lap after punishing lap, while the camera spins, lurches, staggers along. These scenes bristle with horror, and when Sailor, an overage contestant, is dying of a heart attack, the film expresses his agonizing vision by going into slow motion. What results is spooky, deathly, diabolic—perhaps a cross between Holbein and Dante.

But all kinds of scenes are managed with quiet brilliance. Scenes on the dance floor when nothing much is happening beyond the monotonous, lethargic roundelay, or when exacerbated contestants pick fights or just pick away at their partners; scenes in the rest area, backstage, with people often too tired to rest properly, crumpled up in bizarre positions, or bickering, or snatching at pitifully inadequate remedies, or having hysterics; scenes in Rocky's, the entrepreneur-MC's, office, where everything from seedy skulduggery to sterile lovemaking takes place. And even such very minor characters who say next to nothing, like Turkey, Rocky's fat, cigar-smoking assistant (Al Lewis), or the sixty-seven-year-old woman who sponsors Robert and Gloria because they are Number 67 (Madge Kennedy) are vividly conceived in terms of appearance and mannerisms, but are not caricatured or condescended to.

For such things we must be grateful to Pollack's direction and Robert E. Thompson's screenplay (though James Poe gets top screenwriting credit, his contributions do not survive in the final version). Pollack and Thompson have created two especially memorable characters: Gloria, the girl with the deathwish worn on her sleeve, and Rocky, the low-grade, hardened showman, are both absorbing and rich in surprises. At every turning of the film they reveal something further of themselves—sometimes unexpectedly better or worse than we would have thought, sometimes thoroughly fulfilling our aroused expectations. And both are played very nearly to perfection.

As Gloria, that fine little actress, Jane Fonda, graduates into a fine big actress. If there is one thing wrong with the performance, it is the vestige of a Vassar accent; other than that, it is solid, untricky acting, squeezing all the juice out of the part but not chewing up its rind. What impressed me most is that I did not really recognize Miss Fonda—and I don't mean the frizzed hair and other tricks of make-up, good as they are. I mean that the actress here gives an antipodal performance: there is none of the glitter, kittenishness, or jollity that have been her specialties in the past. But even her hardness has (unlike in *Spirits of the Dead*) a lining of humanity, and there is something about her very toughness that repeatedly moves us. And there are even fortuitous benefits: Miss Fonda has fascinatingly long, spatulate fingers—hands that are bony and poignant without being aristocratic or beautiful. They show up splendidly in the two-shots on her partner's shoulders and appear to be the hands of both Death and the Maiden in one.

As Rocky, Gig Young, that ex-matinee-idol-that-failed, makes a spirited comeback. The character emerges sleazy enough, yet not without a hardboiled charm, corrupt but with moments of solidity and even sympathy. His reminiscences of childhood are neither too sarcastic nor too touching; they are aimed at understanding, not empathy. He is not afraid of overplaying the two-bit MC aspect of his role, as overplayed it must be; but he keeps the other aspects in firm control and handles the transitions effortlessly. Young has just the right good looks gone partly to seed, and the properly flexible voice that turns oily in the limelight and greedy in the shadows.

Other roles are very neatly managed, too, both individually and in the here all-important ensembles. Especially imposing are Susannah York and Bonnie Bedelia, two actresses I have previously been less than keen, and sometimes downright down, on. Miss York plays a semirefined, semi-absurd would-be actress, strenuously emulating Jean Harlow, and trying to attract the eye of producers who might wander into the marathon's audience. She does it with a judicious balance of preposterousness and pathos, poise and desperation: the superficiality and flightiness of the character are kept as much to the fore as the naked need for affection, even if only from a vulgar audience, or, lower yet, from sordidly quick sex with another girl's partner. The hysterical scene in the shower is sensibly played much more for the sickness and horror of it than for vulnerability and heartbreak. It emerges, with Gig Young's strong collaboration, as a shattering and humane scene devoid of false heroism or histrionics.

As for Bonnie Bedelia, she is an actress whose appeal lies in some kind of fundamental ordinariness, which she usually epitomizes for other people's delectation, not mine. But here, as a famished, several-months-pregnant Okie wife, in the contest mostly for the food (her husband, by the way, is played with fine, fanatic, dumb-animal anger by Bruce Dern), she manages to be honestly gripping: naïve, confused, downtrodden, yet willingly, tenaciously dancing, plodding, hanging on. When she smilingly sings, out of the pit of her hopelessness, a mendaciously cheerful pop song and a few coins are tossed at her by the audience, the screen fills up with that dauntlessness and endurance that is the countertheme of this dirge with dancing.

Deserving of note, too, are the performances of Allyn Ann McLerie and Red Buttons as overage contestants who nevertheless defy mortality. For in this rockbottom marathon there are no runners gloriously expiring as they announce the victory of a Miltiades, only obscure human beings dragging themselves to exhaustion or death to proclaim obscurely the persistence of the human spirit.

Praise must go also to the make-up department, headed by another McCoy, Frank. It is an awesome sight to see these contestants grow feeble, haggard, ghostly before our eyes; becoming images of shuffling death. Time and all its creeping ravages, so powerfully conveyed by the acting, are as brilliantly evoked by the mutations of make-up.

Hovering over all this is the banal music of the period, suggestively yet unostentatiously chosen and arranged by John Green who, in his previous avatar as Johnny Green, also wrote many of the catchy tunes.

The music reflects, exalts, mocks, and finally provides an aural epitaph for these dancing damned. As for Harry Horner's setting, it is a shrewd replica of an old Los Angeles ballroom that could easily double as one of the lower rings of Dante's Inferno.

But, but, but. There remain the flaws I discussed earlier on, and the ultimate incredibility of Gloria's suicide—at least as presented on the screen. Sydney Pollack says that the last straw is supposed to be the accidental ripping of Gloria's last pair of stockings, and I concede that such an absurdly anticlimactic minor mishap will drive the exasperated person over the brink. But either because the incident is not etched sharply enough, or because too much time (including the seemingly liberating emergence of Gloria and Robert from the ballroom onto the boardwalk) intervenes between it and the shooting, Gloria's death remains unconvincing.

I suppose this is partly due also to her not being made into enough of a loser in other episodes of the film, and to Jane Fonda's deep, vital attractiveness, which even the dark triumphs of make-up, costuming, and performance cannot quite overshadow. Still, although *They Shoot Horses, Don't They?* does not, as a whole, reach the domain of art, many of its aspects and an aura that lingers on establish it as a true and eminent cinematic achievement.

January, 1970

Z

Why should a film based on a fairly respectable novel, telling a story of something bigger (indeed universal) than the events touched upon, involving a large cast acting together in exemplary harmony, having been directed and photographed with great skill, yet fall short of being a work of art?

Z, made from a novel by Vassili Vassilikos, is a fictionalization of the 1963 political assassination of Professor Gregorios Lambrakis, a deputy of the Left-oriented Greek EDA party, in Salonika, where the University of Athens professor of medicine had just delivered a speech against the installation of an American Polaris missile base. What was pronounced an accidental death from being knocked over by a passing vehicle, eventually proved to be a carefully planned assassination organized by the extreme Rightist party with the approval and collaboration of the chief of Salonika's gendarmerie and other high officials.

A young Investigating Magistrate, appointed by the government, turns out to be so much in love with the truth that, despite blandishments and threats from very high sources (perhaps the King himself), he inexorably brings the guilty to trial and condemnation. As a result, the Karamanlis government (it is not so identified—nothing in the film is) falls and, for a while, the Papandreou government takes over. But, with CIA support, the Rightist colonels, *plus royalistes que le roi*, stage their coup, the culprits are freed and reinstated, and the supporters of Lambrakis are jailed, exiled, or assassinated.

The last part of the sad tale appears in the film only as a brief, bitterly ironic epilogue: the body of *Z* concerns itself with what looks and feels like the arduous triumph of justice, and is meant to instill in us elation and hopefulness. With whatever difficulties, at the cost of martyrs' blood and every kind of suffering, the body politic goes from the sickness of warmongering, elitism, religious fanaticism, racism, and despotism to the health of Leftism, pacifism, democracy, freedom and justice for all. (This is, of course, an oversimplification at best, but let us, for the moment, go along with it.) Then, however, comes the epilogue, in which with a casualness that deliberately verges on the sardonic, we learn of the complete reversal of the just ending, the systematic destruction of truth and goodness, and a reversion to conditions even worse than the initial ones.

Although the Greek-born French director, Costa-Gavras, and his coscenarist, the Spanish-born French novelist, Jorge Semprun, have followed their historical novel reasonably closely, they have created a plot that is artistically untenable: the main drift of the film clashes with the epilogue to produce a self-contradictory, self-defeating impact, as of a Tinguely machine that destroys itself. But, you may remonstrate, does not the tragedy in *King Lear* set in just when everything seems to be finally working out for the best? True, with two significant differences. In *Lear* there is a sense of a cruel and unjust universe running through the whole play, and, secondly, the "good" characters are riddled with weakness, impatience, irascibility, gullibility, authoritarianism and other flaws, whereas the "bad" ones often have on their side a certain dash and charm, and a shrewdness verging on sheer common sense.

I am not proposing *Lear* as the measure of all dramatic, let alone cinematic, art; by that standard, few works indeed would make the grade. But the same principles must apply. In *Z,* the bad guys are quite intolerable without exception, and the good guys are as right as Left can be. Well, there is a half-Jewish lawyer-deputy (sizzlingly played by that superior jack-in-the-box, Charles Denner) who is probably too violent—but with what fearful provocation! And there is the Investigating Magistrate, who, though a government man, proves an absolute saint of justice. But there it is again, absolute sanctity so unswerving that when the man—privately convinced there was a murder yet still insisting that, until conclusive evidence is produced, everyone refer to the death as an "incident"—himself, near the end, inadvertently slips into the word "assassination," that one word hits both the court stenographer and us in the audience like a sudden judgment of God.

The Magistrate, then, is one who was accidentally born into the ranks of "Them," and who, had history evolved otherwise, would duly have found his way to "Us." The only two characters in Z who are not black or white are a muckraking press photographer, delightfully played by one of the screen's most prodigiously versatile young actors, Jacques Perrin; and a carpenter who proves a key friendly witness, played with incomparable juiciness by Georges Geret, a character actor on the grand scale of such earlier French masters as Harry Baur, Raimu, and Marcel Dalio. Both these men, though they do great good, do it out of mixed, partly selfish motives. But both of them are, in a sense, peripheral characters; while they affect the course of events, they are politically unaffiliated, outside the ideological lineups that confront each other on the film's prime battlefield.

No less important in removing the film from the range of art is the atmosphere of drama verging on melodrama and sometimes even farce that prevails in it. We are always in the presence, first and foremost, of a plot, and a plot that progresses along melioristic lines from profound gloom to radiant dawn. Characters are barely sketched in; except for that colorful carpenter, they exist only as plot furtherers and ideological mouthpieces. Now to some extent this is the inevitable consequence of trying to tell an elaborate story in all its detailed ramifications with compact efficiency. In other words, the genre itself largely defies art, or, at least, screen art. Costa-Gavras and Semprun have, to be sure, tried to add a little extra dimension to the film by introducing rapid-fire mini-flashbacks, mostly meant to show that all was not quite well in the murdered Deputy's marriage. Also, one of the two murderers is represented as a somewhat comically sinister pederast, but these are rather conventional "humanizing" touches, and remain unexplored.

On the other hand, the dialogue, presumably by Semprun, is generally polished, witty, biting, or flavorous enough to make the onesidedness go down easily. Yet propaganda it is—even though it happens to be on the side of what I firmly believe to be right. There are surely qualitative differences even in propaganda, and this is superior propaganda as well as serious, excellent entertainment. Within this lesser context, one can even enjoy such questionable devices as the chase of the half-Jewish deputy by a car occupied by a single person bent on running him down. It is hard to conceive that a surer way of doing him in could not have been devised, and that efficiency in murder would so defer to cinematic suspense. Similarly, the farcical touches surrounding the arraignment of the high functionaries of the gendarmerie, though very satisfying in a two-dimensional context, would be unpardonable in the framework of a genuine piece of art. It is not that these things may not be true, but the eye of art would select more carefully, or the touch of art would fuse and integrate more suasively.

The performances, all but one, are remarkable. Besides those already mentioned, I must single out the blustering General of Pierre Dux, sometime leading man of the Comédie Française; the cowardly yet superficially punctilious Public Prosecutor of François Perier; the winning, decent, reasonable, and brave EDA Deputies of Bernard Fresson and Jean Bouise; and the loyal wife of yet another deputy, played with fine, understated tension by Clotilde Joano. There is much to be said also for the homosexual assassin of Marcel Bozzufi; as the murder victim, Yves Montand endows his relatively brief role with manliness and dignity.

In what could have been the standard Gregory-Peckish part of the Investigating Magistrate, Jean-Louis Trintignant works quiet wonders. He manages to make imperturbable dedication look human and also a little sad, and can, even from behind dark glasses, flash looks of luminous penetrancy. Only Irene Papas, as the victim's wife, is content to walk through her part with a face frozen into an easy tragic mask. It may be that the part does not permit much more, but seeing Miss Papas pull the same trick over and over again (most recently in the totally negligible *A Dream of Kings*), I wonder whether she is the actress we all took her for or just another gritty face.

Raoul Coutard is a magnificent cinematographer, and his work with light and shadow, sunburst and brooding nightscape, treacherously lovely exteriors and morose interiors is always exciting without falling into mere prettiness. The images remain just a little grainy—the true texture of history on film; and there is brilliant use of large expanses of white against which a little black or red or both can work miracles of coloristic poignancy. The choice of Algeria for location-work is less than fortunate—not because it is considerably closer to the tropics than Salonika, but because this film, which steadily implies that it could be happening anywhere and not only in Greece, should eschew the lush atmosphere and swarthy extras that seem to restrict it to some exotic backwater. The music by Mikis Theodorakis, one of the folk heroes of the Greek Resistance and now ironically deported to Arcadia, had to be smuggled out of the composer's house arrest. It is not so good as its romantic provenance, but it is good enough.*

Good enough, too, is *Z* itself, under the skilled direction of Costa-Gavras. Let it be a message film, oversimplified and propagandistic. It is taut, humane, intelligently constructed, sharply executed, and it is against those colonels who have plunged Greece into barbarism. So do go to see *Z* right away, and do not go to Greece this summer. And ponder our country's role in the ghastly events depicted here.

January, 1970

THE ACTIVIST

It was not until *The Graduate* that Hollywood discovered the potential of the "youth film," the film that is not so much *about* young people as *for* them. To make up for lost time, the industry is flooding us with movies that pander more or less shamelessly to the fantasy life of students and dropouts while pretending to tell it scrupulously "like it is."

In all these films, though to a differing degree, the young are made out to be more honest, brave, and wise than those above thirty, and their idealism ends up triumphing over the jaded, hypocritical, materialistic values of the "old." None of these films, so far, has addressed itself squarely to campus revolt, however—perhaps out of fear that such violent and ardently contested issues might not lend themselves to the sentimentalizing or comic oversimplification (*The Graduate* remains the prime example) that feeds the youthful ego without feeding the elders more humble pie than they can eat.

But youth films are merely the old platitudes stood on their heads. If James Dean, lovable rebel without a cause, was ultimately proved wrong by older and wiser heads, this was no more convincing, and no less so, than Dustin Hoffman, lovable rebel with a shadowy cause, winning out over older and, by redefinition, less wise heads. It is, therefore, much to the credit of a middle-aged husband-and-wife team, Art and Jo Napoleon, to have set out to make a commercially distribut-

---

*Theodorakis has been sprung, in an arrangement with the Greek government, and is now living somewhere in the "Free World," though of course at the time this was written he was still confined in Greece.

able film exploring the life and struggles of college activists fully and forthrightly. Protest against the war and the draft is a film topic that makes the men in Hollywood's front offices as nervous as if napalm were blistering the veneer of their mahogany desks.

Alas, the film the Napoleons turned out under the title *The Activist* falls short, in all but a couple of scenes, even of the mediocrity to which, at best, it seems to be aspiring. Briefly, it is the story of Mike Corbett, a student leader on what can be recognized as the Berkeley campus. He stumbles across Lee James, a pretty graduate student with a sheltered Wellesley background; they fall in love and move into an apartment together. Lee begins to take part in Mike's antidraft activities, including involvement in guerrilla theater in the streets.

A huge demonstration in front of the induction center is being planned, and Lee becomes anxious. Some unnerving experiences—a taste of physical assault, Mike's expulsion from college, a conversation with another long-time activist's girlfriend which indicates that protest is a life-style that never ends—make the girl apprehensive. Still, she participates in the mass demonstration and shares in a bloody and humiliating rout, perhaps partly due to mismanagement by the student leaders. A favorite professor of Mike's invites the couple for a restful weekend in his romantic Big Sur house. There he tries to convince Mike that revolution is something one makes in youth and then grows out of: the nature of man and the world cannot be significantly altered. Mike, having done his bit, should now accept the professor's help to get him enrolled in a Midwestern university where he and Lee could make a fresh start. The girl passionately seconds this plea. But Mike's conscience urges him to fight on; the lovers separate, seemingly forever.

The film, just like this synopsis, is much too pat. Mike and Lee are played by a pair of real-life lovers, both campus activists, Michael Smith and Lesley Gilbrun, who have by no means been parted by events. The very fact that the Napoleons needed this dramatic—and, as they manage it, unconvincing—conclusion, proves that they were more concerned with making a good old-fashioned sob story than with telling the truth.

Indeed, the problem here is not whether Mike can make it with Lee or any other girl, but what will become of him as an antiwar militant prevented from completing his education. The Napoleons need not have come up with answers to this difficult question, only to have shed some honest light on it. But instead of close attention to the plight of this new kind of displaced person, we get another conventional boy-meets-wins-loses-girl story.

The phases through which the film went during production are significant. At first the Napoleons were working from a script; then, having met a personable pair of activists and their crowd, they decided to scrap the script and make a *cinéma-vérité* film, with the students enacting their life stories and telling them in their own words. It then emerged that the students could not express themselves clearly, were limited actors and worse improvisers; some of them were not even disciplined and dedicated enough to show up when needed. So the film had to be made as an uneasy compromise between the two genres, with the writing made up in daily installments and the dialogue kept simple enough for these nonactors to speak. But in view of the Napoleons's previous credits—movies like *Too Much, Too Soon* and TV shows like *Dancing Detective*—I wonder how much less simple their most complex dialogue would have been.

The writing, like the acting, is threadbare, indeed. At one crucial point, Mike tells Lee: "It all boils down to one thing: you've got a brain and a body. If you commit one and withhold the other, you're a phony. That's what liberalism is all about." It is unclear whether this is an invitation to use the body as well as the mind or the reverse, or just a plain invitation to come to bed. It clearly isn't what liberalism is all about. And though ostensibly meant as an attack on liberalism, even that is not absolutely certain. Worse yet is what Mike tells Lee at the height of their amatory ecstasy: "This is nice. You're nice." Now *there* is a subject for a film: a generation that, apparently, has so lost control of expression, of meaningful words, that all a lover can say to his beloved by way of supreme tribute is, "You're nice."

There are two effective scenes: the sequence in which Lee is attacked by an elderly female Bircher with a hose, and the woman's husband and Mike are drawn into the fight that concludes with the man shooting at the bus in which the kids are escaping; and the big demonstration that ends in police brutality and cracked skulls. Though this scene is powerful from the visual standpoint, its logistics are not made clear: the drama of just when, how, and why things went wrong is lost in the scuffle.

The lesson of *The Activist* seems to be this: either, if you are a good enough writer and director, you write your script and direct professional actors. (This does not apply to the Napoleons, as scene after clumsy scene blindingly demonstrates.) Or you make an honest-to-goodness *cinéma-vérité* film, and let the chips and the inarticulateness fall where they may; at least you end up with some raw truth on film. Yet this, too, has its dangers. Since their principal characters were real-life lovers, the Napoleons shot a lengthy scene in which the two really have intercourse. It ranks among the most boring, seemingly interminable sex scenes on screen, conveying neither rapture nor even erotic stimulation. Which merely proves once again that, on film, art is far superior to mere documentary footage.

March, 1970

P.S. I am told that the young couple, Lesley Gilbrun and Michael Smith, did, after all, separate. It would be interesting to know why—could life, besides imitating art as Oscar Wilde pointed out, imitate pseudo-art as well? But, in any case, the break-up came well after the Berkeley riots subsided, and the relationship seems to have fallen victim to peace rather than to war. There may be a real film in that, and I hope the Napoleons don't make it.

July, 1970

PATTON; WOODSTOCK

Patton and *Woodstock,* two lengthy and elaborate American productions, can be viewed as kindred opposites. On the surface, *Woodstock* is a youth film, celebrating peace; *Patton* a middle- and old-age film, glorifying war. Upon closer scrutiny, both films become fuzzy and, in a sense, disturbingly merge into each other. *Patton* is subtitled "Salute to a Rebel," which, ostensibly, means that Patton was in some way anti-Establishment and is, therefore, to be hailed. But as history and the makers of the film know, if Patton was against the military Establishment, it was only in being more maniacal, megalomaniacal, martial, and martinetish. Vaguely demented, perhaps, yet successful because, in the fanatical context of war, the true-blue fanatic has the advantage.

The film, directed by Franklin Schaffner and having for one of its scenarists Francis Ford Coppola (whose work is schizoidly divided between collaboration on "big" pictures such as this and *Is Paris Burning?* and smaller, supposedly, avant-garde films like *You're a Big Boy Now* and *The Rain People,* with something like *Finian's Rainbow* uniting both sides of Coppola's incompetence), is a peculiarly slippery enterprise. The filmmakers have clearly made a film to be read in opposite ways: by hawks, as a tribute to unassuageable aggressiveness that partly pays off; by doves, as a portrait of bloodthirsty militancy, at least partly subdued in the end. It is all rather like that famous message sent by Mortimer to the jailers of Edward II: according to where you put the missing comma, it could mean that the king must die or must be spared. *Patton* has been left carefully unpunctuated.

The film is made in Panavision 150, and the process, apparently, lends itself to unprecedented sharpness of photographic definition—or else, it is the achievement of Fred J. Koenekamp, the cinematographer. Whatever the case, there are scenes in cool tonalities, like views of the desert on an overcast day or dimly lit interiors, that emerge with the sharpness of an etching and are nevertheless color photography. The effect is almost painfully beautiful; thus in a scene in which Patton inspects GI graves in North Africa, featuring a series of extreme long shots all beige, gray, and white, yet with each pale hue very much itself. With Jerry Goldsmith's score here intoning the Patton theme, a kind of distant alarum for muted trumpets that is urgent and mournful and very lovely, the cumulative impact is profoundly enticing. It makes it extremely hard not to be for Patton. At other times, the film suggests much of the ruthlessness, delusions of grandeur, even beastliness of the man, and George C. Scott's performance (such cold blue eyes!) is the ideal vehicle for the concept.

Scott is unsurpassed at portraying a demonically driven man who can, in turn, frighten you out of your skin with a look, a word, the weight of an implication. He also has wit and charm and can make you laugh and rejoice with him—something Jack Palance, for example, could never do. Why, then, isn't *Patton* art, since it has a tremendous ambiguity to explore, and a first-rate actor to explore it with? Does the necessity of fighting back justify a war-lover as commander? Does an anachronistic vision of oneself as an old-style general—a combination Hannibal, Napoleon, and Don Quixote, say—and the successful embodiment of that vision make one into a figure of tragic stature?

If the film seriously addressed itself to these problems, it could have indeed attained artistic importance. But Patton's psyche, motives, background, and private life are not probed, or just barely; no worthy antagonists are pitted against him; the film is devoid of poetry. The people remain two-dimensional, the battle scenes are just proficient battle scenes, the words spoken are prosaic and superficial. Though some of the images, as noted, are striking, that in itself does not make a film a work of art.

During the opening credits I noticed the fairly prominently displayed name of Abraxas Aaran, and wondered what sort of an actor it might belong to. The closing credits identified him as Willy, the pit-bull terrier—the creepiest breed of dog there is, yet so ugly as to be almost endearing. The ambiguity is very much akin to the one with which the movie views its hero; but what can be accepted at face value in a dog needs further investigation and analysis in a general and protagonist.

Woodstock, the film by Michael Wadleigh, ought to be the opposite of a film like *Patton;* but, unsettlingly, it really isn't. The epic of peace and the epic of war exhibit disturbing resemblances, not the least of which is reveling in elephantine dimensions. Though *Woodstock*'s hours of coverage (and extended use of the split screen, usually in threefold images, makes its three hours seem at least six) give you a sense of the largeness of the crowd and the portentousness of the event, the film barely probes the meaning behind the superficies. The bits of interviews with various people are only enough to arouse a curiosity they do not begin to satisfy. What we get instead is the obligatory scenes of nude lovemaking and bathing, and an inordinate amount of the entertainment, which the majority of the throng could neither see nor properly hear, and did not come for in the first place. What is distressing about most of the performers at this mammoth mud-in, apart from their obvious lack of musical talent, is, in most cases, their equally obvious hostility. I mean not just laudable opposition to the war, but also profound neurotic hostility.

I am no great admirer of our national anthem for either its artistic or patriotic merits, but to hear and watch what Jimi Hendrix does to it—something ineffably ugly, inhuman, and hate-riddled—almost had me running for shelter to the nearest American Legion post. In view of what happened at the next major rock rally at Altamont, it was incumbent on the filmmakers to search out the seeds of violence that Woodstock also contained—for instance, in the lukewarm reception accorded the milder performers, and the furious acclaim reserved for the rabblerousers. But this the filmmakers, through blindness or dishonesty, avoided.

April-May, 1970

WATERMELON MAN

Watermelon Man concerns a narrow-minded, loudmouthed insurance salesman, a smart aleck who wakes up in the middle of an ordinary night to find himself turned into a Negro. The idea suggests Kafka's

Metamorphosis: like Gregor Samsa, Jeff Gerber becomes an outcast overnight, and the unexplained transformation could be put to powerful uses. But Melvin Van Peebles, the black director, and Herman Raucher, his white scenarist, opt for flashy, superficial farce with gobs of facile portentousness. The jokes fall short of comic illumination, and the overtones are, generally, ill-considered.

Thus when Jeff is rejected by his ostentatiously liberal wife, he rushes to the apartment of a pale blonde Norwegian secretary, who has yearned for him from the moment he turned black. After a mad night of many-faceted sex, Jeff discovers that the girl's feelings are only black-skindeep. He now calls her a bigot and keeps provoking her until she insults him and yells "Rape!" out of the window. Jeff sneers at her for not loving him for his soul; but when he hurled himself into her bed, was *he* after soul?

Again, we are shown that the insurance business is an unsavory racket. When Jeff turns black, his boss typically wants to exploit him as a prestige Negro on his staff, and sends him out to mulct the still untapped blacks. Jeff quits, only to start, with what seems to me shaky capital, his own insurance business in Harlem, and, presumably, bleed his customers in ways not unrelated to those of his ex-boss. And, as usual in such films, no white over eleven is allowed a shred of decency.

The worst thing about the film, though, is that it makes turning black, once the initial trauma and immediate losses are sustained and risen above, seem rather simple and pleasant. Though the whites become oppressors, Jeff enters into prompt solidarity with blacks of all types, changes from dull Mad-Av clothes to gorgeously wild color combinations and styles, appears to be well rid of a drearily nagging wife, and may at last begin to live. In an attempt to make it all a jot less obvious, the movie's final scene shows Jeff and a motley bunch of raggedy blacks practicing up with mops and brooms for the coming revolution. We are free to view this scene as ridiculous or sublime according to our prejudices, and it is a fitting ending for a morally and esthetically ambiguous venture.

June, 1970

THE REVOLUTIONARY

Last time round it was *The Activist,* now it is *The Revolutionary;* in between, it was *Getting Straight* and *The Strawberry Statement.* The genus is the youth film; the species, youth-in-revolt. And a pretty specious species it has been so far, with the premise that one joins the Movement either to get laid, if one is male; or, if one is female, because one is being laid by someone in it. *The Revolutionary,* be it said for it, makes no such arrogations; unfortunately, that is almost all that *can* be said for it.

The hero of *The Revolutionary* is "A."—a young bourgeois student in an unnamed Western country. He has rebelliously left home to live in a wretched tenement with Ann, a loving, motherly, lower-class girl; they are both members of a radical student group. But A. becomes disenchanted with the organization, which he considers insufficiently militant and too easily manipulated by the politicians, police, and university authorities. He joins a Communist workers' cell, and loses Ann, who has guessed that his interest has strayed: A. is now pursuing Helen, a pretty little heiress whom he has met by chance. A. is expelled from the University by a smarmy dean who won't even state the real reason, A.'s political activities. Called up for the draft, A. rejects his father's offer to use his influence to keep him out of the army.

When he learns that his regiment is about to march against some black militants, A. deserts and warns the blacks, who receive his help with bad grace. Back in his home town, he finds that the Communists, who never quite trusted him because of his bourgeois background, are lying low, awaiting the outcome of the trial of some striking workers. A., who is now hiding out in the greenhouse where Helen conceals him from everyone, loves and is loved by the girl, but can't get her to sleep with him. Disgruntled by the Communists' inaction, he drifts into the orbit of a Yippie-anarchist group, whose leader, Leonard II, picks him up in a bar. They begin together in a small way, by breaking into a pawnshop and giving away its contents to all who ask, and escaping before the cops arrive.

Innocently abetted by Helen, A. drifts deeper into a relationship with Leonard II and his group. They plan the assassination of the judge, should he condemn those striking workers to death. If Leonard's bomb does not go off, A., sitting on a bench the judge must pass, is to throw another one. Leonard's bomb does fail, the judge comes face to face with A., and as the latter struggles desperately to make up his mind one way or the other, the film ends with one of those by now platitudinous freeze-frame cop-outs.

The Revolutionary does not convince us of the ineluctability of A.'s progress—if, indeed, it is a progress. Certain things seem too easy— like deserting and resuming life in one's home town; others seem too fortuitous—like the haphazard way in which Leonard II enlists A.'s services, and, just by sending him a few ambiguous messages, quickly lures him to the stage where he must kill and, very likely, be killed. A. himself is too fuzzy, vague, and unrealized a character: in many ways too dumb for his supposed intelligence; in most ways too passive and dependent for his supposed activism and independence. I am aware that Hans Koningsberger (who wrote the screenplay from his own, rather more believably worked-out novel) wants to illustrate precisely that paradox, but he does not hit upon those initmate details, quirks, turns of phrase, that would fill in his schematic and didactic outline with the cement of humanity. It all comes across as an insufficiently dramatized case history; a case, moreover, in whose historicity it is hard to believe.

There is a grave problem of texture. *The Revolutionary* must have been written with some Continental country in mind, but it was filmed by a director, Paul Williams, who insisted on slanting it toward the United States, yet, for reasons of economy, shot the film in England. The police uniforms, the militant blacks, and all the main actors are markedly American; the extras and the locales are extremely provincial British; and the elaborate mouthings of doctrinaire Marxism are very Continental European as, indeed, may be Helen's virginal innocence. Thus the film lacks any real sense of place, and smacks of a limbo every bit as unearthly as the old M-G-M sound stages. Matters are further unrealized by the casting. Collin Wilcox-Horne is too old and portly for Ann: she does not look like a fellow student of A.'s but like a house mother from some neighboring girls' school whom he has managed to subvert. As Helen, Jennifer Salt is neither pretty nor talented enough, but she does happen to be the leading man's real-life girl friend.

For that leading man, the film is fortunate to have the services of a remarkable actor, Jon Voight. Fresh from his splendid Joe Buck in *Midnight Cowboy* and impressive Milo Minderbinder in *Catch-22,* Voight brings to the part of A. a bumbling seriousness, confused but pure goodwill, and that strange mixture of patience and pigheadedness that alone could lend credence to the character. I wish only that he had not chosen to affect a peculiar, almost Chaplinesque shuffle, perhaps his way of annexing a bit of Ratso Rizzo to his new role. Voight is, in any case, marvelous at conveying that little glimmer of intelligence at the core of darkest stupidity, or the stupidity that lurks inside the most crystalline intelligence.

But it is important not to overlook the shakiness of *The Revolutionary* because of the solidity of Jon Voight. The young filmgoer is in serious danger of being duped by a star system that could become as stultifying as the one that created the Tyrone Powers and Rita Hayworths of yesteryear—a system that would convince him that Jon Voight or Dustin Hoffman or Dennis Hopper is his alter ego, with whom he must identify himself through thick and thin, through cornballs and conmanship.

July, 1970

JOE

We've had the youth film, and now here is the first anti-youth film. I don't think it was planned that way. The scriptwriter of *Joe* is Norman Wexler, once a speechwriter for Bobby Kennedy and present at the fatal shooting; he is also the author of some off-Broadway plays, and, to put it mildly, an eccentric. He is not the stuff of which hard hats are made. Neither is John G. Avildsen, the director and cinematographer of *Joe*, an alert young man who, among other things, photographed *Out of It,* a sympathetic film treatment of high school hangups. *Joe,* I think, was trying to present the polarization of our society—a bigger problem even than the Vietnam war by which it was begotten but with which it will not end—in a realistic light, and without taking sides. But out came something different.

Bill Compton, a $60,000-a-year advertising executive, finds his young daughter, Melissa, in Bellevue Hospital. She has been living in the East Village with a pusher and has freaked out on speed. Compton goes to pick up Melissa's belongings, runs into the pusher and, while beating him up, accidentally kills him. Trying to recover his cool in a bar, he encounters a burly, balding foundry worker, Joe Curran, who is drunkenly inveighing against Negroes, Jews, homosexuals, the welfare society, and, most of all, hippies: he'd like to kill one of them. Compton, unnerved, confesses that he just did. When the pusher's death hits the news media, Joe puts two and two together, and telephonically summons Compton to a meeting. Bill is terrified that he will be blackmailed, but Curran merely forces his bearish admiration and friendship upon him.

Pretty soon the Currans and Comptons are visiting each other, having awkward dinners together, and recognizing certain correspondences underneath their unlikeness. Joe proudly shows off his gun collection to the Comptons; Bill takes Joe to the classy hangouts of the advertising crowd, and they find that Joe can outsmart those flashy four-flushers. A curious symbiotic relationship evolves: Bill has actually killed a hippy, which is the one thing Joe can't do; and Joe has the hate-corroded mind that produces the justification for such a killing—the very thing Bill lacks. Melissa Compton escapes from the posh sanatorium she has been transferred to, and finds out the truth by overhearing her parents talk. Hysterically, she accuses her father and, when he tries to stop her from running away, hurls at him the chilling question: "Are you trying to kill me too?"

Joe offers to help Bill find Melissa, and together, on a wintry night, they scour the Village joints. They get involved with a bunch of hippies looking for drugs, and even produce the stuff that Bill confiscated from the pusher's and Melissa's pad. Ostensibly all in the interest of tracking down the girl, they become part of an orghee (as Joe pronounces it) and have somewhat unlikely sex with the girls. In the morning, they find that the male hippies have made off with their wallets and credit cards, and that the girls have no intention of continuing to see them. Joe beats one girl into confessing where their commune is located, and the two men drive off to a farm in Rockland County to retrieve their lost wallets and egos. Joe produces guns—just to frighten the kids—but when the wallets reappear without money in them and the culprits start running, Joe shoots and kills. Bill tries to prevent him, but Joe persuades him to stop the mouths of these lousy drug addicts who, if spared, would tell the police. As Bill shoots a girl trying to escape, there is a reverse angle shot and we see her face. Perish the thought of my betraying any secrets, but I'll give you a clue: Jephthah. Or, changing the sexes: Medea.

My guess is that Wexler and Avildsen were trying to give us an inexorably Hellenic or biblical tragedy, and at the same time not weight the scales on the side of the underdog. They assumed that the majority of the guaranteed audience for their film—for any film—would be young people, who did not have to be sold on hippies, sex, drugs, the East Village and the rest. So it did not seem necessary to develop the flower (or weed) children of the film into rounded human beings: even if surly, selfish, arrogant, and thieving, they and their life-style would come equipped with automatic acceptance.

Instead, it appeared strategically sound to build up Joe and Bill. Thus Joe—coarse, roistering, foul-mouthed, bloody-minded, bigoted—also has a crude but lively wit, endearing naïveté, fierce though unthinking loyalty, unenvious appreciation of his friend's success, resignation to a life of hard work for relatively little reward. That he is performed by Peter Boyle, an actor who can put a glint of charm into the greatest vulgarities and turn a huge ape into just an overgrown baby, helps enormously. As for Bill, loving father, henpecked hus-

band, guilty but pathetic victim of Mad Av and our cult of the Bitch
Goddess, avenger of his daughter's degradation—only a Rolling Stone
would not be moved to pity for him.

And so the film, perhaps inadvertently, nudges us into rooting for
the combined forces of soft-brimmed and hard-hatted reaction; indeed,
when they start shooting up a nest of cowering hippies who have been
shown lacking a single redeeming feature—unless youth itself be considered one—it is dangerously easy to slip into a reverse-Charles Man-
sonism and feel the same satisfaction one used to get, stupidly, from
cowboys shooting up Indians, and gets nowadays, equally stupidly,
from Indians plugging cowboys. The film is on to something important
when it depicts the gradual warming up toward each other, and alliance between, the know-nothing right and the isolated and alienated
middle. If only their joint campaign against whatever is to the left of
them—even their own children—were shown controlledly as well as
compassionately; less melodramatically and more truly disturbingly; if
more attention were paid to verisimilitude—the police in *Joe* are as real
and visible as leprechauns—and if the hippies were made as sympathetic as the squares; there might be a real film here. Even so, the ideas
that *Joe* overstresses are well worth pondering, and the quieter first half
of the film makes very good, frightening sense.

August, 1970

3

The Youth Film

THIS CATEGORY, for the full impact of which readers are urged to look back over several items in the preceding category, contains films that represent the most important new trend in American moviemaking. If there is a new genre that emerged in the last few years, it is precisely the youth film. And what makes the genre so fascinating is that it is one of the very few aimed at those people of whom it treats. Consider: the western is not really made for whatever cowboys, bounty hunters, cattle rustlers, gunfighters, etc., might survive to this day, but for the city-pent fantasizers who want to dream themselves into saddles, saloons, and heroics that existed in a manlier age or, more likely, never. Similarly, the gangster film, though gangsters still exist and show no appreciable decline, cannot expect to recoup its outlay from an audience of mafiosos, crooked politicians, psychotic killers, and such. But the youth film, by God, is predominantly supported and subsidized by the young people it deals with.

And how does it deal with them? In most cases superficially and dishonestly, self-servingly or condescendingly. Yet many of these films are successful, either because they flatteringly tell youth what it wants to believe about itself, or because youth in its inexperience is unable to spot the condescension with which it is being treated and exploited. This could become a problem: for whereas spies are not likely to get many useful pointers from watching their Hollywood counterparts outsmarting their own shadows, young people might believe the aggrandizing or minimizing mirrors that are being held up to them. All a critic can do is to point out such falsehoods—whether they imply that all adults are guilty of having created this corrupt world, which the shining young will set to rights; or whether they suggest that the young haven't a clue to what ails the world, and are agitating only in order to raise hell and get laid. In fact, the best the critic can do is to strive to prevent youth films from becoming too much of a genre (with all the clichés and lies attendant on typical genre films) and remain, instead, films about people who happen to be young and in some ways foolish, and, in others, wise.

THE GRADUATE

One would like to be able to say that with *The Graduate* Hollywood has finally graduated; if so, the film merely demonstrates the need for postgraduate work. A few taboos are, indeed, broken; but does that make for a good film? I have not read Charles Webb's novel and cannot say how many of the film's flaws are inherited from the book. There again, though, what does it matter? The movie's principal weaknesses are oversimplification, overelaboration, inconsistency, eclecticism, obviousness, pretentiousness, and, especially in the penultimate section, sketchiness. Let us examine these one by one.

Oversimplification is the easiest to spot: all the adults in the film are ludicruous, corrupt, mean, or, at the very least, ineffectual; the two young lovers, on the other hand, are honest, idealistic, pure, lovable, and, if you don't look very closely, not particularly deficient mentally. When they finally run off with each other, the film labors to make us feel that, thanks to them, there's hope for the world; without perceptible resources or qualifications, though, and with familial ire pursuing them, it is an exiguous Eden they can look forward to.

Overelaboration runs through the entire film. When the pilot's voice in the very first shot announces over the plane's P.A. system, "We are about to make our descent into Los Angeles," the film's only moment of subtlety has been used up. Forthwith we descend into underlining, overdoing, dragging out. The party his parents give for Ben, the new graduate, is sheer hyperbole. True, the unsavory genus big businessman, especially the garish California species, complete with females even deadlier than their castrated males, is quickly pinned to the screen. But must the pins be driven into the specimens with a hammer?

Concomitantly, Ben is presented as an idealistic, sensitive, confused innocent, as well as an inordinately tongue-tied, slow-on-the-uptake simpleton, innocence becoming tantamount to obtuseness and clumsiness. I don't think the director, Mike Nichols, intended the youth to be a yokel, but either his comic technique requires such overstatement, or he and his scenarists felt the public cannot comprehend innocence in any less dripping form. For that matter, can we, nowadays, buy the notion of a graduate—even from an Eastern college—who is still a virgin?

Ben bumbles through a large part of the film. His father, oily and officious, must nag and embarrass him without surcease while Mom supplies an obbligato of fluttery giggles. Mrs. Robinson, Dad's partner's wife, the predatory dipsomaniac who seduces Ben, is represented as a sexy gargoyle with perhaps two seconds' worth of incipient humanity allowed her. Many of the scenes are carried to the level of grotesquerie, as, for instance, Ben's birthday party at which he is obliged to give a humiliating exhibition of the frogman outfit his father has bought him. We must crawl inside the rubber suit with Ben, breathe stertorously and galumph with him, dive into the swimming pool with him, watch through his visor, and later even from underwater, his family making asses of themselves. There is a line where satire ends and oafishness begins, and *The Graduate* keeps crossing it as if it had diplomatic immunity.

Inconsistency is at the very core of the film. Many have pointed out that it breaks in two somewhere around the middle—when from outrageous comedy or flagrant farce it switches to sentimental near-drama. Others, championing the film, have argued that the two elements are interwoven throughout, and that true love for Elaine, the Robinson daughter, is supposed to transform Ben into a romantic figure and justify the partial change of tone. I myself am not so concerned with maintaining the unity of tone as I am with safeguarding a certain consistency of character. Here is Ben, the nonstop fumbler, suddenly turned into a master sleuth: the ingeniousness with which he elicits information about the place of the wedding from various people—particularly his resourcefulness with Dr. Smith's answering service at a time of utmost physical and emotional strain—tax my credulity beyond endurance.

This may not be incredible if we assume love makes men out of boys overnight, but we cannot suppose so swinging a film would hold so square a notion. Yet, naïvely and sentimentally, if not duplicitously and jesuitically, that is just what the film proposes. Even here, however, it is inconsistent. The upright and sweet Elaine, for all her love of Ben, allows herself to be hustled off by her monstrous parents to marry another beau—an elaborate, formal wedding, by the way, which, we are to believe, was arranged for and celebrated in something like thirty-six to forty-eight hours.

Minor inconsistencies abound. After carrying on a copious affair with Elaine's mother, Ben still addresses her, even in bed it seems, as "Mrs. Robinson." Mrs. Robinson, who carries on with Ben as she presumably has with many others, casually and out of boredom and frustration, nevertheless is so demonically possessive about him that she will go to satanic lengths to prevent him from a happy marriage with her daughter. The California WASPs are shot through with little New York Jewish touches—as when Ben exclaims in amazement about the Robinsons's mating habits, "In the car you did it?" Finally, the supreme inconsistency is not in any of these lapses, but in the basic impossibility of accepting the sudden change of Candide into an amalgam of Romeo, Don Quixote, and Lochinvar. And in the triumph of such a chimerical figure (lion's courage, serpent's wisdom, goat's stupidity) over the hostile monolith of society.

Eclecticism characterizes Mike Nichols's directorial style. Like a time machine, it transports us to earlier films: *8½, Juliet of the Spirits, A Man and a Woman,* Godard's *oeuvre*—even the embracing primates in the monkey house from *Dear John* are there. Nichols goes so far as to import Eddra Gale, the woman-mountain from *8½,* for a nonspeaking bit part. There are familiar slow fade-ins on characters, overlaps of visuals from one scene with dialogue from the next, shifts in time and place bridged by the same, seemingly continuous movement, tricky camera placements, as inside a clothes closet. The extreme close-up and telephoto lenses are hauled out for spurious reasons.

The old device of pantomime shot through a windshield after the convertible top has been lowered is resorted to at the very moment when hearing the words that bring Elaine and Ben, the car's occupants, together would be most helpful in establishing their supposed intelligence and idealism. And that car, Ben's red Alfa Romeo, a linear descendant of all those ubiquitous, scene-stealing cars in Godard's and Lelouch's films, is on screen more than any character save Ben. Photographed with everything from reverse angle to helicopter shots, and with Simon and Garfunkel's songs obstreperously dogging it, the car very nearly drives the film to vehicular suicide.

Obviousness and pretentiousness appear either in a pure state or commingled. After Ben's father tells him his marriage plans seem half-baked, and Ben, with his typical cute stolidity, replies that they are fully baked, two pieces of toast pop up from a toaster. In a Berkeley frat house, every boy has to be as blond as the California sunshine. Paul

Simon's lyrics alternate between nauseating poeticism ("Hello darkness, my old friend . . . Silence like a cancer grows . . . The words of the prophet are written on the subway wall . . . The sound of silence") and trashy folksiness ("Here's to you, Mrs. Robinson: Jesus loves you more than you can know"), and are set to his and Garfunkel's music that is not so much rock as rock bottom. Nichols keeps reprising these decompositions, until the soundtrack resembles the streets of New York during the garbage collectors' strike. And for supreme pretentiousness, we get a protracted shot of Ben crucified against the plate glass of the choir loft at Elaine's wedding.

Sketchiness afflicts the whole long Berkeley section of the film. The stages of Ben's and Elaine's romance are much too elliptical to convince anyone not a raving swinger or abject square. Sketchiness creeps into the characterizations and performances as well. Dustin Hoffman, a remarkable character actor, is clearly uncomfortable when reduced to a passive booby. Katharine Ross, thanks in large part to the scriptwriters, Calder Willingham and Buck Henry (the final script, we hear, is almost all Henry's), emerges as a pretty cipher. The part of Mr. Robinson is a bundle of dark, inchoate hints. William Daniels does much for the obvious part of Ben's father; the role of the mother is too thankless to give Elizabeth Wilson a sporting chance. Anne Bancroft burns with a black flame as Mrs. Robinson, and succeeds in making this *outré* Fury very nearly human and believable.

The Graduate, in fact, has some effective moments: parts of Ben's seduction, and the entire scene in which Ben tries for precoital conversation with Mrs. Robinson, are pertinent, pungent, and not without poignancy. In the end, though, the film is a piece of calculated pseudoinnocence. Clearly Hollywood has overdone the What Are Our Kids Coming To? posture (and imposture) of righteous indignation. For the first film that considers the generation gap from youth's point of view to go outrageously—and, I think, with a shrewd eye on the box office —in the opposite direction seems equally indefensible.

Ben and Elaine are a younger Bonnie and Clyde, not forced into crime, but just as specious in their heroism, and pitted against just as simplistically villainous a society. That is the trouble with our middlebrow culture and its artifacts: the notion of a corrective is to go to the opposite extreme. If the picture hangs crooked in one direction, those who set out to straighten it push it awry in the other.

February, 1968

ROMEO AND JULIET

A master of the phony (who has the advantage of coming from the land of boloney) has now emitted his film version of *Romeo and Juliet*. In his staging of the play for the Old Vic, Franco Zeffirelli at least had an idea: to convert Shakespeare into a precursor of Arthur Laurents and give us a kind of *West Side Story* minus the music. For three acts that worked quite well. In his film, Zeffirelli has no clear-cut idea, except perhaps to give us a *Romeo and Juliet* for teenyboppers and pederasts. For the delight of the former, we get a pair of lovers so young that their delivery of verse sags with puppy fat, and for the delectation of the latter we get fondly lingering shots of Romeo's bare bottom, and a relationship between the stripling Romeo and the older Mercutio (creepily played by John McEnery) that rivals in intimacy and tenderness the puppy love of Romeo and Juliet.

There is a reason for the theatrical adage that no one under forty can play Juliet properly. The girl may be nominally under fourteen, yet she represents, along with youthfulness, that fruition of the feminine principle that takes years of acting experience on top of years of experience in living to manifest itself. Certainly it is their youthful innocence that makes these lovers lyrical; but only ripe humanity, a sense of really meaning the poetry (not Shakespeare's greatest), can make them tragic. Olivia Hussey (despite a supererogatory layer or two of actual puppy fat) and Leonard Whiting are attractive youngsters, but even if they were much better actors than they now are, they could not make us believe their intenser gestures and expressions, their more piercing utterances. There is a gulf between the words and the faces, between unmarked, unmarred bodies and speeches lined with wisdom and puckered with wit—a gulf of audiovisual dissociation of sensibility.

As might be expected from Zeffirelli, he unleashes a great deal of centrifugality—some of it effective, much of it distracting—and a minimum of respect for the text. When the director cannot divert our attention by avalanches of movement, he resorts to cutting. Thus Juliet's two important soliloquies are omitted, "Gallop apace" and the potion-drinking speech, as is the moving final exchange with Romeo, "O God, I have an ill-divining soul. . . ." Cut, too, are such effective scenes as the wedding feast that turns into a funeral, and the important slaying of Paris, which alone justifies Friar Laurence's abandoning the revived Juliet in the tomb.

One of the apter aspects of the film, besides Danilo Donati's convincing costumes and the generally sound art direction, is the editing by

Reginald Mills. But three other cutters get an unusual tribute: Franco Brusati, Masolino D'Amico, and Zeffirelli himself are credited with something called "screenplay." This consists almost entirely of blue-penciling, though not quite; the "Come vial" soliloquy, which goes on for some forty-five lines, has been rewritten by the scenarists in four words: "Love, give me strength!" I wonder how much each of the trio was paid for writing one-and-one-third words into Shakespeare. I discount the frightened mumblings of "No! No!" by various bystanders during the dueling scenes—surely Brusati, D'Amico and Zeffirelli generously threw those in gratis.

The color cinematography of Pasquale de Santis is merely adequate, and Zeffirelli does not help much with such hoary tricks as framing Friar Laurence's head during most of the potion-preparing scene with a retort curving hammily around the edges of the shot. Another slight disappointment is Nino Rota's music. Rota established himself as one of the great film composers with his work for early and middle-period Fellini films, as well as other brilliant scores, *e.g.,* for Visconti's *Rocco* and Clément's *This Angry Age.* Lately, however, he has declined. Though this score is better than what he did for Zeffirelli's *Shrew,* its simplistic main theme falls as short of Prokofiev (with whom, alas, it must compete) as Zeffirelli does of Shakespeare.

November, 1968

YELLOW SUBMARINE

For a thorough audiovisual sauna, there is nothing like immersing oneself in the *Yellow Submarine.* As everyone must know by now, this is a cartoon feature in which the Beatles are represented by their own singing and musicmaking; for the rest, there are four scriptwriters writing their lines, four actors speaking them, and God knows how many animators under Heinz Edelmann drawing them and their fantasy world. In this Beatliad, the irrepressible four save the good, tuneful folk of Pepperland from the monstrous, music-hating Blue Meanies. Not since the Seven Against Thebes was there so mighty a coalition, and here, moreover, the outcome is pleasanter: the Pop Muses are heard again in Pepperland, and the Blue Meanies are sent to blue blazes.

The film is fun, and an animated feature that holds the interest of adults of all ages (I don't think there are children of any age left) is not to be sneezed at. Visually, every conceivable style is thrown in pell-mell: there is Art Nouveau and psychedelic, op and pop, dada and surrealist, Hieronymus Bosch and just plain bosh. Why does it work? Because of its reckless generosity. The fact that *Jugendstil* is made to rub curlicues with Miró, that expressionism is obliged to lie down with the Douanier Rousseau, that the outrageous *mélange des genres* is served up as demurely as the most ingenuous tossed salad—in short, that it is so unself-conscious—that's what makes it click.

And verbally there is the paronomasia: pun upon pun upon pun. Brilliant ones and appalling ones, all casually flung off and left to fend for themselves as the teaming mind spawns and rushes on. The sight gags and sound gags interbreed, until the film stretches before and behind us like a vast punorama. The songs are particularly well, because particularly offhandedly, illustrated, and only the filmed appearance of the Beatles at the end proves an anticlimax.

Too sappily good-natured, too commercial, too lacking in the old Beatle rebelliousness—these charges have been brought against *Yellow Submarine* with some justification. But this, too, is finally not unmoving. The mixture of naïveté and cynicism, of coziness and exploitation, is the portrait of the authors as not quite so young men and explains where all those flower children have gone.

December, 1968

IF . . .; GREETINGS; CHANGES; THREE IN THE ATTIC

A film of considerable distinction though missed excellence is *If . . .* by Lindsay Anderson. Anderson's only other feature film was *This Sporting Life,* which struck some powerful attitudes but remained hollow at the core. *If* (if I may be permitted to drop the ellipsis) is much more effective while it chronicles the faintly surreal realities of English public-school life than when it enters the domain of the surreal whole hog. The story of three musketeers of nonconformity in a tradition-sodden English school functions admirably on the level of smug authoritarianism crossed by petty defiance; but the final holocaust would have required both more imaginative writing and, in the director, the unlikely combination of a Jean Vigo and a Luis Buñuel.

We are told how Mick and his two henchmen, Johnny and Wallace, begin by resisting, quite naturally and naturalistically, the authority of the prefects, or "whips," of College House, only to end by staging a bloody, and entirely surrealist, revolution. The ludicrous and dismal aspects of English boarding-school life (I, too, experienced them briefly) are caught with droll and dismaying precision, but are then escalated into hypertrophic horror. The infiltration of the surreal is not uncleverly managed. The pompous and sanctimonious chaplain hits a junior-school boy over the head during class with plausible brutality; the next one, however, is punished by the chaplain's hand disappearing under the lad's shirt front and doing something unmentionable there. The housemaster's wife who, until then, was a model of vacuous placidity, is suddenly seen wandering nude through the boys' dormitory. Ever stranger strands crop up in the fabric of things, but they are not shown as one person's vision, rather as a world slowly turning psychotic.

This may sound defensible, even challenging, on paper; on the screen, it comes out untidy, indeed pretentious. Perhaps if the central part of Mick were more fully developed and more dynamically acted (not that young Malcolm McDowell is bad, mind you), one could enter the fantastic through his psyche and find it more acceptable. Or if the bizarre little subplots—like the various homosexual motifs—were more than just hinted at and the surreal elements were shown flashing forth *equally* in all of them, the iffiness of *If* might be more controlled. Additional funds might have helped, too; the picture was, apparently, shot piecemeal over a protracted and often penurious period. Thus color photography had to be abandoned at times for monochrome, resulting in what looks like an arty visual crazy quilt, for which Miroslav Ondriček, the gifted Czech cinematographer, should not be blamed. As in *This Sporting Life,* one gets a feeling of richly sculptured individual scenes, but a deficient sense of the whole and somewhat nebulous continuity.

Still, David Sherwin's script has many racy moments, Lindsay Anderson's direction is always textured and full of gusto, and a cast of mingled newcomers and old-timers blends into a flawlessly incongruous cross section of bankrupt paideutics. The funny or cruel scenes work very handily; it is only the apocryphal and apocalyptic material that fails to persuade. Yet the film is never uninteresting, seldom unspirited, and there is some sort of intelligence even in its miscalculations.

Something similar can be said about *Greetings,* by two young New York filmmakers, Brian De Palma and Charles Hirsch. It is a loosely concatenated set of episodes involving two young men trying to coach their friend in flunking his Army physical—or, rather, psychical; the obsession of one of the trio with solving the JFK assassination, even if it means using the bodies of otherwise inclined bed partners for complicated ballistic computations; and the adventures and misadventures of all three with a variety of girls. There is much flippancy both in individual scenes and in their joining, the color photography is less than expert, and there are shenanigans worthy of the underground film at, say, its second most self-indulgent.

Nevertheless, *Greetings* is saved by its spontaneity, zest, and easygoing wit that sometimes penetrates into satire and sometimes contents itself with zaniness. One is reminded of the good early specimens of Beat poetry—of Ginsberg, Corso, Ferlinghetti, and others like them—when the movement was fresh and frisked all over geography, pornography, prosody, and tarnation. The acting is winsome and has a certain jaunty insouciance about it that makes even its lapses seem intentional. Precisely because it makes no demands on our sympathy and commitment, *Greetings* earns our amused benediction.

When the West Coast crowd tries to make a youth film, the results tend to be disastrous; Hall Bartlett's *Changes* is a pure abomination. It is the incoherent account of a wealthy, mawkish, platitude-mouthing dropout from Berkeley who wants to see the world and figure things out, and so proceeds to race up and down between San Francisco and Los Angeles in his Porsche, until he wrecks it in expiation for driving an idiot girl to suicide. Thereafter he depends on the kindness of motorists who pick him up and pretty young women who take him in (sometimes, conveniently, the two are the same). It is unclear on what he lives or what he wants; or how, at the most unlikely times, he manages to be in Big Sur; or why, wherever his skulking and maundering takes him, the landscapes and seascapes are gorgeous, as if there were no dreary flatlands in California, and no world at all beyond it.

The youth is involved in one more stereotyped situation than the next, and the dialogue in this script by Bartlett and Bill E. Kelly never fails to cement the stereotypes with sticky clichés. People arrive and depart for no good reasons; mate and separate at random; love, withhold love, commit suicide as aimlessly as motes jiggle in a sunbeam; and, all the time, peddle truisms as portentously as if they were pushing dope. Platitudinous despair follows on platitudinous delight—consisting mostly of slow-motion frolics with certain shots held well beyond the limits of civilized endurance.

Richard Moore's color photography is redolent with arty coyness, and the leading man, Kent Lane (which sounds more like a suburban address than a human appellation), accomplishes the difficult task of being at once brutish and effete. Of the girls, only Michele Carey is prepossessing, but even she is afflicted with a Liz Tayor voice, though that is still preferable to the conglomeration of pop songs on the sound track; these are so monotonous they make the drum beats with which they alternate sound positively melodious. Sex and rebellion (presumably so as not to offend the Motion Picture Association's raters) are totally bloodless, the former consisting of bathing-suited slow-motion rolling in the sand, the latter of some anodyne footage of a protest march that wouldn't demilitarize a kindergarten sand lot.

The entire film was sired by *A Man and a Woman* upon *The Graduate*, and emerges a worse mongrel than either parent. Bartlett's directorial flair consists of things like having his hero wander through a peaceful old-fashioned graveyard while the sound track crepitates and explodes with all the noises of the Vietnam war. Or of having the stony-faced protagonist look on endlessly as a little boy and girl float across a playground in slow-motion pursuit of each other. When he finally leaves the most charming girl who became his mistress for no fathomable reason, our hero sends her a copy of Thoreau inscribed "Your [*sic*] alwa's [*sic*] with me." How he could have lasted two years at Berkeley, even if he had majored in Tree Surgery, is a mystery.

No less nauseating, though occasionally more diverting, is *Three in the Attic*. Based on what must be his equally sleazy and smart-aleck novel, Stephen Yafa's screenplay concerns Paxton Quigley, a New England college stud who is servicing simultaneously three girls from the neighboring women's college: a haughty, intellectual WASP, a sassy Negro sexpot, and a weird Jewish flower child. When they discover his game, they imprison him in a dormitory attic and come to him by turns, one every hour on the hour, for sexual satisfaction. A pipe-smoking woman dean detects the activities of our succubae, but utters merely a gentle reprimand. Paxton is drained of almost all his vital juices when the two other, less involved girls convince the WASP, whose love-hate knows no bounds, that Paxton must be released—after a fortnight of round-the-clock performing. He has to be rushed by ambulance to the nearest hospital, but eventually all ends well, with Paxton winning back the affection of the chief succuba in the baggage trunk of the Greyhound bus on which she was about to escape him.

The dialogue is replete with college humor-magazine repartee (second-rate college), and one sometimes cannot tell whether it is meant to be funny. Or, rather, when Paxton arouses Tobey's most ardent yearning by quoting an alleged bit of Kierkegaard at her, this is obviously intended as a joke. Yet as one laughs, one isn't sure whether one is not in fact laughing at the author and director who thought this was so terribly clever. Another unappetizing feature of the film is that, though its subject is copulation, it was directed by Richard Wilson with a tape measure and stop watch: the moment a zipper reaches a danger area, we cut to something else. While the smut flows liberally, anything that looks like a healthy bit of sexuality is doled out like water to a caravan lost in the desert. That, doubtless, is how the film got its R rating (minors admitted only in the company of adults) instead of the X it so richly deserves. Better yet would be to give it a new rating, XX: no one under or over sixteen admitted.

March, 1969

LAST SUMMER

Grace is almost completely lacking from the Perrys's *Last Summer*. The team that gave us *David and Lisa* and *The Swimmer* is giving it to us again. The feeling I get from a Perry film (except for *Ladybird Ladybird*, which was sheer disaster) is that it is made by commercially oriented amateurs: for an interesting amateur effort, it is too slick; for a satisfactory commercial movie, it is too amateurish. In the present case, Eleanor Perry adapted a novel by Evan Hunter—in itself a guarantee of non-art; whereas Frank Perry directed with concentrated artiness to create a gem of corrupt childhood, a sort of combination *Turn of the Screw* and *The Bad Seed*.

The story concerns Sandy, Peter, and Dan, three neglected rich kids in their middle teens and sexually restless, summering in Fire Island beach houses. They meet over a wounded seagull pretty Sandy has found on the beach and, with the help of the two boys whom she fascinates, nurses back to health.

At first, it looks as if the triangle formed by these children thrashing about in the last stages of virginity might provide them with a constructive alliance against the irresponsible parents they are saddled with. But when Sandy starts shedding the top of her bikini; when they begin telling one another unpleasant truths about themselves—harmless enough, yet something we feel Sandy is using to subjugate the boys with; when the boys start speculating about laying Sandy, and each fondles one of her breasts at the movies or else the hands of all of them jig around in her lap; when Sandy joins a computer dating service under false pretenses and first hatches, and later performs, mischief; and finally, when the recovered seagull is forced to fly at the end of a string like a living kite and pecks Sandy in self-defense, whereupon she bashes its brains out and tells the boys it has flown away—serious trouble is in the offing.

Rhoda arrives on the scene—a precocious, unattractive, vulnerable adolescent—and the unholy triangle gradually forms a phalanx against her. In the end, pinioned by Sandy and Peter, she is raped by Dan, and we are to understand that something shattering and tragic has come to pass: at least one life, Rhoda's, and possibly also that of Peter, the most decent of the three callow *farceurs,* is going to bear the mark of "last summer." But alas, the Perrys, barely equal to the seriocomic body of the film, are floored by the demands of the ending. (I dare say Evan Hunter was no help to them, either.) We are left with a hasty, hugger-mugger, inconclusive conclusion—or rather, one that strikes attitudes of conclusiveness without knowing how to drive its points home.

Insufficiencies abound. Actually, the dialogue works reasonably well much of the time, but it is directed in a keyed-up manner, the actors whipped up into the self-conscious effervescence of a bubble bath trying to make like a geyser. The kids end up hurling themselves into their lines rather than letting them well up from within, as scene after scene is overstressed.

There is trouble also with the *mise en scène.* In a way, restricting adult presences to one brief scene with a grown-up and an adult party glimpsed in silhouette at a distance is the right idea, because all the needed information about the remiss parents emerges from the kids' conversation. But making an effective chamber film—in the manner, say, of Bergman's *Through a Glass, Darkly* (itself only a partial success) —is a tricky business. There is, moreover, something peculiar and unconvincing about these vast stretches of Fire Island seemingly inhabited only by four kids and some gulls.

The kids themselves, with the exception of Cathy Burns (Rhoda), are not particularly good actors, and Barbara Hershey (Sandy, and not a kid any more) looks, regrettably, much better with her bikini top on than off. Miss Burns, on the other hand, is an extremely accomplished little actress, but also insuperably homely—she looks, in fact, like a pink beach ball with a few limbs and features painted on it. There is no excuse for Rhoda being a positive freak, and making us feel she is damned lucky to have been raped at all. (By the way, it is typical of the prevailing directorial sloppiness that Dan, though a virgin, executes the rape with the utmost speed, precision, and efficiency.)

Again, when Rhoda tells about how her mother lost her life on a silly bet, the scene, though in some ways played down, is still allowed to stick out much too conspicuously as a set piece meant to twang away at the heartstrings. And like the final boom shot in *David and Lisa,* the closing helicopter shot in *Last Summer* is pure pictorial grandiloquence.

Does *Last Summer* make a cinematic contribution? Well, it does show a little more adolescent bitchiness and sex play than we have seen (except perhaps in *If . . .,* before they stupidly cut it), and its youngsters certainly talk "dirtier" than previous movie kids. It is on your evaluation of the importance of this contribution, I am afraid, that your appreciation of the film will have to depend.

July, 1969

EASY RIDER

Easy Rider is a vaguely underground film made by youngish men who are, in one or another sense of the word, independents—even hippies of sorts. Thus Dennis Hopper, who directed, co-authored, and co-stars, was an Actors Studio hotshot who abandoned all that for the hippie scene. And Peter Fonda, who produced, co-authored, and co-stars, is an actor intimately associated with the drug world. As for the third co-author, Terry Southern, he is, if not a hippie, a hipster *par excellence.*

The film concerns Wyatt and Billy, motorcycle hippies from California, who smuggle (rather unconvincingly) cocaine out of Mexico, sell some immediately to a rich pusher and, with the rest secreted in their gas tanks, zoom off to New Orleans and the Mardi Gras. On the way, they have various encounters: with a toothless farmer whose Mexican wife and large brood share his quiet contentment; with another hippie who leads them to a commune struggling to survive on meager crops in a scorching summer; with two girls from that commune whom the restless young cyclists take to a swimming hole for some aestival dalliance. In a small Southern town, the brutish constabulary throws them into jail, where they meet George Hanson. Hanson, the lawyer and black sheep of a prominent family, has drunkenly placed himself in protective custody lest his wrathful father catch up with him. In the morning, he gets the young men out of jail, dons his disused football helmet, and happily goes along for the ride.

In another small town, the local rednecks and police taunt and humiliate the trio. They are forced to sleep outdoors and are set upon in their sleep by the ruffians. George is killed. Wyatt and Billy get to New Orleans, where they have a strange relationship with two whores whom they take on an LSD trip. Then they continue on their way to Florida, from which Billy, like Ratso in *Midnight Cowboy,* expects salvation; but what makes sense in a denizen of the Bronx slums is incomprehensible in a Californian.

Wyatt, though, feels they blew the whole thing. The landscape, no longer open and unspoiled, is industrialized, suburbanized, shanty-towned. Two bruisers in a pickup truck drive past and provoke the boys. Billy gives them the finger, is shot and mortally wounded. When Wyatt speeds off to get help, he too is gunned down.

Easy Rider has great surface impact. The boys' love for their bikes and the road is rapturously conveyed; the landscape is uplifting and various ways of embracing or brushing past it are eloquently depicted. George Hanson, the lawyer who is a child at heart, believes that superhumanly intelligent Venutians have infiltrated our world and deplores his countrymen's fear and hatred of those who are free, is a beautifully realized character. Laszlo Kovacs's photography has a pleasantly informal, spontaneous look. The bestiality of the herd-men to the outsider comes as a cruelly convincing reminder of the hate that rips America—perhaps the world—asunder. Yet upon closer scrutiny and speculation, only one thing in the film holds up completely: Jack Nicholson's dialogue and performance as George Hanson.

The presentation is one-sided. Hippies are basically free, good, and love mankind and life; the others are envious, hateful, murderous slaves. That Wyatt and Billy have scarcely more conversation than do their motorcycles, that they live by dope-smuggling, and are hooked on the stuff, that their relationships with girls are trivial if not meaning-less, that their freedom is considered a noble end in itself rather than the road to anarchy, is all meant to be swallowed like a happy-pill without questioning. The fact that the commune, unversed in agricul-ture, may face starvation is not meant to throw doubt on its sanity. George's ideas about the Venutians are not intended to invalidate the wisdom of his pronouncements. And when Wyatt finally concedes, "We blew it!" we are left unenlightened about what, when, how, and by whose fault.

I would willingly sympathize with these kids if their case were better argued, if the logic of it all were not simply that the victim is *ipso facto* innocent. But though the central plea leaves me cold, there remain the dignity of the exteriors, the spry sauciness of the rock numbers on the sound track, the good eye in many of the shots, and the ability to convey the cyclist's passion. Still, I wouldn't be surprised if this film that so aches to achieve spontaneity were chiefly remembered for its artful transitions, whereby the next scene is sneaked into the end of the current one with shots of the next locale dizzyingly vibrating through what is present.

August, 1969

MORE

Barbet Schroeder, the twenty-seven-year-old producer of several newest-wave movies, has come up with his own firstling called *More*. This is the story (allegedly based on fact) of a German student who heads south for the sun, starves, and gets involved in crime in Paris, picks up at a wild party a moody, abstracted American girl about whom he is warned, falls into bed with her, and finally follows her to Ibiza. Estelle is mysteriously involved with a tough ex-Nazi, a big hotelier on the island; Stefan manages to get her away from him and they go to live in a secluded villa on the rocks overlooking the sea. Unfortunately, Estelle brings along a *tertium quid*—and I don't mean her girlfriend who visits and is made love to by both Estelle and Stefan, but a large quantity of heroin she stole from her aging lover. She is hooked on the stuff. Stefan tries to save her from the Big H, but is himself soon enslaved by it.

The heroin comes at the end of a *gradus ad Parnassum:* First there is pot and hash, pep pills, and what looks to my untrained eye like opium. After a stormy mainliner experience, the lovers return to town and Stefan goes to work as a bartender for the ex-Nazi. The lovers undertake a cure from heroin by means of—yes, indeed!—LSD. But soon Estelle is back dallying with the ex-Nazi, which drives first Stefan, then her, back into the arms of horse. At last, apparently on purpose, Stefan takes a double dose of shit and dies—just in time, for I have run out of synonyms for the stuff. Estelle doesn't even attend his paltry funeral.

For those who want to explore the details of drug-taking, *More* may prove a fairly exact manual. For those who want to revel in nudity, there is plenty of it. As Stefan, Klaus Grünberg looks all right naked, but cannot act very much. As Estelle, Mimsy Farmer neither looks good nor acts well. Indeed, the interminable nude swimming, sunbathing, and lovemaking sequences suffer considerably from the pair's lack of charm. The film was made mostly in English, which Grünberg speaks with unseemly Teutonic gutturals. Even more unpleasant, though, is Mimsy Farmer's breathy Marilyn Monroe-Jackie Kennedy English, in which "charcoal," for instance, is pronounced "chuhkuh," the uh's representing gusts of breath. An altogether dispensable girl, this Mimsy, looking and acting like a cross between Sandy Dennis and a young Lizabeth Scott, with added suggestions of Jean Seberg and a death's-head. During the nude gambols—how they gyre and gimble in the wabe!—Mimsy displays a small and flaccid enough bosom and a large and square enough bottom to make the toughest mome raths outgrabe on the spot.

This is a supreme example of that new kind of film in which things happen for no reason, illogically and unbelievably, while the dialogue, if it is forthcoming at all, merely obfuscates the issue. The masters of this mode are Godard and Chabrol, and it is not for nothing that Schroeder here collaborated with the latter's scriptwriter, Paul Gégauff. Miss Farmer helped translate the laconic and moronic dialogue into somewhat stale hip English, and like, man, it's not *More,* it's the most. The film is photographed in rather amateurish color by Nestor Almendros, but Ibiza is a wildly photogenic place, and at times these Balearic balnearics look better than the primitive filmmaking deserves. The movie's chief purpose, apparently, is to be a pendant to Mies van der Rohe's famous dictum, "Less is more"; the reverse is now equally evident.

September, 1969

ALICE'S RESTAURANT

Alice's Restaurant is a film afflicted with a lack of attitude. Let us clarify: art is not expected to—is, in some circles, expected not to—have preconceived notions about life. But a universal sympathy is different from galloping indecision. Arthur Penn, the director and co-scenarist, apparently cannot make up his mind whether he laughs with or laughs at the hippies and their world. Either attitude is possible; in the hands of a very great artist, which Penn emphatically is not, the two might perhaps coexist. Here, the warring attitudes produce fragmentation and nervous dishevelment. The breath is pummeled out of the spectator, and the meaning out of the film.

The other scenarist, Venable Herndon, might have something to do with it. Though his name makes him sound like a medieval English theologian, he has in fact none of the "sweet lovable personality" *The Cambridge History of English Literature* finds in the Venerable Bede. Herndon's best-known play, *Until the Monkey Comes,* though by no means untalented, is one of the nastiest dissections of modern youth. In *Alice's Restaurant,* perhaps because of an inchoate difference between the two scenarists, a strange ambivalence obtains: the free-swinging sexuality of Alice and her consort, Ray, is contrasted with the chastity and monogyny of Arlo Guthrie; the exaltation of a commune living in a deconsecrated church is contrasted with the pathetic outcome of the experiment, which, even so, is viewed much more favorably than the other world of adult squares.

Indeed, even a seemingly kindly, idealistic landlady, an old friend of Woody's from "the Movement," proves to be a harpy: in exchange for a loan, she would extract from Arlo a pound of fleshly love. But, similarly, the charming young groupie, sniffling from a bad cold yet ready and stripping, her adolescent body unhampered by a rheum at the top, is equally tainted. She wants to make it with Arlo because "someday he may be an album." Arlo, like the gallant troubadour he is, rejects Reenie (deliciously embodied by Shelley Plimpton), just as he later rejects Alice. And that is as indicative as anything of the movie's central schizophrenia: the hero of a swinging world, a chaste Galahad! Later, he finds conventional happiness with Mari-chan, the film's most improbable character. Played by an extremely pretty, fashion-modelish Oriental girl (Tina Chen), she is supposed to be some little lotus flower that just happens to be employed in a Stockbridge pottery workshop. Not bruddy rikery.

Or take the character of Shelly, the prototypical motorcycle and heroin addict, who, if anyone, should personify the pathos of the wilting flower children. Instead, he is almost as much of an oversimplified flat line drawing as are the more obviously caricatured neo-Keystone Kops of Officer Obie. Penn's direction is spotty: the funeral scene, despite the lovely singing of Joni Mitchell's penetrating "Songs of Aging Children," is staged with the ultimate of deadly artifice. But the Army physical, although by now a bit of a comic commonplace, is managed skilfully and emerges, except for an obvious travesty of a tough noncom, filled with fresh and humane humor. Dede Allen was, once again, Penn's imaginative film editor.

September, 1969

THE STERILE CUCKOO

For a more eccentric kind of sentimentality in the youth film, there is *The Sterile Cuckoo,* the first picture directed by Alan J. Pakula, who was previously Robert Mulligan's producer. Alvin Sargent wrote the screenplay from a successful 1965 first novel by John Nichols, which, like most of Mulligan's films, I managed to miss. So I would come to this film quite unbiased, except for glowing reports from those who saw it before me about how marvelous Liza Minnelli is in the title part.

Cuckoo is the story of Pookie Adams, who meets Jerry Wayne on the bus taking them to their neighboring colleges in upstate New York. They are both freshmen: Jerry a budding entomologist, as nice and staid and ordinary as they come; Pookie a severe neurotic (or worse) who considers everyone a weirdo or a creep. She keeps descending on Jerry and, by and by, with her misanthropy and glib talk and availability, fascinates, cajoles, and browbeats him into an affair with her. Jerry loves her, but Pookie's possessiveness and emotional blackmail—not to mention her antagonizing everyone around—drive the young entomologist back into his protective carapace. He asks for a month's respite. Pookie, hurt to the quick, leaves school and vanishes. When she reappears, she is an emotional wreck; all Jerry can do is send her back to a father who has never forgiven her for causing his beloved wife's death in childbirth, and who is almost always on trips away from home.

It is a simple, oversimplified, unconvincing little film. Whereas the sentimentality in a film like *Goodbye, Mr. Chips* stems from the romanticizing exaggeration of a real enough ambience, that of *The Sterile Cuckoo* belongs to the Cloud-Cuckoo-Land colleges remembered from films like the June Allyson musical, *Good News* (1947). Here, as mysteriously as in Bluebeard's Castle, no other real presences exist besides Pookie and Jerry, and, fleetingly, Jerry's roommate. Pookie and Jerry shuttle between a rickety motel room where they practice their unplatonic brand of puppy love, and the picturesque open spaces around Hamilton College, where the novel is understood to take place and where the filming was actually done. These outdoor wandering and lovemaking sequences, photographed in undistinguished colors by Milton Krasner, and full of consciously lyrical long shots and conscientiously rhythmic dissolves, perilously approach equivalent scenes in *Changes*—that is to say, rock bottom.

I repeat, there is not a single teacher around, and other students are lay figures occasionally scurrying by, or seen at one of those movie junior proms that would make a sardine feel confined. Or during its aftermath, with someone strumming a guitar as artfully scattered couples discreetly pet in distant prospect and chiaroscuro. Pookie's "tragic" background is sketched in with few and unconvincing strokes; Jerry's is left blank.

A typical example of the filmmakers' confusion is the Easter vacation: Jerry is staying over to catch up with his work, and Pookie lives with him in his room in connubial bliss and acrimony. Pakula cannot decide whether Pookie is a dangerous nut who disturbs the hell out of her serious friend, or whether Jerry is a humorless grind who spoils Pookie's delightful sport.

Perhaps we are to overlook all this for the sake of that brilliant character, Pookie—lovable, horrible, bright, foolish psychopath in the making. But if a girl is as abnormally standoffish and world-hating as Pookie is, would she—could she—play the undauntable, irresistible enchantress to Jerry? And if she can do that, would she not, on some sick level, also dazzle and subjugate at least some of the creeps and weirdos? How, one wonders, does she take care of herself and survive during a lengthy disappearance she laconically describes with "I was in Boston"? Nor is her attitude toward her pregnancy and miscarriage (unless they are more of her fabrications, which the movie does *not* seem to suggest) consistent with her pathology.

And Liza Minnelli? Though some of her kookier lines recede as swiftly and irretrievably as her chin, her outbursts of joy or panic are authentic and often affecting. But she tends to do too much, her whole body shaking like an overworked steam engine, her eyes carrying on like gaskets about to burst. Despite some talent, she cannot fake charm or acceptable looks. For a fugitive moment we can fool ourselves into believing that she is a *jolie laide,* but forthwith she reverts to her usual mixture of Judith Crist and the Emperor Tiberius.

December, 1969

PADDY

Most of the new movies are "youth films," with which there is nothing intrinsically wrong. At the crossroads between art and the market, the American film has almost always unherculeanly opted for the market. At least now it addresses its pandering to an audience with an enthusiastic if indiscriminate feeling for film, rather than to the previously postulated faceless audience whose one presumed feature was near-imbecility. There remains, however, the important question of whether a youth film takes up the concerns of youths or merely caters to their cravings and delusions of grandeur.

Paddy, an Irish import, is not really a youth film, except insofar as its eponymous hero is young, restless, and searching for an undefined fulfillment rather than willing to settle for a steady but routine job and a fine but basically conventional, marriage-bent girl. Perhaps because the locale is Dublin, where youth rebellion seems confined to catching the boat for London, everything is pretty tame in *Paddy.* But the film is not without its charm, its moments of earned pathos, and a pervasive sense of incommensurability between an old dispensation and a new one. It is, in fact, a sort of lesser, Hibernian *Alfie,* lacking the earlier film's poise and sharpness, but with the same sexual symbology for social unrest.

Paddy is a footloose lower-middle-class youth of, say, twenty, who works his way up from butcher's delivery boy to insurance company clerk, from apparent virginity to a rich double life pleasuring two complementary women, only to end up chucking it all. One woman is the lusty widow, Claire Kearney, as generous with her money as with her somewhat *faisandé* charms; the other is the pretty, young fellow office-worker, Maureen. Maureen wants to marry Paddy, whom she truly loves; Claire is content merely to keep him, in both senses, as long as possible. And Paddy has further sexual adventures, such as a threesome with a bizarre girl artist described as a masochist (a word that puzzles Paddy) and a dandified young man from the insurance office; or a buoyant teen-age pickup on the train returning from a weekend with Claire, now living in County Wicklow.

There are also adventures of the mind, consisting mostly of Platonic dialogues in a pub with Harry Redmond, a self-styled poet who has never written a poem but whose talent for scrounging is as incontestable as his garrulity that earns him free drinks. Other than that, Paddy has a family to contend with, consisting of a tough, demanding widowed mother, a grouchy older brother and a dying younger one, as well as a sizzling malcontent of a sister, handsomely played by Ita Darcy. His good-natured floundering from girl friends to friends, from friends to family, makes for a jolly, rambling, sometimes affecting film. But, and it is a but as big as Nelson's Column, it has all been done before, often much better.

One problem is that the layabout's wit and wisdom of Harry Redmond never reaches the standards set for this sort of thing by Joyce and

O'Casey. Another is that the film was at least partly aimed at an Irish audience, which meant abiding by strict sexual censorship—the genuine scene of lovemaking has to be played fully clothed, in the manner of *A Stranger Knocks*. And though there is much *talk* of canes and whips, what we *see* is always decorously out of sexual sync. The color photography by Daniel Lacabre, a former assistant to Claude Lelouch, falls short of Lelouch's work, though the fault may in part be that of Pathécolor, a process I do not recall ever having yielded masterpieces of color cinematography.

But the director, Daniel Haller, has, on the whole, directed with a fluid brio, failing only in a young-love montage sequence, which is photographed in the standard television deodorant-commercial manner. (A new cinematic vocabulary for young-love-in-bloom sequences is desperately needed.) What Haller does get, though, is nicely varied moods and tempos, giving you the impression of watching something more substantial than Lee Dunne's screenplay, based on his own novel, actually provides. Another prepossessing element is the restrained rock score by John Rubinstein, which includes a title song that, for once, really works, instead of being a nuisance and embarrassment.

The acting is beautiful with a couple of exceptions. As the middle-aged dispenser of eternally young blarney ("Get married? I'd rather go to work!"), Milo O'Shea of the wildly bifurcating eyebrows simply lacks charm. The actor seems to be sweating oil, his speech is tallowy, and his eyes exude a sickly-sweet pustulence; one cannot imagine why people would buy him drinks instead of hygienically throwing them in his face. And as the rich Irish-American tourist out to hook him, Peggy Cass once again displays her standard mixture of ugliness and aggressiveness unsupported by any talent, which in some quarters passes for being a character. This can happen only on stage or screen; imagine serving up a dead vulture and pretending it is Thanksgiving turkey.

But Des Cave is a truly engaging Paddy: a lout full of delicate feelings, with a face that combines naïveté with shrewdness, and a manner that can leap from tentativeness to self-assertion at the drop of a neckline, if not a hat. Dearbhla Molloy is devastatingly dead-center as Maureen, making you feel both the girl's youthful givingness and grace and the conventionality underneath with a oneness that rightly defies easy categorization. And Maureen Toal coaxes every bit of humor and pathos out of the part of the aging mistress, without ever letting the characterization lapse into crudeness or stickiness. The others are equally good, with only Judy Cornwell overdoing the eccentric artist.

When all is said, *Paddy* is still only a fair little film—which, however, is enough to make it loom large over most current offerings.

May, 1970

HI, MOM!;
THE MAGIC GARDEN OF STANLEY SWEETHEART

There is, first, *Hi, Mom!,* by the same duo that made the delightful *Greetings!* Once again, Charles Hirsch is producer and co-scenarist with Brian De Palma, who also directed; once again some of the same performers appear in roles that evolved from those in the previous film; and once again there is an exclamation point at the end of the title. And there the similarity ends, for *Hi, Mom!* is, regrettably, an almost total waste of time. The filmmakers have run out of ideas: they either try to milk the same situations as before (making Peeping-Tom sex films), or if they come up with something new (militant Black Theater that humiliates and manhandles white liberal audiences), they stretch it out as desperately as beggars their last crust of bread.

There are even more basic problems. *Hi, Mom!* is clearly improvisatory cinema, an enterprise that requires true brilliance somewhere. It may be in the director (*e.g.,* Fellini, in some of his earlier films), or it may be in the performers (*e.g.,* Nichols and May—though they worked on the stage, which lends itself better to the genre, and their best routines were not improvised). Here, however, brilliance is not forthcoming, although Allen Garfield contributes a juicy bit as a pornographic film producer. Robert De Niro and Jennifer Salt, who have the principal roles, are not prodigal enough with verbal invention, and even their expressions, gestures, and intonations lack the final comic polish. And whereas *Greetings!* had a unifying plot device—how to stay out of the Army—there is no such central motif here, and the film switches from a parody of porno filmmaking to a parody of educational TV programming (extremely superficial) to a parody of Black Theater (extremely laborious) to a parody of . . . I could go on, but let me leave a stone or two unturned, in case you do want to see the film for the sake of your fond recollections of its predecessor. It needs to keep its few mild surprises undivulged.

A more elaborate youth film is *The Magic Garden of Stanley Sweetheart,* based on a semiautobiographical novel by the then twenty-two-year-old Robert Westbrook, Columbia University dropout, former film assistant to Sidney Lumet, maker of underground films, author of a book called *Journey Behind the Iron Curtain,* and son of Sheilah Graham. Unfortunately, it is that last datum that is most indicative. For the book is a flashily superficial bit of sexy plot-concocting, gussied up with derivative "modernist" fictional devices, such as extensive fantasies, a book-within-a-book, sequences based on speculation by one character about another, etc. The main attraction remains the juvenile polymorphous sex-and-drug scene, with the obligatory rock background, and, because this is fundamentally the old college first-love-and-sex novel in new dress or undress, an occasional reference to Kant or Kenneth Patchen.

Actually, it is more about Kant's homonym. Here is a typical passage: " 'Oh, groovy,' she moaned. Or was she mocking him? 'Fuck me, man.' Stanley was about to oblige when he noticed that his prick was hanging most limp between his legs." Patently, the trouble lies in those four-letter words, "most" and "legs." The "most" is a shabby way of achieving originality—a mere superlative will never take the place of imaged evocation; and the "legs" is mere word-mongering. Where else could it be hanging: between his ears?

Badly written as it is, the novel does contain a rudiment of structure and some attention to form; the film drifts along as aimlessly as its hero, reducing the plot and characterization to an even barer minimum, and the actresses to maximum bareness. Yet it is dishonest even in its attempts at daring. Though the dirty words are there, they are used frugally rather than, as in the book, as a kind of baser basic English. Though there is much nudity, the hero never displays his genitals, most or least limply; and even the girls are disrobed unevenly: the one that comes nearest to incipient stardom, least of all; the one that is a comic greaseball, and thus funny rather than sexual, the most. And sex, being by now by far the least censorable thing, fares infinitely better than the inchoate political and social comment in the novel, which, sketchy and innocuous as it is, gets summarily excised from the film.

There is evidence also of much haphazard cutting of the finished product: the character of Dr. Arthur Osgood, though still prominent among the screen credits, does not once appear; and the ending, as it now stands, is too amateurish even for these filmmakers—Westbrook, who wrote his own screenplay, and Leonard Horn, who directed. The key character, Danny Rosenberg, a frail, homely, tormented Jewish musical prodigy, becomes a big, blond, sexy, extroverted rock musician, with the Jew and Juilliard in his background equally soft-pedaled. The latter is mentioned once, the former not even that often.

The discothèque sequences are especially offensive with their pretentious and pointless trickery, and the rock score is undistinguished except for one rather fetching tune by Michel Legrand to which, however, the new Hollywood-hotshot songwriting team of Alan and Marilyn Bergman have contributed their usual disfiguring lyrics. Victor Kemper's cinematography is poor, and the acting nonexistent, with the possible exception of Holly Near's fat Fran. Had I not seen Michael Greer do well on the stage, I could not have deduced ability from the droopy-faced slouch that is all we get here. Victoria Racimo is a sexy face and body, and Dianne Hull is not even another pretty face, just another good body. The rest, including Don Johnson as Stanley, cannot get any kind of vote because they failed to register.

May, 1970

GETTING STRAIGHT

By far the slickest and most odious of the current youth films, however, is *Getting Straight,* which is as crooked as they come. Purporting to be an outspoken seriocomic satire on what goes on in our universities, the film, directed by Richard Rush from a screenplay by Robert Kaufman, would play both ends against the middle, if it had a middle. As it is, it has only the two extremes: a horde of inhuman, computer-wielding, reactionary university authorities, occasionally leavened by a mere cynic or amiable nonentity; and a rival horde of black and white student militants who seem to be protesting only because they cannot get laid, or so as to be able to get laid immediately after or even during the worst campus fracas. The melees depicted are particularly grating, with both militants and militia shown at their worst, and the tone switching irresponsibly from snide humor to heart-tugging gore. Even this absurd oversimplification and manipulation might, up to a point, stand, if only the standpoint would stand still. But no; repeatedly the suggestion is held out that either teaching or student revolt may have an inherent dignity, and equally consistently the idea is kicked over by a cheap gibe or freewheeling foolishness.

Something might still be salvaged if the protagonist, Harry Bailey, a veteran of Selma and Vietnam who returns to the university to get an M.A. enabling him to teach, were a character whose changes had a meaning. But Harry fluctuates between a supposed vocation and feeding his pupils trivia (not to mention having his girl grade them), between belittling and endorsing the student activists, between wanting to make it at any cost and throwing it all up for a moronic jest. The last shot has him, a failed would-be teacher and failed revolutionary, quietly falling to screwing his girl, while fiercely muddleheaded campus fighting rages all around. So we might assume that the message is sheer nihilism; in that case, however, the repeated gestures toward commitment of some sort are smelly red herrings; and for a truly nihilistic film, characters like the hero, the heroine, and the black militant are treated with highly dishonest sentimental leniency.

Richard Rush's direction is all fast, hollow cleverness, matched by Laszlo Kovacs's photography, a continual shuttling of focus between foreground and background, so that some part of the image is everlastingly submerged in an arty blur. Elliott Gould is allowed to get away with a lethal dose of Method mugging as Harry; as his deliciously WASP girl friend, Candice Bergen's pseudoacting continues not to improve. By some dire misconception, if a pretty girl makes faces, screams, and assumes agonized attitudes, the result passes for a performance. Even that whining voice of Miss Bergen's makes one wish Papa's ventriloquizing would come to her aid. The film contains the obligatory nudity, though not for Miss Bergen, whose insufficiencies force the prying camera into truly Pascalian leaps—from shoulders to toes, usually. Yet the main trouble is that awful moral and ideological blur which, going the camera one better, manages to besmog foreground and background simultaneously.

May, 1970

LET IT BE

The new Beatles film, *Let It Be,* is only for worshipful teenyboppers and middle-aging intellectuals hell-bent on being with-it. Sloppily photographed and casually spliced together, it could pass for a home movie, except that an unfunny funhouse is not a home. One is aware, especially now that their break-up has been announced, that the Beatles have progressed from the beatific stage to canonization, and that their fingernail parings have become priceless. *Let It Be* is a collection of audiovisual nail parings, but not without a certain morbidly sociological interest.

For this purpose, it is appropriate to consult the film reviewer who has attained the highest degree of that kind of interest, Judith Crist. "It is a delight," she writes of this movie, "not only for its music but for its closeup . . . of the four young men who have affected the lifestyle of one generation and—look around you and then back to photos of the fifties—at very least the appearance of several generations."

I myself could not find a single outstanding song in the film, but that is not the point. The question is whether changing the "lifestyle" of one generation and the appearances of however many Mrs. Crist thinks have zoomed by since the fifties (including perhaps those old-timers who haplessly sport the hippie look) makes someone a delight to look at. (The Beatles, by the way, have not changed the appearance of Mrs. Crist, as you can verify by checking a two-page advertisement in the women's magazines that features eight pictures of the lady; the ad is for Pristeen, a product describing itself as a Feminine Hygiene Deodorant Spray.) One would first have to demonstrate the esthetic value of this new look, which Mrs. Crist neglects to do.

Paul McCartney, a chubbily handsome young man, appears quite pleasant with, or despite, his generation-shaping look. But the others! Particularly grubby are John Lennon and his worse half, Yoko Ono, who sits, smug and possessive, almost always within touching distance of him. Flouting, it would seem, even minimal sanitary measures, their hair looks like a Disneyland for the insect world, and their complexions appear to be portable bacterial cultures. This would be of small importance if one generation, at any rate, were not determined to emulate their example, and if the spectacle were not touted by adult reviewers.

I am no inveterate Beatle-baiter, having enjoyed *A Hard Day's Night* and *Yellow Submarine,* as well as some Beatle records. But very little of this transcends the mass-culture, pop-music level, for all the hard days' nights the Beatles may have put in studying the sitar or Stravinsky. At one point, Lennon mumbles a bit of impromptu rhyme, something like "Isadora Duncan/Goes for Telefunken," and that is about the height of wit in *Let It Be.*

We witness several recording sessions and one improvised concert on top of the Apple building that stops the surrounding traffic; we see the inscrutable smirking of Yoko (truly, in Wilde's phrase, a Sphinx without a secret); and there is much middling music-making and muddled smalltalk. Galt MacDermot, the composer of *Hair,* once told me during an interview that he expected rock to be a passing musical fashion, and I wonder whether it isn't about time for it to pass. But, I suppose, rock has become the international anthem of the youth revolution, and while that movement lasts, so will rock. Which brings us to the central point of the film: that the Beatles, visibly, are not that young any more. As if sensing this, they disport themselves with a certain lassitude; I note a forced gaiety in Paul and John, a bemused quizzicality in Ringo, and downright gloom in George. In some of the film's sequences, John displays an open sore on his Adam's apple—symbolic, perhaps, of the canker in the Apple.

June, 1970

THE STRAWBERRY STATEMENT

What is pornography? Or what is pornocinematography? The question is frequently asked and even more frequently, and boringly, answered. Yet it is a subject one cannot entirely avoid at a time when so many new films, directly or indirectly, touch upon it—or, more often, burrow into it. There are even some films around that have hardly any overt sex in them but manage, nevertheless, to generate a subliminally pornographic atmosphere.

Such a film is *The Strawberry Statement*, based on James Simon Kunen's book about the student revolt at Columbia University and with a screenplay by Israel Horovitz, the respected young playwright. Because the film could not be made in its natural habitat, it had to be transferred to San Francisco and a mythical institution; furthermore, a conventional plot about a rather dopey student romance was added. What makes the film especially repulsive and, in a sense, pornographic is the steady suggestion that perhaps the principal reason for which students join the Movement is to get laid, a theory we are already acquainted with from the pioneer work, *Getting Straight.*

Now if sex is the prime mover, or movementer, the subject should be explored with honesty and attention to detail; in the film, nothing like that is actually done—one scene of instant fellatio as a reward for supposedly revolutionary activity was cut after the first New York screening. As the film now stands, what little sex there is in it occurs outside the revolutionary context. If the idea, however, is that student sexual hopes are, in fact, frustrated, the film equally fails to make that point. And if, as I believe, sex is not the chief cause of student revolt, films like this one are cruelly unfair and exploitative.

In *The Strawberry Statement*, we are always encouraged to envision the orgy just around the next turn of the reel, but all we get is puppy-love, puppy-politics, and Stuart Hagmann's, the director's, insufferable manipulations. His maniacal use of the zoom lens makes that instrument second in hatefulness only to a dentist's drill. Actually, it is as if Hagmann were giving the camera incessant hotfoots, making the poor thing leap like a demented creature and land in the unlikeliest places. When it is not zooming, the camera seems to be passed back and forth between a spastic dromomaniac and a whirling dervish. The film makes you seasick. Add to that cutenesses and clevernesses of every kind, like a high crane shot of the singing students seated and swaying in a perfect Busby Berkeley circle, and you have true visual obscenity matched by the glaring vulgarity of a bad rock soundtrack.

The great sequence to which all builds up is the police bust, staged and shot as part ballet, part *Walpurgisnacht,* part bloody Invasion of the Body Snatchers (*viz.,* pigs), and featuring such symbolic delights as club-wielding cops leaping out from behind an immense American flag hung over the proscenium of a stage. For the action takes place in a high-school gymnasium-cum-auditorium, and this, along with the other locales in the film, is synthetic. The absence of a real university complex adds a topological unreality to the various other kinds the film flaunts. I have no doubt that the police can be brutal, just as students can be stupidly provoking, but the execution of this scene wallows in every kind of falsity. As the heroine, Kim Darby clearly belongs in a Walt Disney picture about high-school hi-jinks, and the rest of the cast is not much more convincing. I can only hope that Hagmann goes back to TV commercials, where his neo-baroque talents can be fully appreciated.

July, 1970

4

Sex

HOW FAR the film has gone toward sexual emancipation in the last few years! When you consider that as recently as in 1963, in Bergman's *The Silence,* some rather chaste masturbation footage and a fairly briefly and dimly seen bit of copulation in a movie theater were considerably trimmed down by the censors—or precensors! The earliest film in this section, *The Fox* (1968), has already moved well beyond in masturbation, and, the following year, *I Am Curious, Yellow* goes considerably farther in all sorts of directions, including oral sex and male nudity—considered more outrageous than female nudity by a society as patriarchal as it is puritanical. Needless to say, the process of liberalization, like most blessings, is not unalloyed: besides filmmakers who have important truths about sex to convey, the open door admits every kind of opportunistic hack whose sole aims are titillation and turning a quick buck along with an incidental stomach or two.

But the good of it, I believe, far outweighs the bad, though the films in this category, except for the two mentioned above, are chiefly exploitational. The category was arranged, however, to show precisely the growth of sexual permissiveness. The real gains will be perceived more readily in other categories where the sexual freedom may not be the prime concern, but constitutes an important additional artistic means nevertheless. One of the unquestionable good things about this freedom is that, because it is equally available to film artists, it may to some extent undercut the success of skin flicks. For the film artist can, among other things, make his sexuality more powerful than that of the crass skin-flick-maker. As for the possible harm pornography on film might cause, I discuss the problem in several of the following pieces. But I can summarize my position by saying that I consider the danger of sex films' provoking sex crimes no greater (and no less) than that of car-racing films increasing the number of highway accidents.

GETTING FURIOUS OVER "CURIOUS"

My two subjects may seem far apart. One is the recent Court of Appeals decision permitting the showing of *I Am Curious, Yellow,* a Swedish film whose seizure by the United States Customs Office had been upheld by a jury trial in the U. S. District Court. The other is the new ratings for films by the Motion Picture Association of America, whose Code and Rating Administration supplies films with letters like G, M, R, or X, which may vastly influence their fate. Yet these subjects are related. As Hardy's poem "The Convergence of the Twain" demonstrates, an ocean liner and an iceberg, created thousands of miles apart and seemingly unconnected, may come together in a disastrous conjunction.

I Am Curious, Yellow (the *Yellow* to distinguish it from a sequel or alternative version, *I Am Curious, Blue,* which, incidentally, struck me as much less good) is the work of an able Swedish filmmaker, Vilgot Sjöman, a disciple and protégé of Ingmar Bergman. It concerns a young girl's search for identity in contemporary Sweden, in the course of which she rummages around in all accepted values: political, social, and sexual. Lena's investigation of foreign policies, nonviolent resistance, distribution of wealth, women's rights, family problems, etc., is supplemented with her quest for a good sex life, and there are scenes of nudity, copulation, and oral intercourse handled with frankness but also with wit and style. And the sexual problems are shown as relating to the other ones in the process of self-discovery.

The District Attorney's office elected a jury trial, presumably counting on the greater puritanism or obtuseness (assuming that these are separate virtues) of a jury than of a judge. Despite the favorable testimony of film critics, psychiatrists, clergymen, sociologists, and a famous novelist (there was also some hostile ecclesiastic testimony), the jury found against the film, which, according to law, means that (1) its dominant theme appeals to the prurient interest; (2) it patently affronts contemporary community standards for the representation of sexual matters; and (3) it is entirely without redeeming social value.

The film remained confiscated and prohibited from showing in the United States.

Grove Press, the importer, took the case to the Court of Appeals. Here an almost unprecedented thing happened: a jury decision was reversed, and the film approved for exhibition to adults. The chief judge, however, violently dissented from the majority opinion, which was itself somewhat divided. The Government is now pondering whether to appeal the decision to the Supreme Court. Meanwhile, what happened in the lower courts gives us ample, albeit rather gristly, food for thought.

The basic formulation of the problem dates from some eighteen-and-a-half centuries ago, when the great Roman poet Juvenal asked in his "Sixth Satire," "But who would guard the guardians themselves?" Or, to put it into our context, how and by whom can arbiters of morality be appointed? Chief Judge J. Edward Lumbard, in his dissenting opinion, states: "When it comes to a question of what goes beyond the permissible in arousing prurient interest in sex, the verdict of a jury of twelve men and women is a far better and more accurate reflection of community standards and social values [than the decision of] circuit judges in their middle sixties who cerebrate in the ivory tower of the judiciary." This promptly makes one question the validity of Judge Lumbard's opinion, since he, too, must be in his sixties and do his adjudicating in the same ivory tower with his colleagues rather than in Yankee Stadium or Grand Central Station.

But let us look more closely. Judge Lumbard opines that "the jurors are drawn from all walks of life" and adds in a footnote that "they ranged in age from thirty-two to sixty-eight years and engaged in widely varying occupations." Now this happens not to be true. The very first potential juror was peremptorily dismissed by Assistant District Attorney Schilling—because his walk of life was teaching history at Columbia University. Clearly, an intellectual and, therefore, unrepresentative.

The ages of the jurors may have varied, but observe that though they included some of those sexagenarians whom Judge Lumbard finds suspect, not one of them was between the ages of twenty-one and thirty-two—the age group of a very large portion of our population, a still larger one of our moviegoers, and precisely the one to which the problems and conclusions of the film most urgently address themselves. And though there may have been a certain range of occupations, it is noteworthy that the only juror whose field was even remotely related to the question at hand—whether I Am Curious, Yellow is a work of art with a serious purpose, or a piece of gratuitous, unhealthy trash—was an editor of Reader's Digest Books. It would seem to me that the world of Reader's Digest is as far removed from the world of art and genuine intellect as anything that calls itself "Books" can be.

That is my point. According to law, a man is to be tried by a jury of his peers. A film and its maker that have artistic and intellectual pretensions are thus entitled to be pronounced upon by a panel of artists and intellectuals. So I would argue that neither the said jury nor the three circuit judges are the proper choice of arbiters; in Sweden, it was precisely a panel of the sort I mentioned that pronounced the film unobjectionable. But if choice there must be between jury and judges, I opt for the latter—because of their more extensive education and, presumably, higher degree of civilization.

Two positions are possible. One can argue that the decision is up to the expert—the engineer in engineering matters, the clergyman in religious ones, the philosopher in philosophical ones, and so on; or, on the contrary, that it is the common man, frail, exposed, susceptible, but the backbone of society, who must pronounce on the issue. If, in the case of *I Am Curious, Yellow,* we conceive of the matter as esthetic and moral, it means that it is arguable that estheticians and moralists, i.e., artistic, intellectual, and spiritual experts, must pass on it; in other words, artists, educators, psychiatrists, and clergymen. And, if worse comes to worst, judges.

But if one takes the other position—that it is all up to the average man, the ordinary consumer, the large masses—then it is precisely the large masses that must decide, and twelve men and women, even if they include butchers, bakers, and candlestick makers, are *not* the large masses. Under this option, in fact, everyone must be allowed to make up his own mind. But when Judge Lumbard exalts the twelve jurors over his two fellow judges because of "their less pretentious positions in the community," the word "pretentious" gives away the show. Either Judge Lumbard is fed up with his colleagues, in which case we may justly accuse him of the very unjudicial, unjudicious, and mind-befogging condition of pique; or he is against the thoughtful, specially trained, cerebrally oriented person and favors the ordinary, the average, the commonplace. God forbid that the future of the arts should fall into such hands.

Again, I stress that minors are not at stake here: they will, in any case, be excluded, and what was under litigation here is merely the suitability of the film for adult consumption. But if, as Judge Lumbard, Assistant District Attorney Schilling, and others of that stripe feel, a film such as this is obscene and damaging to adults viewing it, the obvious question is what happens to the psyches of the various people appointed or self-appointed to act as censors? It is, of course, common knowledge that customs officials, policemen, district attorneys, state and city censors, members of church and patriotic organizations have a much higher and stronger moral sense than ordinary people. But even they must suffer the damaging consequences of repeated and prolonged exposure to obscene material. And jurors being, as we are told, plain unpretentious people, less hardened and resilient, they must incur dire moral lesions from even a single compulsory viewing of an obscene film.

The only safe and sanitary way, then, of dealing with such highly dangerous material is for the Government to pick an individual by lot and have him view all suspect films in strictest isolation. He would thereupon report to judges and juries on the content of the films in carefully diffuse circumlocutions and de-fused euphemisms, and the cases would be judged on the strength of the deposition of this Federal Moral Scapegoat. After one year of service, the contaminated FMS would be deported to a desert island where he could do no further damage to society.

That brings us to the other issue: the ratings of the MPAA and its Code of Self-Regulation. This, ostensibly, affects only minors. A film rated G is for general audiences; one rated M is for mature audiences, with "parental discretion advised." A film rated R is restricted, with minors admitted to it only in the company of an "adult guardian"—but who will prevent the guardian from being the nearest dignified-looking pervert the youngster is able to pick up? A film rated X is forbidden to all persons under sixteen, but "this age restriction may be higher in certain areas." It is not specified how much higher, but I assume that sexagenarian judges will, in all cases, be admitted.

Ratings present serious problems. Thus in small towns with few movie theaters, the exhibitors may not show X films at all, lest business fall off. Or the exhibitor may pick up his very own pair of scissors and, unbeknown to all, snip out whatever makes the film X in his opinion; the law unfortunately, is of no use against depredations of this order. Or again, and there are already instances of this to hand, a producer may dictate to the filmmaker what he may or may not include in a film being shot, so as to avoid a possible X-rating. Thus we have not only self-censorship (as it is somewhat loftily called—for if a film by

Antonioni is objected to by a Mr. Shurlock of the MPAA, how does that constitute *self*-censorship?), but also pre-self-censorship.

Let us, however, consider the rating system with reference to its presumptive forte: the warning signal to parents of children aged one to unspecified. Here the issue is once again: who are these raters, encoders, or censors? The director of the operation, until the first of this year, was a Mr. Geoffrey M. Shurlock, a seventy-four-year-old former Englishman living in Hollywood, which immediately exonerates him from any suspicion of sexagenarianism or ivory-towerishness. Indeed, Mr. Shurlock's educational background is exemplarily univoried: he merely attended the now defunct Theosophical Institute of San Diego.

Shurlock has just been made special consultant and replaced by his former assistant, Eugene G. Dougherty, about whom I know only what Jack Valenti, head of the MPAA, has said: that his "rational good judgment is acknowledged throughout the industry." I prefer people whose judgment is less tautologically admired by the industry, but I cannot quarrel with another new staff appointment, a trained child psychologist with varied experience.

The rest of the staff consists of a former A.P. reporter and four others of indeterminate previous occupations, though they all have degrees from colleges or universities. What makes me wonder, though, whether the appointments are truly ecumenical is that three out of the four are graduates of Catholic institutions, and two of them got degrees from Santa Clara and Gonzaga Universities, which suggests either a truly remarkable coincidence or rank parochialism with perhaps a touch of cliquishness thrown in.

I ask myself whether it would not be more useful to parents if they took a little time out to read one or two reviews of the films in question; with a minimum of effort they could find a couple of publications whose critics strike them as congenial and reliable. To these they could subscribe, or just read them in the library. This might actually be preferable even to setting up a Rating Board consisting of professional film reviewers—inasmuch as the New York Film Critics' Circle recently picked *The Lion in Winter* best picture, and *War and Peace* best foreign picture of the year.

Ratings, it would seem, are needed less by films than by film critics. Any critic voting for *The Lion in Winter* should be given a rating of X, meaning "not recommended as reviewer for any film aimed at the over-sixteen audience." And any critic who voted for *War and Peace* should be given a rating of R, meaning "to be admitted to films with adult pretensions only in the company of an adult guardian who can explain to the critic the difference between pretension and achievement."

February, 1969

THE FOX

The characters in D. H. Lawrence's *The Fox* are, according to F. R. Leavis, "lower-middle-class and ordinary." In the film version, the class has been slightly upped while the ordinariness has been strenuously diminished. Much is made of masturbation and lesbianism, and relatively little of Lawrence. I recall the annotated reading list of one of my high school English teachers, which included *"Of Human Bondage:* a lesson from Spinoza, not deep." The current film might be described as "a lesson from Lawrence, not Lawrence."

The most obvious weakness of the film is its exaggerated literal mindedness: March, the more intensely alive of two young women living together on a little farm, has to be shown in a long, rapturous masturbation sequence—and, in typical Hollywood fashion, even onanism has to be played as a love scene. Thus March masturbates in front of a mirror and a mute duologue ensues; that this suggests narcissism, inconsistent with her generous character (as the movie has it), did not seem to bother any of the film's fabricators. Again, the lesbian scene between March and the delicate, infantile Jill is Hollywoodized into something like elder and younger sister going to sleep together, with one chaste good-night kiss for a send-off. Even this is much too explicit, however, for what in Lawrence's story is subliminal and unconscious, and in its all but everyday normality, far more disturbing.

The work was felt to be in need of updating, yet its meanings are closely bound to its World War I setting, when the fumbling uncertainties of man-woman relations were in a transitional period and when men, moreover, were scarce. The scriptwriters, Lewis John Carlino and Howard Koch, first transplant the action from the edge of an English village to what looks like the core of the Canadian wilderness, making the whole thing seem exotic and eccentric (what are these girls doing in Ultima Thule?) and shifting the emphasis to some sort of woman-against-the-elements outdoorsiness. Then we switch to a simplistic contest between heterosexual and homosexual love, reassuringly won by the former.

In the novella, the action takes place in an England the protagonist finds small and oppressive, from which he wants to escape to Canada with his chosen woman. In the film, the hero is going to take March from Canada to, of all places, Vermont, which I can explain only as an aberrant craving for maple sugar. The original story is vivid and meaningful because no one in it is a type: the hero is only a boy, March is a shy creature for all her assuming the male role vis-à-vis Jill, and Jill is neither so cute nor so weird as the film (or Sandy Dennis) makes her out to be. Consequently, there is a far more intricate and subtly ambivalent set of interrelations at work, and, as Graham Hough has remarked, "the aesthetic surface is never broken by symbols that call attention to themselves." The surface of the film breaks out in a horrible rash of symbols.

Still, there are compensations. William Fraker is a not untalented color photographer—he is much better here than he was in *Games*—and he has conveyed the spur-like sting of the wintry outdoors as palpably as the sensuous warmth inside the girls' cottage. The screenplay has its moments of quiet conviction (Carlino is a sporadically gifted playwright), though most of the awkward beauties of Lawrence's dialogue, almost compulsive in its simplicity, are unhappily missing. Mark Rydell has directed with little urgency despite some purple cross-cutting, but Lalo Schifrin's score (*The President's Analyst* and *Cool Hand Luke* were also scored by Schifrin) is ingenious, musicianly, and free from the greasiness of standard studio orchestrations.

There are two beautiful performances. Anne Heywood's March, sensitively modulated and broodingly suggestive, is easily the most Lawrentian element of the film. Her work exudes intelligence; so, too, with perhaps a little more emphasis on low animal cunning, does that of the fox. In the crucial confrontation scene between Miss Heywood and the bushy-tailed marauder, both perform stunningly. I hope this unbilled vulpine charmer will not retire from the screen. (May I suggest *Lady into Fox* as a possible starring vehicle?)

Keir Dullea is adequate as the man: he looks right and at least does not do anything wrong in a role that the screenplay reduced to utter banality. That brings us to the film's sorest point, Sandy Dennis. Pauline Kael has aptly observed that Miss Dennis has "made an acting style out of postnasal drip." It should be added that she balances her postnasal condition with something like prefrontal lobotomy, so that when she is not a walking catarrh she is a blithering imbecile. She has carried that most repugnant of Method devices—taking one or two trial runs on every sentence, if not phrase, one utters—to the level of a tic: her every line of dialogue issues in triplicate, ready to be notarized. Superimpose on this a sick smile befitting a calf's head in a butcher shop, an embryonic laugh that emerges as an aural stillbirth, and an epic case of fidgets, and you have not so much a performance as a field trip for students of clinical psychiatry.

One final point of interest. Hollywood has, as usual, gone to work on the characters' names. Thus Nellie March becomes Ellen March (more like a starlet, that); Henry Grenfel turns into Paul Grenfel (only sissies and pot bellies are called Henry); and, best of all, even March's favorite hen is elevated from Patty into Edwina! Hollywood is a great little maker of images; too bad so few of them have anything to do with film.

March, 1968

HERE WE GO ROUND THE MULBERRY BUSH

If you can imagine a cross between *Tom Jones* and *Peanuts* taking place at and around church theatricals and high school orgies in provincial England, you more or less have the essence of *Here We Go Round the Mulberry Bush*. If you can't, don't bother to try. But you might want to see it, anyway, for one powerful reason: young Judy Geeson in the altogether is the loveliest sight in movies so far this year, and unlikely to be outstripped by later contenders.

Disconsolate at the sight of so much utter, unattainable loveliness, I recalled a device of Pierre Costals, the novelist-hero of Henry de Montherlant's *Les Jeunes Filles*. To facilitate his envisaged parting from a new conquest, he unearths on the very first going to bed together a "safety exit"—some flaw he can fix upon when he wants to end the affair. After desperate scrutiny, I could fault Miss Geeson only with a hyperexcrescence between her incisors and bicuspids; but then I would gladly give my eyeteeth to—and for—her any time. I cannot say as much for the direction of Clive Donner, which gets worse with each successive film. It's high time to bring on Blitzen.

March, 1968

BELLE DE JOUR

The truly disconcerting film of the day is Luis Buñuel's *Belle de Jour,* the story of a rich, beautiful, frigid, masochistic housewife, unhappily revered by her surgeon husband. She has dreams in which she is humiliated, tortured, raped, killed; finally she finds her way into an exclusive little bordello. Here, under the tutelage of a madam who combines the best features of maternalism, lesbianism, and sadism, she undergoes (always only from 2–5 P.M.) a good many humiliations for real. This brings her closer to her unsuspecting husband. Unfortunately, her favorite client, a grisly young punk, tracks her to her luxurious home, and, out of jealous frustration, shoots the surgeon.

The loving spouse ends in a wheelchair, bereft of speech and paralyzed. He may or may not be on the road to recovery when a sinister family friend tells him the whole truth. Now that her husband seems utterly pulverized, our completely self-abased heroine can, blissfully and as his equal, share rock bottom with him. Her anxieties and evil dreams have left her. Instead, she has a good dream, of the two of them healthy and happy together. This last is, one assumes, a hideous irony.

How much of this nonsense (and even though *some* of it makes clinical sense, it *is* nonsense) is Buñuel and how much the novel it is based on, I can't say: not for anything in the world would I read another book by Joseph Kessel of the French Academy. I gather the dream fantasies as well as the two brief flashbacks to the heroine's childhood are Buñuel's, as is that elusive ending. So, too, is a daydream in which an aging, crazed duke performs on Belle de Jour (as the heroine is called from 2–5; from 5–2 she is Séverine) a mock ceremony involving incest, necrophilia, onanism, and sacrilege; perversity coupled with anti-Catholicism is as dear to Buñuel as to Sade. Buñuel or Kessel, it is all trashy because superficial: none of the characters, least of all Séverine, is as real and moving as, for example, the Uncle in *Viridiana.*

To be sure, the Hakim Brothers, those revolting producers who get good men to make bad pictures for them, precensored the film, and (one learns from *Sight and Sound*) a juicy thing or two, especially in the Duke episode, was never even released. This is Buñuel's tragedy: he could make the greatest works of film pornography ever—nothing to be sneezed at—but no one will subsidize him. Instead, he is forced to make more or less respectable films, which he nudges as best he can toward pornography, and which, as a result, tend to fall between two stools (no pun intended).

So in *Belle de Jour* there is almost perfect decorum: whips leave no marks, shouts and squeals are minimal, nudity is almost subliminal, and perversions are intimated but left in the twilight of ambiguity. There is much suggesting of weird but unclarified nastinesses which, in fact, makes the film rather more smutty and unpleasant. Moreover, the screenplay by Buñuel and Jean-Claude Carrière (the collaborator on the even more unfortunate *Diary of a Chambermaid*) tries hard to be clever and profound, but succeeds mostly in being coy and portentous. And the film is full of Buñuel's private symbols (on top of such public ones as shoe fetishism): visual or aural references to cats, children skipping rope, asphodel seeds, cowbells. They remain, regrettably, purely personal obsessions.

Nevertheless, and almost sadly, the presence of a master is felt in the film. The rhythm of the writing, the color changes, acting tempos, camera angles, the whole editing—all this is perfect. There is not one extraneous shot, nor one that is missing. Disparate elements are embraced in a self-possessed, lucidly enchanting flow. A directorial cleverness, such as an unexpected high-angle-shot, calls no attention to itself; the whole construction is a model for student directors to learn from. The color cinematography by Sacha Vierny (of *Marienbad* fame) is subtly voluptuous, the set design and decoration unostentatiously sumptuous, and Yves St.-Laurent's wardrobe generates more lustful yearning, among female viewers at least, than any of the film's sex.

The acting is uneven. Catherine Deneuve is lucky in having a lead that requires little more than beauty and abstractedness; Michel Piccoli, as the odious friend, and Françoise Fabian, as a whore reluctantly playing the part of the domina, are very good; Francisco Rabal and Pierre Clémenti, as a pair of punks, are appallingly bad; the others are mostly adequate. The one brilliant performance is that of Geneviève Page as the madam: every *oeillade*, every innuendo is made to count, and nothing ever rises above the level of pregnant understatement. If only the rest of the film were up to her—but there I go dreaming like a frustrated *bourgeoise.*

May, 1968

THÉRÈSE AND ISABELLE

In *Thérèse and Isabelle*, based on what must be an ineffably dreary autobiographical novel by Violette Leduc, the middle-aged Thérèse returns to the boarding school, a converted château, in which she had a brief but passionate love affair with a schoolmate, Isabelle. As Thérèse (Essy Persson of *I, a Woman*) wanders around the empty school, closed for summer vacation, and sees her face reflected in the water of a familiar toilet bowl, voices, figures, her former self—the whole past comes to life. Radley Metzger, the producer-director, and Jesse Vogel, his scenarist, revel in cutting back and forth, throughout the film, between an unconvincingly middle-aged Essy Persson and an even more unconvincingly teen-age one.

The ineptly told story is that of the gropings of two girls toward lesbian fulfillment, until, shortly after consummation, Isabelle, suddenly and preposterously, disappears forever. The sex scenes are ludicrous because Metzger, a producer and distributor of skin flicks who made an improbable fortune with the impossible *I, a Woman,* has (a) set himself up as a director, for which he has no talent whatever, and (b) attempted to make an art as well as sex film without the faintest notion of what art is all about. Here is a case of acute dissociation of sensibility: while the soundtrack groans with the overripe sex prose of the authoress, a cross between Jean Genet and Faith Baldwin and a heavy one to bear, the screen shows two naked females languidly lolling about, or, if they are doing anything, doing it reflected in a bulbous, distorting vase or hidden by some interposed object.

To be sure, there are suggestions of cunnilingus, *soixante-neuf,* as well as the longest and clumsiest masturbation scene on film—to which poor Georges Auric has composed dutifully dreadful cunnilingus and masturbation music. The whole thing tries desperately for both art and pornography, and flops resoundingly as each and deafeningly as both. Essy Persson has an ugly face, squat body, unsightly bosom, bad legs, stubby fingers and no acting ability. Anna Gaël (Isabelle) has a lovely face; fine, but for her supposed age, overripe body; and modest acting talents. The official brochure invokes a comparison with *Mädchen in Uniform,* but in its vulgarity the film is more of a *Mädchen in Cunniform,* and in its antiquity a *Mädchen in Cuneiform.*

June, 1968

BARBARELLA

Barbarella is a barely tolerable entertainment. Granted, almost any film that starts with Jane Fonda in the nude is doomed to going downhill from there. But at least Miss Fonda, even if approximately clothed, remains omnipresent, lending grace, suavity, and a jocund toothsomeness to a foolish comic strip that emerges, in the movie version, a foolish comic strip. Terry Southern is the northernmost among some eight, mostly French or Italian, perpetrators of this science-fiction grotesque, a kind of Candy in the sky with zircons.

There are some interesting props and actors (in that order) involved, but they are put to flabby and self-indulgent use. Typical of Southern and of Roger Vadim, the director and Miss Fonda's husband, is the submersion of some vaguely funny lines and situations in masses of spurious chic and gutless parlor sadism. By the latter I mean a flaccid, jaded appeal to our baser appetites, always liberally doused with essence of cop-out, resulting in an elucubrated, anemic pornography. The only episode approaching true wit is one in which the cosmos-trotting heroine is to be tortured to death inside a pleasure machine, an orgasm-organ; but that is a brazen plagiarism and vulgarization of a superb invention in Alfred Jarry's *Le Surmâle*. For this (or any other) film of his, Vadim deserves that Miss Fonda leave his bed and boredom, not to mention his cameras.

November, 1968

I AM CURIOUS, YELLOW

After one has testified for it in court and seen the testimony excerpted and misprinted in a book; after one has spent an evening in Stockholm discussing it with its maker, Vilgot Sjöman; after one has written a polemical piece defending it in the *Times* and stood up for it in a radio debate—one is somewhat tired of *I Am Curious, Yellow*, and would just as soon not have to review it.

Sjöman's controversial film concerns the quest of a girl called Lena Nyman for her selfhood: political, social, and sexual. Politically, she demonstrates for various left-wing causes, especially nonviolent resistance; socially, she has organized a group of young people to go around with tape recorders and interview people about whether Sweden is a classless society, the findings to be studied by the Lena Nyman Institute; sexually, she is experimenting in depth with a lover, her twenty-fourth. Lena also has family problems with her father, in whose house she lives: he had gone to fight Franco in '37 but quit after a couple of weeks; now he works in a frame shop, is mistrusted by his daughter and despises himself.

The film functions on several levels. There is Lena as a character in the story, but there is also a real-life Lena, who has an affair with the director-scenarist Sjöman (as she did in real life), then goes on to having one with Börje Ahlstedt, the actor who plays her lover in the film. What complicates matters is that we often see Sjöman and his crew making the film and getting into the Pirandellian act; that there are as many real moments of *cinéma-vérité* as bits of staged *cinéma-vérité* and "story" sequences; that there are authentic interviews with men like the brilliant young Swedish Cabinet member, Olof Palme, and imaginary ones with Yevtushenko, Dr. Martin Luther King, and the King of Sweden; and there is even a fantasy where the government adopts nonviolent resistance as the official policy. It becomes hard, indeed impossible, to tell which level is up; whether, for instance, a lovers' quarrel is part of the fiction or of the framework, and whether the framework itself isn't really fiction.

Sjöman achieves a hyper-Pirandellian conundrum, some of it amusing and some merely a bother. Nevertheless, the point that fantasy, fiction, wishful thinking, and reality are all equally meaningful and, in some senses, interchangeable, is made well enough. And Lena's struggles to achieve nonviolence in her various selves—as a political and a private person, as mistress and daughter—are animatedly chronicled in their partial victories and considerable setbacks. Particularly fine are the scenes with the father (played touchingly by Peter Lindgren), full of unresolved conflict and, on his part, scrupulous evasiveness. Scarcely less good is Lena's imaginary encounter with the King, and some of the responses of anonymous interviewees are of all too human interest.

But these things tend to escape notice, for attention avidly focuses on the sex scenes. Lena and Börje make love in various places, moods, and positions. There are tender lovemakings and querulous ones; some in fun, some in fury. There is oral sex and, in a dream sequence, castration. Defiantly, the lovers copulate on the balustrade of the Royal Palace; experimentally, in what is said to be Europe's oldest tree. Though varied, the sexuality is never erotic. (Whether that makes the film better or worse is a question I leave open.) Unerotic, first, because neither of the young people is particularly attractive—Lena, in fact, is downright bovine, but her liveliness is almost as good as loveliness. Unerotic, secondly, because the sex scenes are full of humorous or unglamorous details, which prove distinctly anaphrodisiac.

Artistically, the film has its weaknesses. Sjöman shot too much footage, so that he ended up making two versions of *I Am Curious: Yellow* and *Blue,* named after the colors of the Swedish flag. I have seen *Blue,* a much weaker film though not without its moments, and must regretfully report that some pieces that belong in one film have ended up in the other, contributing to the depletion and confusion of both. For example, an infestation with body lice that Lena passes on to Börje in *Yellow* is explained by a dalliance *à trois* with a married couple in whose car Lena hitches a ride in *Blue.* And there are motifs that seem insufficiently developed, while others are dawdled over.

Peter Wester's cinematography, which tries for a spontaneous newsreel look, is at times a bit too slapdash. Finally, the film never probes deeply enough, precisely because it probes away in so many directions. But *I Am Curious, Yellow,* is interesting in its shimmering, multifarious approach to life in Sweden today, in its frankness about sex, and in the considerable step ahead it marks in Vilgot Sjöman's artistic development.

March, 1969

LA PRISONNIÈRE

The most disappointing film of the moment is the reputable Henri-Georges Clouzot's *La Prisonnière,* which induced Claude Mauriac to write: "My throat is choked up, my heart bowled over." Actually, the film is an impossible conglomerate of "profound" statements about art, life, and the psyche; pornographic titillation; and old-fashioned boulevard melodrama of passions. On top of which, the psychology is either rudimentary or ridiculous, the profound statements are superficial when not downright false, and the love triangle uninteresting because of the shallowness and sketchiness of its participants. As a last indignity, even the pornography is derivative and, instead of building up to ever greater excitement, commits the sin against the unholy ghost of petering out into romance.

There is some handsome color photography cunningly intermingled with black-and-white shots, and there is a stylish and fearfully contemporary milieu bristling with kinetic as well as more traditional art—in fact, Jacques Saulnier, the veteran art director, comes off as the hero of the occasion. Clouzot himself merely strikes one as painfully *passé* and even more painfully striving to be "with it." As for Claude Mauriac, who continues, "I want to be by myself, I am so moved," we can guess just what he was moved to; but praise in such spurts is spurious and ephemeral.

April, 1969

TEOREMA

If Pier Paolo Pasolini's *Teorema* is not the worst film ever made, you can't blame it for not trying. A mysterious, handsome Stranger appears, no one knows whence, at a party given by a wealthy Milanese industrialist. Pretty soon the whole household is in a dither. The elderly maid is about to commit suicide from sheer frustrated desire, but the Stranger obligingly hops into bed with her. In no time—in bed, on a sun deck, in the bushes—he has done as much for the industrialist, his wife, their son and daughter.

Then a telegram summons him away. The maid goes back to her parental farm, where she cures a boy of eczema, has her hair turn miraculously to silver, eats only a soup made of boiled nettles, levitates above the barn roof, and ends up by having a friend bury her in a building site, leaving only the eyes exposed, with a puddle of tears forming slightly to the left of them. The daughter becomes catatonic and must be carted away by men in white. The son turns into a fanatic abstract painter who will cover a canvas, à la Yves Klein, with solid blue paint, and then urinate on it—abstract peeing, no doubt. The mother becomes nymphomaniacal, cruising about in her sports car and picking up youths, singly or in pairs, to have intercourse with—either back at their pads, or in a ditch beside a church. In between, she looks straight into the camera and emits a fearful howl. The father gives away his factory to the workers, goes to the railway station and almost follows a trick into the men's room; instead, he throws off his clothes then and there and hurries off to a wilderness, glimpses of which have appeared, like a refrain, throughout the film to the accompaniment of quotations from the Bible. Mother-naked, father faces the camera and emits the howl mother emitted before him. The end.

But do not for a moment assume that the story proceeds by any sort of narrative logic. It jumps around in fragmented Godardian non sequiturs that arise from nowhere and trail off into nothing. At the slightest sign of a little consecutive action, Pasolini whisks us off to some unrelated nonincident, or to that wilderness with cloud shadows scurrying across it and another unrelated biblical quotation streaking across the soundtrack. The film actually begins with a quite ungermane bit of staged *cinéma-vérité* in which workers are sounded out on their feelings about the factory's being turned over to them, so that the film proper is a long flashback leading up to this Marxist miracle in Milan.

Nor are you to think that there is anything like meaningful dialogue in *Teorema*. The advertisements proudly proclaim that though there are only 923 words in the film (it is not clear whether that includes duplicates), it says everything. There is no doubt that it says everything; unfortunately, however, without saying *something.* Pasolini has declared that the film is largely about the "cage of words" in which we are all cooped up, from which the Stranger, who represents (you have guessed it!) the Divine, extricates us. Yet since there is almost no talk, and what there is comes mostly after the visitation, it would seem that, if cage there be, it is the Stranger who tosses us into it. But, then, a cage of 923 words spread over an hour and a half has bars far enough apart for an elephant to walk through.

What of the visual elements? The color cinematography is handsome to look at, but what is *it* looking at? Apart from a few brief exteriors, mostly close shots of the actors doing vague, indefinable things. As the Stranger, Terence Stamp is generally sitting around nursing a Mona Lisa smile and reading Rimbaud in a Franco-Italian edition. (Why our liberation from words should be accomplished by a divinity reading words, and why that divinity, even if we grant its being Italian, should not be up on its French, is left unexplained.) The rest of the time he is mounting the rest of the cast, sometimes without the removal of clothes. Truly, God works in mysterious ways.

Behavior here is a series of poses. The daughter vacuously holds out her photograph album to the Stranger and says nothing, perhaps by way of preparation for catatonia. The Stranger and the son look through a book of reproductions of the paintings of Francis Bacon: Rimbaud, Bacon—we see what kind of sexuality the divinity likes in an artist. There are, in fact, a great many male crotch shots in the film, almost as if it were told from the point of view of a homosexual worm. This may account also for the weirdness of the two younger actresses. Mother, we are told, is played by Silvana Mangano. But since she is always, even in bed, wearing thick, chalk-white, heavily rouged and mascaraed pancake makeup, rather like a *kabuki* mask, she might as well be enacted by Utaemon XIII, or whatever numeral the current star female impersonator of the Kabuki Theater bears. The daughter is played by Anne Wiazemsky, in private life Mme Godard, possessed of the face of a horse, the teeth of a rabbit, and the expression of an amoeba. The combination of intense lack of talent and looks with scenes of hermetic emptiness represents a new high in minimal art, cinematic division.

At a Museum of Modern Art screening of *Teorema,* Pasolini explained to the audience that the Stranger is "a hypothesis," the sex "metaphorical," and the family a typical Milanese, or European, middle-class family. I thought of asking him a biological question: when

five members of a typical Milanese middle-class household are meta-
phorically screwed by a hypothesis, what is the issue? But the answer
is obvious: what is begotten is *Teorema*.

/Though the title, quite plainly, is the Italian for "theorem," people
keep referring to the film as "Theorama," either because they think it
is named after the process in which it is shot (like Cinerama, only more
divine), or perhaps because they assume the title to be an obscure
Greek word meaning "rammed by God." In discussing the film with
the poet Giuseppe Ungaretti, I asked what he thought of this mixture
of faggotry, Marxism, and Christianity. "Awful," he said, "but, you
know, the second and third ingredients are not to be taken seriously."
And he pointed out that whereas the men don't come to such bad ends,
the women get the works.

Teorema is totally vapid as film, yet might it not be valid as a parable?
Frankly, I can't see how this God (Pasolini has also said—what hasn't
he said?—that the Stranger is not Christ, but "the terrible God of
Creation") reaches those five people: though the mystics have put
erotic tropes to good use, I cannot take this by-the-numbers intercourse
seriously even as a metaphor. And why do the five react as they do?
What is the meaning of their reactions? Why should the buggered son
become an action painter *ipso facto,* and the humped daughter a catatonic? Why not the reverse? Why should the mother become a whore
and the servant a saint? Social class can't be the answer; the father, too,
is rich, and he gives away his earthly goods to become an eremite. Why
shouldn't the mother become a painter? She painted her face heavily
enough. Why don't they all become pizza vendors, or clowns in a
traveling circus, or a rock group called God's Very Own or The
Grateful Had?

Stamp's appearance suggests, if anything, a Caravaggio angel. The
angel as sexually ambiguous—asexual, bisexual, androgynous—has
fascinated pederastic painters and writers. Wallace Fowlie has written
about Rimbaud's "angelism," and idealized catamite angels appear in
works as diverse as those of Cocteau and Allen Ginsberg. It may even
be that *Teorema* is a conscious or unconscious homosexual pun: "Divine" is a favorite epithet among inverts, and the hero-heroine of
Genet's *Our Lady of the Flowers* is called Divine. The ritual of the
Catholic Church, with its quasi-transvestite garb, its florid panoply, its
celibacy, its choirboys, has always appealed to homosexuals; and the
sadomasochism that frequently accompanies inversion has found rich
pabulum in St. Sebastian and other holy martyrs. The problem with
much—though not all—of this art is that the inversion colors the con-

version, that God plus sodomy yields a perversion we might call godomy.

This would account for the *sessualità metaforica,* as Pasolini labeled the sex in *Teorema.* The homosexual milieu tends to be more promiscuous than the heterosexual (something that heterosexuals often envy), and the easygoing, geometrical way in which this Stranger covers everyone has distinctly homosexual overtones. It further explains his pretty, tight-trousered looks, and why the mother picks up young boys rather than mature men. It might even explain the sadomasochist overtones: the daughter, in her catatonic state, digging her fingernails deep into her palms (felicitous suggestion of the Crucifixion as well!); the servant eating boiled nettles and having herself entombed; the mother being brutally used in a ditch. It's a metaphoric sexuality all right, but what the metaphor stands for is not all that divine.

Most interesting, however, is the reception *Teorema* has been getting. In Europe, it became highly controversial, receiving last year in Venice the Prize of the International Catholic Film Office, only to have that Office revoke the prize this year. The film is now being prosecuted in Italy, possibly at the instigation of the Vatican, and Pasolini might have to go to prison. The cultist cinema magazines of Europe have proclaimed *Teorema* a masterpiece; in America, conversely, it is the reviewers for the mass media that have been most rhapsodic about it. Vincent Canby of the *Times,* while he clearly disliked the movie, was humbly respectful, advocating that it "should be seen at least twice" for full understanding, and blaming the healthy laughter with which it was greeted by a preview audience not on anything like the film's absurdity, but on the regular feature at that theater, *Baby Love:* an audience that had come to see so ribald a work was, in his opinion, obviously unequipped for Pasolini's profundities.

In the *New Yorker,* Penelope Gilliatt wrote a rave review intended, she tells me, as a put-on. But quotable ironies like "I thank Pasolini and Heaven for it," by helping its advertisers, lend support to *Teorema.* A phrase likening the film, no matter how slyly, to "a piece of geometry that the Deity Himself might have thought it wise to spend six days on," can nicely befuddle the less than ideal reader—aside from putting dangerous ideas into the deity's head. It used to be a favorite subject of Scholastic disputation whether God, being ominpotent as well as immortal, could destroy himself. That question, at least, has been answered: by making a film like *Teorema*—easily.

May, 1969

SUCCUBUS

Pornography has discovered intellectual pretension. In books, this has been going on for some time, the best known recent examples being *Story of O* and *The Image,* where, for instance, torture sessions are decked out with references to Christian martyrs. In the movies, *La Prisonnière* seems to have led the way: when the sadist hero wants to show his intended victim a pornographic slide, he slips it in among projections of handwriting specimens from Hugo, Lamartine, Rimbaud, and Valéry. In *The Libertine,* a timidly pornographic film that serves chiefly to confirm Catherine Spaak's absolute lack of talent, we get references to the Strega Prize and Wilhelm Reich—but only in the Italian dialogue. In the subtitles, the former dwindles into a Book-of-the-Month-Club selection, and the latter vanishes altogether.

Much more spectacular in its pseudoliteracy is a German import, *Succubus,* a collaboration of no-talents of various nationalities starring Janine Reynaud, a thirty-year-old Patou model, as the devil's tool for the destruction of men. The program tells us that "the role stamped an indelible finis to her original desire to become a dentist," but ninety minutes of *Succubus* without Novocain are not substantially different from several hours of root-canal work. Throughout the film, mixed in with inept nude scenes, kindergarten sadism, and gauche murders are word games in which people hurl names like Heine, Kafka, Faulkner, Robbe-Grillet, and Charlie Mingus at one another; they also extol the films of Buñuel and Godard; and there is a character at a bacchanalia who hortatorily recites satiric verses by Wilhelm Busch.

Two of the best moments occur when the subtitles render Stockhausen as Stockholm, and when someone on the German soundtrack who was supposed to lament (I guess) that "Hebbel and Kleist are no longer performed on our stages" goofs, and says instead "Hegel and Kleist." There is also a dumpy seminude bit player who performs clumsy high kicks in a night club while reciting *"Aber die Fahne ist nicht dabei"* etc.—from Rilke's *Cornet!* According to the press release, the film concerns "Lorna, a reality-displaced nympho-necrophile who wanders in a catatonic trance from man to man, kissing and killing as she goes. . . ." If you think that might be stimulating to watch, believe me, a good production of Hegel's *Phänomenologie des Geistes* would be every bit as aphrodisiac.

June, 1969

COMING APART

It would hardly be worth reviewing a piece of pretentious juvenile pornography called *Coming Apart* by one (or is it two?) Milton Moses Ginsberg, if it had not received laudatory notices in certain high-toned journals like *Life* and the *Saturday Review*. It purports to deal with the crack-up of a psychiatrist as photographed by a camera the good doctor himself has hidden so that it can catch the action on a nonpsychiatric couch where most of his couplings, as well as his coming apart, conveniently take place.

A host of dreary or demented women in various stages of disrobement and psychic disarray conduct clumsy dialogues and fornications with our hero, who sounds and acts not quite bright enough for a village veterinarian, let alone a hip shrinker. All sorts of cinematic tricks are used in conjunction with the stationary camera, but nothing can disguise the vulgar and ostentatious mind misinforming the picture. Typically, such mental illness as a woman's intense masochism is treated as a big joke, whereas we are to view the psychic maunderings of the hero, played by Rip Torn as a hallucinated Texas cracker, with infinite concern. The performances are amateurish, ranging from Sally Kirkland's unhinged exhibitionism to Viveca Lindfors's narcissistic attitudinizing, perfect subjects for a *genuine* psychiatrist.

November, 1969

MYRA BRECKENRIDGE; FREEDOM TO LOVE; CENSORSHIP IN DENMARK; BEYOND THE VALLEY OF THE DOLLS

With *Myra Breckinridge*, at last, we are in mid-obscenity. I have not read Gore Vidal's novel, but, having read some of his more ambitious efforts, I assume sophisticated pornography would be just about his speed. Whatever the novel may be like, it surely cannot be this sort of witless, lip-smacking, consistently inept cop-out. The story, as everyone knows, concerns Myron Breckinridge, who, after a Scandinavian operation, becomes Myra. Equipped with physical beauty, knowledge from within of both sexes, and expertise in Hollywood lore, she sets out to capture both the men and the women of filmland today, and tomorrow the world. The movie turns all this into a dream, and cleans up the comically lewd incidents by reducing comedy to oafishness and lewdness to suggestive smirking. That kind of deliberately halfhearted —or, in this context, halfarsed—cleaning up is the real dishonesty, the real smuttiness of the enterprise. For the sexual acts are now performed by half-clothed Barbie dolls with carefully castrating camera angles, and if the dirtiness is not for real, it must be for dirty.

Michael Sarne, the director, who already proved his lack of talent with *Joanna,* and who here also collaborated on the unspeakable screenplay, uses as a refrain clips from old movies that are meant to comment ironically on this supposedly new one. A whole montage of clips from bronco-busting to bursting dams is intended to explain what happens when Myra is buggering Rusty, whom she has strapped to a table. Both in execution and in concept (and here Vidal must claim his share of the glory), this scene marks the latest nadir in major-studio bad taste; a record previously held by *Candy.* What makes it all genuinely pornographic is not the homosexuality, which most reviewers irrelevantly castigated, nor the bisexuality, which Vidal so proudly advocates. The onus lies in the eagerness of the film (and, I dare say, the book) to make us squirm. Squirm for the sufferings of the victims, squirm for the joylessness of the tormentors, squirm for the moral superiority imputed to this Myra (that is not even carried through in the film), squirm for the filmmakers who imply that this is good unclean fun. And squirm for a director who thinks that actors as untalented as Raquel Welch and Roger Herren can do anything but further cheapen the proceedings.

Still another dimension in horror is the casting and display of Mae West, fully clothed and perfectly mummified, as a nonstop sex talker and performer, playing endless sexual prologues and epilogues with young men who allegedly service and even desire her. These scenes are exquisitely stomach-turning, but, unfortunately, not without several grains of truth to them. At the gala preview of *Myra,* Mae was mobbed by thousands of adoring fans, some of whom brandished Mae West Fan Club placards inside the theater, while others tied up traffic, broke down police barriers, and smashed glass display cases outside. Inside and out, they did their best to knock the old lady, already insecure on her pins, completely off her feet.

Miss West, who is seventy-eight, but according to the *Times* "looks years younger" (well, maybe two), was bedizened with a couple of feet of platinum wig, yards of ermine and white satin, and more solitaires than you would think it possible to fit on ten shrunken fingers. Yet I had the feeling that there were people of all ages in that adoring throng who would have gladly crawled into bed with her. I cannot, so

shortly after struggling to analyze Miss Streisand's appeal, be expected
to undertake the analysis of Miss West's. But I suppose it must have
to do with her death-and-menopause-defying act, with the sweet notion
that Americans might still enjoy the benefits of a full sex life in Forest
Lawn, lucky stiffs that they are.

A further minor though distinct horror is the presence of Rex Reed
in the role of Myron. I had hoped that this campy butterfly and self-
styled critic—who was cast, I am told, so as to make certain things
about Myron obvious without the script's having to spell them out—
would at least be able to portray himself on screen so that, on the
strength of his success, we would be rid of him as a writer. No such
luck. Reed's movements resemble Birnam's toward Dunsinane, his
lines dribble from his mouth like moist mashed-potato mix, and his
facial play is a permanent pudgy pout. In short, his acting is on a par
with his writing. Come to think of it, none of this should prevent him
from plying both trades with equal kudos.

Among the new films are two major sex-documentaries—or whatever the term is for the growing mass of films that purport, seriously
or spuriously, to shed light on sexual problems, but depend for their
success on the prurient expectations they can satisfy or, more likely,
arouse. If I call these two films major, it is because of their greater
éclat. In the case of *Freedom to Love,* this consists of the script, direction,
and on-screen presence of the eminent sexologists, Drs. Eberhard and
Phyllis Kronhausen. Alas, this married pair of worthy sexual enlighten-
ers looks like a powerful argument for absolute abstinence, and the
film itself is nothing but a collection of chats with still other experts,
snatches of plays and paintings with sexual subjects, and clumsy enact-
ments of situations where legalized prejudice harasses the innocent
pursuits of lesbianism and intercourse with a ripe and willing fifteen-
year-old.

Despite its well-intentioned and ill-delivered narration full of statistics and impious platitudes, the film will convert no one to anything;
even less will it turn on the most willing thrill-seekers. Among the
filmed interviews, there is one with Kenneth Tynan in the London
Playboy Club, and, as creator of *Oh! Calcutta!* and cynosure of Bunnies
seen bustling around him, the once justly admired critic stands every
chance of becoming yet another unthinking Reed, a fall from eminence
I would deeply regret.

A much more spectacular film is *Censorship in Denmark,* whose one
point is that there is virtually no censorship of any kind in Denmark,

and, the sexual crime rate having declined there, isn't it a wonderful thing? Now I am all for no censorship, except in the case of children, and I am all for the decline of sexual crime (though the figures have not yet yielded unambiguous conclusions), but I am not at all for this movie. It is, I am afraid, hard-core pornography—which does not make me want to ban it, either, but does make me wish it were at least good hard-core pornography. It treats us mostly to views of pornographic stills, the shooting of pornographic films, and the enactment of live pornie shows.

What we see was not staged directly for this film, but only recorded or rerecorded by it, thus diminishing its chance to stir up our healthy lusts and appetites. What is worse, the performers recorded look, at best, average and perform (or indulge) without genuine passion. Pornography can only work if it arouses our desire to get into the act. For that, the people and their passions must draw us in.

Censorship in Denmark also features a lot of interviews with typical pornography dealers and consumers, as well as with tourists and curiosity seekers. These prove about as pale as the ones with the experts in the previous film. *Censorship* gets around our censors by being ostensibly a documentary about Denmark. I admire its ingenuity more than its achievement, though it does bring to our screen for the first time an ejaculating penis. May it not prove seminal!

We come next to the most peculiar movie of all, *Beyond the Valley of the Dolls,* a film Russ Meyer, the *doyen* of skin flicks, was hired to do for Fox. It so pleased the powers there that Meyer was promptly signed for a three-picture contract. It also caused a law suit by Jacqueline Susann, who considered her own *Valley* lowered by titular association with this blue movie, which goes to show that the grass always looks bluer in the other man's valley. But the film, awful, stupid and preposterous as it is, is also weirdly funny and a real curio, rather like a Grandma Moses illustration for a work by the Marquis de Sade.

Russ Meyer's appearance is that of a former prizefighter now operating a successful chain of South American brothels. But a brothel-keeper with delusions of intellectual grandeur who imagines himself to be Hugh Hefner. Enlisting in the Signal Corps as a combat photographer at the age of eighteen, Meyer, in peace time, converted from violence to sex and became a purveyor of nudies. In his first hit, *The Immoral Mr. Teas* (1959), an aging, paunchy, voyeuristic delivery boy develops the dubious gift of seeing clothed women as naked. After numerous odd experiences with his queervoyance, he seeks therapeutic help. When even his female psychiatrist is revealed to him nude, he accepts his manifest destiny.

Reviewing the film for the first issue of *Show* (October 1961), Leslie
Fiedler made a number of interesting points. "In *Mr. Teas,*" he wrote,
"there was not only no passion, but no contact, no flesh touching flesh,
no consummation shown or suggested." The partial nudity "existed
chiefly to titillate [Teas's] impotent desire." There was "never *complete* nudity. Sitting, for instance, in a café, gnawing on an obscenely
large slab of watermelon, Mr. Teas finds that the waitress who serves
him has become quite naked, except for the merest doily of an apron.
. . . What we are shown when the [censorship] rules are observed is
not female flesh, but pin-up pictures—moving pictures of moving pin-
up pictures, life twice removed. . . ." Teas "inhabits a world of prefabricated fantasies . . . manufactured for men powerless to evoke for
themselves even the intangible shadow of sex."

Now we come to Fiedler's key observation: "Nowhere is there a
pimple or blemish or sagging skin or untoward wrinkle or mottled
flesh. The loving, patient camera (not really a movie-maker's camera
at all, but that of the still photographer) that follows the play of light
and shade on haunch and hollow finds no human imperfection, not
even goose flesh or beads of sweat. Such girls seem more like fruit than
flesh—hothouse fruit, serenely perfect and savorless, not to be touched
or eaten. Only looked at. Unreal. Unreal. Unreal. This is the sadness
of *Mr. Teas.*" Fiedler concludes by wondering whether the filmmakers
were "really aware of the implications of the movie," and "would like
to believe that Meyer [whom he calls Meyers] knew all along not
merely how funny but how sad *Mr. Teas* really was."

I go along with all of Fiedler's points, but cannot share his assumption that Meyer was not "merely exploiting the mindless audience"—
and neither, I am sure, could Fiedler, in the light of Meyer's subsequent career. While Fiedler went on to busts of a different kind, Meyer
stuck to bigger and bigger bosoms, bigger and bigger skin flicks. In
none of his films is there any trace of insight or intelligence to justify
Fiedler's ingenious but extrapolative exegesis. At most there has been
a "middle period," as Richard Schickel calls it, in Meyer's work, when
violence along with suitable moralizing preponderated.

But in describing the latest period of the *oeuvre* (preceding the
present film), Schickel notes a happy return to sex: "The films are in
color, less moralistic, more surrealistic. The humor is conscious, the
editing snappier, concern with character and motivation less careful. . . . In these pictures characters tend to be led around by their
insatiable, but relentlessly cheerful, sexual appetites." Schickel's article
(*Harper's,* July) concerns a Russ Meyer retrospective that was presented by a Yale Law School student group; it brought Meyer and his
new co-scenarist, Roger Ebert, to New Haven, along with a bevy of

Meyer starlets, and generally created a mild stir, though it is debatable whether it succeeded in establishing Meyer as an *auteur.*

Beyond the Valley of the Dolls cost a million and a half, which in Meyerian terms is a superproduction; *Mr. Teas* cost $24,000 and grossed over a million. The higher production cost means that bosoms now come in all sizes from medium to mammoth, in both black and white, and, above all, in far greater profusion than before: what used to be a mere constellation has become a Milky Way. It also means that Meyer was equipped with a co-scenarist, the aforementioned Mr. Ebert, film critic for the Chicago *Sun-Times* and, by all accounts, a rather fey put-on artist. As a result, the film emerges curiously schizoid: Meyer's exaggeratedly male, aggressive, brainless lustfulness (or bustfulness); and Ebert's smartass, campy, in-joking put-ons. It is as if Harold Robbins had collaborated on a novel with Gore Vidal: the mating of two antithetical but equally *outré* sensibilities produces schizophrenic pornography that is so scatterbrained, self-contradictory, funhouse-distorting-mirrory, that it cannot fail to make you laugh.

The film concerns a three-girl rock group and their young manager, Harris. Arriving in Los Angeles, they are taken over by a twentyish pop-music tycoon, Ronnie "Z-Man" Barzell, who renames them The Carrie Nations. (Barzell is the first of a series of caricatures from real life in which the film abounds.) The leader of the group, Kelly, has come to claim her part of a large inheritance from her pretty young aunt, Susan Lake, head of a swinging ad agency. But her willingness to cut Kelly in on a generous share is opposed by Susan's dastardly, scheming, and evilly middle-aged lawyer, called Porter Hall—a typical movie-buff in-joke, Porter Hall having played the villain in numerous B-movies of the thirties and forties. Although Kelly is Harris's girl friend, she falls under Z-Man's baleful spell and is soon shacking up with a pretty blond boy from his *demi-monde,* Lance Rocke, who ought to be a homosexual gigolo but is presented as a heterosexual one. For no visible reason, Kelly also has sex with her enemy, Porter Hall, who wears socks and shorts to bed.

All this drives Harris to despair, or, more precisely, into the arms of Ashley St. Ives, a rising sex star and dedicated nymphomaniac. When he fails to perform as a nonstop satyr on the back seat of her Rolls-Royce ("It's my first time in a Rolls!"), a moonlit beach, and other choice locations ("We did it swinging from a chandelier, standing up in a canoe; let's make it in bed for a change!" he laments), Ashley calls him a fag and goes off with someone who just happens to be on that deserted beach, ready and willing to service her.

Meanwhile Casey, the second girl in the group and a senator's daughter, who was always somewhat squeamish when Harris and Kelly were making it in front of her—alerting us to her lesbian tendencies—has been popping the pills rather hard. Having seemingly similar problems, she and Harris now end up in bed together. In an access of postcoital revulsion, Casey swings over to a predatory lesbian fashion designer, Roxanne, who later helps her get an abortion for Harris's zygote (yes, folks, that one misstep with Harris bore bitter fruit) in return for Casey's body.

The third girl in the trio, Petronella, is black. At one of Z-Man's mad soirées (where everything goes, from naked dancing, through homosexual oral sex, discreetly suggested, to heterosexual intercourse in a sunken marble bathtub the size of a Hilton swimming pool), she gets involved with a hard-working young Negro, Emerson Thorne, who is putting himself through daytime law school by being a waiter at Z-Man's parties, the night school of life. At another such bash, Petronella is picked up by the world heavyweight champion and epigrammatist ("If you don't live for now, you might as well just roll over and take the full count!"), Randy Black—no interracial intercourse in Meyer's reverently box-office-watching film! Emerson catches Petronella in flagrante, is roughed up by Randy, but soon reconciled with his repentant sweetie.

A bit thereafter, Harris attempts to commit suicide by jumping from the rafters onto the studio floor where The Carrie Nations are taping a telecast under Z-Man's Svengalian eye. Harris is not killed, merely confined to a wheelchair; the now equally repentant Kelly lovingly returns to her dear paralytic.

Z-Man decides to throw a mini-orgy à quatre, and invites Lance, for whom he apparently secretly lusted all along, and the by now happy lesbian couple of Casey and Roxanne. After much drinking and drugtaking, Lance is made to wear the tiniest leopard briefs, the girls assume diaphanous lounging garments, and Z-Man, finally revealing his true identity, dons the garb of a campy, comic-strippy Superwoman. His butler, a beefy German and ex-Nazi, rumored to be Martin Bormann, serves in full SS regalia.

The girls are soon off in a bedroom, where Roxanne, without her belly touching Casey's, and though apparently neither a tribad gifted with an abnormal clitoris nor equipped with a dildo, manages to make Casey have an orgasm just by rubbing against her. This suggests that lesbianism is one thing whose technique escapes Meyer and Ebert; another is the English language. When Casey had qualms about that abortion, for example, she exclaimed, "After what happened last night, this could be the only child Harris could conceive."

Z-Man has got Lance in a different bedroom and, as Superwoman, urges him to come "in the arms of she who is every man's dream." (It may be, after all, that it is inverts who are especially cursed with bad grammar, as a Meyerian badge of perversion.) When Lance refuses to oblige, Z-Man ties him up (we are not shown how he managed it) in a humiliating posture, and disrobes, revealing his even truer identity in the form of two tiny tits, the shape and size of halfeaten ice-cream cones. Lance laughs and calls him a freak, and hell having no fury like a Superwoman scorned, Z-Man snatches a sword from one of the mounted suits of armor and decapitates him with a fine faggoty flourish, the blond head zooming off in a perfect parabola.

All this to the music of the Polovetsian Dances (or, more symbolically, "Stranger in Paradise"). Since the Nazi butler is a witness to the crime, Z-Man chases him out into the ocean and, to the music of the Ride of the Valkyries, repeatedly perforates him in mid-surf, making the green one red.

Fetching a revolver, Z-Man visits the girls' bedroom. Casey is wandering about in a wide-meshed negligée; she always needs some kind of artificial support for her breasts which, unsupported, would flop right out of the low wide-screen frame. But Roxanne is there, sleeping the sleep of the just fagged-out, and he inserts the gun between her sensually parted lips. Roxanne, without waking, begins to give the gun a blow-job; lesbians, in their sleep, apparently revert to relative heterosexuality. As if to punish her for such duplicity, Z-Man pulls the trigger, and a geyser of blood comes gushing out of her guilty, dying mouth. Next, Z-Man chases Casey about to the tune of the 20th-Century Fox theme music, having caught her making an SOS phone call to her friends.

In response to the call, Emerson, Petronella, and Kelly grab a car for Z-Man's Xanadu; even Harris, wheelchair and all, tags along. In a mad scramble, Casey is killed—her entire face blown off in an oral death seemingly reserved for wicked lesbians. Petronella is merely wounded in the arm, her brief unfaithfulness to Emerson condignly but mercifully punished. Z-Man is likewise killed, but the good, long-suffering Harris is rewarded: in the heat of battle, he bravely leaps out of his wheelchair and deservedly regains the use of his legs. Here the film might end (you realize that I was giving you the merest thumbnail précis) but we are in for two more desserts.

There is, first, a recapitulation of the film's highlights, with what may be Meyer's voice telling us in didactic tones where and to what extent the characters went wrong, and how they were punished or redeemed —justice being infallible in the Meyerian macrocosm. This is followed by an "Epilogue" in which we see a joyous triple wedding: Kelly and the now nimbly mobile Harris, Petronella and Emerson, and the gullible but decent Aunt Susan and a faithful old suitor who has come to reclaim her. He is called Baxter Wolfe (the mute *e,* as in Rocke and Thorne, lending cachet to the character), is played by an actor who looks like a cross between a prognathous bull and a curly-lipped runt, and must be the incarnate spirit of this dualistic film. Porter Hall, reduced to a bum, tries to stare in at the ceremony, but the blind is drawn in his face.

Now this film is true pornography. There is sex and intercourse all over it, but staged and photographed to look merely like an unusual way of playing mahjong. The couples are of various sexes, ages, colors, yet it all comes out identically homogenized. There is a fair amount of fleeting nudity, but it is all breasts, some few behinds, and nary a crotch. The women are objects of lust and infinitely lascivious; the men merely reach for what is ceaselessly dangled at them. Except for one freak, all the women, even the walk-ons, are gorgeous, or, rather, what Meyer considers to be so. (Significantly, two of his leads are ex-*Playboy* playmates.) There is no stab at believable characterization or narrative; everything simply leads to yet another prettified and disembodied scene of sexual activity. It is meant to turn you on, but the only people it can arouse are those whose idea of sex is totally divorced from reality.

This, I think, is the important distinction: whether a film incites to masturbation or leads to intercourse. There seems to exist a pornography for potency, and a worse pornography for impotence. The girls who, in Fiedler's phrase, look more like fruits than women, who bring an entire beauty parlor into the sheets with them, who make love like mechanized rubber dolls, and who emerge from lovemaking absolutely unruffled and with only the one desire to start all over again— these are truly pornographic inventions. And when they are encased in a lurid and libidinous plot that makes neither sexual nor even melodramatic sense—and has the gall to end with a moral preachment and a sense of justice that one would have thought died out with Victorian lady novelists—the product is true-blue onanistic and sadistic pornography.

Yet even this, it would seem, requires an idiot belief in what one is doing. If Russ Meyer did not believe in his work, did not, for all the camp Ebert was allowed to bring into it, take that work and himself seriously, there would be no real pornography—only the obscene gestures and posturings of a *Myra Breckinridge.*

The sick double standard (Meyer's bestiality, Ebert's campiness) of the film is perfectly mirrored in its use of language. This can be brutally crude—"Carnal desire? My arse!" or "You're a groovy boy; I'd like to strap you on sometime!"—as well as disgustingly syrupy and sanctimonious—"And if love is in you, then gentle will be all your steps as you walk beyond the valley of the dolls." Both these modes, if indeed they be two, may be assumed to be Meyer's contribution. But there is also an arrogant, smark-aleck, finally even viler camping around with language, as when the narration for a crazy montage sequence about Los Angeles is all rhymed doggerel, or when Z-Man declaims in mock-Elizabethan fustian, "You varlet, you serf, you buggering knave! . . . You will drink the black sperm of my vengeance!" Related to this is the pretentious use of supposedly prestigious or "in" references, such as Z-Man's description of his flirting with Kelly as "a little make-out session between Count Dracula and Mary Wollstonecraft Shelley." These, we may be sure, are Roger Ebert's contributions.

Corruption of minors and the like are hard to demonstrate, but this sort of sabotage wreaked on the language is unmistakable and a defilement. What goes for the language, of course, goes for the movie as a whole. Accuse it of vicious affectlessness, and its makers will plead, "Just good campy fun." Accuse it of sick jokes that stick in the craw, and the makers will declare condescendingly, "The laughter is meant to turn into shivers, that's what makes you aware of the underlying moral purpose." In other words, you can have it any way; something for everyone—campy intellectual, long-faced moralizer, or swinging voyeur. Clever, but not so clever as it is swinish.

July, 1970

SOMETHING FOR EVERYONE

Heaven help sex in *Something for Everyone*, the film-directorial debut of Hal Prince, the Broadway producer-director. The movie is not only slapped together ineptly, not only pretentious, unfunny, and obvious, it is also a prime example of disguised homosexuality at its distorting worst. True, there is an overtly homosexual part of the plot, which, for the first time in a major-studio release, shows male homosexuals kissing, however stagily and awkwardly. That is not objectionable. What is objectionable is the covert slanting of the film toward making heterosexual relations unappetizing, and toward turning moral values upside down. The novel on which it is based, Harry Kressing's *The Cook,* is said to be something rather better and quite different. What Hugh Wheeler, a flabby and floundering Broadway playwright, has scripted here, is a broadened version of *Teorema* and *Boom!,* a sexually polymorphous fantasy with a little black humorlessness thrown in.

Take, first of all, the women. Angela Lansbury plays a German countess; she is descended, she says, from Attila the Hun and is the widow of a scion of Barbarossa—or, as Miss Lansbury pronounces it, "Barbarosa," further decreasing an already minuscule credibility. Miss Lansbury looks like an aging female impersonator gone sloppy, who allows himself to be photographed in costume but without a wig—a bisected androgyne, woman below, man on top. God only knows where the notion that Miss Lansbury has class originated; perhaps her vestigial lower-middle-class English accent passes for that in our informed show-biz circles. She is, in fact, common; and her mugging, rattling-off or steam-rollering across her lines, and camping around merely make her into that most degraded thing an *outré* actress can decline into: a fag hag. Typically, though this Countess von Orenstein spouts the most arrogant drivel, we are to take it as Wildean wit; though she behaves like a snobbish cow, we are supposed to see in her a high-strung thoroughbred.

Opposed to the Orensteins are the parvenu Pleschkes, supposed to embody all that is loathsomely nouveau riche and coarse; and worst among them, naturally, is Frau Pleschke, portrayed as a prototypical pushy, long-cigarette-holdered vulgarian. But her daughter, the alleged ingenue of the film, is played by an actress called Heidelinde Weis, who is boring as a performer, unattractive as a woman, apparently at least as old as her mother (forty if she is a day), and even more profoundly dishonest and corrupt. That leaves the girl juvenile, who turns out to be the chief villain of the film. As played by Jane Carr (who was acceptable in *The Prime of Miss Jean Brodie*) and directed by Prince, she is an unmitigatedly repugnant weirdo, a sort of overweight child bride of Dracula.

The plot tells of a penniless but richly calculating young German immoralist (Michael York) who lands a menial job at the impoverished Countess's fabulous castle by way of a little murder, works his way up the servants' ladder through every kind of intrigue, including sleeping with the Countess's young son, and arranges for the wealthy Pleschkes to make the castle solvent by getting their daughter, whom he also beds, to marry the aforementioned son and lover. He then conveniently kills off in an "accident" all three Pleschkes, seduces the Countess, and is about to become master of the castle, only to be blackmailed by the odious and obese nymphet into marrying her instead. Michael York is a supremely monotonous actor and has, moreover, the head of a blond rat. But he has good legs which, in their mini-lederhosen, the camera keeps lovingly hugging. His sex with the young son (Anthony Corlan, a sullen, dimensionless performer) is also lovingly dwelt on; whereas heterosexual sex is always shown as hasty, sordid huggermugger.

But it is not only sexual values that are prestidigitated with. In a typical death-wish fantasy, the only character in the film permitted to have solid moral values is a saturnine old butler whose room is plastered with photographs of his late father, an SS colonel, of whom he speaks with admiration and adoration. We are told that the butler himself was only old enough to be in the Hitlerjugend, though he looks to be about the age Goebbels would be now. The scene in which he defies his captors (to whom our hero has betrayed him—we are to believe that no one before had penetrated into the butler's room), notably a Nazi-witchhunting mayor presented as a figure of vulgar fun, very clearly stresses his filial love, dignity, and courage. And when he says something about none of these good burghers being worthy enough to have cleaned his father's boots, the scene is written, directed, and acted so as to make us accept this as the truth.

I submit that the entire film exemplifies a kind of vengeance on the heterosexual world by a mentality resenting its real or alleged compulsion to dissemble and hide its predilections. In retaliation, anything that the so-called normal world considers healthy and decent—and some of it, so help us, *is* healthy and decent—is systematically trodden underheel. *Something for Everyone,* described in the program as a "contemporary fairytale" (I don't know about the contemporary), is a thoroughly unsavory film. But I think that the lion share of our indignation should be directed at a society that through obsolete laws begets needless concealment and falsifying strategies. I am not sure that heterosexuals will be all that happy with the spate of overtly homosexual films that will gush forth once inversion becomes legal, but at least the films will be more honest, will probably not idealize Nazis, and will not depict women as horrors—if they bother to depict them at all.

August, 1970

5

The New Violence

THE PROBLEM of violence on screen has been raised again in
connection with certain gangster movies and the new western,
which is often more violent than the old western—though, at
other times, it is its gimmickiness that makes it seem more violent
(or, conversely, less violent) than it actually is. In either case,
there is a manipulativeness at work that needs careful assessment.
Both the gangster film and the western, in any case, are striving
for consciously symbolic effects, contemporary relevance, or, at
the very least, greater sophistication. A typical example of this
sophistication is self-parody, a genre kidding itself. Whether any
of these approaches or devices can rescue these two "mythic"
American film forms, infuse them with artistic validity, remains
to be seen.

Certainly along with greater sophistication comes the attempt
to raise these forms out of the realm of mere entertainment into
that of art. Films like *Stagecoach* and *Brute Force* did not consciously aspire to the level of art, and, to some extent, therein lay
their salvation. But films like *Bonnie and Clyde* and *The Wild
Bunch* do wish to be works of art, probably because the American film wants to elevate its heritage to a status coequal with that
of the European film and the myths, history, culture, and art it
has had to draw upon. Thus attitudes toward bloodshed—its
psychological, social, and political implications—become more
important than plot and suspense, and radical reinterpretations of
the killer, whether in cowboy duds or gangster suits, are the
order of the day. I am inclined to be skeptical about the artistic
possibilities of either genre, except, perhaps, in isolated instances.
My reasons for this should emerge from the following pieces.

THE QUESTION OF VIOLENCE

A great deal has been written lately about violence in the movies, and if I now presume to advance my opinions on it, it is because I am not going to tell you either that there is too much of it on screen, or that it does not really matter how much of it there is. Instead, I will ask you to consider what violence truly is, and then how it can be used: artfully or artlessly, inartistically and anti-artistically.

The first point about violence is that, like sex, it is more than just a device to bring thrill-seekers into movie houses—though even if it were only that, it would not be demonstrably and necessarily a bad thing. (I am, of course, not speaking of children, whose movie-going should be supervised by adults.) At the very least such violence might be cathartic, harmlessly purging our harmful urges. But our concern should be less with whether such violence does damage to us than with whether it damages the films it appears in. *Bonnie and Clyde, In Cold Blood,* or *The Dirty Dozen* will not turn young persons who otherwise would have become subway trainmen, linotypers, or architects into bank robbers, murderers, or commando raiders (or whatever that butcher's dozen should be called). But the way violence is used in those and other films may render them unpalatable on esthetic rather than moral grounds, and so, despite initial acclaim, turn them into ultimate artistic and commercial failures.

Violence, again like sex, is part of our lives: it enters into our feeling, our thinking, and, in one way or another, our doing. To represent it, therefore, on screen—even in certain heightened or stylized forms— is to tell us something about our environment and ourselves. But, except in situations like total war, violence is only one element in the pattern of life, and can best be represented by one strand in the pattern of the work of art. This can be the main, but seldom the only one. Perhaps the most helpful comparison would be to a color on the painter's palette: blue, for example.

A painter may want to explore the possibilities of that color, and, like Gainsborough, paint a "Blue Boy." Even here, however, blue is not the only color; if the face, say, were blue, the picture would not work at all, except perhaps as a study of a boy who had been locked in a refrigerator. Yet realism must not constrict us. Franz Marc painted blue horses, which, as everyone knows, are about as frequent as unicorns. But their blueness implies something: a yearning on the artist's part for a brighter, more colored world; or the suggestion that a beast is nobler, more extraordinary than we are commonly aware of, which is brought home to us by translating one aspect of it into the fabulous. Then along comes a painter like Yves Klein, "le Monochrome," who covered entire canvases with a flat spray of blue. Forthwith blue loses all meaning, except for the "artist" and his dealer, for whom it means money, and for the gullible client, for whom it means (as he believes) prestige.

Like the color blue, then, violence can depict a condition; or, by isolating that condition from its context, comment on it analytically; or, by establishing some correspondence between the condition and an underlying truth, convey something deeper than the surface events. On the other hand, it can be used for sheer exploitation. The most obvious basis for differentiation is quantitative: the film that has the most violence in it is usually the least meaningful because, almost always, the least disturbing. Not only does excess tend to cancel itself out by becoming repetitious and boring, but also filmmakers who mass-produce violence (or sex) are not artists enough to know how to make it count. There is nothing less sexually arousing than the cheap skin flicks that play around 42nd Street, which are so unsubtle as to become unsuggestive. In the same way, films like *Khartoum, The St. Valentine's Day Massacre,* or *The Dirty Dozen* reduce violence to the equivalent of shadowboxing by the repetitiveness and perfunctoriness with which they approach it. Some of this is, of course, done deliberately, so as not to run into censorship trouble or lose the valuable kiddie trade, but much of it is ineptitude. Too much blue, the wrong shade of blue, or blue not surrounded by the right colors to make it stand out.

More important than *how much* is *how* violence is used in a film. As has been noted, the reason the violence in *Bonnie and Clyde* upset some people is that it was more real and believable than what usually passes for it in American films. Thus the people frightened by it were not so much frightened by violence as by reality. *In Cold Blood* is disturbing to some viewers for a similar reason: though the murders are not so graphic as in *Bonnie and Clyde,* they are known to be true rather than fictional, and promptly they begin to bother some people intensely—for most Americans, reportage is truer than art.

Yet though I think that both these films fail, they do so for reasons virtually unconnected with violence. As far as that is concerned, both films, though in different ways, are purposive and efficacious. What is trash, however, is a film like *The Penthouse* or *Point Blank,* in which violence is not just faithfully depicted or used to make some social or psychological point with, but gussied up and wallowed in. In such films, violence, usually conjoined with sex, is smirkingly made to subserve lust for power and plain lust; the product is a tribute to sadomasochism rather than an effort to understand it. Even this would not be unduly offensive if it were not covered with a veneer of moral indignation, social comment, or hypocritical meliorism—and a very thin veneer, lest any of the underlying nastiness be obscured by it.

The truth about violence is that it is most effective—and most meaningful—when used sparingly but magisterially. Thus the scene in Bergman's *Persona* in which the nurse leaves a piece of broken glass for the barefoot actress to step on is as cruel and quietly violent as anything in films. The "accident" occurs offscreen and we only hear the slight cry of pain; but there is such avid expectation of that pain on the nurse's face, followed by such triumph and letdown, that this brief scene becomes more shattering (and more profound) than all of *In Cold Blood.* Similarly, the straightforward way in which the nurse tells of an orgy she once participated in—a scene without flashbacks that merely shows a narrator and a listener, two women becoming united in a peculiar relationship—is infinitely more sexual and laden with significance than all the sex scenes in the *oeuvre* of Roger Vadim, which consists almost entirely of sex scenes.

But even flagrant violence is far more effective when used sparingly and in a strategic position in the film. In the opening scene of *Paisan,* which, along with the final one, is a high point of horror in the history of the war film, the two deaths occur quickly, casually, irrationally, just when things seem to be going well for the G.I. and Carmela, and for the Allies in general. It is the randomness of the soldier's death and the cruel irony of the girl's, both barely noticeable when they occur, that constitute the violence of the effect. And of its meaning. And what is violence if not that which is communicated—transferred in all its painfulness from the film to us—rather than countless gory deaths and lovingly spelled-out tortures that end up by numbing or nauseating us?

The death of the young lovers in Andrzej Wajda's powerful *Kanal* is not even shown. The scene is etched with cruel irony. The dying boy cannot see the grating which, at the last moment, cuts off the freedom toward which the pair has crawled through blood and rivers of excrement in the sewers of Warsaw. The girl, uninjured but clearly dooming herself to die by her lover's side, tells the boy beautiful lies, and there we leave them. Yet the violent brutality of that immobile, inanimate grating the Germans have put there does not leave our memories.

So there are three main kinds of violence on film: the ineptly overstated kind, which proves eventually boring; the sadistic one, which is finally nauseating; and the artistically meaningful one, which is thereby moral. None of these seems ultimately harmful, though one of them is certainly distasteful. But there is another kind of violence becoming rampant in film today, a violence that I consider sinisterly deleterious. Not that I am for censoring it: I do not consider censorship an intelligent or efficacious weapon. If such a weapon exists, it is perceptive criticism.

The violence I have in mind is affectlessness on the part of the filmmaker: violence done to coherence, causality, point of view, responsibility, form—any of the things that might hold a work of art together. I am thinking of that vast area of contemporary film whose pinnacle is Godard and whose nadir is Warhol, and which, for all its enormous width, has but a few inches to separate its top from its bottom.

In the films of Jean-Luc Godard there is no respect for anything: meaning, communication, significant form, men, women, or life. There is no respect even for what has distinguished most previous avant-garde movements: rebellion in the name of greater freedom. Godard's rebellion is just for the sake of infantile self-indulgence. In his work, there is no affection that does not reek of affectation, no jest that is not merely a rude gesture, no movement that has motivation as well as motion to it. True, there are ostensible moral purposes in Godard. *Alphaville,* for example, pretends to be against mechanization and dehumanization; but its hero, when he is not mechanically mouthing prestigious quotations or elephantine platitudes, is himself all inhuman brutality. *Pierrot le Fou* purports to be against a world of advertising and conspicuous consumption; yet what it offers as an alternative, the mindless, feckless, and finally feelingless relationship of its hero and heroine, is at least as repugnant.

The manner of Pierrot's suicide is typical of Godard's approach. Pierrot wraps several bundles of sticks of dynamite, which have mock-serious slogans printed on them, around his head, and sets the fuse on fire. He changes his mind, curses profusely, tries in vain to stomp out the approaching flame, and goes up in an explosion photographed so as to suggest nuclear cataclysm. An offscreen voice recites a stanza from Rimbaud's "L'Éternité." There you have the essence of Godard: the one vaguely sympathetic figure of the film does away with himself in the way in which Jerry the Mouse usually disposes of Tom the Cat. To make the demise more ridiculous, there are those slogans on the dynamite, and our Blue Boy has painted his entire face cobalt blue. The childish affectlessness of it all is, on the one hand, further ridiculed by Pierrot's cursing and chickening out; on the other hand, it is aggrandized by the visual reference to the atom bomb, and the aural one, totally irrelevant but intellectually prestigious, to Rimbaud.

Godard clearly does not have the faintest idea where he is going with his scene, his film, his *oeuvre*—so he blithely goes off in all directions simultaneously. It is an act of consummate pretentiousness, irresponsible violence, and vacuity. It is also (as near as I can guess) a put-on that ends by taking itself seriously and thus puts itself on. This is the worst, the suicidal, type of violence in the current cinema: the film that does violence to all form, including its own. That is something that neither Beckett, the supreme Absurdist, nor Genet, the intransigent rebel and outlaw, would dream of doing.

March, 1968

BONNIE AND CLYDE

Agnès Varda tells me she liked *Bonnie and Clyde* because "it is violent without being sadistic." I doubt that there is much difference between the two when violence is dwelt on with such clucking solicitude. At the utmost one could call such violence unconscious sadism. But that may be even more attractive to the asinine audiences that guffaw their way through the film; overt sadism is kinky, whereas this is just rousing shooting the hell out of people. As directed by Arthur Penn from a screenplay by Newman and Benton, the well-known slick-magazine writers, the picture is clever trash. The formula is hayseed comedy bursting sporadically into pyrotechnical bloodshed and laced with sentimental pop-Freudianism.

The technique is artful, though derived from Godard—quick little vignettes ending in verbal or visual punchlines following one another at breakneck speed. A group of semimoronic naturals gather around an impotent youth and an infantile girl for an extended crime spree that shifts from the absurd and mildly funny to the childishly cruel and murderous. The explanations implied befit a primer of abnormal psychology for junior high schools, and that the whole romp is based on a true story does not bring it more than an inch closer to truth. It is outfitted with considerable authenticity of period and place, however, and photographed cannily in sometimes striking, sometimes slick, color.

But the whole thing stinks in the manner of a carefully made-up, combed, and manicured corpse. Crime may have its funny side, but here, for long stretches, it has nothing but funny sides. To switch then, without warning, from belly laughs to bloodbaths and produce facile shock effects is added dishonesty. Between murder as fun and murder as Grand Guignol there is little to choose from. The audience is invited to have a lark either way, and responds to the invitation with unappetizing explosions of laughter and applause. The acting is good, but slop is slop, even served with a silver ladle.

October, 1967

This follow-up review was published three months later.

Since it seems to be customary to have second thoughts on *Bonnie and Clyde,* here are mine. They are in no way a palinode, only an amplification of what, I feel, I originally stated with excessive laconism.

What is basically wrong with the film is not so much violence as hero worship. The point at which the disaffected intellectual and the footloose lowbrow meet is their shared love for the outlaw. Arthur Penn and his scenarists combine the sentimentality of the second-rate intellectual with a first-rate roustabout's amorality, and out come a Bonnie and Clyde who are all bumbling charm, naïve cleverness, derailed ingenuity. Critics who have seen them as bunglers are myopic; for all their limitations, imposed on them by an unjust society exacerbated by the Depression (here immature sociology joins hands with amateur psychiatry), they are witty, inventive, fun-loving, and alive—which is more than you can say for any of the other characters in the film. The policemen are faceless nonentities; the sheriff and the self-righteous father, downright repulsive. Bonnie and Clyde, moreover, are even physically beautiful—star children among the toadstools.

The message is that in a capitalist society, and a bankrupt one at that, the outlaw is a far finer fellow than the inane solid citizen who plays into the hands of the exploiters on top, quietly tightens his belt, and even rats on the guys who rob the rich man's banks. The robbers don't exactly turn the loot over to the poor—even this fanciful hagiography daren't go that far—but they do make a few Robin Hoodish gestures that ring even falser than their specious context.

Now, the robber can in certain extreme situations be a hero—at any rate, a flawed tragic hero—as in Kleist's *Michael Kohlhaas,* which Penn & Co. would have done well to ponder. But to argue as they do that in periods of social injustice (which means anywhere this side of Utopia) the outlaw is clearly superior to the staid, plodding citizen is sentimental nonsense and moral truancy. The truth of the matter is that those little shopkeepers and bank clerks, dim and dull as they may have been, were, provided they were law-abiding, immeasurably better people than all your robbers and murderers. That is the simple fact that

Bonnie and Clyde, with its puerile antihero worship, militantly ignores. Again, I cannot help being made uncomfortable by the biographical falsifications. A work of art has the right to take liberties with history, but does a piece of non-art have the same rights? Certainly, if the subject is someone like Alexander the Great, about whom there are not enough facts available, and those that are may not be facts. Equally obviously, where one enters areas that cannot be documented— thoughts, intimate conversations, private moments—fiction is in order. But where the time is barely past, and data, no less than living memories, still abound, I wonder whether gross distortions of fact can be condoned. All the more so as the movie begins with pictures of the actual Bonnie and Clyde, and has narration (dropped later on) in the manner of genuine documentaries and faithful restagings of history.

Esthetic prettification provides the final dishonesty. We get scenes that are stifling in pretty-prettiness (the esthetic equivalent of goody-goodiness), such as the reconciliation in the wheat field with little clouds passing over the sun to produce a fretwork of light and shadow, laughter and tears, analogous to the thunder and lightning in the murder scenes of hackneyed thrillers. Worse yet is the reunion with Bonnie's mother, photographed as a Grant Wood filtered through Puvis de Chavannes, through enough filters to outfit the rose window of Chartres Cathedral.

The film's estheticizing continually obtrudes on and obfuscates moral values. Thus, with one highly debatable exception, the crimes and killings performed *by* the Barrow gang are all picturesque, humorous, cozy or, at worst, matter-of-fact affairs. But the violence performed *upon* the gang is always made as harrowingly inhuman as possible. This is explained by the champions of the film as the outlaws' belated awareness that death is real, and the grave their goal—in other words, a rude moral awakening. But, in fact, Clyde makes it clear, in an idyllic scene, that had he to do it over again, he would do exactly the same. He has learned nothing. Fair enough, if only the filmmakers did not so resoundingly applaud him for it. That very confession, made amid the joys of a finally consummated affair, emerges as a heroic *non serviam!* and the brutalities preceding and following it merely serve to underscore the outlaws' courage in shouldering their cruel and unjust fate with round, unblinking eyes.

The point is driven home by the staging of the lovers' death. They are mowed down by a barrage from innumerable guns, sniping out of craven concealment. This much is historical fact, I dare say. But they die a love death that is a superimposition of *Romeo and Juliet* on *Tristan und Isolde.* It is done in lyrical slow motion, without disfigurement of

their physical beauty—perfectly inconsistent with the previous naturalism in mutilations and gore. Bonnie is shaken by the shower of bullets
as if by the spasms of orgasm, while Clyde choreographically rolls over
toward her, star-crossed rather than bullet-riddled, his dying hand
reaching out for the beloved straight out of Shakespeare's Verona.

When this syrupy piece of idealization is considered, as it has to be,
the final comment on the story, there can be no doubt about the
intentions of Penn and his collaborators. What we witness is not the
death of a pair of tawdry criminals, but a *J'accuse* hurled at the material-
ist society that led these innocents to the slaughter. I am for all assaults
on materialism, but when the attack is launched by such a frail and
leaky cockboat, it is doomed to sink into sentimentality, bathos, anti-
art, and, worst of all, inhumanity.

January, 1968

IN COLD BLOOD

I have not read the book *In Cold Blood,* but, I'm afraid, I have seen the
movie. Not that it is so bad as Hollywood products go; in fact, it marks
a slight step up for its director, Richard Brooks, best remembered for
reducing *Lord Jim* to pablum and *The Brothers Karamazov* to pulp. He
has served as his own screenwriter, and from even a cursory scanning
of the book I can tell he meant to be faithful to it but was defeated by
three problems: the book's superabundance of detail, much of it barely
relevant but arguably more interesting than the more pertinent stuff;
the shifting, inchoate, self-contradictory sympathies and antipathies
lurking under Capote's mask of impassivity; and the need to make it
all "filmic," as that term is conventionally understood—having the
proper suspense, climaxes, visual effects, and so on.

To handle the detail correctly, Brooks went to the exact locations
—only to prove, once again, that the camera photographs the photographer. Yes, this is the Clutter home; yes, that was shot in the actual
courtroom; but Brooks does not capture the *genius loci.* He can show
you what a place looks like, not how it feels to be or live in it. The
significant detail is missing—whether it is something about the upholstery of a chair or the precise proportions of a room. Few of the places
he shows us seem used: the people and their ambience assume no other
relationship except the flimsy one of contiguity.

The problem of point of view is even graver. The movie (and this seems to be true of the book as well) continually shifts its ground: now it is full of compassion for the victims, now for the murderers; now it makes you root for a speedy comeuppance, now for mercy and abolition of capital punishment. Even secondary figures, like the detectives or Perry's parents, are seen through this ceaselessly whirling perspective that is both emotionally and intellectually self-defeating. In a long book this might be less bothersome, because time and space function differently there (the film is not long by today's standards). But a movie about criminals cannot be both *The Asphalt Jungle* and *White Heat*, both *Rififi* and *Hands on the City*. I do not mean that a film cannot dramatize conflicting positions with some feeling for all of them, but that it cannot assume a basic editorial stance and then change it around with impunity. Complexity is one thing, inconsistency another.

If, on the other hand, the idea is to be strictly documentary, you cannot have didactic colloquies between a seasoned crime reporter and an Ivy League tiro right in the shadow of the gallows, with soured humanism dribbling from the former and anguished humanitarianism gushing from the latter. You cannot have obvious sympathy for one of the killers and almost none for the other, no matter if one of them is superficially more likable. You cannot bring in Freud—on the most elementary level, to be sure—when it is convenient; and throw him out on his ear when that suits your purpose.

As for making the film more filmic, this leads into such bizarre bits of hamminess as having the hangman's face turn into that of Perry's father; or equipping the soundtrack with a portentous, hypertrophic score by Quincy Jones; or having Conrad Hall photograph it all in the flashiest chiaroscuro. And it turns Truman Capote into a figure called The Reporter—a grizzled, canny, humane though cynical, wonderfully virile regular guy. As played by Paul Stewart, he is, on top of all those other good things, the archetypal Jewish "mensch." To sum it all up, there was something rather queasy about Capote's enterprise, and Brooks's addenda make it only queasier.

Yet beyond all this the film has its good points. Chief among these is the acting of Scott Wilson and Robert Blake as the killers. There are adequate contributions also by other performers, and some of the nonprofessional Kansas types provide genuine local colorlessness. The atmosphere of provincial bus terminals and small-town department stores cannot but yield a certain fascination. There is also the sense of danger skulking on the highways—as in an episode where the killers contemplate doing away with the next motorist who'll give them a lift, when chance, curiously, takes over. Altogether, because this is a true story, the role of chance in human lives and deaths is conveyed with authoritative awesomeness. For all this ability to constrict the throat, however, *In Cold Blood* barely grips the heart, and it provides the mind with confusingly varied, only mildly tempting, cafeteria-style food for thought.

January, 1968

THE WILD BUNCH

Seemingly the most debated film of the summer season is *The Wild Bunch*. One need only glance at any two reviews to get some idea of the critical divergence. To me, Sam Peckinpah's latest western appears neither so good as Vincent Canby would have it, nor so loathsome as Judith Crist proclaims. It is, rather, an important bad film, avoidable by people who want genuine art, but recommended to all those interested in the faltering steps by which the American cinema might titubate into maturity.

There is no doubt that Peckinpah has a nice sense of time and place; that his locations and groupings, as well as the faces and peripheral activites that fill a shot have the right look and feel about them. But he is much less sure about the staging of the main action in a scene, except where seedy debauchery or sudden flare-ups of violence are concerned. He is quite apt to fall into sentimentality and substitute a liquorice stick for his usual wormwood. The dialogue rides high and wide from the awful to the quite acceptable, but the dominant strain runs to things like "Well, why don't you answer me, you damn yellow-livered trash?" Peckinpah is half Indian, and that may have induced our guilt feelings to turn him into an *auteur* before his time; it may also give him a keener understanding of his subject matter.

The Wild Bunch deals with a group of hardened outlaws who, in 1913, find themselves hemmed in on all sides: by the railroads with their bounty hunters, by the vanishing frontier, and by their own advancing years. The plot is fairly typical and not worth detailing; it records the last—ingenious, brutal, heroic—capers of the gang. Reduced to four, they are finally forced by their loyalty to a butchered comrade to take on the entire division of a semi-bandit Mexican general. After wreaking conspicuous slaughter, they are themselves finally riddled to death.

Despite an inventive twist or two, the plot settles all too comfortably into the usual western groove with all the beloved mythic commonplaces. But there are differences. The world of Peckinpah and his co-scenarist Walon Green is predominantly evil; there are no really good people anywhere, only the less bad and the much worse ones. The members of the gang stick together and have a certain code by which their leader, Pike, can, albeit with difficulty, make them behave. The men who hunt them down or exploit their services, on the other hand, are cruel, greedy, generally craven, and have no code whatever. One of the outlaws, Angel, is a Mexican Indian; his village seems to be full of good, exploited people. Yet his girl leaves him to be the mistress of Mapache, the swinish general. Later, it is Angel's own mother who betrays him.

Women are represented as particularly untrustworthy, and, next to women, children. Throughout the film we see kids enjoying the bloodshed and brutality around them and, whenever possible, joining in the fun, if only by torturing animals. Pike is brought down by the combined bullets of a Mexican prostitute and a little Mexican boy, both of whom shoot him in the back. In the case of the children, it may be the example of the adults that is to blame, but corrupt they are, and this is something new in a western. Except for Angel's concern for his villagers (he sacrifices his share of the loot for them), and the dignity of some of these folk, there are no unalloyed positive values in the film —even the gang's solidarity is labile and continually threatened from within. But Pike is idealized, and here the film goes soft. His opposite number, Deke, a former gang member who to save his own skin reluctantly leads the bounty hunters, is a considerably more ambiguous character, yet he too is sentimentalized.

The reverse side of the coin is the turning of the railroad people into absolute rotters, the U. S. Cavalry into bumblers (quite an innovation!), the Mexican soldiery into feckless layabouts, the bounty hunters into scum (this, at any rate, we don't question), and the plain townsfolk into arrant fools. All this is not so offensive here as in *Bonnie and Clyde,* from which much of the film derives, because there is less obvious sympathy drummed up for the members of the gang, except perhaps for Pike and Angel; but even in their behalf no easy sociologizing is trotted out.

Pike's motto is "When you side with a man, you stick with him; otherwise you might as well be some kind of animal." Whereas the unresonant "animal" is not much better than the lush vibrato of "damn yellow-livered trash," such literary weaknesses have a way of being absorbed by the able filmmaking. Yet that, too, is uneven. Take, for instance, the scene where the gang is leaving Angel's village. The entire population lines the main street on both sides, women rush up with sundry farewell goodies, everyone is singing a schmaltzy Mexican song. The camera is on a dolly, the point of view of the departing horsemen, and we are treated to a cordon of picturesque physiognomies, among which we single out the compassionate lineaments of the village elder. We would like to think this is tongue-in-cheek, but no, it is pure treacle.

The film has a good many of these oversimplifications, exaggerations, or platitudes along its lengthy way. But then, again, there are powerful images: an ugly, mannish Mexican woman in Mapache's camp, who sits in full military gear suckling an infant; chickens scurrying underfoot and underhoof at the damnedest times; Pike trying to mount his horse and falling off because an old leg wound acts up as his men make sarcastic remarks; and, immediately afterward, Pike getting into the saddle and riding defiantly ahead.

This last is truly lovely: Peckinpah is a master of the rear tracking shot, for which he uses a telephoto lens. Here Pike rides on, his shoulders squared against the gibes, the horse and rider jogging up a sandy slope until they suddenly disappear over its edge. The tele-lens clings to the figure, lovingly flattening out the landscape around and for the rider; the camera seems to bob with him out of sympathy, and a terrible decency pours out of that careworn but gallant back. When the figure vanishes from the image, we feel the stab of loss.

There is an equally fine rear tracking shot following a reverse pan as the four outlaws go forth to liberate Angel from Mapache's hands; here, from the back, the posture and the way of holding his weapon characterizes each man. At this point, the smoke of the campfire makes the image blur and swim before our eyes, and the scene becomes appropriately hallucinatory and ominous. There is a curious, devil-may-care bravado about these four silhouettes pacing and pacing and pacing into the lion's maw.

Lucien Ballard's cinematography is skillful but his colors are insufficient; the blues and beiges predominate, absorbing the flesh tones and virtually exluding the warmer colors of the palette. Jerry Fieldings's score is serviceable and unobstreperous but a long shot from, say, Ennio Morricone's for the Italian western *Once Upon a Time in the West*, where the score almost becomes a participant in the action.

With the editing of Louis Lombardo, we are once more brought up against *Bonnie and Clyde*. Even more than that film, *The Wild Bunch* revels in bloodletting; not since baroque poetry and mannerist painting have there been such human fountains, blood spurting from them in manifold jets. They are photographed either in slow motion or, conversely, in a quick montage of single-frame or very short takes. The result is, first, that a great deal of horror sneaks in subliminally, making it more bearable but still present; secondly, that much of the dying takes on a balletic quality which, again, makes it easier on the eye, though ultimately more appalling. Indeed, there is too much gore in the film.

The objection requires reflecting upon. Can one remonstrate with the frequency of refrains in a ballad? Can one cavil at the number of holes in travertine? The gore is of the essence. But cannot the essence be defective? By the use of slow motion, Peckinpah makes these deaths look rather like the similarly decelerated performances of shot putters or high jumpers in Riefenstahl's and Ichikawa's great films of the Berlin and Tokyo Olympiads.

The man whose face is suddenly bathed in crimson perspiration and who sinuously gravitates to the dust is a twin of the pole vaulter who has just cleared or not cleared an improbably high crossbar. The gun arcing away from him is the now useless pole, and he the winning or defeated athlete-hero hitting the sandlot. Win or lose is unimportant, what matters is the nobility of the sport. But killing and dying for sport should not look Olympic or Olympian: the gods who kill us for their sport should not get off the hook so cheaply.

But was it not so in Homer? Doesn't the *Iliad* chronicle, catalogue, itemize, deaths and the details of dying? True, but those are for us the least worthy parts of the poem—and hasn't the epic as a genre bit the dust precisely because it depended overmuch on war and violence and unlikely derring-do? Is not the epic as such an infantile form of art in both senses: a primitive art form and one appealing to puerile minds? The film, to the extent that it wants to achieve maturity, must outgrow the western.

There are no particulary noteworthy performances in *The Wild Bunch* (though Jaime Sanchez as Angel is winning without becoming sticky) nor particularly bad ones. The right kind of face and appropriate stance become the performance (William Holden, for instance, does not look Pike enough). But that is a kind of shorthand, not art: it is much more closely related to traffic signs than to metaphors.

August, 1969

TRUE GRIT

Worthy of succinct notice is *True Grit,* an amusing, unassuming western, antiheroic with a vengeance. Everybody here, villain or justicer, is at best fallible and at worst inspiredly erratic. Under Henry Hathaway's leisurely direction, the story and dialogue (screenplay by Marguerite Roberts from the novel of Charles Portis) gallop along briskly or bumblingly, as the case may be, and achieve, along with the acting, a style best described as realistic caricature. There is a slight, consistent heightening or lowering into absurdity, but there is also a strong feeling for the unvarnished preposterousness of everyday existence. The whole thing is a controlled joke, but one that you are more inclined to believe than most ramrod-straight tales of how the West was won. Robert Duvall heads a good group of supporting players, and John Wayne and Kim Darby do very nicely at acting at acting (*sic*).

Violence in *True Grit* is used sparingly and strikingly. It flares up now and again, briefly, paroxystically, hideously; whereupon the film once again reverts to an even temper, indeed cheerfulness. Hathaway could have derived this idea from the films of Kurosawa, which have similar pacing. Needless to say, when the violence erupts in this manner, and when, moreover, it unfurls at a speed a little greater than our eye can comfortably cope with, the gain in effect, as well as in believability (or, perhaps, *because* of its believability), is immeasurable.

September, 1969

BUTCH CASSIDY AND THE SUNDANCE KID

Butch Cassidy and the Sundance Kid is George Roy Hill's comic western with a plethora of supposedly stylish devices leading up to a bloody ending—in other words, *Bonnie and Clyde* rides again. The attempt is to be both very attentive to period flavor, and wildly "now." Thus we get the quasi-imperceptible switch of Conrad Hall's photography from the sepia tones of yesteryear to the artfully understated colors of just yesterday; the continual dependence of William Goldman's script on standing every possible western convention on its brainless head; the endless wisecracking of Paul Newman and Robert Redford in a language and humor that are half a century too early and half a continent too easterly for their historic time and place.

No need to go into the plot. It jollies up and glamorizes these outlaws' careers in much the same way that *Bonnie and Clyde* did those, but, in broad outline and detail, depends even more on smart one-upmanship. Paul Newman, as Butch, treats us to his usual smooth and soulless performance—rather like an aircraft piloted by remote control; Robert Redford, as Sundance, is fresher and racier, but he, too, runs out of tricks to sustain the dimensionless writing. As his girlfriend, Katharine Ross is rapidly losing her youthful bloom without sprouting any compensatory growth in artistic stature. And Hill's direction, like Goldman's scenario and Hall's cinematography, is too adorably and calculatedly puckish, as if the film had been made by a bunch of corrupt koalas. Most meretricious of all is Burt Bacharach's score, a systematic despoliation of Kurt Weill, with the main theme's opening bars lifted straight out of *Johnny Johnson.*

December, 1969

TELL THEM WILLIE BOY IS HERE

Tell Them Willie Boy Is Here is not a film we would ordinarily have to consider. It is a western that is in some ways a little above average, and in other ways rather below. The dialogue has a laconic bite to it, the framing of shots is sometimes quite nice, Conrad Hall's color cinematography (actually color and black-and-white superimposed) achieves disconsolately bleached-out hues for the daytime desert, and a truly ghostly quality for the night sequences. Robert Blake and Robert Redford give decent, but not extraordinary, performances as an Indian who kills in self-defense and a sheriff who admires him but must, for reasons of political pressure and hysteria under the Taft Administration, hunt him down. This is as far as the credits will go.

The debits include every kind of lack of probability. There is anachronism—people in the first decade of this century behaving in post–World War II manner; political and social symbolism which, rather than human realities, is made to determine the course of events; contrasts between Indian lovers (natural, good) and white American lovers (unnatural, neurotic), driven in with a sledgehammer; slurring or skipping of large chunks of plot in the interest of grand, mythic effects; Katharine Ross, who is both improbable and bad as an Indian maiden, and Susan Clark, who, as a woman doctor from Radcliffe, is just plain bad.

The reason the film is fussed over, however, is that it was made by Abraham Polonsky, one of the victims of McCarthyite blacklisting, who was kept from work (other than some anonymous, and probably inconsequential, script collaboration) for twenty-one years. But, as I have written before, the Hollywood Ten were all of them less than artists of consequence, or even of any kind, and it took blacklisting to make them important. Polonsky, on the strength of an acceptable gangster film he wrote and directed (*Force of Evil*), and a quite good boxing movie he wrote the script for (*Body and Soul*), became an *auteur*, so that his current return to film is being celebrated as if it were a major artistic, even historic, event. But *Willie Boy*, despite its minor virtues, remains a mediocre film, trying hard to imbue its clipped statements and portentous gestures with existential and symbolic significance, and not succeeding very well.

February, 1970

6

Declines and Pratfalls
of Major Directors

WHAT IS it that militates against a master-filmmaker's artistic
longevity? Why is the creative span of brilliant cinematic talents
shorter than that of a racing-car driver? Why does a Fellini or
Antonioni, a Kurosawa or Bresson or Truffaut, after films of true
greatness, grind to an ear-splitting halt, or flounder on and on to
the antipodes? We know what causes shortlivedness among min-
ers. But what is cinematic silicosis? Some answers emerge from
the reviews that follow; here are some others.

There is always the gifted filmmaker whose movies don't make
money and who finds it hard to get backing. Partisans of Renoir
and von Stroheim can cite them as examples; I prefer to name
Olmi and De Seta. I am, however, more concerned here with the
catastrophic lapses of major talents, or with their woeful declines.
One reason for this is that film is a very rapidly consumed
medium. We know that a novel takes longer to produce than a
film—it certainly takes us a longer time to read, even longer if
it first has to be translated, and we are quite inclined to let the
novelist rest up between books for a year or two. A painting,
even if only in reproduction, hangs around on our wall. But a
film goes down in two hours, and disappears from the theaters
in a couple of weeks or months, and already we want to know
what the filmmaker is working on now and how soon we'll get
to see it. Film, moreover, still appeals chiefly to the young, and
the young are notoriously impatient. They want to get the next
spoonful before this one has been properly swallowed, and the
pressure on the filmmaker is at best heavy, at worst inhibiting.

More importantly, film is considered an avant-garde medium,
an art whose possibilities have hardly begun to be explored.

There is some truth in this, and the filmmaker may feel obliged to indulge in continuous and conspicuous experimentation lest he fall behind the times. A poet, for example, may evolve a personal style gradually and continue refining that style at leisure without becoming old hat: poetry has become an aristocratic art and an unremunerative one, and forthwith the pressure of vulgar demands is off. But given the hysterical pace of film and the filmmaker's corresponding fear of obsolescence, a Fellini or Antonioni may abandon his personal mode before its possibilities have been fully realized, or, at any rate, exhausted, for the sake of something unviable or merely unsuitable to his particular genius.

Furthermore, there is still a widespread resistance to the notion of film as art; I even know film reviewers who doubt that film can be an art, and others who positively wish to prevent it from becoming one because they really enjoy trash more. They are comparable to men who can enjoy sex only with whores. In any case, if film is viewed as an entertainment only, a commodity, a subject for party chitchat, it becomes incumbent on it to keep coming, just as newspapers, magazines, telecasts, consumer goods, must keep coming at us lest we die of ennui. Thus to maintain his market value, a filmmaker may be pressured into producing far more regularly and frequently than his spirit moves him—certainly more often than a composer, say, is expected to cough up a new composition.

Finally, because film is an eminently social art, it is the social and political climate that provides the filmmaker with subjects and, at times, usually after periods of inhibition, shoves him into a phase of fertility. Thus the end of World War II and the downfall of Mussolini provided Italian filmmakers with the impetus and opportunity to tell all about Fascism, the war, and its aftermath. Thus also, in Poland and Czechoslovakia, during their all too brief political thaws, a plethora of splendid films gushed forth. As these privileged eras gradually or suddenly come to an end, things revert to the normal and pedestrian.

ROSEMARY'S BABY

Rosemary's Baby is yet another Roman Polanski horror film. When he made his first, *Repulsion,* there were rumors that it was all this gifted director could raise money for. When he made *Cul-de-sac* and *The Fearless Vampire Killers,* there were rumors that the producers had cut or re-edited, and seriously damaged the films. With *Rosemary's Baby* there are no more mitigating rumors: Polanski likes to make trashy films, and he makes them as routinely as anyone else. Nothing about this film suggests the talent that once gave us *Knife in the Water* and *Two Men and a Wardrobe;* the few vaguely suspenseful moments could have been made by any reasonably competent hack.

Just as some of the bosomy nude shots of Mia Farrow must have been faked in, whoever directed this picture must have been the brilliant Polanski's dopey *Doppelgänger,* if not indeed his Hollywood stand-in. The lone authentic bit of horror in the film is Ruth Gordon's performance: a sort of self-serving, nonstop tuneless singsong issuing from a decrepit butterfly that thinks itself the Empress Theodora, it is easily one of the most offensive spectacles of any year and does make *Rosemary's Baby,* whenever it is on view, perhaps not horrifying but certainly disgusting.

July, 1968

THE BRIDE WORE BLACK

Strange things are happening to form in films. Thrillers don't thrill any more, romance does not seem very romantic, tear-jerkers don't jerk a single tear. I am not sure whether the old forms are no longer viable, or whether the current crop of filmmakers have simply lost their understanding and love of these forms, without, however, coming up with anything better. It may be a period of transition, but it feels more like entropy.

Consider François Truffaut's latest, *The Bride Wore Black.* Based on a trashy mystery novel by William Irish, it tells of a girl on the verge of suicide because her childhood sweetheart was sniped down on the church steps just after their wedding. Instead of killing herself, though, Julie decides to avenge David's death. It seems that there was a group of five men involved in the sniping; one by one she seeks them out, makes them fall for her, and kills them each more bizarrely than the one before. Truffaut has called the film a love story; others have taken it as a tribute to his master, a Hitchockian thriller. In fact, it is neither; it is a piece of junk.

If the film were a real mystery, we would have to follow Julie as she tracks down the five men; as it is, we do not even find out how she unearthed their identities—after the shooting, they split up and discontinued all contact among themselves—let alone how she managed to discover their whereabouts. Moreover, the mode of killing would have to make sense: if she found that poison works easily, as it did with the second victim, she would stick to that. But no, she goes to precarious and absurd lengths to perform grotesque executions—at least one of which strikes me as physically impossible, and two others as extremely improbable—presupposing well-nigh impossible conditions.

So these killings are there mostly for their unfunctional, estheticizing weirdness, suitable to Edgar Poe but not to the efficient, modern mystery. Furthermore, there is never any suspense: everything proceeds so effortlessly for Julie, and there is such an aura of (unconscious) camp about it all, that we never doubt she will polish off her five little Indians.

In what sense, conversely, could *Bride* be a love story? Julie's love for David is shown in one brief and rather inept flashback, and in one quite prosaic affirmation of it by Julie herself later on. The fact that she is willing to kill for that love still does not make it a tangible presence to be empathized with. Yet a possibility does present itself. Truffaut intends Julie to be, as he said in an interview, the "absolutely chaste woman." And she is on a sacred, death-dealing mission. If this were a study of sexual pathology, of a virgin getting her kicks from what seems to be a holy crusade but is in fact profane, prurient killing, the film might have its impact and meaning.

Indeed, there is a clumsy step in that direction: Julie seems to be falling for the painter who is her penultimate target (she shoots him with the bow and arrow with which she poses for him as the chaste huntress, Diana—but, of course, not until she has posed for him for a good, long time; we shall call this the Artemis artifice). It doesn't work. To begin with, casting Jeanne Moreau as a virgin is about as convincing as casting Lassie as a vegetarian. Then, neither Truffaut nor his co-scenarist Jean-Louis Richard qualifies as a psychic deep-sea diver. All we get is the improbable adventures of a blank, two-dimensional avenger dressed always in black or white—whether for symbolism or for mere color contrast hardly matters.

Finally, Truffaut has tried to create an imaginary landscape: he has shot scenes pell-mell around Paris, in various parts of the South of France, and even in England. The idea stems from *L'Avventura,* where a somewhat imaginary, mythic Sicily was created. But in that highly stylized masterpiece, where landscape and architecture must correspond to human moods rather than to topography and actuality, such license is justified. Here it merely looks arbitrary, derivative, modish, and, above all, gratuitous.

What do we get then? A thriller, perhaps even a psychological thriller, without thrills and without psychology. Dimly aware of the moral void—a Julie killing five people of whom only one can be truly guilty—Truffaut tries to make each victim somewhat irrelevantly blameworthy (a playboy, a satyr, a bit of a fascist) but not too much so lest we lose sympathy for him. This lands Truffaut in equivocations, all the more so since each victim is allowed only about fifteen minutes on screen, or less than enough for complexities to reach a stage beyond the sophomoric.

One is left with two very sad bad tastes in the mind. The first pertains to Truffaut: he is clearly not a sophisticated, discriminating, broadly intelligent person on the evidence of his last three films shown here. His first three were quite wonderful, but patently or latently fed on personal experience. Once this was used up—disaster. The other sadness concerns Jeanne Moreau; at a relatively early age, she already looks ravaged and utterly spent. Damn it, it is my youth, too, that she is prematurely dragging down with her.

It may be added that Truffaut does display, here and there, a directorial nicety, and that Raoul Coutard continues to be one of the world's finest cinematographers—too good for this film as he is too good for Godard. Among the performers, the lovely Alexandra Stewart is wasted on a non-part, but the subtle Michel Bouquet suggests a hotbed of petty convolutions with his portrayal of an aging and impoverished provincial swain.

August, 1968

STOLEN KISSES

No step ahead, alas, is François Truffaut's new film, *Stolen Kisses*, unless we count the giant steps backward taken by his last three films; in that case this marks a few modest paces forward again, in the direction of his splendid early achievements. *Stolen Kisses* is once more that special Truffaut blend of sentimentality and screwiness, of an alert eye, a spunky technique, and a respect for the zaniness of life. But this loose sequence of adventures and misadventures befalling Antoine Doinel (the child hero of *The 400 Blows* and youth hero of Truffaut's episode in *Love at Twenty*) upon his dishonorable discharge from military service—"You have pull," grumbles the CO, "you must have Communist friends!"—is too aimless, casual, slight. One wonders why film exhausts its major talents so quickly.

The answer is, more than anything else, quick imitation. If a writer evolves a new technique, it takes a relatively long time for it to become understood, accepted, and emulated. Film, however, displays its novelties perspicuously, palpably, immediately—there are no serious problems of translation, dissemination, interpretation, and film is mass-produced and mass-consumed everywhere. By the time a Fellini or Antonioni makes one or two genuine Fellinis or Antonionis, there have sprouted all over the world dozens of pseudo-Fellinis, scores of pseudo-Antonionis. The more filmic your invention, the more it is copied.

Thus Truffaut's ending of *The 400 Blows* with a freeze shot has been parroted in a short time by so many films that it has promptly become one of the most vacuous cinematic platitudes. Similarly, Resnais's fragmentation and scrambling of the time-and-place sequence in *Hiroshima, Mon Amour* has become overnight an accepted—almost conventional—mode of film structure, applied rightly or ridiculously to everything from psychological studies to trivial love stories. The most superficially cinematic filmmaker of our time, Godard, is also the most aped; the most intellectual and "literary" one, Bergman, remains the least imitated or imitable. Truffaut's misfortune is to be so engagingly, seductively, accessibly filmic that his imitators have exhausted him before his time. But in addition, I dare say, there is a lack of substance in his vision.

Stolen Kisses opens and closes with a charming Charles Trenet song, sung by Trenet himself on the sound track, *"Que devient-il de tout cela?"* The song contains the phrase *"baisers volés,"* which is the film's title and provides a theme for Antoine Duhamel's otherwise undistinguished score. "What has become of all that?" is indeed the prevailing mood of the film as young Antoine Doinel fluctuates between a sophisticated older woman and an only slightly less sophisticated *gamine* (not to mention an occasional prostitute), and goes from job to outlandish job. The tone is one of youthful turbulence and pathos recollected in wistfully smiling tranquillity, and Truffaut is a master of bittersweet buffoonery down to such details as an embarrassed man's black-gloved hand clasping its nakedly white mate in pained bewilderment.

When a husband catches his wife in bed with another man and is urged by his private eye to cause a fracas, instead of throwing a handy vase at his unrepentant spouse, he removes the long-stemmed yellow irises from the vase and pelts her adulterous bosom with these angry caresses. Again, when Antoine sends a *pneumatique* to the married woman he worships but wishes to give up in the manner of the hero of Balzac's *Le Lys dans la vallée,* the camera lovingly follows the whole uniquely Parisian and by now somewhat antiquated procedure of delivering the *petit bleu* through a network of underground tubes. A magician performing tricks in a night club provides the accompanying patter in sweetly silly doggerel. And there is a *poésie de deux sous*—a puerile yet insinuating lyricism—about everything Truffaut does in this film (as in *Shoot the Piano Player* and *Jules and Jim*) that unabashedly sashays into our souls.

But also at work is a very contemporary absurdist touch. Antoine, shaving before his mirror, suddenly begins to intone, over and over, three names, each for something like a minute. First it is that of the older woman (she is married to the man for whom he works as a business spy, and seems unattainable), then that of the young girl (she seems to have lost all interest in him), and lastly his own. It is a litany of despair, and a magic incantation, and a scientific attempt at dissecting a precious name. As Antoine, with suitable grimaces, rings ever more frantic changes on, tries to wrest ever more essential meaning from the three names, a bizarre spell emanates from the screen. Is this poetry or absurdity—the folly of youth attempting to find the true pitch of reality, or the existential anguish of mortal man trying to grasp the fleeting identity of the beloved and the self?

Or take the closing scene, when Antoine has finally (if anything in this makeshift, zigzagging existence can be called final) settled on the young girl, and sits with her on a bench as a man who has been following the girl throughout the film accosts them. We thought he was a private detective but discover that he is a clandestine suitor. Declaring his definitive and immutable love for the girl, he assures her that she will belong to him and gives her a little time to break off such temporary relationships as the one with Antoine. After the man stalks off, the stupefied young lovers also leave, commenting about his complete craziness. With this the film ends: absurd and sentimental, but more absurd than sentimental.

Truffaut's tone is both modern and reminiscent, both sweet and acerbic. It is like a poem by Jacques Prévert, or an old photograph of a first love whom the change of fashions has made slightly ridiculous-looking. It's likable all right, this *Baisers volés;* yet from someone whose first films were so innovative, so individual and challenging, we want more. So Antoine stumbles into and fumbles such jobs as soldiering, hotel night-clerking, and private investigating, to end up as a TV repair man (for how long?); so he goes from a lightning affair with the married woman to a more viable one with the girl (for how long?); so what? The penetration of the artistic medium and of human nature, the keener illumination of the Now and the Always—what has become of all that? Not much.

The acting and direction of actors are good. Jean-Pierre Léaud continues to be the quintessential Parisian dropout, but under Truffaut he is not so loutish and dreary as under Godard. In the smaller parts, Michel Lonsdale is *primus inter pares* as a thriving businessman obtusely puzzled by his unpopularity. Claude Jade is pretty and typically French as the ingénue (her bad legs merely add to her typical Frenchness), and the gifted Delphine Seyrig would be marvelous as the older woman but for two things. One is that, after seeing this film in Paris last fall, I caught her in a mediocre play by Jean-Claude Carrière (who is, among other things, Buñuel's unfortunate scenarist); Miss Seyrig was brilliant in the play, but she was using exactly the same persona as in *Stolen Kisses:* same looks, same delivery, same mannerisms.

This brings us to her other problems. She is a disciple of Lee Strasberg and has turned to a kind of Method acting: excessive tinkering with her words, arrested development in her phrasing, an inward and downward pushing of the voice. There may have even been Method improvisation in her big scene, which would account for the bad grammar of *"toutes les femmes sont exceptionnelles—chacune à leur tour."* Miss Seyrig's natural talent is far greater than the Method, and it is a pity to swap *pâté de foie gras de Strasbourg* for chopped chicken livers *de* Strasberg.

Distressing, though, was the presence in the film of André Falcon as the head of the detective agency. Twenty-one years ago I went to the Comédie Française to see *Le Cid,* featuring the then ruling *jeune premier.* Comes the famous tirade, and the blond, wavy-haired, stocky young man delivers it with every odious rhetorical curlicue, every street-corner oratorical gesture, every bit of *emphase* that passes for greatness in that venerable showcase of theatrical antiquities. During the prolonged and thunderous ovation that followed, I had ample time to decipher his name on my darkness-enshrouded program: André Falcon. Last year in Paris, I saw Sacha Pitoëff's appalling production of Pirandello's *Henry IV,* and, in a generally poor cast that included Claude Jade, there was one performance that managed to surpass even the wretched Pitoëff and his worse wife in sheer horror. Who was this stocky, grizzled, ineptly gesticulating Belcredi? A look at the program: André Falcon! And here he is again, an eyesore in *Stolen Kisses,* further proof of Truffaut's sentimentality—in this case about a quondam star of the Français.

March, 1969

SPIRITS OF THE DEAD

Spirits of the Dead is a trilogy of tales from Poe. The first episode, "Metzengerstein," was directed by Roger Vadim, making little further comment necessary. There may be worse filmmakers than Vadim, but no one can surpass him in spiritual rottenness. His is a megalomaniacal interior decorator's world inhabited by campy marionettes. His orgiasts have sawdust in their heads, veins and glands, and Vadim, for all his sexual shadowboxing, cannot even rise to that nadir of eroticism, dishonest titillation.

Here, at best, one can get a laugh out of Jacques Fonteray's costumes, the ultimate in Folies-Bergère medievalism: we are treated to sheer medieval nightgowns, see-through medieval bodices, bared medieval midriffs, and any number of interesting fashions to be burned at the stake for. The chief *frisson* is that Jane Fonda's love interest is played by her brother, Peter, but since he cares more for his horse than for Jane, and perishes before either passion could be consummated, no new frontiers are conquered. Particularly disheartening is the indifferent cinematography by the great Claude Renoir.

"William Wilson," the second episode, directed by Louis Malle, is equally remote from Poe's story, equally inept. If there is anything worse than Alain Delon in a starring role, it is Alain Delon in a dual role. Also around is Brigitte Bardot, voice dubbed, face daubed, and, although playing a woman of the world, looking more like a spirit of the dead than anything else in the movie. Again there is disappointing color photography by a fine cinematographer, Tonino delli Colli.

But the real disappointment is the third episode, Fellini's "Never Bet the Devil Your Head." Fellini's segment is considerably superior to the others, but vastly inferior to the old good Fellini, who, it seems, will never come back. In this freely updated tale, Toby Dammit, a bibulous, played-out English movie star (well acted by Terence Stamp, whose presence may account for jocular allusions to Pasolini, though there are in-jokes of every kind) comes to Rome to do a western that is to be an allegory of the Christ story. He is willing mostly because he has been promised a fabulous sports car as part of the deal. From time to time, he is haunted by a little girl playing with a large ball, who, as we later discover, is the Devil.

There is an award dinner in Dammit's honor at which the usual decadent Fellini revelers watch Toby make a drunken fool of himself as he garbles a speech from Shakespeare; he then shocks them all with an embarrassing confession of how he ruined his life. He runs from the dinner, jumps into his new sports car, races madly through sleeping villages, and comes up against a fallen bridge. A wire is strung across the road to keep motorists away. Toby bets the Devil his head that he can ride his Ferrari across the chasm. The car makes it, but Toby's head is neatly sliced off by the wire. The sinister little girl picks it up and proceeds to use it as a new ball.

The film is not much better than this outline. Occasionally, the dialogue has some bite to it, and there is one scene in a television studio where Toby is being interviewed that is genuinely funny and knowingly directed. But mostly there is that typical Fellini bustle: people being whisked about in cars or buttonholed and harangued by busybodies; accosting or being accosted by mysterious women to no particular avail; talking at cross-purposes and stifling amid various forms of jaded opulence that always manages to include members of the clergy and the film industry. The award dinner, Fellini's umpteenth go at a bacchanalian gathering of the international *beau* and *demi monde,* comes across as a neon-lit stereotype. And the frightening thing about it all is that it probably prefigures quite accurately the further boring orgiastic bustle to which we shall be subjected in Fellini's *Satyricon.*

Even such a scene as Toby's maniacal night drive, where, as in some other sequences, Fellini tries for expressionistic or surreal effects, fails to achieve the desired excitement. Giuseppe Rotunno, another excellent cameraman, comes to grief with a series of heightened coloristic effects that refuse to coalesce into a world of a different color. And the very idea of the Devil as an impudent little girl seems to be cribbed from Buñuel's *Simon of the Desert.* Fellini has stumbled into the same pitfall that is already crawling with our novice *cinéastes:* swirling, aimless movement mistaken for the pinnacle of filmic expressiveness. The name of the ailment is cinematic dotage, but Fellini is not old enough for a second childhood.

September, 1969

THE DAMNED

The number of year's-best lists that feature *The Damned,* the votes it garnered at various critics' polls, the long lines of the damned queueing up outside the theater where it is playing, the sheer prestige of its maker, Luchino Visconti, make unavoidable a brief assessment of that director's career.

There is no more overblown, self-inflated and preposterous reputation in film than that of Luchino Visconti. I have not been able to see *Ossessione,* but on the basis of *La terra trema* I am willing to admit that he was one of the fathers of neo-realism. What of it, though? The film is vastly inferior to the neo-realist work of Rossellini, De Sica, and the early Fellini, and, in art, getting there first is far less important than doing the most with the discovery. As I look at Visconti's later output, I find it pretentious, posturing, bloated, and empty under all the window-dressing.

A film like *White Nights,* admired by Pauline Kael, strikes me as the ultimate in pseudo-art; movies like *Senso* and *The Leopard* are made for the greater glory of set and costume design, and emerge as equal kitsch despite the superior novel on which the latter is based. *Rocco and His Brothers* begins satisfactorily in a vein that was, however, more or less exhausted by 1960; but as it goes on, it becomes more and more the usual Viscontian strident pseudoprofundity devoid of human authenticity and artistic vision. *Bellissima,* which I recall imperfectly, seems to me worth reviving, if only to enable us to determine why we may have overestimated it—Magnani's performance, perhaps.

The Stranger is Visconti's most palatable film, largely because he stuck close to Camus, had a superb cinematographer in Giuseppe Rotunno, and some marvelous acting, notably from Mastroianni and Georges Geret. Usually Visconti is, besides other bad things, nonactor-prone, allowing such erratic performers as Burt Lancaster, Claudia Cardinale, Alain Delon, Farley Granger, Maria Schell, Michael Craig, and Jean Sorel, among others, to foul up his films. For all I know, Visconti may be a good operatic stage director (his *Figaro's Marriage,* the only such work of his I saw, was resourceful and, until the grandiosely overdone last act, highly effective); but his films always tend toward grand operatic gesture at the expense of subtle, searching honesty.

And something else. In his highfalutin and vacuous monograph on Visconti, Geoffrey Nowell-Smith writes, "his work has a devious consistency"—a phrase illustrative of the critical doubletalk and double-think that parlays men like Visconti into greatness. What there is in his films, though, is a "deviate consistency," taking consistency in the sense of texture. In almost all the Visconti films known to me, the director alludes to, suggests, toys with homosexuality, keeping it, nevertheless, subliminal, marginal, or thinly veiled. It is regrettable that instead of his bogus Marxism, for which he has no genuine understanding, Visconti should soft-pedal this other theme of his, for which he seems to have much more profound concern.

Thus *Sandra (Vaghe stelle dell' Orsa)* goes in for all kinds of foolish attitudinizing about fascism, and politico-sexual mystery-mongering, but might have amounted to something had it not falsified the impact of a monstrous mother on her children as producing incest rather than, much more believably, inversion. Still, such is Visconti's prestige that *Sandra* won the grand prize at Venice, very possibly the worst film to be so honored.

In a sense, *The Damned* is an extension and elaboration of *Sandra,* which did not need elaboration, only oblivion. It is, as customary with Visconti, a very long film whittled down from an even longer one, and crammed full of disparate elements, mismanaged in themselves and mutually conflicting. We begin in 1933, at a family dinner of the mighty Essenbeck clan, a faintly disguised and grossly fantasticated version of the Krupps. Presided over by steely old Baron Joachim von Essenbeck, the evening is complete with entertainment by the younger members of the family, which extends from young Günther's sensitive cello playing to young Martin's outrageous transvestite impersonation of Marlene Dietrich as Lola-Lola in *The Blue Angel.* (It is typical of the film's non-artistry that, instead of letting the able actor do his own impersonating, Dietrich's recording of a song is grafted onto the sound track.)

This beginning, with the various members of the family, including friends and retainers, shown in their behind-the-scenes as well as on-the-scene stances, is the first and last effective sequence of *The Damned,* vaguely reminiscent of a family chronicle like *Buddenbrooks.* Indeed, Thomas Mann is paid a dubious compliment by having the film's most melodramatic villain named Aschenbach, after the very different protagonist of *Death in Venice.*

The various family hates, rivalries, and intrigues are not, however, sketched in with noteworthy clarity or skill—only the bustle and ritualism of upper-class life in that era are well conveyed—and with the dialogue and characterization we are in for rough sailing right away. The script, by Nicola Badalucco, Enrico Medioli, and Visconti himself, is undoubtedly trashy even in Italian; in English, it is a total mess. There is bathos like "I accepted a ruthless logic and I can never get away from it"; dime-fiction lushness like "It's a young hate, pure and beautiful"; and sheer junk like references to "your tiny little arse." Worst of all, it has been couched in that not quite ungrammatical yet less than couth translator's English that falls chillingly on the literate ear. And, of course, it is dubbed into a variety of accents ranging from British to low-comedy that have traditionally left Hollywood smilingly unconcerned.

The Damned, included in the ten-best Pantheon of both Vincent Canby and Judith Crist, is meant to be tragic and terrifying, but it emerges as the ludicrous flailings of puny puppets in inscrutable, wooden frenzies. "It's an object lesson, a morality tale, a tragedy of historic proportions!" shrieks the puppeteer, and all we see is the bashing together of stupid, wooden heads, while our notions of what it may all mean remain dim and unrewarding. Luchino Visconti is supposed to have made the original cut of the film five hours long; he can, and probably does, claim that half of that, which is what remains, isn't enough—though we might have expected him to have learned something from the inordinate length and subsequent enforced cutting of some of his previous films.

The artist must work within his medium, and, in the case of the film, part of that medium is time: the time an audience is able to endure without squirming, falling asleep, laughing out of the wrong side of the mouth, vomiting, or having to leave. The greater the artist, the longer he can hold his audience in thrall, but in no case can he do this beyond a certain point, and in most cases he will prefer to stop well before that point is reached. There is no evidence that a film can last beyond three hours without attenuating itself out of existence or bludgeoning us into a state of obliviousness. But considering the kind of writing, directing, and, above all, thinking Visconti subjects us to with *The Damned*—the banalities, platitudes, bathos, sensationalism, dishonesty—every minute is sheer presumption.

We are never given a sense of what the greatness and glories of the Essenbeck family consisted of before the *Götterdämmerung* (the pretentious European title of the film), what values, joys, achievements, were to be lost. True, we see Friedrich Bruckmann, the lover of the widowed Baroness Sophie von Essenbeck, coveting the steel empire; but a Bessemer converter at work while hyper-Wagnerian music churns away during the credits is all the feel of empire we get. And true, Albrecht Schönhals, an always commendable actor, does a nice job suggesting the head of the mighty clan, Baron Joachim; but his various accomplishments and activities are not conveyed: there is no sense of greatness or usurpation, of nobility or exploitation. Wealth and stiffness are all the script allows.

Even shadowier is the scheming yet ultimately weak Friedrich— uncomfortably played by Dirk Bogarde, who seems aware of how his Britishness obtrudes on the proceedings, and possibly even of the shoddiness of the film itself. What is Friedrich Bruckmann's story, how did he rise this high at the Essenbeck works, how did he get to be Sophie's lover, what makes him aspire to the top? Less clear yet are the various minor Essenbecks, their relationships, motivations, indeed their very identities. There is, for example, the couple, Herbert and Elisabeth Thalmann (whom the program and, for all I know, the script misspelled as "Thallman"), whose exact place in the family is uncertain; if we care to trust the untrustworthy program, Elisabeth is Joachim's grand-niece.

At the initial dinner party, the various attitudes and backgrounds should have been cogently presented. They are not. Nephew Aschenbach is an SS villain, son Konstantin is an SA bully, Thalmann a cliché of a liberal, Elisabeth a lovely and anxious wife, Konstantin's boy a sensitive intellectual who does not want to inherit the factories, and so on. Finally, during this fateful night which is that of the Reichstag fire, the old Baron is murdered in a most perfunctory way, while the excitement focuses on beautiful but hard Sophie's weird son, Martin. He is to be the central character of the film, and, characteristically, he does not make sense.

Martin is conceived as a homosexual: we see him delighting in his drag Dietrich act, adoring and secretly loathing his glamorous mother to whose skirt tails he clings while spewing forth that ready, impudent wit that serves as the homosexual's offensive-defensive weapon. Yet this same Martin is suddenly revealed as a molester of girl children, who does something awful to one of his little female relatives under the grand piano on the night of the murder. But we do not find out what, or what the consequences were, or why he is not given some kind of treatment or even sequestered.

Later on, we see Martin living in a back-street apartment where he maintains his blowsy artiste-mistress, Olga. He now seems capable of a fairly standard heterosexual relationship. Not for long, however; he does his dreadful thing to the landlady's small daughter, who proceeds to kill herself. (Here Warner-Seven Arts insisted on cutting a shot of the girl hanging from a rafter, thus making the sequence even more muddled and mystifying than it already was.) Now you might think that Olga is just a front, and that Martin's heart is not in this affair, but not a bit of it. He is jealous of her, wants to keep her in bed with him as much as possible, and is still her lover at the end of the film.

I submit that all this is nonsense. Martin clearly detests his mother —one of his childhood drawings shows him murdering his *Mutti*—yet feels dependent on, even chained to her. This, though Visconti makes it a trifle schematic, is a credible homosexual syndrome. What is not credible is Martin's seduction-rape of his mother, complete with cunnilingus (her reaction is likewise less than convincing, but we'll come to that later), and the subsequent mock-wedding-cum-genuine-murder ceremony he stages for her and Friedrich.

Here is the notorious Viscontian fudging at work again. In *Rocco and His Brothers*, for example, the filmmaker introduced the character Morini (played with utmost sinisterness by Roger Hanin), an unlikely specimen who preys sexually on prizefighters. Now while we know about inverts who specialize in seducing brawny heterosexuals, and about others who jeer or browbeat undecided young boys into sex with them, Morini's humiliation technique with someone like Simone would most likely have resulted in mayhem. Violence, to be sure, doesn't always occur, but Morini is too experienced and clever to risk it. Visconti plainly knows the homosexual milieu, yet falsifies it for the sake of sensationalistic effects or pseudomoralistic toying with the subject, whatever suits his disingenuous purpose.

But Martin's deflowerings (or whatever) of little girls are certainly relevant enough to deserve the analytic and artistic exploration they never get; there is not even the sense of pity Fritz Lang was able to inspire in us for the rapist and killer of children in *M*. And when Martin joins the SS, and, in exchange for diverting armament from the SA to them, acquires the power for evil he lacked before, Visconti again fails to show how the young man adapts to, profits by, or is further corrupted by the SS. Visconti may not be interested in the problem psychologically, but since it is, in fact, his political theme, the crossbreeding of private and public vice, he must explore it. He doesn't, and the film, far from making a significant statement about Nazism, history, politics, remains a lurid piece of fumbling sensationalism.

Characters like Sophie, though of key importance, are illuminated even less. She is shown, simply and dishonestly, as power-hungry, domineering, and lustful. Nothing about how she became that; why she picked Friedrich, of all people, for her instrument of conquest; whether, and to what extent, she cares for her son, and what sort of marriage it was that produced him; and how her feelings for Martin change, if they do. When Martin has possessed her, she becomes, without apparent transition, a raving dope fiend; if she is as tough as we are led to believe, a little incest would not matter that much.

Sophie's makeup and costuming, as well as her script and direction, are such that this lovely woman (played by the beautiful Ingrid Thulin) emerges even sexually very nearly repellent. Particularly tendentious is an extreme closeup of just one of her breasts: to show this spread across the vastness of Cinemascope, the nipple roughly the size of the Matterhorn, does not, as in Baudelaire's sonnet about the giantess, instill the desire to *"dormir nonchalamment à l'ombre de ses seins"*; rather, it fills us with a Brobdingnagian horror, even as the whole Sophie becomes a figure from an antiheterosexual nightmare. In the last analysis, she is raped not by her son, Martin, but by her director, Visconti.

Speaking of the cinematography, it is the no more than adequate work, ranging in color from evocative to garish, of Armando Nannuzzi, an old standby, and Pasquale de Santis, a new one (he also photographed Zeffirelli's *Romeo and Juliet* with unsteady success). But the photography at its worst cannot match the melodramatic obviousness of scenes like the one in which Aschenbach maneuvers Martin into the SS, or the one in which Aschenbach and Sophie contend for ascendancy over Martin, with Aschenbach's threats getting the better of a mother's hisses. How much more meaningfully this sort of thing is done in, say, the original version of Hochhuth's *The Deputy,* or in Zuckmayer's *The Devil's General,* or even in the caricaturing of Brecht's *Arturo Ui.*

But the prize pratfall is the Night of the Long Knives, the SA orgy at a lakeside resort, during which Roehm and his SA were surprised by Himmler's SS and, for all practical purposes, wiped out. In this scene, and only in this one, the dialogue is in German, as if for such a historic occasion nothing short of the most reverent *verismo* would do. The scene at the resort is one long, flaccid transvestite revel, with men in varying degrees of drag and disrobement lolling and loping, cavorting and moseying around. Occasionally, even a few beefy tarts get chased about a bit, for good measure. It is not just that these sequences are tacky, theatrical, and maudlin, all of which they may well have been in reality. The cheap thing is the lack of a point of view. When a disarrayed young transvestite is languidly stretching himself on a postcoital, dawn terrace, an undercurrent of wistful tenderness seems implied; at other times, all is porcine vulgarity. But the melancholy is banal and facile; the swinishness sensationalistic, disconnected, noncommenting. Yet the scene, if I may put it so, drags on and on.

Exploitation of sexuality in films is always unattractive. It becomes more so when it postures as art or history, as it does here. And it becomes superlatively unprepossessing when the filmmaker seems to be exploiting something close to his heart, something he would like to make an honest and humane statement about but lacks the courage to render in any but a smirking, splashy, jesuitically quasi-condemnatory way. For none of these SA homosexuals is shown as loving; none exhibits, like the members of that famed phalanx of Epaminondas, eagerness to save his lover. Everyone merely tries to save his own skin, having indulged his own glands.

Though Konstantin is a victim of this massacre, while Friedrich and Aschenbach are among the killers (the former, to be sure, under duress), we learn nothing new about these three crucial characters. Still, the scene is presumably meant to be highly revealing, staged as it is in ever so much more detail than, for example, the book-burning.

What need of further elaboration? Visconti's *The Damned,* with its flamboyantly vapid score by Maurice Jarre, is a cinematic dime novel —or, better yet, the equivalent of a Menotti opera with a late Tennessee Williams libretto. Thus the last scene, the mock marriage Martin stages for his mummy and her lover, after which they are ordered to take poison, is surely the quintessence of Grand Guignol, arty division. It is hard to believe that Friedrich and Sophie could not have escaped to Switzerland or Sweden, or that in all this time they would not have gotten married, or that Martin, however much of a beast, would act as his mother's executioner.

None of this matters to Visconti, who has Sophie looking like Blanche DuBois playing Pierrot Lunaire, and Friedrich re-enacting Prince Rudolf at Mayerling. The Krupps should have had it so bad! And while the newlydeads are sprawled out on a sofa, Martin, glorious in his jetblack SS uniform, dances with his Olga.

Helmut Berger is effective as Martin, an easy enough part to play, and Charlotte Rampling looks pretty and gallant as the tragic Elisabeth Thalmann. Ingrid Thulin, basically unsuited to the part of Sophie, is further undone by Visconti. Bogarde is uncharacteristically ineffectual as Friedrich. The others do what they can, dubbed and duped as they are. There exist bad films about whose merits one can debate; *The Damned* is not one of those.

January, 1970

THE MILKY WAY

Of all filmmakers who can lay claims to being major, none is so hard to evaluate as Luis Buñuel. He has not made a single film that can honestly be pronounced unflawed, or as near to it as mortal skill can come. His best films have impact rather than achievement. Buñuel is good in patches—marvelous patches, to be sure—that can crop up even in such basically unsound films as *The Age of Gold* or *El*; whereas his best work, like *Los Olvidados, Viridiana,* or *Simon of the Desert,* though more consistently good, may lack the bravura of the lesser films.

The two hallmarks of a Buñuel film are peculiar, often sadistic, sex; and religious excess, often cruel, and usually viewed with irony. The two are generally intertwined, and the result can be splendidly baroque and bizarre. But, in both his favorite realms, Buñuel has a way of bogging down. If subsidized and encouraged, he could make superb pornographic films; as things are, he feels obliged to bring in perverse sexuality surreptitiously or marginally—as a dream, an allusion, a sur-real fantasy—thus dissipating much of its power and even reducing it to maundering private symbolism.

In religion, Buñuel seems to be striving desperately to rid himself of his Catholicism, perhaps even of all belief, but he just has no talent for atheism. His love-hate for the religion he thinks he has sloughed off has a way of assuming ludicruous, convoluted, and, as in *The Exterminating Angel,* infantile forms; it tends to lack the directness and force of such swift kicks in the rear as are administered in even such a commercial film as *M*A*S*H.* I am not saying that ambivalence cannot be artistically fruitful, but Buñuel's constant tergiversations and ambiguities become, finally, exasperating.

The Milky Way strikes me as an occasionally amusing but essentially slapdash, turbid, self-indulgent film, and I defy the hordes of enthusias-tic reviewers, both high and low, to give a cogent interpretation of more than two-fifths of what goes on in it. The film concerns two vagabonds, Pierre and Jean, who go on a pilgrimage from Paris to St. James of Compostela in Spain; a star is once supposed to have guided pilgrims to the tomb of the Apostle James, buried there, and the two men follow that stellar trajectory. But the prime heavenly high road is the Milky Way, an emblem of Christianity's path through the ages; and so the film also dips into the past, to depict incidents from the lives of famous Christians, anti-Christians, and heretics. To tie the two levels together, a prefatory narration tells us that the Milky Way is known as the Road of Saint James in many European languages—not exactly true, but let that pass.

We are treated to a series of religious-picaresque episodes in which past and present run parallel, or vaguely connect, or seem to correspond to each other. But even when a meaning is deducible, Buñuel's evaluation of it tends to remain inscrutable or ambivalent. Thus most reviewers have seen in this film a ruthless satire on Catholicism. Yet to no less a critic than Stanley Kauffmann, the film is "a vision that lifts the history of the Church off the ground and sustains it through an idea of faith that is larger than any pettifogging theological pedantry." I myself see Church, Christ, and even God attacked in this film, but with a hate that, like Lord Alfred Douglas's love, dare not speak its name.

Right at the start, the tramps encounter a mysterious and commanding figure, whom the program identifies as "the Stranger," and Kauffmann calls "a prophet." This powerful personage refuses alms to the tramp who says he has no money, but richly rewards the one who shows that he has some. I am reminded of God's helping those who help themselves. The Stranger then foretells that the pair are to beget upon a whore two children, to be named You-Are-Not-My-People and No-More-Pity. These were the words of the Lord to Hosea, which provides us with a second clue to the speaker's identity.

The Stranger walks away, and suddenly is seen leading a bow-legged dwarf by the hand; the latter, equally out of nowhere, releases a white dove. The one has become three: a harsh father leading a stunted son who lets go a pointless pigeon—the triune God! And, surely, if the analogy of the path of Faith through the ages and across the sky with that of the two representative present-day men is to hold, we must begin where everything begins, on earth as in heaven, with the Trinity. But what a Trinity!

So, too, the film ends with the old and young tramps arriving at Santiago (Saint James) de Compostela, but being diverted by a whore (of Babylon?) from the shrine. She tells them there are no pilgrims to beg from there, ever since it has been discovered that the buried body is not that of the Apostle, but of the heretical Bishop Priscillian, and that they should instead beget on her two children, You-Are-Not-My-People and No-More-Pity. Pierre and Jean go off into the bushes with her. Now so mercilessly named a progeny can only be twin Antichrists, and, indeed, when the Lord gave those instructions to Hosea, he added that he would have no further compassion with the House of Israel: "for ye are not my people, and I will not be yours." Begotten at God's behest by hobos on a whore, they will be pitiless scourges of a humanity that refuses to be the people of God. Irony may lurk here:

considering what God is like, would one want to be his people?

Two more clearly identifiable characters of the film are Christ and the Virgin Mary. Kauffmann thinks them portrayed with beauty and reverence, in the colors of the Piero della Francesca frescoes at Arezzo. Yet if you look at the film without preconception, you notice that Jesus, as played by Bernard Verley, is a smug young chap with a shifty, downcast gaze, who often sounds smart-alecky; his mother, as played by Edith Scob, looks like a sentimental, mass-produced Saint Sulpice figurine of the Virgin. She acts sticky-sweet, talks with a simper, has at least one other child (contrary to Catholic doctrine), and when she tells Jesus not to shave off his beard because he looks so much nicer with it, I fail to see how this can be taken as a pious tribute.

Jesus, by the way, is never accorded his full complement of a dozen disciples, only a desultory three or four, and at the marriage at Cana things really become ludicrous. While Jesus tells a quasi-biblical parable that is in fact a most un-Christian paean to usury, his mother watches him raptly across the table and dotingly exclaims, "Isn't he marvelous?"

At the very end of the film, the bums having given the whore the rush, two blind beggars get their sight restored by Jesus. Then, as Christ and his followers hurry on, the beggars are shown, but only up to their knees, groping onward with their canes, practically stumbling into a crevice. Buñuel does not show their faces in this last shot, so that one might think that these fumbling, blind feet belong to somebody else. Yet I am clearly reminded here of how another Buñuel film, *The Age of Gold,* ends. A text there identifies Christ emerging from a castle as the Duke de Blangis, one of the heroes of Sade's *The 120 Days of Sodom,* who, with three fellow libertines, tortured, maimed, and horribly killed a seraglio of beautiful girls and boys along with other victims of this criminal lust. Indeed, Christ, looking supersanctimonious, is shown finishing off a not-quite-dead girl who tries to stagger out of the castle.

Buñuel, now older and more prudent, does not make his attitudes as obvious as that in *The Milky Way,* but, not really restoring the sight he pretends to restore, his Christ is still a wolf in lamb's clothing. And, what is more important, the film is a mere trifle wrapped in a triple cloak of befuddling obscurantism.

Most reviewers saw in *The Milky Way* the "massive assault on the Roman Catholic Church" that Brad Darrach of *Life,* vogue word and all, at least had the courage to identify. Several others merely hint at this, while still others equivocate. And so, regrettably, does Buñuel himself. Take the episode where the tramps, on a stormy night, find shelter in a shed. Jean, the younger and sassier one, is amazed to find the elderly Pierre believing in God. Jean steps out into the tempest, bares his chest, and challenges God to strike him down. Nothing happens. But as Jean reenters the shed, lightning strikes a nearby hut. "It didn't hit me, after all," Jean remarks. "Imbecile," Pierre retorts, "do you think God is at your disposal?" Now what does this mean? That religion fraudulently interprets random but vaguely applicable phenomena as not accidental and irrelevant but proof positive of the existence and omnipotence of God? Or the opposite, that miracles can be explained away by atheists, because the inveterate scoffer, not satisfied down to his least whim, can always find something inconclusive about them? The incident is deliberately ambiguous.

In another episode, the tramps are stumbling on, exhausted. Pierre's shoes are about to expire, the soles having almost completely left the vamps. A fancy sports car roars down the pike and ignores Jean's plea for help. "Break your neck, you bastard!" Jean shouts after the car, and turns away from the road not expecting anything further. A few seconds go by, then crash! The car has been reduced to a John Chamberlain junk sculpture, the driver is dead, and in the back sits an antiquely garbed youth, smirking. (The program identifies him as the Devil, and, since he is played by the loathsome Pierre Clémenti, one is willing to lend it credence.) Jean exclaims that he was not aware of another passenger before. No, says the youth, it was Jean's imprecation that put him in there. He then instructs Pierre to take the dead man's gorgeous shoes, which Pierre does.

What of this now? The implication seems to be that whereas God does not obey our commands, the Devil heeds them. But if the driver was uncharitable, perhaps his whole life long, he may have deserved this punishment. Yet, why, in that case, must the punishment wait on an irreligious tramp's demanding it? Or is the punishment unjust, our own evil wishes wreaking havoc on other people? Then why is this illustrated in terms of a stony-hearted rich man who races his car past poor, pleading voyagers? A rich man, moreover, whose shoes fit the victim of his contumely as if by divine Providence. It is all extremely confusing, though it makes a provocative splash on the screen.

To obfuscate matters further, the Devil turns on the car radio, gets a peculiar Spanish sermon, then turns the radio off. This, like a good deal of what follows, may be a veiled dig at Franco's Spain, though none of it becomes clear. In fact, the last, Spanish section of the journey is full of events so bizarrely surreal—people stepping from the present into the past and back again, strange bedfellows materializing out of nowhere in people's beds, and many more—that I can no longer speak of loose ends in the plot, only of a screw loose somewhere. I do not mean to say that surrealism equals madness, but I do think that the way in which Buñuel casually introduces it into a realistic context, and as casually drops it again, is artistically and psychically suspect.

There are, to be sure, parts of the film that are perfectly plain and unequivocal, such as the duel between the Jansenist and the Jesuit, in which the two are ready to kill each other over points of dogma, only to depart, a while later, arms slung around each other and perfectly reconciled. The point is that, however great the doctrinal dissensions, the Church always restores its solidarity and solidity, holy water being thicker than bad blood. But both the quarrel and the reconciliation are ineffably petty.

Such scenes make simple points in a moderately dramatic way; yet even if all of them worked, which they do not, the result would be less than commanding. So I kept hoping for some orgiastic or brilliantly perverse sexuality to dazzle me, but whenever Buñuel is on the verge of it, he backs away. Take the scene played in Latin (with a veritable Babel of Latin pronunciations) where the heretical Bishop Priscillian justifies fleshly indulgence as giving the Devil, who created the flesh, his due. The more the flesh is mortified through sexual excess, he argues, the more we can detach our souls and render them unto God. But the orgy this builds up to is barely adumbrated. After the Marquis de Sade, in another sequence, has lectured a chained and bloodied victim on the idiocy of her trust in God—the scene is actually from *Justine*—and she continues to defy him with her faith, he moves toward her to let her have it. Blackout. Again, a nun's crucifixion is played almost for laughs, the sadomasochism Buñuel could depict so brilliantly, left unexplored. The real Buñuel refuses to stand up.

Just as many episodes in the film are obscure and ambiguous, the overall meaning remains inscrutable. The whore (a part on which the gifted Delphine Seyrig is wasted) tells the tramps that there is no point in going on to the shrine—ever since it has been revealed that the bones buried there are Priscillian's and not St. James's, pilgrims no longer come and the tramps would find nobody to hustle. And, as I said, the three go off to procreate a pitiless offspring. Pierre and Jean, with their typical names (used to similar effect by Maupassant in his novel, *Pierre et Jean*), are humanity led astray from its pious destination—exactly as the other Way of Saint James, the path of Christianity through the ages, has strayed from sanctity to heresy.

Or is this negative interpretation correct? The tramps, after all, are only doing what the God-figure predicted and, very possibly, wanted from them. And if it is true that the relics are Priscillian's, that too may be for the best; perhaps what is needed is an untrammeled self-fulfillment, a carnal religion, which the tramps' offspring may institute. But, again, the whore may easily be lying to the tramps, God having prophesied their monstrous paternity as punishment for them and mankind for getting sidetracked—and the former interpretation holds.

The mind boggles. Some of the blame may devolve on Jean-Claude Carrière, who previously collaborated with Buñuel on two of his worst films, *Diary of a Chambermaid* and *Belle de Jour*. The color photography by Christian Matras, one of my three favorite French cinematographers of the old school (the other two veteran masters being Roger Hubert and Claude Renoir), functions unobtrusively and effectively. Among the actors, few get a chance to act. Two come off best: Julien Bertheau, as a maître d'hôtel who spouts Catholic orthodoxy as he exudes headwaiterly punctilio, but practices perfect uncharitableness; and Agnès Capri, the *diseuse,* who teaches her little girls to recite fierce anathemata as if they were the poetry of "our great poets, Racine, Lamartine, and Henri de Régnier"—a juxtaposition that is in itself an anathema.

Bewildered by all the references to Photinus and Cleobulus, Marcion and Nestorius, a puzzled young woman-reviewer asked me if I could recommend any reading matter that would fill her in on these things. I suggested Migne's *Patrologia* in 300-odd volumes; it might take a while to read, but less long than to unscramble *The Milky Way.*

February, 1970

ZABRISKIE POINT

Sadly, now, I must report on the first major film disappointment of the year 1970, *Zabriskie Point.* Ever since Michelangelo Antonioni announced that he was making his initial film about and in America, I have been wondering what the collision of that irresistible mind with this immovable Leviathan would be like. It now appears that Antonioni's view of the U.S.A. is no more incisive or subtle than that of your average cultivated, snobbish European, which is enough for some semipertinent, semi-impertinent generalizations, but not for an insightful work of art.

The idea materialized for Antonioni, apparently, when he stood on the lookout platform at Zabriskie Point and gazed across the gypsum-and-borax dunes and declivities of Death Valley. Here, with the salt-like crystals blowing about him, the vision crystallized: America as a desert, a death-trap, the bleached and pulverized bones of once living hills and valleys. In it, a few young people are trying to plant new life, by making love and also war—on materialism, racism, capitalist despotism. The film turns out to be, I am afraid, the case of a man who finds a button in the street and has a suit made to match it.

Let us consider the plot. Black and white student revolutionaries at a Los Angeles university plan a demonstration and the takeover of a building. One young man, Mark, walks out on the meeting in disgust. He says he is prepared to die, but not of boredom. He later says that he will join the activists when they are determined to win, not just to fight a losing action. A young girl, Daria, is seen trying to retrieve a book she left on the roof of the Sunny Dunes Development Co., but is refused admission until its chief executive, Lee Allen, who happens to be passing by, takes her under his wing. Later we learn that she became his secretary and, presumably, mistress. Meanwhile, a large group of student and faculty demonstrators are being booked at a police station; when Mark tries to bail out his roommate and does not kowtow to the police, he is roughly tossed behind bars with the rest.

Mark and a friend purchase guns with the utmost ease when they tell the dealer that they must protect their womenfolk in a borderline neighborhood. "One more thing about the law," another salesman warns them, "if you shoot them in the back yard, be sure to drag them into your house." At a later demonstration, a Negro student is wantonly shot down by the police on the pretense that he is carrying a gun, which he is not. Mark reaches for his weapon to shoot one of the cops, but before he can do so (at least that is how I interpret the elliptic editing here), somebody else does and Mark decamps. His roommate tells him on the telephone that he or someone like him was caught by the television cameras on the scene of the shooting. Mark goes to the airport, picks a likely plane, and, despite protests from the operations tower, takes off.

Daria, meanwhile, is supposed to meet Lee at his Xanadu in Phoenix, Arizona, where there is to be a business meeting. She is driving down in an old Buick she borrowed, and causes Lee, who doesn't know where she is, much concern. While Lee is watching a ghastly Sunny Dunes TV commercial in the company of his assembled staff, he gets a phone call from Daria, already in the Mojave Desert, asking him to help her locate some town ending in "ville or something" where she is to meet a guru to meditate with. It turns out she is in the very town (not ending in "ville" or anything like it), where the bartender blames the guru's crowd for local unrest. She does not find him, but is rushed instead by a bunch of ten-year-olds who want "a piece of arse." She has a hard time escaping from the kids, then drives on.

Flying in fine fettle over the desert, Mark spots Daria stopping to get water for her tank from a roadside container. (The hairy young man must have a bald eagle's eye to be able to tell from that height, and at his speed, that the girl below is attractive.) He proceeds to buzz her car in the most spectacular stunt flying I have seen in some time (how does a mere student come by such aerobatic skills?) until she gets out and scrawls an obscene message in the sand. He drops a red nightshirt for her, and, on a desert landing strip, they meet.

They go off to get gasoline for the plane, but end up off Zabriskie Point, gamboling in the gypsum. She: "Don't you feel at home here? It's peaceful." He: "It's dead." She turns on, and he tells her how he became a dropout. Pretty soon she turns to him, he drops on her, and they start balling in the borax. Scores of other nude or seminude couples and triples appear scattered across the lunar-looking landscape and perform some rather peculiar sexual games, a veritable hippie Thebaïd. I take them to be Daria's vision, and they promptly vanish.

A state trooper chances upon Daria in the desert—Mark has hidden behind a latrine; the cop questions and eyes Daria suspiciously, and Mark, from his hideout, makes ready to shoot him. Daria stands between the gun and the policeman, who, finally, drives away. It emerges that Mark is the fellow she heard about in the newscasts who stole a plane. When she asks if he might also be the one who shot a cop, Mark says he was beaten to it by another gun. Why did he steal the plane? "I needed to get off the ground." Why does he now choose to return it, knowing the risks? "I want to take risks." So Mark, Daria, and an old painter who lives in the desert repaint the plane: naked breasts, weird faces, psychedelic sex and antiwar slogans. "They may not even think it's a plane. Some prehistoric monster with its genitals hanging out." Mark flies back to L.A., and the foregathered police kill him without warning.

Daria hears of Mark's death over the car radio, in between the rock music she keeps listening to. She stops in front of some totemic cactuses but cannot weep. She arrives at Lee's superranch-style house curving around a mountainside boulder. It is Frank Lloyd Wright on the outside, and frankly wrong inside, full of vulgar furniture and bibelots. By the pool, sleek young women gossip. In a grotto, Daria steps under a spray of water and cries for Mark. Inside the house, Lee and some businessmen bicker about the proposed Sunny Dunes housing development here. Daria watches through the plate glass, horrified. Lee spots her and directs her to her room. Instead, she starts driving away, but stops a short way off. She fingers the red nightshirt and steps out of the car. Looking back at Lee's house with loathing, she has another vision: the house explodes with a blast resembling an atom bomb's. Some half-dozen times the house blows up, seen from ever closer by, at last from almost inside the explosion.

Next, there is a series of slow-motion shots, showing the contents of the house and the poolside furniture floating through the blue air, like bacteria in a tinted preparation under a microscope. Exploding clothes, TV set, refrigerator, food, books, magazines, glide through the azure, led by such recognizable coryphées as Kellogg's K, Wonder Bread, Look magazine, an eviscerated fish, a chicken and a lobster in a doomsday ballet. Daria smiles and drives on into one of the most succulent sunsets ever photographed, the sun going down like a giant Sunkist orange oozing California orange juice all over the sky and screen.

If this signifies the end of a corrupt old society to be followed by a younger, better one, I wish it did not look quite so much like one of those billboards *Zabriskie Point* has been mockingly lingering over all along. Antonioni has made the one thing I would not have believed him capable of: a naïve film.

A thorough oversimplification of the American problem it is, a series of tendentious posters—sometimes very beautiful—that neither embody nor encourage speculation. The young activists, whether Black Panthers or white leopards, are aggrieved, victimized, and assassinated by a police that treats them at best with cold cynicism, at worst with murderous hatred. Now there may be a good deal of truth in this, but in order for it to work artistically, it has to be made at least dramatic, and preferably also believable. There is not a decent gesture or word out of any cop here; the least offensive reaction from one of them is the dumb amazement of the highway patrolman who finds Daria seemingly alone in the desert. But even this fellow has a glint in his eye and may be revolving in his head, while the camera executes a circular pan around the godforsaken landscape, a quick tumble in the dust with the defenseless girl.

It is the unhappy gunhappiness of the cops that is their salient feature. They shoot a Negro student because, as they shout to justify their act, he has a gun on him, though, quite clearly, he hasn't. They shoot Mark without warning because, beleaguered, he tries to ram one of the patrol cars with his landing plane. How, by the way, did that much police get to be lying in wait for him, as if by appointment? How can Mark, in all that pea soup, even find Los Angeles and the little airport? Why no bullet marks on the plane, no blood on Mark? It is as if in this scene, as in several others, only the nastiness mattered, and there was to be no concession to anything as vulgar as verismilitude.

These cops are also ignorant and dehumanizing. When a fellow they are busting gives his occupation as "associate professor of history," the recording policeman objects that this is too long and puts down "clerk." He would more likely have put down "professor" or "teacher," but that, for Antonioni and his scenarists, would be too nice. When the same policeman asks Mark for his name, and is given the *nom de guerre* "Karl Marx," he first has to ask how "Marx" is spelled and then enters the Christian name as "Carl." These oafs, clearly, don't even know the name of what they are fighting.

But other members of the Establishment—and, in this film, almost everyone who is not a student blends neatly into a dehumanized Establishment—are equally unsavory. Thus even the food-shop owner, who says he cannot give the unknown Mark a sandwich on credit, for then he would have to give one to all who ask, takes on a sinister coloration in this context, simply because his statement, though uttered in rational, unhostile tones, makes him less than a saint or character out of Saroyan. Although Lee (Rod Taylor) worries about Daria, we are made to feel this could not be concern for a mere human being, or even an employee, but only for a mistress who might prove unavailable to him and turn his impending trip into all work and no play, thus making him an even duller boy than he already is.

And that brings us to the elliptical editing that makes *Zabriskie Point* a duller, less affecting film than anything in the Antonioni canon. A great deal, for example, is not told us about the heroine of *Red Desert*, but at least her sickness is illustrated and explored in enough ways to achieve a certain dramatic validity and so confer on her a measure of interest and dignity. In *Blow-Up*, much is indicated only by the tiniest clues, and even those are not devoid of ambiguity; but at least they are there. Here, we do not know how Daria gets her job with Lee, what their exact relationship is, and if it is sexual, how much it means to either participant. Accordingly, it becomes impossible to assign any moral value, positive or negative, to the actions of either character toward the other, or to fit their relationship into the moral framework of the whole film. In *Zabriskie Point*, foreshortening becomes, all too often, crippling amputation.

There is a graver problem, too. Antonioni's previous feature films, starting with *Cronaca di un amore*, indeed even his short subjects, all have considerable social significance; *Zabriskie Point* is his first film to have political significance. Here we are no longer concerned with an alienated bourgeois society, stagnant, dispirited, despiritualized, and only spuriously alive in the areas of sex and pelf. Here we are contemplating the Movement, which fancies itself a revolution and may in fact be one—at least so it appears to Antonioni. But in a revolutionary context we need to know who the adversaries are, where exactly they stand, what they propose to do about each other, and how much humanity they are ultimately capable of.

In a merely social context, we can do with less information. Thus in *L'Avventura* we need not know whether Corrado and Giulia, the eternally sparring couple, will stay together, or whether Sandro and Claudia will ever get married. Married or unmarried, these people merely have the choice, not even of different circles in hell, only of this or that *bolgia* within the same circle. In a political context, however, in a revolution, we must know with how much feeling a given combatant is endowed, for it is ultimately on the degree of his humanity that *we* must judge him, whatever other criteria history may choose to invoke.

Antonioni seems to take the superiority of the young over their elders for granted. The guilt of the adults is meant to be self-evident from their surroundings: chrome-and-glass offices crammed full of computers, closed-circuit television, telephones, dictaphones, control panels, gadgets—circumstantial evidence, perhaps, but not quite enough for the judicious viewer to pass judgment. Antonioni the pamphleteer, the poster-maker, the agit-prop filmmaker wins out over Antonioni the artist.

There is, for instance, a magnificent shot of Lee enthroned behind his desk in a glass office that Antonioni had specially built on top of a skyscraper. The shot is from the floor, diagonally up the tycoon's legs, past the control panel under the top of his dolmen of a desk, up along, still diagonally, the complacently backward-leaning figure, then out through the plate-glass window, where an American flag battens on the breeze, and beyond that to a swarthy, neo-Moorish office tower. There was intense blue light on the actor (its heat, I am told, almost unbearable), to create the same steely blue within as without. The angle and the palette are those of El Greco, and the whole thing looms chill, gaunt, and gigantic in the camera's slightly astigmatic eye.

Such an image, for all its artistry, is dishonest because it tries to tell through a single picture what can be shown honestly only through a series of dramatic images and words. In short, through an action. There are times when one picture's speaking louder than a thousand words functions to the artist's detriment: a political argument must persuade through its cogency, not through its loudness. What is more persuasive about the film is the skill and obsessiveness with which it records the various forms of advertising that dominate the scene, from billboards to TV commercials, from colossal papier-mâché figures to slogans on the backs of taxicabs. Here the repetitions and juxtapositions begin to make a case, except that the concept of California (or America) as one vast gallery hung with stationary and mobile advertisements had become a bit of a commonplace even before Antonioni.

When it comes to making his young people eminently lovable, Antonioni is rather at a loss for adequate images. We wonder why Daria, the free spirit, the happy-go-lucky flower child, should so quickly and easily become the mistress of a tycoon who must stand for everything she abhors. All Antonioni can do is simply not show us how it happened. To depict Mark and Daria's immediate mutual attraction, the best he can manage is to have the kids meet cute—indeed, supercute.

Their antics in the desert are no more convincing than their air-to-ground courtship, and their dialogue, poorly post-synced, sounds stilted and is delivered without conviction. The histrionic insufficiency of both youngsters (Daria Halprin and Mark Frechette), the sloppy plotting and writing, the overuse of zoom and telephoto lenses, the obtrusion of film clips from the San Francisco State demonstrations in the middle of staged sequences in Los Angeles—such things make it hard for us to care about Daria's conversion from flower-childishness to supposititious activism, yet that, if anything, is what the film is about.

Nobody, however, changes noticeably in this film, even if some shadows come to gesticulate a little differently. Mark may pick up a gun, and Daria may blow up a house or a whole society in her mind, but if these paper cut-outs flutter in slightly different directions, does that mean development of character? Antonioni loves these young ones, presumably for private, sentimental reasons to which he is entitled; but that he should expect us to fall for them, to share his undramatized predilection is an act of pure hubris. What Antonioni has made here—whether deliberately or unconsciously, I cannot say—is a Godard film.

Just as in Godard, we get billboards and slogans, zeroing in on bits of lettering, visual puns, characters hurtling from one gratuitous act to the next, the camera zooming off somewhere for no particular reason (say, onto an escarpment at the far end of Death Valley), storytelling and editing so elliptical that characterization is jettisoned, omission of key details (did Mark shoot that policeman or didn't he?), coincidences and illogic rampant, reveling in revolution and destruction. Pauline Kael has rightly likened the relish in those final explosions (the house, I have been informed by better mathematicians than myself, blows up thirteen times and is shot by seventeen cameras) to Vittorio Mussolini's notorious comparison of Italian bombs dropping on Ethiopia, as seen from the air, to roses unfurling in full bloom. There is a nastiness here, a glee in destruction, unearned by what the film has been able to demonstrate; though this does not quite reach Godardian proportions, it is nevertheless similar in kind.

Now it is perfectly all right for an outsider like Antonioni to make a film about America, but he is then unwise to ignore the advantage in telling the story from the privileged position of an observant foreigner. To try to tell it from inside out, as Antonioni does, is courting disaster, most promptly perceptible in such verbal infelicities as Daria's remark to Lee about not digging work, only digging it when she needs bread. Or take Mark's flatfooted comment after the sexual act, "I always knew it would be like this." In itself, that would be merely banal; following upon Daria's vision of scores of copulating couples, the line elicited giggles from audiences and had to be cut well after the film was released.

So it goes when a movie has two Italian scenarists, Antonioni and his *fidus Achates,* Tonino Guerra; an English one, Clare Peplo, Antonioni's girl friend; and two very different American ones, Fred Gardner and Sam Shepard. Gardner is a former *Ramparts* journalist, an expert on campus activism and the Movement; Sam Shepard is a leading avant-garde playwright whose vision is extremely idiosyncratic.

Zabriskie Point represents the uncoordinated thrashings of this disparate quintet. Yet the problem goes beyond that of too many cooks: it is a case of cinematic language and spoken language not meshing, indeed contradicting each other. Antonioni's filmic style is complex and overpowering, whereas the dialogue tries hard to be swinging, loose, cool. Thus for Mark to explain the purloined plane with an offhand "I just needed to get off the ground" is to undercut the sophistication of the filmmaking, and to undercut it to no meaningful, artistically expressive purpose. The dialogue is even worse, though, when it tries to be poetic, as when Daria exclaims, " 'So anyway' ought to be one word—the name of some place or river, Soanyway River." I doubt that in Italian Antonioni would have let that pass.

There remains, on the credit side, Antonioni's way with his camera, although Alfio Contini, his new cinematographer, strikes me as less gifted than some of his predecessors. (I say this on the further evidence of *The Libertine,* also shot by Contini.) There are some overwhelming images here—as well as others that are overdone or just ordinary. Let us examine three beautiful ones.

Having just heard the radio announcement of Mark's death, Daria stands with her back to the camera in front of some giant cactuses. There is a wind, and in it all kinds of lesser vegetation jiggles and writhes around those colossi; they, however, tower immobile like a living Stonehenge, a green monument to imperturbability and survival. Or take a mere shot of a trash can at the airfield: a yellow can inscribed with "NO OIL PLEASE" in large red letters, while the background of hangars and sky is all gray or grayish blue. The colors and composition here are worthy of a painting by Morandi, and as quietly instinct with atmosphere.

Atmosphere of a different kind is achieved in the scene in the bar of the little desert town where Daria looks for her elusive guru. The faces, conversations and silences; the rhythm of the small incidents and smaller talk—funny, peevish, disquieting—in fluid juxtaposition; all this supremely evokes some typical corner of America, some ultimate cranny of loneliness. The imagery and mood here are strongly suggestive of Edward Hopper, particularly at the conclusion of the scene, when Daria's car spurts out of the frame and the camera passes through a window to linger for the last time on an old-timer seated at the bar, craggily staring beyond his glass of beer into a future that does not exist.

Although this failure of *Zabriskie Point* is dispiriting, it is hardly an excuse for the yelping and growling horde of currish reviews that have been sinking their teeth into Antonioni's ankles. It is as if the artistic failure of the film were compounded by a foreigner's presuming to sit in judgment over us, which, heaven knows, is his right as much as anyone else's. The fact that this judgment is made in clichés is probably more apparent to us than to him, and to non-American viewers it may seem much more pertinent and revealing than we would surmise. This does not make *Zabriskie Point* a valid work of art, or a valid view of the United States, but studying it may shed some light at least on why Americans look so deceptively like ugly Americans even at home.

What is probably most disconcerting about the film is the absence of the Antonioni look, so unmistakable since his Trilogy. A young German critic suggests that the desert sequences look like an Italian western; some of the L.A. shots remind me uncomfortably of Demy's *The Model Shop;* and much, as I said, is Godard. And a Godard film we do not even need from Godard, let alone from a master like Antonioni.

March, 1970

FELLINI SATYRICON

Fellini Satyricon is barely satiric and a huge con. This adaptation of Petronius's first-century novel has had its title extended to *Fellini Satyricon* in order to distinguish it from a "cheapie" *Satyricon,* quickly thrown together in Italy to cash in on this film's prestige. The new title happily also distinguishes it from Petronius's delightful book, of which it is a thoroughgoing vulgarization and subversion. In fact, without having seen the cheapie, I take it to differ from this dearie only by its less lavish vulgarities.

For the umpteenth time, then, let me say that the film adaptation of a classic, be it the Bible, *Madame Bovary,* or *Huckleberry Finn,* has grave difficulties whether it tries to be faithful or not. If it stays close to the original, it finds the fictional devices unassimilable or only awkwardly translatable into film; if it takes liberties, it ends up, being usually made by lesser men than Flaubert or Mark Twain, proportionately inferior to the original. First-rate cinematic talents tend not to bother with adaptations. Fellini, too, was once a first-rate filmmaker; in those days he made *The White Sheik* and *I Vitelloni,* and left Petronius alone.

This is no place for a detailed analysis of what the Roman patrician, epicurean, and *elegantiae arbiter* at Nero's court has done in his book (or, rather, may have done, for what remains is somewhere between a sixth and a tenth of the work). But even from the surviving fragments we recognize the operation of a witty, skeptical, critical and, above all, fastidious mind. Although the book deals with assorted unwholesome and unappetizing matters, its tone admirably eschews both the porcine and the priggish. Petronius must have been as amused as he was repelled by the things he describes. I imagine him as an ironic aristocrat who, in pursuit of his varied sexual pleasures, came into contact with a variety of low-life characters and observed their menial machinations with the same artistic detachment with which he noted the more ambitious vices of the rich and exalted.

What is clear from the remnants of the work is that, despite its picaresque and episodic character, it had structure and cohesion, and that, along with the larger satirical social canvas, it provided well-developed, precise character studies of its principal personages. It is thus absurd to claim, as some have done, that Fellini has been faithful to the original by fragmenting his film and making the transitions between scenes brusque and confusing. He has been faithful to the termites of time that have gnawed away large chunks of the work— not to the work itself.

The main difference between Petronius and Fellini is that the former was telling a story with a subtly understated moral purpose, whereas the latter has pasted together a number of sensationalistic images, and even if you should admire them visually (as I do not), you cannot begin to guess what they are meant to say—if indeed they mean to say anything. On the rare occasions when Fellini follows the book, he does it in an outrageously splashy, *nouveau riche* fashion, as if a new millionaire's wife were wearing all her jewelry at once, including some on parts of the body better left unadorned. If, for example, Petronius writes, "I saw, as if through a fog, Giton standing at the far end of a street," Fellini constructs a whole surreal set, something halfway between giant baths and an enormous cloaca, swathes it in real (well, mock-real) mist, and thinks he has created a powerful image. Actually, it is Petronius who created an image. When, exhausted by the search for his beloved, Encolpius finally sees him, it is as if through a fog that has descended on the perfectly ordinary street—the wear and tear of frustrated love casts a pall on an everyday street scene. To make the setting extraordinary and the fog seemingly real, however, is to miss the point and merely indulge one's infantile fantasies.

Consider a typical episode: Encolpius and Giton on Captain Lichas's ship. In the novel, it is a realistic but complicated set of relationships involving Lichas, Tryphaena, Encolpius, and Giton in a tangle of contradictory loves, jealousies, and hates. In the film, decor and situations are gratuitously weird: the ships are out of Bosch or Leonardo's fantastic drawings; Lichas defeats Encolpius in a creepy wrestling match, and then, though in this version married to Tryphaena, proceeds to wed him in accord with Roman ritual. But it is the beefy Lichas who assumes the role of the bride, with the traditional bright saffron veil, and Alain Cuny makes her—him—a new but unsavory dish of mincing beef.

When, during this shipboard episode, Petronius has the sailors hunting fish with their tridents, Fellini has them hauling on board with pulleys a huge, monstrous fish. Like so much in the film, it has no structural function whatever. But there was that closing scene in *La dolce vita* with the enormous ray, to which this creature may be a fishily self-serving *hommage*.

In the introduction to his 1566 translation of *The Golden Ass*, the other famous Roman novel, William Adlington wrote: "I trust that the matter shall be esteemed by such as not only delight to please their fancies in recording the same, but also take a pattern thereby to regenerate their minds from brutal and beastly custom." Fellini not only delights to please his fancies in recording them without any care for pattern, moral or otherwise; he sinks deeper, clearly delighting in brutal and beastly customs. The lupanars of Petronius are sordid and sometimes comic; the Fellini bordellos are vast, surreal, full of quaint, exotic sights that are meant to tickle and fascinate. Fellini the artist always had a showman inside him dying to get out, but low budgets and fidelity to his early experiences kept Fellini from letting the showman get the upper hand. Now given complete freedom, the showman avenges himself by keeping the artist locked in.

Fellini Satyricon is a giant magpie's nest: bits of literature, art, information lifted from all over and tossed into this lengthy film; but disparate shards, however artfully or artlessly scrambled, do not arrange themselves into a single, original vision. There was a splendid chance here for filling in the lacunas with appropriately picaresque episodes Fellini and his co-scenarist, Bernardino Zapponi, could have invented. The basic structure is there. Encolpius, a young loafer living by his bisexual wits, hires himself out to men and women alike, stealing as well as taking from them. His traveling companion and true love is the pretty young boy Giton, who is already as much of an all-around whore as his lover. Another young idler, Ascyltus, of much the same moral persuasion, is picked up by Encolpius for a little sex one night in a park; a traveling trio is formed, and now Ascyltus too wants Giton. Encolpius is the handsomer and more thoughtful of the two rivals, but Ascyltus is tougher and endowed with an enormous organ that enables him to make people and influence friends. He thus influences Giton into leaving with him, all the more easily because Encolpius is pursued by the heavy ire of Priapus, the licentious god whom he has in some way offended. Priapus has taken away his potency, and Encolpius can satisfy nobody: lover, beloved, or himself. Though Giton prefers Ascyltus, Encolpius abducts him, and they escape in the company of Eumolpus, an aging and unsuccessful poet, with a chip on his shoulder, a verbose song on his lips, and knavery in his heart. The Encolpius-Giton relationship has in it the seeds of all those great future fictional affairs in which an older lover, insanely jealous of his young and fickle beloved, nevertheless makes up continuous excuses for the flighty creature, literally begging to be hoodwinked.

Out of their adventures, both extant and to be filled in, a lovely film could have been made. Take, for example, Petronius's tale of Philomela, the woman who prostitutes her young son and daughter to Eumolpus, posing as a rich man who might make her his heir. The former Fellini would have turned this into a rollicking, ghastly, hilarious episode; the new Fellini simply omits it. Instead, we are given pointless sequences such as the one about the albino hermaphrodite, worshiped as a demigod in a dark cave by the sick and crippled who hope to be cured by him. A brutish soldier, with the help of Ascyltus and Encolpius, abducts him; in a desert, the creature dies of thirst, the abductors have at one another, and the two youths finally manage to kill the soldier. Besides alluding to phony-miracle scenes in *Cabiria* and *La dolce vita,* the sequence accomplishes nothing, does not fit into the scheme of things, and sheds no new light on the main characters.

Fellini and Zapponi pilfer from everywhere. The suicide of the unnamed patrician and his wife (how Lucia Bosè has lost her looks!) is clearly derived from Tacitus's account of the death of Petronius, with a little of Sienkiewicz's *Quo Vadis* thrown in. As a tragic episode, and irrelevant, too, it is doubly jarring here. While the patrician is bleeding to death, his wife utters the two first lines of Hadrian's famous epigram on his own departing soul: so truncated and misapplied, they lose all meaning. The laughing audience watching Encolpius's combat with the Minotaur (a particularly unmotivated and foolish episode) and celebrating the festival of the god Mirth is filched from the fourth book of Apuleius's *Golden Ass,* where, however, it is properly integrated. The threatened casting of Eumolpus into Trimalchio's blazing ovens seems derived from the torturing of the Christian boy in De Mille's *Sign of the Cross.* Even the artwork on various walls is scavenged from diverse sources and carefully scrambled: Pompeian frescoes, mosaics from the Naples Museum, Picasso's *Tauromachy* crossbred with cave drawings, Persian miniatures blown up to mural size, cuneiform inscriptions, and what have you.

Anachronism pops up now and then: a ship has radar, an art gallery features a doubledecker minibus that whisks jaded visitors through it, a character suddenly talks German for no reason. There is a Babel of tongues throughout the film: Italian, both high and low; Latin, often with a German accent; Greek; and a number of non-Indo-European languages, some perhaps invented. The macaronic dialogue dislocates us to no good purpose—we knew all along that the ancient world was as heterogeneous as ours. But worse than needless anachronism is a kind of setting or situation outside any time and place, with no dramatic or psychological justification.

Such a scene is the one at the outdoor bath where our heroes stop on the way to Trimalchio's dinner. There were, of course, no such baths: a large, irregularly shaped pool in the middle of an arid plain, and around it a burning forest of man-sized tapers. In the pool, scores of naked men and women, tightly packed, jumping up and down in unison, and uttering pointless exclamations. It is all photographed with red gelatins, to yield a facile garishness. By the pool, vaguely sexual activities are in progress, but the scene has no profile. Sexuality is thrown in throughout as part of the ambience; thus during a tracking shot we might catch sight briefly in the background of men watching two nude girls, side by side on all fours, wiggling their arses in unison. It is not sexy, funny, sensational, or even decadent, but it is typical of the puerile sexuality of the film.

Sex takes quite a beating in *Fellini Satyricon.* It is always either ludicrous or horrible, and if it is at all passionate, it is pederastic. This is not so in Petronius, where Circe's infatuation with Encolpius, and the youth's ardent but vain efforts to regain his potency with her, have a genuine serio-comic urgency. Nothing like that in the film, where women, if they are not already old, ugly, obese, or sick, behave in a fashion to make them repellent. The exception is an enchanting slave girl who seems part Oriental and part Negro, and is played by Hylette Adolphe. She runs around in exquisite seminudity and burbles away deliciously in some strange shlurpy language. This lovely innocent, too, is thrust into a troilist relationship with Ascyltus and Encolpius.

The other women are all racked with lust or blood lust. There is the sleek witch who is cursed with quite literal fire between her thighs (Petronius once uses this as a metaphor); there is the raving, ravaged nymphomaniac who has to be carted about spreadeagled and tied with thongs to the four corners of her wagon, to be mounted by any passing male who can be pressed into service; there is the overripe matron who lies in the middle of the arena waiting to be satisfied by Encolpius before a throng of circus-goers; there is the idiotic wife of Trimalchio and the cruel one of Lichas; and so on *ad nauseam.* Only love among men is allowed some little dignity.

Even the continuity is faulty. After we have seen the nymphomaniac tied to her cart by leather straps, we get a closeup of a single wrist bound with a rope. After we have seen, in closeup, the corpse of the hermaphrodite decompose into what seems to be melting lemon sherbet, a long shot shows him in one piece again. And I defy anyone to give a coherent account of Ascyltus's death as cut, or chopped, by Fellini—this despite the fact that his editor was the excellent Ruggero Mastroianni. But, then, the cinematography of the no less excellent Giuseppe Rotunno has likewise been forced into what I can best describe as visual noise.

There is little room for acting in such a film: besides the usual dubbing there is the drubbing of the actors by the *mise en scène.* Surprisingly, Martin Potter manages to make something almost human out of Encolpius, and, as Eumolpus, Salvo Randone also has a good moment or two. Hiram Keller, a graduate of Broadway's *Hair,* plays Ascyltus with a histrionic range extending from leers to sneers. Max Born's Giton is a greasy imp, and Mario Romagnoli, the popular Roman restaurateur who plays Trimalchio, should have stayed in his *trattoria*. The women, as already noted, have even less of a chance.

The randomness of the film is typified by the scene in which a young emperor stabs himself before being run through by his legions. There's no such thing in Petronius, and Nero, who was to die somewhat similarly, was no boy. But it gives Tanya Lopert, the mannish daughter of Fellini's former American distributor, a chance to make a perfectly gratuitous appearance.

What has Fellini wrought? He himself said in an interview with Alberto Moravia—in which the fatuity of the answers is surpassed only by that of the questions—that he eliminated history from his film, leaving only "an immense tableau vivant whose meaning eludes us." I suggest to Fellini, to whom I also award the title of *arbiter inelegantiae*, that one cannot, as a filmmaker, eliminate history. But one can be eliminated by it.

A subsequent review, written for The New York Times:

Petronius's *Satyricon* was about something. There were real people in it; relationships which, though farcical, mattered because they involved genuine feelings; and there was a plot. Encolpius the drifter's love for Giton, the young bisexual whore, and his rivalry over him with the stronger Ascyltus, is a sort of homosexual Roman "Lolita," pathetic as well as ludicrous, and, above all, recognizably human.

The rats of time have nibbled away at this first-century novel, and we are left with its decimated bones. But better that than the bonemeal *Fellini Satyricon* has ground them into, the better to fling them in our eyes. There is no excuse for the chaotic magpie's nest Fellini has made of the work, depriving it of any meaningful structure, tossing into it garbled bits of literature, history, art history, languages from ancient Greek to modern German, obviously self-serving allusions to his own earlier films—everything out of whack, topsy-turvy and gratuitous—unless astounding the bourgeoisie can be called a valid motive.

Most of all, Fellini has dumped into the film his dreams. And what an uninteresting lot of dreams they are: a stage production in which a hand is really chopped off, a slave ship whose captain, dressed up as the bride, forces the young hero to marry him; a combat with a Minotaur who turns out to be a neo-Steve Reeves in a bull mask; a Roman emperor who is a woman in drag stabbing himself before his legions perforate him; a nymphomaniac who is dragged about tied spreadeagled to her cart and for whom her husband has to round up studs; an albino hermaphrodite, supposed to be a demigod but, when abducted, dying of thirst in the desert. Now such things may sound interesting on paper, but they are not so in the film, where they are situations in search of a development, wisps of plot lacking even the consistency of a specter.

They are, in fact, random images dredged up from Fellini's subconscious (significantly, none of them has an analogue in Petronius) and left unexplored, unintegrated, unfinished. It would be good if Fellini, and others like him, realized that undigested dreams, the raw material of the unconscious, do not make telling works of art. Because, paradoxically, they are less varied than reality, even invented reality. The fantasies of lust and blood lust are always desperately similar to one another (hence also the boredom of pornography) because the human unconscious—Jung, it would seem, was right—is not really individuated. It spews up images of carnality, violence, fear and frustration that have a way of being interchangeable with everybody else's. It is only on the level of conscious, analyzed, shaped art-making that the differentiation, the form-giving, the stamp of originality is achieved.

A typical such dream scene has a large number of guests, midway to Trimalchio's feast, stopping off to jump up and down in his big, weirdly shaped swimming pool in the middle of nowhere. A forest of tall tapers is burning alongside the pool; the naked men and women are in separate groups but bouncing about in unison; the whole scene is shot in red monochrome for added creepiness. While some of the main characters are lolling around poolside in vaguely sexual activities, the bodies inside are intoning an inscrutable chant. All around, there is a desert landscape, and nothing happens. Now why did everybody jump on Antonioni's desert love fiesta in *Zabriskie Point,* whereas nobody attacked this equally clumsy and even more irrelevant scene in *Fellini Satyricon?* Because, I suppose, Fellini's film is so set up that nobody expects it to make sense; it is all one vast sexless but subliminally titillating orgy of idle, meaningless image-mongering. Because the whole thing just washes over you, you don't worry if any one part won't wash.

But there is also intellectual pretension. For no reason at all, in the middle of the tomfoolery, we are to get a quick whiff of high tragedy. A patrician and his wife are about to commit suicide so as not to fall into the barbarians' paws. With infinite tenderness (or what Fellini here takes to be that) they bid adieu to their children, off to relatives; their slaves, off to freedom. Then they sit down to a last frugally elegant meal, the husband opening his veins, the wife reciting the Emperor Hadrian's epigram, which he improvised on his departing soul, and thereupon stabbing herself. Now there are elements in this demise taken from the death of Petronius, as reported by Tacitus. But turn to the historian's account (it is reproduced, for example, in the Penguin Petronius) and you will see how much fuller, more humane, bittersweet rather than tragic yet ultimately piercing an exit-scene from life it is, to which Fellini's pyrotechnics cannot hold a Roman candle.

And why should the wife be reciting the first two lines of Hadrian's poetic farewell? It was written a century later, it very clearly belongs to Hadrian, and the first two lines without the remaining three barely make a point. Worse yet, though it is fine for Hadrian to patronize his "errant, flattering little soul," it is hardly fitting for a loving wife to make light of her beloved husband's parting breath. So what is the whole scene doing in this context? Showing off Fellini's, and Zapponi the co-scenarist's, homework in Classics 12B.

What about the famous "visuals," the ultimate defense of idiot movies that have nothing to say, as if films were children that should be seen but not heard? The first point here is that, although film is a visual medium, it is also, like it or not, an aural one, and even visually we have every right to demand from it something more than treating human beings as if they were so many Albers squares to be arranged according to size and color. Whatever one may think of the merit of pure abstraction in painting, to treat flesh and blood, the human face and body merely as a unit in a color scale, an oval or triangle to be fitted into an abstract composition, is to join, however tacitly, the vast antilife movement, the often quasi-liberal processes of dehumanization rampant in the world. Art had better chop off its arm than lend a hand to this movement. Fellini's film is full of grotesque, overpainted faces, veritable physiognomic palimpsests; misconceived torsos and pointlessly preening behinds; drooping bosoms for which this unnecessary exposure is just another flattening blow.

Yet all this might be pardonable if it were meant to arouse our dormant sensualities to newer, friskier life. But not at all: these visual anaphrodisiacs are meant to freeze the blood in our organs—without, however, proposing any alternative vision. The men in the film are all either asexual or homosexual—which would be all right if homosexual love were treated with sympathy as well as irony, as Petronius treated it; but Fellini makes it all just swishy-washy. The women, except for one or two figures that scarcely register, are all ravening predators or coarse-fibered dolts. Yet even such jaundiced views might serve some satirical purpose if only there were genuine wit here, or some real vision other than Panavision, or whatever the wide-screen process might be, used here to express the narrowest views. The very continuity is slovenly, illustrative of Fellini's haphazardly improvisatory filmmaking. Leather thongs binding a woman become, in closeup, ropes; a body decomposing in closeup, emerges in a subsequent long shot recomposed.

There is much more to be said about this unhappy film, part of the gradual decomposition of what was once one of the greatest talents in film history. Neither what I have said here, nor other things I discussed in my *New Leader* column, can exhaust the issue. But *Fellini Satyricon* strikes me as a gimcrack, shopworn nightmare.

March–May, 1970

THE MISSISSIPPI MERMAID

François Truffaut's *The Mississippi Mermaid (La Sirène du Mississippi)* was greeted both here and abroad with almost unanimous displeasure. On the whole, I agree that this particular siren can be easily resisted. Truffaut makes two kinds of movies: a kind that is autobiographical, or at least fraught with autobiographical implications, and generally good; and a kind that emulates one of his masters, Hitchcock, in plot and supposed supense, and is, generally, bad. The last of the second kind, *The Bride Wore Black*, was so foolish as to be intensely embarrassing; *Mermaid* is almost equally preposterous, yet I found it rather less dislikable.

The Mississippi Mermaid is based on a thriller by the same American writer who, under a different pseudonym, wrote *The Bride Wore Black;* and Truffaut's screenplay once again changes the novel's locale besides taking other liberties. Louis Mahé, a rich tobacco manufacturer on Réunion Island, a French possession in the Indian Ocean, poses as his own employee and gets himself a mail-order bride, Julie Roussel. She turns out to be quite different from and much prettier than her picture, which she explains by having been too shy to send her own photograph. This already is absurd: Belmondo needing a mail-order bride? And even though Julie turns out to be an impostor (her lover, with her assistance, killed the real Julie on shipboard), the idea of Catherine Deneuve as someone who could even pass for a mail-order bride passes understanding.

The rest of the film concerns Mahé's furious pursuit of Julie, who robs him of a fortune, and how vengefulness turns into abject adoration. The pair end up living together after he rescues her from a cheap dancehall, the fortune having ended up with her former lover, now serving a long prison term for cop-killing. But Mahé, too, is driven to kill the very private detective whom he himself hired to find Julie, and all this for a girl who, when they are hunted by the police and all the money is gone, starts slowly feeding rat poison to him.

We now come to the grand Truffaldian climax. Earlier, when Mahé tried to shoot the faithless, thieving cheat, she urged him on—life no longer meant anything to her. Whereupon Mahé discovered the strength of his love and chose to continue the marriage. Now he finds that she has lied once again for the sake of the money he could still raise by selling his tobacco factory. It is his turn to tell her he loves her so much he doesn't care if she kills him, if that is what she wants. Things come full circle: this time it is Marion (that is her real name; she was orphaned and had a terrible childhood that made her tough and whorish) who seems overcome by the man's love. She announces that she has at last learned the meaning of love and wants nothing more than to live with Louis. She discontinues the rat poison diet, and through a snowy landscape they flee toward Switzerland. Will they make it? Will they be happy or has Marion been lying yet again?

It sounds corny, and so it is. The theme, to be sure, was a favorite in French literature even before it reached its apogee in Proust. It is the story of Manon and des Grieux, but the film lacks the simple unself-consciousness of Prévost's narrative; it is the tale of Carmen and Don José, but the film lacks the brutal honesty of Merimée's ending, to say nothing of the sheer passion the novel generates. *Mermaid* comes closest, perhaps, to Pierre Louÿs's *Woman and Puppet,* out of which von Sternberg made a campy, overrated film with Marlene Dietrich, and Julien Duvivier a flabby and flavorless one with Brigitte Bardot.

The idea of turning an essentially spineless spine-chiller into a passionate and tender film, using the mystery story only as a pretext (as Truffaut so successfully did in his earlier and very fine *Shoot the Piano Player*) is an attractive one. If your actors are Belmondo and Deneuve, though, you are beaten before you begin. Belmondo can act—in films like *Two Women, Monkey in Winter,* and *La Viaccia,* he has made this clear. But he needs a stronger script, a more eloquent part, or just a better partner. In any case, he is not a great enough actor to turn dross into gold. Mlle Deneuve can portray a cool clotheshorse with a schoolgirl emotion or two very nicely, as in *La Chamade;* beyond that her histrionic pittance will not stretch.

The love scenes between Belmondo and Deneuve could not ignite a leaky gasoline tank, but oh what a younger Edwige Feuillère, Jeanne Moreau, or Simone Signoret—even opposite Belmondo, and still more opposite Gérard Philipe—could have done for this film! Up to a point, anyway, for the banalities and absurdities finally are too thick. As things stand, Truffaut does best with some lighter touches, such as Deneuve stripping on a forest road and driving a passing motorist to the point of not being able to see either the forest or the trees he drives into. Or, again, the scene in which Belmondo hides Deneuve's panties in his shirtfront and turns the search for them into an aphrodisiac game ending with both him and her (though not simultaneously) getting into her pants.

There is frequent evidence of a fine director in control. Thus there are good camera movements, effective without calling undue attention to themselves. Notice how the scene in which Mahé awaits his bride at the dock of the steamer Mississippi (hence the unconvincing title) is built up. Observe the suspense Truffaut can get out of whether a girl getting off the boat is or isn't Julie. Consider the tempos of the film. The whole first part in Réunion Island is really exposition to be gotten over with as quickly as possible. Truffaut succeeds in maintaining a breakneck pace. Without however neglecting a certain amount of local color and minimal yet effective characterization of such minor characters as Julie's sister and Mahé's business adviser. It is harder to determine whether the small part of the private eye is Truffaut's achievement—for it is a gem—or that of Michel Bouquet, an actor who can insinuate his subversive charm into any role.

Denys Clerval's color cinematography is competent, but all that can be said for Antoine Duhamel's score is that it is used with economy —though here parsimony would have been even better. Mlle Deneuve gets in, as usual, an Yves St.-Laurent wardrobe, and the two were clearly made for each other. If one cared to descend into triviality— and a film like this will drive one to it—one could speculate on the contributions of certain *couturiers* to the images of certain stars: St.-Laurent's to Deneuve's, Chanel's to Delphine Seyrig's, Givenchy's to Audrey Hepburn's, and Cardin's to Jeanne Moreau's. Whichever way you slice it, *Mermaid* is a trivial film, but it does reveal one formerly hidden, or partly hidden, talent: Mlle Deneuve's bosom, which turns out to be very much better than the previously exposed square shoulders and somewhat wilted cube of a behind would have led one to expect.

April, 1970

RIDER ON THE RAIN

Fighting off age is the problem of that once remarkable director, René Clément. Ever since his inspiration left him, the maker of *Forbidden Games* has shuttled between a few commercial ventures (only one of which, *Purple Noon,* succeeded even on its own terms) and long periods of silence. Now he has come up with the most Hitchcockian of thrillers, *Rider on the Rain,* and reviewers have rushed in with hosannas for paradise regained.

The film can certainly compete with Hitchcock in some respects, but that is no unalloyed blessing. It means preponderance of plot and technique at the expense of everything else. Indeed, the characters in this screenplay by Sébastien Japrisot do not nearly make sense—beginning with a rapist who lets his victim become untied after the rape, hangs around the house for not even a crazy reason, and allows a rackful of guns to stand there waiting for the victim's reprisal. True, he is a madman; but he is also quite smart enough to elude an expert pursuer. That sleuth is a U. S. Army colonel in civvies who finds it necessary to pose as a sadistic blackmailer to get the truth out of a mere housewife, and, naturally, ends up falling in love with her.

And there is the housewife herself, gentle as a dove and hard as nails, too frightened to make a call to the police or simply confess her victimization to her husband, but quite ready to walk unaccompanied into a Parisian crime den, full of gangsters and prostitutes. Add to this weird coincidences and calamitous misunderstandings enough for Dumas père to stretch out into a tetralogy, and you have as hokey a thriller as can come from the crassest of Hitchcock imitators, in whose ranks we must include the maker of *Topaz* and *Torn Curtain* himself.

Yet Clément does manage individual scenes quite nicely, and there is an intermittent density of texture and atmosphere in the film. But there is also that carelessness which permits the heroine to be raped in the nude, only to be seen, in the aftermath, dragging herself about with a pathetically half-fallen stocking on one leg. Again, the U. S. colonel, played by Charles Bronson with his customary beefy cuteness, speaks the most flawless literary French, yet pronounces it in the worst American tourist manner.

The subtitles add their own irresponsibilities, translating *"Et puis je m'en fiche"* ("What's more, I don't give a damn") as "And then I ran away." Marlène Jobert turns the heroine into a blob trying very hard to act pixieish, and makes me think back sadly to the glories of Danielle Darrieux and Micheline Presle in similar roles. At least Annie Cordy is good as the heroine's once wayward, now sober mother, and, in a small part, Jill Ireland is genuinely sexy. Andreas Winding's color cinematography is finely balanced; but I do long for Clément to try, once again, for something more.

June, 1970

7

Ingmar Bergman

INGMAR BERGMAN is, in my opinion, the truest, most self-sustaining, least exhaustible genius of the cinema. As Robin Wood notes in his monograph, "It is Bergman's distinction to have established himself as a great, and central, artist in an age peculiarly inimical to great art. His greatest quality is his capacity for development, which is also the drive towards the attainment of human fullness." No other filmmaker, as I see it, has achieved such fullness, which is both a variety—the continuing elaboration of themes and elucidation of problems; and a unity—the blending of all Bergman films into a sustained questioning of the universe, a heroic struggle to come up with a clearer understanding of the questions at least, where answers seem to be increasingly unobtainable. As Bergman's *oeuvre* evolves, we see at last that it is less fruitful to speak of echoes and parallels, to arrange the films into groups like the first and second trilogies (in the manner of Peter Cowie, for example), than to perceive all of them as a continuous structure, something midway between a Balzacian *comédie humaine* and a Proustian *recherche du temps perdu*.

To give only one example, but a basic one, Bergman is relentlessly concerned with opposing poles within two persons, or one and the same person, or simply within human nature. For these poles he has devised the symbols *A* and *E*. As early as in *Smiles of a Summer Night*, *A* and *E* (usually as self-contradictory as they are antithetical) appear as the irresponsible dilettante yet successful lawyer *E*german, and the imaginative, artistic actress yet also practical, purposive woman, Desirée *A*rmfeldt. In *The Magician*, whose proper title is *The Face*, *A* and *E* coalesce into the one person of Vogler, the doctor-hypnotist, both healer and quack, artist and charlatan, whose Christian names are Albert Emmanuel. In *The Silence,* the conflict is between two sisters, Anna and Ester, rivals for the affection of Anna's son. Anna is sensual, promiscuous, mindless; Ester, intellectual, artistic but with sterile, incestuous, and lesbian tendencies. In *Persona,* the situation becomes even more complex: the apparently profound yet devious actress, Elisabeth, and the seemingly straightforward yet troubled nurse, Alma, are each subdivided into two personalities, but, at crucial moments, both women merge into one, without, however, being able to achieve a stable fusion. And, finally—except that, happily, there is as yet no finis to Bergman's inquiry—in *A Passion, A* and *E* appear in reduplication as two interacting, entangled pairs, Anna and Andreas, Elis and Eva. Why *A* and *E?* I can hazard a guess: because they are the first two vowels of the alphabet, and vowels, unlike consonants, can have an independent verbal existence. But they are vowels that in Latin, German, Swedish, and other languages can be fused into another vowel or diphthong, "ae" or "ä."

In the four films discussed here, Bergman's most recent works, a gloomy world-view progressively darkens to the point of total hopelessness and despair. In *Shame,* a somewhat rickety but functioning marriage succumbs when the world itself goes mad with war: fragile cultural values, precarious individual relationships, cannot survive political chaos. But in *Hour of the Wolf,* though the setting is the same little island, there is no civil war and life could be idyllic and peaceful. Yet the marriage of Johan and Alma collapses from internal difficulties: the madness of the artist, tormented by private doubts and demons that drive him to his destruction. Between these films comes *Persona,* where the conflict is between two women, who are also the two sides of one woman and, perhaps, all women; and who, probably, further represent the clash of the creative, neurotic personality with the seemingly healthy and uncreative one. The love-hate of the two principals, though it yields a relationship both can, up to a point, feed on, does not produce mutual fulfillment, completion, rest. The bleakest view of all, however, is that of *A Passion,* in which the four principals—very different men and women—can find no happiness in a variety of relationships, both in and out of marriage. If you add Anna's dead husband and Andreas's wife who walked out on him, and consider all the interactions of this sextet, you are truly left with a sense of the impossibility of loving, of men and women as each other's doom.

It is with utmost interest that I await the further progress of Bergman's investigation of life; it is a measure of his greatness for me that he is the one filmmaker in the world whose concerns fully concern me. There may be a ray of hope in Bibi Andersson's monologue in *A Passion* in which she speculates, qua Bibi Andersson, about the future of Eva, the torn character she portrays: she assumes that through altruistic care for greater unfortunates than herself, Eva may find fulfillment. Is this a real hope or yet another chimera? If anyone can tell, it is Bergman, in his coming films.

PERSONA

After seeing Ingmar Bergman's *Persona* twice, I still cannot be sure that I understand it. What I am sure of, however, is that something difficult and elusive is struggling to gain form and recognition here; that, unlike in a film such as *Accident,* the complexity and obscurity are unavoidable, and not merely gratuitous mock-profundities. Never before on film has the derailed psyche been more penetratingly examined, never before has the drama been played so consistently beneath the surface, yet without the slightest sacrifice in palpable excitement. The whole film appears to be shot from inside out: the tormented and tormenting soul is not so much viewed as allowed to express its own views, to impress us with its awesomely human inhumanity.

The film begins with a mysterious sequence of unrelated images. Inside a projector, a film runs off the sprockets and an arc light sputters; scenes from old-fashioned cartoon and Keystone Kops comedy; inner organs being pulled from a sheep; a spider in extreme closeup; a nail being hammered into a hand; various winter landscapes, including a house with a snow-covered, spiky, wrought-iron fence. Then what seems to be a morgue: the sound of water (or formaldehyde?) dripping; an old man, a crone, a boy laid out and covered with sheets. A telephone rings. The boy curls up as in a womb, but is forced to awaken. He puts on glasses and starts reading *A Hero of Our Time.* A woman's face begins to appear to him, in and out of focus, on a translucent wall or screen. It is actually the blended face of two women, the heroines of the film about to begin. He stretches his hand toward the apparition, but her eyes close and she fades out.

Bergman himself has said about *Persona,* "On many points I am unsure, and in one instance, at least, I know nothing." There is a certain "subjectivity" or "arbitrariness" in the scenes included: "For this reason I invite the audience's fantasy to dispose freely of what I have put at its disposal." It seems to me that those initial images represent the pitifully limited efforts of art (film) to grasp reality; then diverse forms of fear, cruelty, loneliness, including the spider-God of Bergman's Trilogy. Then the final isolation, death—non-being out of which we are summoned into life. Again art (Lermontov) is to teach us how to live heroically, but unheroic we (bespectacled) reach out to the *Ewig-Weibliche*, mother or woman, for help. She eludes us; her eyes close in grief or exhaustion.

Persona concerns a young nurse, Alma, who is to look after Elisabet Vogler, a famous actress who has lapsed into absolute silence. A woman psychiatrist tells Alma that the patient's mind and body are perfectly sound, but that she simply stopped speaking after a performance of *Electra*. Different explanations suggest themselves. We see Mrs. Vogler in her hospital room in anguish as she watches on the TV screen a Buddhist monk's fiery self-immolation—what is the death of one Agamemnon to the horror of Vietnam? From a letter from Elisabet's husband that Alma reads out loud to her, we learn that something has gone deeply wrong with that marriage. As emerges from an admonitory speech of the woman doctor, Elisabet may simply be essaying yet another role: finding it impossible to be real, she prefers to sham muteness. Thus her condition may be caused by the inflamed world, the cooling of the flesh, or by an artful devil within, a devil connected with her art.

That Elisabet is to be taken as a symbol of the artist is confirmed by the fact that she is called Vogler (i.e., fowler) like the hero of Bergman's *The Magician*, who more manifestly embodies the artist. Like Vogler in that film, she, too, is first seen in a black wig (for Electra) and then in her natural blonde hair. Like the Magician, Elisabet is an equivocal figure: there is good but also considerable falsity in her. And her silence is evil—just as in Berman's *The Silence*, noncommunication, however innocent-seeming, is always bad. Significantly, when a romantic play reaches Elisabet over her radio, she laughs; when she hears some austerely classical music, she is close to weeping. The possibilities of communication seem to begin where the word ends. But has the word failed us, or we the word?

The woman doctor sends Alma and Elisabet off to her seaside villa for what is to be a therapeutic summer. The two young women take to each other, even communicate through shared aestival experiences, but Elisabet persists in her speechlessness. Alma (the name may come from the Latin "nourishing, bountiful," from the Celtic "all good," or from the Spanish "soul.") confides more and more in Elisabet. Is this therapy, friendship, or, as Alma in a later desperate moment fears, exhibitionism? She tells the alertly, indeed avidly listening actress about her first unhappy love affair, about her current engagement to a decent but plodding fellow who considers her a "sleepwalker," of her work which she enjoys and hopes to go on with.

She also tells Elisabet about an incident on a beach where she and a highly sexed girl sunbathed naked and were observed by two very young boys. They seduced the boys and even passed them on to each other, Alma experiencing the greatest sexual satisfaction of her life. An abortion resulted, about which she still feels guilty. Barely perceptibly, Alma and Elisabet begin to merge. First it is their clothes that progressively resemble each other; then we see shots of them in which their bodies seem to fuse. Later there are little hugs and similar endearments. Then comes a nocturnal scene during which Alma repeats aloud some affectionately cautionary whispers of Elisabet's, thinking the words her own. It could be a dream but it isn't: almost completely alike in their diaphanous nightgowns, the two women merge in an embrace. Next morning, Elisabet denies everything with a shake of her head.

Alma reads a letter of Elisabet's she is supposed to mail; she learns that the actress is really having fun with her, studying her as a subject for her art. There follows a series of fights and reconciliations in the course of which Alma manages to make Elisabet step barefoot on a potsherd (a beautifully staged scene), Elisabet bloodies Alma's nose, Alma threatens to throw scalding water in Elisabet's face and elicits a screamed "No, don't!" after which the silence resumes even thicker. There is a scene in which Alma runs barefoot over rocks after Elisabet, pleading and humbling herself. Unforgiven, she lapses into a terrifying dream.

In this dream Alma begins by asserting her superiority over Elisabet. The latter's husband, blind in the dream, arrives and makes love to Alma, thinking her his wife, as Elisabet abets and watches. The crypto-lesbian experience with two girls exchanging lovers on the beach assumes a deeper meaning. Alma, who awake kept asserting her insignificance vis-à-vis the great actress, now transcends her. In a frightening scene, Alma tells Elisabet how she, the actress, tried to avoid maternity but, trapped into it, proceeded to make her boy an emotional cripple. To illustrate that this is sheer projection, as well as insane identification with the other, Bergman gives us the scene twice: first focusing on the (guiltily or innocently?) cowering actress, then on the malignly triumphant nurse. Thereupon the two women's faces contract into a split but single tortured countenance.

Alma suffers a frightening breakdown in her dream: she talks nonsense (in which, however, the blending of egos is implicit), beats a table and then Elisabet, rends her own arm and gets the wound sucked by the actress—samaritanism or vampirism? She even implacably forces Elisabet to repeat after her the word "nothing"—giving her speech only to take away meaning.

In the morning, the women, silent and hostile, pack their respective bags. Alma puts on her uniform again and we see her catch a bus back to town. We don't see Elisabet leave, but there is a shot of her playing Electra again. Does this mean that, cured, she resumes her work? But it is the same shot we saw when we were told of her breakdown. It may thus be a mere flashback, saying that her abdication continues. And Alma? Can she go back to her old life as if nothing had happened? And why do we see only Alma leaving? Could the entire tale have taken place in Alma's mind—was there only one person all along, assuming various "personas," i.e., actor's masks? At this point the film once again jumps off the sprockets, as it did also after the first big quarrel between the women, suggesting that art cannot resolve this problem: life is too much for it.

Sven Nykvist's cinematography—I think black-and-white photography can achieve no greater heights—manages to abolish the boundaries between dream and waking. Liv Ullmann's actress and, even more so, Bibi Andersson's nurse, are overwhelming characterizations, the one making silence, the other chitchat, supremely eloquent. Bergman's dialogue, rhythms, and *mise en scène*—the hospital, all vacuous white austerity; the seaside, beautiful yet also harsh; the women, with their jolly day-clothes, frilly nightwear, or dreamily mingling blondenesses generating ephemeral warmth—are masterly every step of the arduous way.

I can only guess at the ultimate meaning. The artist and the ordinary human being need each other, but this is a love-hate, a fight for absolute power over the other. Their complete communion is illusory and painful—only a dream, a nightmare—yet also real enough, perhaps, to mark them both. Life and art batten on each other, art sucking life's blood, life trying to cajole or bully art into submission, into becoming its mirror. The result of the strife is madness, whether feigned or real hardly matters. Relatives, lovers, friends, all who are sucked into this conflict, suffer along with the principal combatants. The end is, at best, a draw. And, with luck, a magnificent film.

May, 1967

HOUR OF THE WOLF

A film by Ingmar Bergman that does not work is saddening in itself, and when the failure comes as a sequel to the magnificent *Persona,* it is that much more disheartening. *Hour of the Wolf* returns to the problem of two people's interaction and interdependence to the point where two destinies become, or threaten to become, a single fused one. This time the question is to what extent can the lover help the beloved who is torn between sanity and a world of visionary horrors, the madness that (Bergman seems to feel) imperils the artist with its cruel yet cajoling lure.

A painter, Johan Borg, disappears from a small Frisian island where he spends the summers with his wife, Alma. The film reconstructs, from Johan's diaries and Alma's confessions, the events that lead up to the disappearance. First Johan begins to see demons and to sketch them; then they appear to his pregnant wife as well. They are a rich, eccentric group inhabiting a dilapidated château, and among them seems to be Johan's former mistress, Veronica. In a climactic scene, Johan and Alma have dinner with this company and are humiliated and divided against each other.

Johan's madness—if that is what it is—gains; he is particularly afraid of that hour before dawn when nightmares and hauntings preponderate, when most deaths but also, paradoxically, most childbirths occur: the hour of the wolf, as Swedish country folk call it. Finally, one of the ghostly crowd—if such they be—leaves a gun with Johan, who shoots his wife and thinks he has killed her. The painter runs off to the château, where he is subjected to all kinds of horrors; his host, the Baron, announces that he is now Veronica's lover, then scurries off across walls and ceilings.

After watching an old lady (the superb Naima Wifstrand) remove her face—an especially brilliant bit of filmmaking—Johan is made up *en travesti* by the sinister Archivist Lindhorst, and invited to make love to the nude, seemingly dead Veronica on a stone catafalque, while the Baron and Baroness and their ghoulish crew leeringly watch. Under the triple assault of homosexuality, necrophilia, and exhibitionism, there cracks a noble mind. Alma runs after Johan into the woods, where he is attacked by the entire company, led by Curator Heerbrand. Lindhorst changes into a bird of prey to deliver the *coup de grâce.* Alma is left to bear the child—presumably in the wolf hour—and to wonder whether by falling in with her husband's demonology and visions she loved him too much or not enough.

Thus, roughly, the plot. What this is, though Bergman does not tell us so, is an improvisation on themes from E. T. A. Hoffmann, the great German romantic storyteller. In *The Magician,* Bergman had already appropriated a thing or two from Hoffmann's weird fantasies. In *Hour of the Wolf* the borrowing is chiefly from "The Golden Pot," but there is also a faint parallel to the story "Don Juan," in which a performance of the opera *Don Giovanni* figures rather as *The Magic Flute* does in the film. There is, moreover, a sudden and unintegrated appearance in the film of Maestro *(Kapellmeister)* Kreisler, the hounded musician, who is Hoffmann's alter ego in two of his major works. In Hoffmann (who was a composer and conductor as well as a writer), Kreisler is called Johann, just like Bergman's hero; thinking this to be a dig at poor old Fritz Kreisler, American audiences giggle inanely.

In "The Golden Pot" (1814), which no less a man than Thomas Carlyle first translated into English, the student Anselm is torn between two realms. There is the supernatural one of the Archivist Lindhorst, who is a demon prince and sometimes changes into a salamander or vulture, and his lovely and loving daughter Serpentina, who can turn into a little green snake. And there is the philistine, bourgeois world, typified by Rector Paulmann and his merry, calculating daughter Veronica, who loves Anselm but settles for the prosaic Registrar Heerbrand when he is appointed Counselor. Earlier, Veronica enlists a hideous witch to help her win Anselm; yet the student ends up happily married to Serpentina, and is translated by Lindhorst to their magic castle in Atlantis. Lindhorst's world is that of art and the spirit, of white magic; Veronica's is that of middle-class stolidity, which, once the black magic of its youthful seductiveness has worn off, must lose out to the creative imagination.

In *Hour of the Wolf,* we find a Lindhorst, Heerbrand, and Veronica not unlike those in Hoffmann, although the symbology has been inverted. The world of the spirits, for Bergman, becomes the seigniory of evil: the supernatural corrupts the artist who is exposed, precariously balanced, corruptible. (To be sure, in other stories, such as "The Mine at Falun," Hoffmann too saw things in this way.) Along with these reverse-Hoffmannian figures we get typical Bergman characters: the patient wife, Alma, bears the same name as the sympathetic nurse in *Persona;* Veronica's last name is Vogler, the same as the disturbed actress's in the earlier film.

Unfortunately, the real and the unreal in *Hour* do not mesh. Hoffmann's supernatural is acceptable to us because even his natural world is remote, romantic, fabulous. In Bergman, however, the real is too near to us with toothbrushes, radios, revolvers. And a demon that drives a jeep is simply not a demon, or even the raw material out of which the overexcited mind can make a proper demon. Consequently, instead of the real perfectly suffused with the superreal, we get the mundane and the hallucinatory each in its corner—except for one or two marvelous scenes where the two indeed coalesce.

There is a contradiction in Bergman's mind. In a recent filmed interview, Bergman spoke both of not believing in God and of actual demons that chased him out of habitations. Regrettably, the interviewer was not astute enough to ask how a cosmos can be at the same time godless and demon-filled; in any case, it is this kind of discrepancy that damages the film. There is even a sequence, deliberately overexposed, in which Johan kills a little boy (again, shades of *Persona*), about whose meaning Bergman himself, I suspect, remains unclear.

There are scenes, or at least shots, of great beauty, such as the grisly dinner party that aptly absorbs elements from Fellini and Buñuel; or the slow, choreographed entrances of the Baron and Veronica; or, contrariwise, the sudden and chilling appearances of the old lady with the hat and of Heerbrand at the hour of the wolf. Sven Nykvist's dependably inspired camera is there to catch the most haunting compositions, trajectories, varieties of shade and texture, capturing as many nuances in black and white as the richest palette could with color. A rowboat at dawn gliding past rocks; a penumbral lamp between darkling faces; Johan's sharp, shadowed profile bisecting Alma's tear-lit face against the gloaming of the Scandinavian night; Johan striking match after match in front of his slitted eyes in a vain attempt to domesticate the horror of the wolf's hour—so many master images!

My own two favorites are, first, Alma's anxious face in the dark room comforted suddenly by one, and then two disembodied hands—the rest of Johan is submerged in night. And, secondly, Johan and Alma embracing in the late afternoon light on the threshold of their cottage; in the brisk wind, the laundry on the clothesline flaps hostilely around their faces. It reminds me of my favorite lines from Hölderlin: *"Sprachlos und kalt, im Winde/ Klirren die Fahnen."* (Speechless and cold, in the wind/ The weathervanes are clanging.)

The cast, headed by Max von Sydow, Liv Ullmann, and Ingrid Thulin, is splendid from top to bottom and the sound track, often using electronic music, is one of the spookiest within memory. Yet the film tells us remarkably little about the crises of The Mad Artist, or of those of the loving woman who tries to save him.

April, 1968

SHAME

Ingmar Bergman's *Shame* is a war film almost not about war. It is about the *condition humaine,* for which war serves as metaphor. Eva and Jan Rosenberg, married seven years and childless, are former philharmonic musicians. A civil war has been rampaging through the country for years. They now live in an island cottage with an orchard and greenhouse, and sell fruit for a living. A bad heart—this, too, will prove partly metaphorical—has kept Jan out of the army. The couple have all but accepted war as the natural state of affairs: they hear its percussion, observe troop movements, but are left alone. It is an incomprehensible war, particularly to artists. Only when Jan has a toothache does he wonder if the dentist is still there; inscrutable and devouring, war is tolerated as long as it leaves thee and me reasonably unscathed.

It is a Friday morning, with the everyday irritations and petty sloppinesses encroached on by strange signs. Jan relates a dream he has had: they were back in the symphony orchestra, playing the slow movement of the Fourth Brandenburg Concerto (remember the significance of Bach on the radio in *The Silence* and *Persona?*)—that *was* peace. Jan has a bothersome tooth but exaggerates the pain; he is too lazy to shave. Eva has to do the accounts and get the car ready. Church bells are heard ringing—mysteriously for a Friday. The phone also rings, but whenever Eva picks up the receiver, no voice answers.

Some tanks go by. Eva and Jan fetch the lingonberries they are to deliver to the mayor. Jan bumbles and they have a tiff. Reconciled, they finally drive off. The camera has been hovering close to them: a few medium long shots, but mostly closeups, some of them extreme. Often a two-shot is held for a very long time, like the one over Jan's shoulder, our gaze riveted on Eva's radiant aliveness.

The station wagon rolls out into the landscape and into a long shot of great and disquieting beauty. Not only does the car glisten ominously, the whole landscape has a strident, metallic quality, as if you could cut yourself on the light it reflects. The couple stop by a nervily splashing stream to get a fish for dinner from Filip, the grizzled fisherman. The sound of the river is one of the very few natural ones that we shall hear on the sound track; mostly there will be sounds of war, or silence—never background music. Filip warns Eva about approaching enemy movements. The Rosenbergs' radio has once again not been functioning; Jan, the escapist, thinks it is better so. He also thought, as he watched Eva get the fish, how much he loved her, how beautiful she was. She laughs and exclaims, "Only from a distance."

On the ferry to the mainland they meet the mayor and his wife off to see their soldier son. All around them armament, bustle, tension. The lingonberries will be deposited with the maid; but the four of them must get together again one of these evenigs to play chamber music. Bergman uses the device of shooting a head in very tight closeup, but leaving just enough space around the edges of the frame for suggestions of surrounding upheaval to form an agitated halo. On the mainland, the Rosenbergs have received enough money to treat themselves to a bottle of wine. They go to Lobelius the antiquarian— the graciousness of wine is now sold along with other antiques. Lobelius has been called up; his baggy uniform is pathetic, as are his relationship with his housekeeper and his pitiful hope of getting an administrative job because of a bad leg.

The interior of the shop is tenebrose, yet here Sven Nykvist, Bergman's camera wizard, deploys some of his greatest artistry. The images become extremely sharp, glossy, ripe with chiaroscuro—as we remember them in the dinner party scene in *Smiles of a Summer Night.* Lobelius shows his friends his most precious object, a little twosome of Meissen figurines making actual, tinkling music. All three watch and listen raptly. In this piece of eighteenth-century porcelain the past comes alive; so too, as they sample the German wine they are about to buy, the affability of yesteryear returns. Eva gently pats a stray curl on Jan's temple. The camera follows her gesture and pans around the room, picking out statues, pictures, clocks—an anthology of bygone well-being. When we come back to the Rosenbergs, they sit side by side, transfigured. Parting from Lobelius is halting, awkward, full of stabbing silences.

Back at the cottage, an idyllic outdoor dinner of fish and wine. The couple, tête-à-tête, are lovers again; they talk of having children after the war. Eva worries about her husband's potency in the most fondly fumbling way. Touchy though he is, Jan is in such a good mood, nothing can unsettle him. Why not make babies right now, he suggests, and adds that he is no determinist. Stumped by that word, she replies, "I don't give a damn what you are, as long as you fix the sink." That is woman's practical wisdom. As they withdraw to make love, the hand

of the man is seen in extreme closeup picking a daisy from the table
vase for his lady. More than a gesture of love, it is a pious offering to
the goddess of the hearth.

Later that evening terrible things happen. A patrol warns the Rosenbergs about enemy parachutists. Air-to-ground battle: a man para-
chutes into a tree of the forest that surrounds the cottage. Eva rushes
to help him, Jan is being cowardly. But the paratrooper in the tree is
dying. His comrades now encircle the cottage. Instead of killing the
couple, they film an interview with Eva, asking her tough, confusing
political questions to which she gives honest but apolitical answers.
When it is Jan's turn, he collapses; the patrol that came to warn them
now counterattacks, and the invaders are drawn away.

Bombardment. Eva huddles close to the distraught Jan and tries to
warm him with her creature heat. A closeup shows their faces, hers
slightly above and behind his, filling the screen. It is a kind of *Pietà*.
In the morning, they frenziedly load a few belongings into the car and
head for the sea. Jan again proves his incompetence. He suggests they
take some of the chickens along for food; can he cut off their heads,
Eva asks. No, but he can shoot them with his rifle. He proceeds to miss
one at point-blank range. "Oh God, I'm tired," Eva groans in disgust.
(People who question Bergman's sense of comedy should have their
noses rubbed in this scene.)

They drive through a landscape of death, reminiscent of the plague-
ridden countryside through which the knight and squire of *The Seventh
Seal* rode. The dead lie in horrible, undignified postures and groupings
—death has caught them *in flagrante* with life, in desperate dalliance
with survival. A tracking shot (the car) moves relentlessly forward, and
the Guernican images it captures are tossed aside as quickly as they are
picked up. Yet, for being almost subliminal, these visions are more
infernal: they explode not on the screen but, like delayed-action
bombs, in your mind.

Through a wooded landscape full of forest fires to a sea that is
blocked off by abandoned and destroyed armament—and, suddenly,
the corpses of children. Eva runs out of the car to bend over a little
girl sprawled out like a discarded doll. There is a closeup of Eva's face
against an ashen sky, her eyes torn open by grief. This woman will not
have children, ever. She tells Jan to drive back home; it is not clear
whether they return to survive or to perish with their house.

After a night of bombardment during which her whiter hand clasps
his darker one for comfort, Eva and Jan rise to survey the damage. In
one of the most haunting sequences of the film, the two stand incredu-
lous before the devastation around them. In the background, the forest

is burning: hideous balls of fire are climbing up slender, virginal birches and ravishing them. But also—irony or hope?—there is bird song; clear, liquid bird song on the sound track. And the sound of water dripping from a faucet. Perhaps life *can* go on. Later, in a darkened interior, Jan removes his precious viola from its case. In a beautiful, perhaps too deliberately composed shot, with chiaroscuro worthy of Georges de la Tour, the two heads bend over the instrument and, with it for hypotenuse, form a triangle. He tells her the story of Pampini, who made this viola and died of the cholera or something— Jan does not remember. Art survives disaster; but what of the artist?

This somewhat self-conscious scene is redeemed by a beautifully humane one. An attempt of the Rosenbergs to make love is foiled by Jan's getting a cramp in his leg. That night, when Eva asks Jan to join her in her bed, his childlike alacrity makes clear that he is seeking her, and she receiving him, as a mother, not as a wife.

The next few sequences are too dense, too rich to be cited in detail. The Rosenbergs, along with many other people suspected of collabora-tion, are herded into the headquarters of the island authorities who have repulsed the invaders. There are marvelous shots of the Rosen-bergs' heads bobbing up and down on a sea of driven humanity. The couple is roughly questioned about the film they made for the enemy: another voice has been dubbed in for Eva's, and it spouts collaboration-ist propaganda. Other people are treated worse than they, though Jan insists that during a brief separation from Eva he was brutally beaten.

They are now surrounded by the victims of interrogation. Some are badly hurt, one is a corpse. The horror is magnified by the fact that this is a converted schoolhouse; at dreadful moments the camera catches innocent children's drawings on the walls or scraps of disused learning on a blackboard. A cynical doctor ministers to them lackadaisically. Amid all this, Eva blurts out the second dream in the film. She feels as if she were in a dream, not hers but someone else's (the Good Lord's, we presume), and wonders: "What happens when that person wakes up and is ashamed?"

There is a ghastly mock execution scene, more frightening than a real one, but Mayor (or Colonel) Jacobi, who is in command here, spares his friends the Rosenbergs. In his office, Jacobi explains that he knows their innocence and that they were hauled in only to set an example to others; his instructions were not to hurt them, and he assumes they were obeyed. Jan eagerly confirms this. Eva gives him a quick, wither-ing look, which Bergman's camera brilliantly keeps in the middle distance, showing it from Jacobi's observant point of view. They leave. Jacobi is revealed as not only shrewd but also tired, defeated: in ex-treme closeup, his cane pulls an antiquated heater closer to his chilly self, as he tries in vain to concentrate on his newspaper. Noises of trucks carrying off the condemned streak across the sound track.

The Rosenbergs live in relative comfort now; Jacobi supplies them with various amenities. We see him come to visit, bringing Eva a family heirloom and Jan a first edition of a Dvořák trio he hopes they will all play someday. As they sit around the table, he becomes momentarily sinister. "The sacred freedom of art," he snorts, thunderously bringing down his cane on the table; and then: "The sacred slackness of art!" The Rosenbergs are embarrassed by his presence; Filip the fisherman has warned them against this nexus.

Jan dozes off. In the bedroom, Jacobi, who has become her lover, hands Eva a large sum of money, his life's savings. She refuses it, and it remains on the bed as Eva leads Jacobi to the greenhouse where, she says, they must conduct their clandestine intercourse. There we see Jacobi's head in Eva's lap, just as Jan's had been in an earlier scene. He only took the *gauleiter's* job, Jacobi explains, out of fear of active combat. He, too, is pitiable.

At dawn, Jan wakes up, lights upon the money and perplexedly pockets it. Then he sees Eva and Jacobi emerge from the greenhouse. The scene is brilliantly staged. He pads halfway up the stairs and sits down. The camera shoots through the balustrade, disclosing only his legs and feet encased in thick, silly-looking socks; we hear his reiterated "Eva!" among thin, puling sobs. He rises, staggers against a wall, and we see his chest, in ludicrous pajama tops, grievously heaving.

Jacobi is captured outside the cottage by Filip, who is a partisan leader, and his men. For a large ransom—they need funds—they'll let him go. Jacobi asks for a loan of the money he just gave Eva; Jan disclaims any knowledge of it. The cottage is viciously ransacked—even the rare viola and the seemingly invulnerable chickens are now destroyed; finally, the place is burnt down. Filip hands Jan a gun; to prove his political cleanness, he must execute Jacobi. Recoiling at first, Jan warms to the task and kills with gusto—in a scene unsurpassable for controlled terror. Jacobi's body is carted off with cans of food and other loot piled on top of it. Jan hands Eva the money: again, she just looks at him. When, later, she becomes hysterical, he slaps her; this only makes her cry harder.

They walk through a landscape of scorched tree skeletons even more horrible than the previous one with dead bodies: nature itself seems to have been exterminated. A young deserter surprises them in the greenhouse; he has a gun, but drops it from fatigue and hunger. Eva feeds him, and his head, too, comes to rest buried in her lap. Eva—woman, wife, mother; all men, like unicorns, press their horny heads against her womb. But war has transformed Jan from a pacific coward into a belligerent one; he kills the boy for his boots and for the place he has reserved on a rowboat leaving for the mainland. Eva refuses to follow Jan. "Easier if you stay!" he retorts—and then she does trail after him like a frightened dog. She, the once pure and strong one, has capitulated; to save her life, she loses her soul. As they make off, the camera briefly catches in the background a pitifully small, black funeral procession heading for a half-ruined church.

In exchange for Jacobi's money, Filip, who is sailing the boat, takes on Eva and Jan with the other refugees. Food and water run out; the motor breaks down. One night, as the others sleep, Filip gives Jan, the only watcher, a leaden, fellow-in-guilt look and quietly slips overboard. Vacant sky and sea keep reappearing as a baleful refrain between shots of this derelict boatload struggling to survive. One morning they have run aground on what proves to be a floating island of dead men in full fighting gear and life belts. The boat creaks as if in pain. Only with utmost effort can it be extricated from this shoal of clinging dead.

Another dawn. Extreme long shot of the boat adrift. Then closeup of Eva's and Jan's adjacent heads, as in a sequence long before. She tells a dream she has had. She is carrying her little daughter through a strange town; suddenly she notices a panoply of roses spilling over a garden wall. Beautiful—but an airplane comes and sets the roses on fire. And it's still not awful because it is so beautiful! Hugging her child close Eva realizes she must remember something someone said—but she has forgotten what. End of film.

The third dream is the key. What Eva has forgotten is the two previous dreams: Jan's memories of Bach and her own righteous indignation against a cruel God. Everything has become absorbed by the naked, ignoble hunger for this horrible but still lovely life. It does not matter whether she and Jan survive: those to whom the condition of total war has become the human condition are dead, anyway. Liv Ullmann, Max von Sydow, Gunnar Björnstrand portray the principals. Like their supporting cast, they are superb.

If I have related plot and technical highlights in such detail, it is for a reason. Shame is so tightly packed that you can fully appreciate it only on second seeing. This review hopes to make it possible for you to start, as it were, with a second viewing.

January, 1969

THE PASSION OF ANNA

Ingmar Bergman's *A Passion* (released here as *The Passion of Anna*) records the interplay of four people on the small Swedish island where Bergman lives, the microcosm into which he likes to fit his far-ranging universal visions. The main character is Andreas Winkelman, a man who has relegated his feelings as far inside, and other people as far outside and away from him, as possible. He has, we learn at one point, been in prison: he had passed bad checks, been drunk, and violently resisted arrest. We also gather that his wife, a sculptress, left him. From the vast number of books in his house, we deduce that he is some kind of littérateur. We do not even know how these few data interrelate, if indeed they do. Yet this sketchy Andreas is the perfect carrier for the psychic disease he suffers from, and its articulate mouthpiece.

Certain island neighbors begin to impinge on his life. Anna Fromm comes to use his telephone when hers is out of order, makes a highly emotional plea to someone called Elis with reference to her dead husband and child, is rebuffed in some money matter, and departs distraught. In the handbag she leaves behind, Andreas discovers a farewell letter from her late husband, also called Andreas. The letter points out that though the couple love each other, they cannot help inflicting reciprocal psychic and physical torture, and must separate. When Winkelman goes to return the letter, Anna is asleep, but her dearest friends, Eva and Elis Vergérus, invite him in; he politely refuses.

He does, however, come to dinner one day. Here he learns that Elis is a famous architect who has been commissioned to build a cultural center in Milan, though he is totally cynical about the project, culture, and life in general. His wife, Eva, appears to be a charming, easy-going young woman, placidly dependent on her husband, yet Andreas has previously come upon her dozing in her car in broad daylight, because of a fierce insomnia she suffers from at night. But the big surprise of the evening is the somewhat mousy Anna's vehement tirade against cynicism, disbelief, and lies; as she holds up her memories of a happy, truth-telling marriage that sustain her through life. Andreas remembers the letter from his namesake. That night, having been invited to sleep over, he is awakened by the screams of Anna, who has had some dreadful nightmare.

Next morning, Elis takes Andreas to the handsome old mill he has turned into a studio; tells him about the car accident in which Anna, who drove, escaped with injuries, while her husband and child were killed; and shows him a huge, carefully filed collection of photographs. These, taken by himself as well as clipped from all over, show human beings and faces in every kind of situation, but particularly in emotional crises. It emerges that the dead Andreas was a potential genius, and that, though they loved each other, he and Anna fought constantly. Although Andreas promises to pose for Elis, he is upset by the architect's cynical bitterness, especially by the casual revelation that Elis's wife had been the dead Andreas's mistress, "quite above board."

Andreas goes on a binge, howls his name across the winter landscape, collapses, and is eventually dragged home by Johan Andersson, a lowly firewood-peddler, to whom he has been kind on occasion. Eva, bored and restless during one of Elis's absences on business, comes to Andreas and has a brief fling with him, all the while protesting her love for her husband, whom she cannot meaningfully reach. Andreas goes to Elis's studio to be photographed; Elis extracts a confession of his crime and imprisonment, but agrees to underwrite a bank loan for him, even engages him to write up his architectural notes, thus obligating and subjugating Andreas all the more. We learn from Eva, in an effusion of sympathy, that Andreas and Anna have become lovers, and the rest of the film concerns their unsuccessful affair. By slow stages of attrition, they reach the point where each comes close to killing the other and must, finally, part.

Now *A Passion* does have a central weakness: a good deal of it has to be taken on faith, on somebody's word; we do not even find out such basic things as the source of Andreas's income. But it is a weakness that reinforces two of the main themes. First, that things are not as people say they are—because all speakers lie, deceive themselves, or are simply ignorant—and still we sometimes have to believe them, for there is nothing else to go on. Second, that people so utterly lose the sense of their identity that their professions, like everything else about them, become irrelevant, interchangeable. The fact that Andreas's house has no electric light and can nevertheless harbor a functioning TV set and other electrical appliances is a genuine inconsistency, but a slight one.

What enchants in *A Passion* is the evocative power of the photography, although this is only Bergman's second color film. Sven Nykvist, the cinematographer, has caught in the outdoor shots a thin, almost constipated color: the austerely wintry woods and blur of a distant sea, the anemic skies with a beclouded sun that looks like a reflector beam rendered impotent by fog—these have a way of emerging as faintly tinted lithographs, beautiful but chilling. Yet it is indoors that Bergman and Nykvist work their greatest wonders. In every indoor sequence a certain color or color combination significantly predominates, without the obtrusiveness of such experiments in recent films by Fellini, Antonioni, and others.

Thus in a moment of contentment, like the dinner party, everything is an opulent bronze color, a bronze that happily subsumes the flush of animated faces and the gold of candlelight. When Eva comes to visit Andreas, they play a favorite dance record from his student days, "Always Romantic"—it is almost the only time there is music on the soundtrack—and, for a while, the whole film goes red. This is introduced by a quick shot of a light streaming through a red pane on the front door: Bergman admits that he is about to use a filmic device, but one that faithfully records the red light of nascent passion turned on in the mind. It is not a harsh, declamatory red, like that of the pool scene in *Fellini Satyricon;* it is rather the coral glow of healthy cheeks or remembered sunsets, appetizing rather than strident.

Even more impressive are the seemingly natural color tonalities that are nevertheless emotionally slanted. The morning after Andreas's and Eva's dalliance, things take on a lividly viridescent cast—the hues, as it were, of faint nausea, shame, regret. Again, during Winkelman's and Anna's last car ride in a downpour, everything around them is in the silver-gray, gunmetal domain: the colors of metallic, cutting truth. And what makes the grayness even chillier is that it follows a sequence with a burning stable, all flaming red. Throughout the film, color schemes not only express moods but also contrast pointedly with the colors of what has been or is to come.

Sometimes, however, it is the combination of several colors that is brilliantly provocative. So, in Elis's studio, the architect tempts Andreas with a liquor cabinet suddenly flung open. From among the very white walls there gleams out a dazzling array of variously colored liquor bottles, a veritable hoard of the Nibelungs or some other devilish treasure. Elis himself, in black and white quasi-clerical garb, surrounded by flame-red cardboard boxes, looks like a priest of hell.

The most eloquent device is the use of color and movement together. Thus the dinner party is all static closeups of burnished, warm gold, casting its grace over the solo arias each quartet member delivers in high style. But just as Anna finishes her paean to truth and love, Bergman cuts to a shot we have already seen: the dead Andreas's tortured farewell letter, with the camera moving in extreme closeup across the typescript. The letter is on grayish paper, particularly sobering after the golden glow, and the intense magnification gives the typed characters pathetically frazzled edges. The inexorable lateral movement of the camera, in strong contrast to its previous indulgent lingering over a face, is especially suggestive. This was the movement of the typewriter cylinder as the first Andreas wrote the words that were vainly trying to free him from his impossible relationship with Anna; and it is also the movement of the perusing eyes of the second Andreas, who, despite this dark knowledge, will be drawn into an equally gray affair with the woman. A lateral seesaw movement, then, that unites the two Andreases.

Or take the scene where Andreas and Eva begin their brief affair. Coming after an incarnadine sequence, it is all grays and blacks. Paradoxical but right: there is nothing "Always Romantic" about this fling, a mere humdrum, furtively snatched anodyne. And so, in front of a twilight-gray window, two faces in black silhouette play out an amazing ballet of teasing little comings together and drawings apart: the two dark, wavy lines of the profiles dance a *pas de deux* whose fluctuations are equally beautiful as human lovemaking and as sheer animated abstraction. Finally, the profiles merge in a long kiss and sink out of the image, leaving behind only a window frame dividing the film frame into unequal gray parts. Through the upper, larger one we dimly perceive a red barn: something like an abstract expressionist painting by Rothko or Gottlieb. And during all these pleasant preliminaries to sex with Andreas, Eva is telling him of her frustrated love for her husband, Elis.

Sound is no less important than sight in *A Passion*—whether it is dialogue, poetic, piercing, cogent; or simply sound: church bells, hammering, heavy breathing, the crisply impersonal clink of dishes during a loveless breakfast or, in an ugly, humiliating outdoor fight that follows, the crying of wind and crash of waves from afar. Bergman manipulates natural sounds as if they were notes in music: when desultory sheep bells become the very voice of melancholy isolation; or when a drunken Andreas bellows out his name into the silent recesses of winter, hoping for some answering voice to confirm his identity, and the obbligato of rusty and guttural foghorns offers only a mixture of mockery and indifference. And when Andreas eagerly fumbles with the papers he finds in Anna's bag, the unfurling of that letter with its message of physical and psychic violence is magnified in volume from a mere crinkling to a premonitory, doomful clatter.

These sounds sometimes echo one another. At the climax of Anna's horrible Easter dream (which in its themes, images, tone and shift to black-and-white photography alludes to the dreams of the heroine of *Shame,* and may very well be an outtake from that preceding and related film), Anna comes upon the mangled body of her dead son. We see her scream repeatedly, but the only sound we hear is the ticking of a clock. It is time that is the true enemy, the traducer who delivers us to death; the sound of the clock (which accompanied some previous scenes with cheerfully hypocritical innocence) churns away like a sick heartbeat about to explode. And this is an Easter dream; so much for resurrection.

What does get resurrected is that ticking. At the very end of the film, when Anna may have intended to drive both of them into death, she nevertheless answers Andreas's last question with words that are full of genuine love and humility. Then she drives off, perhaps forever. Now Andreas is left alone on the soggy, muddy road, and we see him in a long shot pacing hither and yon. But this is no ordinary pacing: one direction is that of Anna and staying together, the other is that of continued loneliness and exile from experience. As he keeps reversing his way, the camera slowly comes closer, as if to discover some resolution in his face. At the same time, the image, already grainy, begins to decompose even further, and, once again, we hear that ominous ticking of the clock. When the camera closes in on Andreas, overexposure makes him only just visible: he collapses in the mud, unable to choose either direction. Over the ticking comes the narrator's voice: "This time his name was Andreas Winkelman," and the film ends in a white-out. Yes, and the last time his name was Andreas Fromm. But that, surely, is not the only parallel intended. Another time his name will be yours, mine, Everyman's.

What is the philosophic content of *A Passion?* The insufficiency of life, the central hollowness beneath the sporadically rich surface. Note how brilliantly Bergman turns his spare chamber quartet into a prodigally orchestrated symphony. Andreas the brooder is complemented by Elis the inquirer (his last name, Vergérus, is that of the doctor in *The Magician,* another ruthless dissector in search of an ultimate truth), but an Elis who has to admit that his photographs provide no answer to the riddle of life. Anna, the self-deluding seeker for truth through love, is complemented by Eva, the unfulfilled wife who resorts to little affairs, dabbling and mendacious. And from here the film extends farther, upward and downward.

Upward there is the Vietnam war, which briefly but harrowingly appears on a television set. Downward there is the devastation in the animal kingdom wreaked by a maniac loose on the island, who goes about slashing sheep to death, hanging puppies, and setting horses on fire. People suspect the humble recluse Johan, Andreas's friend, and with vicious, blind cruelty drive the wood-peddler to death. Yet the crimes, for Johan was innocent, continue. Now there is a scene in which all these themes coalesce. Andreas and Eva are watching the

Saigon chief of police gleefully executing away when a dull thud outside draws them from their TV set. A bird—it must have been frightened, Andreas says—accidentally collided in the dark with a wall of the house, and is now in agony. Andreas has to kill it with a stone, much like the stones with which the islanders hounded Johan to death.

But the simple Johan became suspect after a lost law case drove him into seclusion, just as Andreas withdrew after his unhappy bout with the law. The bird has to be killed; yet how horrible is its blood on Andreas's hands! It died because of darkness, aloneness, fright; in a similar lonely state of panic Andreas became an outlaw. So loneliness makes us suspicious and suspect; all of us are hangmen and victims, both of others and ourselves. And the death of the bird coincides exactly with the Vietnam executions on TV.

Bergman's overall mastery is accurately reflected in his mastery of detail. Two examples out of many: when Eva and Andreas have become lovers, there is a closeup of her face, horizontal across the screen, framed from below by Andreas's shoulder and beard, and from above by his bent arm around her. But this enfolding is not circular: what encloses and partly cuts off Eva's face is a lozenge, a diamond shape. Even the protection of intimacy we offer one another is not rounded and soft; it is diamond-hard and cold. And, again, when Andreas and Anna are having that terrible last fight in the rain-battered car, a toy bear suspended from the rear-view mirror jiggles between their faces grotesquely and piteously, duplicating the motions of Andreas's dachshund, which the maniac had hanged from a tree. The fine thing here is that no obvious symbol, no one-for-one comparison forces itself upon us. Rather, there are suggestions of several things: that the maniac, though Johan has died miserably, is still on the loose; that there are objective correlatives for our anguish in the world around us, inanimate things that fill up with our anger and hurt; and that what twists and trembles between Andreas and Anna, love turned to hate, is as deadly as any killer's madness.

As usual, the acting of Bergman's "repertory company" is magisterial. Liv Ullmann's Anna is a characterization of inexhaustible variety, ranging from healthy peasant to self-deluding rationalizer, from avenging angel to cracked porcelain figurine, which the touch of truth will shatter. When she tells Andreas about her marriage and the fatal accident, in a series of closeups in which the camera angle varies ever so slightly yet brilliantly, and the color of her eyes is picked up by the blue-green fabric of her armchair, she exudes an elemental womanliness and humanity that contrast profoundly and pitifully with the untruths she is uttering. Bibi Andersson's Eva is like Blake's Songs of

Innocence and Experience recited simultaneously: this is someone playing an existential game, but you never know (any more than she does) whether the game is knowing or naïve, whether she is kicking the ball or whether she is herself the ball that is being kicked. Take the marvelous little scene when, after the night of lovemaking with Andreas, Eva gets into her car and is about to drive off but jumps out and—with a strange, out-of-context intensity—kisses the bemused Andreas seeing her off. Then she leaps back into the car and really drives away. That kiss, though; what was it? An attempt to turn fleshliness, retroactively, into sisterliness? The farewell to a passion that cannot continue, but wants to die with a crescendo? Or just a spontaneous outburst of tenderness from a woman whose impulses are squelched by her husband? There is something so rich in the lapidariness of Miss Andersson's performance that all three meanings inhere in the single gesture.

Then there is Erland Josephson's architect, cynical, smug, full of quiet bravado, yet subtly revealing fissures in his façade. When his wife and Andreas share a moment of tenderness at his studio while he is turning off a radio playing Bach, and then comes back in warningly humming the melody (the only other, almost subliminal, appearance of music on the sound track), the ominous expression on Elis's face subsumes pain, vindictiveness, and the visible effort to cover up the rift in its composure. Josephson conveys this welter of conflicting impulses in the record time of, I estimate, three seconds. As for Max von Sydow's Andreas, I am exhausted from the labor of ferreting out new superlatives, which every successive performance by this actor requires. His great talent lies in perfectly fusing strength and weakness, as if they had been run through a blender, so that what comes out is so much of a piece that you do not know whether a given movement or inflection is an upsurge of power or a paroxysm of impotence. He can look noble and beautiful when he is saying something abject or terrible; he can do something contemptible and make it appear the essence of manliness. He is, in short, a master of ambiguity.

And speaking of ambiguity, *A Passion* contains a curious, much debated device. At four points the action of the film stops, and one of the four principals (each gets his turn) is given the chance to discuss, as an actor or private person, the character he or she is portraying. What the problems of enacting the role are, what the portrayer thinks the mainsprings of the character to be, what the character might develop into after the end of the film. One justification for the device is that it comes at moments of almost unbearable tension, and provides relief—to be sure, not comic relief, but relief through Brechtian distancing. It also affords a more expressly analytical view of the character, in accordance with Brechtian precepts, and a chance to evaluate him in the additional context of the actor's opinions. Finally, the device permits us to see how different these actors are in real life, how far beyond their quotidian selves their artistry has taken them.

The film has been exploitatively renamed in America by United Artists *The Passion of Anna,* with supposed suggestions of a woman in heat. But it must clearly be *a* passion: Anna's, Eva's, Elis's, Andreas's —anybody's. All these passions intersect, merge for a moment, feed on and destroy one another. Together, they spell a passion of suffering, like Christ's, only here the collective Calvary of all mankind.

June, 1970

8

French Film in Eclipse

EVER SINCE the thirties, French films have been among the most artistic or, at least, accomplished films made anywhere. In the late fifties and early sixties, with the advent of the New Wave, France came to the forefront of cinematic prestige, and its influence was felt literally everywhere. Since then, however, what shocking slippage! And I speak not as one afflicted with fashionable Francophobia, but as a confirmed yet disgruntled Francophile. Not only have the major French directors, discussed for the most part in other sections of this book, declined steadily; but even the new talent coming up proves, on inspection, no talent at all. I except from these charges films like Malle's *The Fire Within,* Alain Jessua's *Life Upside Down,* and Robert Enrico's *Zita*—but even their makers soon stagnate. As for the others, they are, at best, sound bits of commercial filmmaking—sometimes with political significance (*Z*), sometimes new variations on the old French triangle (*La Femme Infidèle*), and sometimes merely good slick thrillers (Jacques Debray's *Borsalino*). Rare as even these things are, they fall short of being works of art, generally very short indeed. On the other hand, hollow pretentiousness abounds in any number of forms, from Rohmer's *My Night at Maud's,* with its sophomoric philosophizing, its rhythmic and visual aridity, its narrative and psychological blind spots, to films like *Benjamin* or Claude Sautet's *The Things of Life,* which pretend to probe human nature but are just so much verbal and visual attitudinizing.

I suppose that the single worst influence on the French film—as, indeed, on all film, but felt most strongly, for obvious reasons, in France—is Jean-Luc Godard. Sometimes openly, sometimes more insidiously, his contempt for plot, characterization, scrutable sequence, and, finally, humanity itself, has in ways hard to pinpoint affected any number of filmmakers. The influence is clear on such films as Agnès Varda's *Les Créatures,* Edouard Luntz's *Les Coeurs verts,* Michel Cournot's *Les Gauloises bleues,* for example; but, I think, even the films of Alain Robbe-Grillet and Marguerite Duras, though based on their equally questionable fiction, may derive some of their incoherence from Godard. Indeed, such older filmmakers as Clouzot and Clément seem likewise to be striving for a bit of the Godardian look in their recent films—*La Prisonnière, Rider on the Rain*—with disastrous results.

It is, I dare say, the backlash vote against all this radicalism that enables certain old-fashioned, even boring, but polished directors like Henri Verneuil to maintain themselves beyond their actual usefulness, and that encourages younger men, like Yves Robert, to follow in their footsteps. Other filmmakers latch on to a surface "modernity" and snobbish chic to gloss over their timeless triviality, thereby inflicting on their films a split personality. Philippe de Broca and Claude Lelouch are cases in point. But the impoverishment of the average product is less worrisome than the failures of the peak achievements. And the trouble here lies with the state of French culture itself. The *nouveau roman* strikes me as a typical blind alley; *musique concrète* is no better; French painting and, with the three very considerable exceptions of Beckett, Ionesco, and Genet, French theater are likewise in a sad state. But it all seems to derive from the intellectual climate set by men like Lévi-Strauss, Saussure, Bachelard, Barthes, and a few others. It is not that these men have failed to make a contribution to certain specific disciplines, but that their grandiose or far-fetched notions invite indiscriminate application and misapplication—as, for instance, when the *Cahiers du cinéma* critics and others of their kidney start spouting structuralism, semiology, etc. Films like Doniol-Valcroze's *Le Viol* or Chabrol's *Les Biches,* to name only a couple of examples, seem to derive their appliquéd pretentiousness at least in part from the cultural climate, simultaneously grandiose and pettifogging.

TO BE A CROOK

A few words must be said here about an earlier film by Claude Lelouch, the maker of *A Man and a Woman*. Just released, *To Be a Crook* confirms my impression that Lelouch is possessed of a formidable technique, which, as technique, can almost do no wrong. The story is Godardian in its grotesque unbelievableness, and there is (need I say?) hardly any probing of character. But Lelouch can manipulate a camera, if anything, too spectacularly well, so that the only fault is an occasional rambunctious piece of self-satisfaction. (It suffices to compare what Lelouch has done for car racing in *A Man and a Woman* with what John Frankenheimer does with very much greater resources in *Grand Prix:* the one is imaginative and artistic in its technique; the other merely an elaborate, cloying bit of craft.)

Lelouch, moreover, can make a filmic trick, say, the courting of a deaf-mute girl, not only an excuse for brilliant cinematic effects, but also instinct with tenderness. If his matter is ever allowed to catch up with his manner—and things being what they are today, there is no great cause for hope—Lelouch could become one of our better filmmakers.

February, 1967

LA CHINOISE

There have been ages of intellectualism, ages (many more) of antiintellectualism, and now at last we have got an age of pseudointellectualism. A fellow bottles a certain amount of noise and silence, writes a couple of windy books to justify it, and it is called music. Another makes a deathmask of a hamburger that died of elephantiasis, and, behold, it is art. Not, of course, until suitable manifestos have been published to prove it. Somebody else creates a traffic jam on Long Island, which, when duly and dully written about, becomes a Happening. Still another fellow stages a bit of fellatio before a paralyzed camera, and forthwith you have been blown in body and mind—with the help, to be sure, of reams of grandiloquent hogwash in the organs of film unculture. A quartet of hairy simians introduces a sitar among its electric guitars and sits at the platitudinous feet of a guru whose truisms will set us free, and, presto, we have absorbed the lore of the

Orient: East and West shall forever be meat for the gogo-grinders.

The object is to have culture without cultivation, knowledge without learning, art without effort, and intellectual superiority without intellect. The put-on and send-up thrive in every art form, and, put upon as we are, we must put up with it or shut up. The perfect weathervane of this climate is Jean-Luc Godard, the ultimate in instruments for registering the winds of change, because he also makes the wind he registers. "In *La Chinoise,*" says Pauline Kael of the *New Yorker,* "the heroine wants to blow up the Louvre; someone threw a stink bomb into a party at the Museum of Modern Art last week. We don't have time to catch up with the future that is already here, and Godard is already making movie critiques of it. . . ." A stink bomb is to a real bomb, I suppose, as the Museum of Modern Art is to the Louvre, and if, as Wilde observed, nature imitates art, there is no reason for a bunch of naturals not to imitate non-art.

La Chinoise, already hailed by Renata Adler, Pauline Kael, Richard Schickel, Joseph Morgenstern, and Andrew Sarris, among others, as a major film, is, in my opinion, a piece of mitigated trash. There is the excellent color photography of Raoul Coutard, and Francis Jeanson comes in briefly to talk a little sense. For the rest, Godard, his material, his pretentiousness and undisciplined garrulity, are boring when not exasperating. "It is fiction," says the heroine about her experience, "but it has brought me closer to reality." Godard himself does not so much confuse fiction and reality as totally lack a sense of either: he cannot create a believable fiction and he firmly believes that whatever floats into his head or camera is *ipso facto* real. So he wallows in a no-man's-land between meaningful fiction and digested reality, a Disneyland for those who want to escape from both art and life.

The film concerns a quintet of boys and girls who set up a Maoist cell in the apartment of a friend's parents gone away for the summer. The handsome flat is quickly repainted in loud colors, the walls are covered with Maoist (or, in the kids' favorite phrase, Marxist-Leninist, slogans), blackboards with more slogans, and pinups of every kind— mostly political, like Mao, Castro, Malcolm X, but also broadsheets, newspaper photographs of the Vietnam war, comic strips and mod fashions (the heroine reads, in a typical shot, the *Peking Information* bulletin right under pinups of miniskirted models), and, of all things, a portrait of Novalis. This head of Novalis is later voted to become the target for some bow-and-arrow practice. (Here, by the way, is a case in point. Under no circumstances can I imagine Godard, or even his Teutonic alter ego, Hans Lucas, reading the esoteric works of that mystical German romantic, but anything Godard stumbles upon gets stashed into that magpie's nest that is his cinema.) In this ambience, the kids run a messy household, harangue one another with Marxist-Leninist homilies, and make (we guess) haphazard love.

The group consists of Véronique, a student of philosophy at the new branch of the Sorbonne at Nanterre (a working-class suburb of Paris); Guillaume, her boy friend and self-styled Brechtian actor; Henri, who works for an Institut de logique économique, whatever that may be; Kirilov, a painter; and Yvonne, a country lass who came to Paris to be a prostitute, is now maid to the group, and, when money is needed, still turns a trick. Kirilov, of course, is named after the character in *The Possessed*, and commits absurdist suicide after reducing to the absurd Ivan Karamazov's famous phrase: "If Marxism-Leninism exists, everything is permitted." On this slender connection, Godard arrogates to his papier-mâché character, about whom he tells us nothing, all the depth and prestige of the Dostoevskian namesake. Guillaume's last name is Meister—he is, of course, a new Wilhelm Meister. There is a scene in which he stands between a pretty girl who removes her bra and a leering hag; each woman knocks on a glass door to either side of him, and there is a text: "LA VOCATION THEATRALE DE GUILLAUME MEISTER." If Godard has read Goethe's early and sketchy *Wilhelm Meisters theatralische Sendung*, the Ur-*Meister*, I will sit through *La Chinoise* five times in a row; but with this scene our *cinéaste* annexes, or so he thinks, the glory that was Goethe and the grandeur that was Heracles choosing between two women at the crossroads. Véronique's last name is Supervielle; the silly girl who incessantly mouths Maoist slogans has nothing whatsoever in common with the subtle poet Jules Supervielle, but the presence of his name increases the intellectual aura.

The film dawdles along or leaps about in typically Godardian *non sequiturs:* short, disconnected, sometimes inscrutable scenes tied together only by arcane intertitles or coy shots of *La Chinoise* being actually filmed by Coutard and a film crew. There are skits about the Vietnam war: a copy of Chairman Mao's "little red book" being thrown at a toy U.S. tank and stopping it; Guillaume, in a symbolic paper-tiger mask, speaking into a telephone, "Hello Kosygin, is that you?"; Yvonne, in Vietnamese peasant costume and bedaubed with catsup, yelling "Help, Mr. Kosygin, help!" as two model U. S. fighter planes buzz around her and, in the pinup behind her, the Esso tiger crouches above the word "Napalm." There are scenes in which Guillaume monologizes about how Marxism-Leninism helps him with his acting; or in which Véronique discourses about her yearnings to blow up the Sorbonne, the Louvre, or the Comédie Française, while Kirilov or Guillaume marches around the apartment reading aloud Mao's aphorisms, which permits Godard to play games with the sound track: one voice fading in and out over another, sometimes drowning it out.

There are scenes of domesticity. The group is awakened in the morning by Kirilov, who runs around the place with a Pepsi in one hand and a radio blaring out the *Internationale* in the other—frequently he traipses across the bed in which Yvonne and Henri are sleeping, and again the sound zooms in and out on the sound track. Presently our group is out on the balcony, doing one brief setting-up exercise to a rhythmically intoned saying of Chairman Mao. Another time, Véronique is helping Yvonne with the dishes and simultaneously explaining to her some simple Marxist-Leninist proposition in even simpler terms. Godard's camera tracks compulsively back and forth, often along the balcony to pry on the group through several windows. The blank outer walls and the gaudily painted shutters provide an interesting counterpoint to the bustling and noisy group within, but Godard reiterates the device well beyond our saturation point.

Most of all, there are the standard Godardian sequences in which a character lengthily speaks into the camera in answer to questions from Godard faintly audible on the sound track. This is supposed to be *cinéma-vérité*, but as the answers are being piped by Godard into earphones concealed under the copious hair of male or female performers, it really isn't. And even if it were *cinéma-vérité*, what a bore it still would be! The characters dribble commonplaces; *e.g.,* Yvonne: "In the country, women are completely disoriented," which Godard tries to relieve by feeding her the word *"déboussolées,"* far too big for the likes of Yvonne. Or, again, Guillaume: "I want to make theater, real theater . . . Something like Brecht or Shakespeare . . . Mao's thoughts can be of help to me." Or Véronique: "Gradually I realized that it was right, after all, philosophy in a workingmen's suburb." And so on.

Godard the jokester is always ready. Let someone say "countryside" and, bingo, we get an intercut shot of the country; let someone mention "chickens" and, forthwith, there are chickens scampering across the screen. There is the typical Sorbonne humor: "One class overthrows the other—I am in philosophy class"; or, as the camera shows a crucifix being overshadowed by hundreds of "little red books" piled onto bookshelves, Guillaume's and Véronique's voices intone antiphonally, "My God, why have you forsaken me?—Because I don't exist." Blackout. Again, Véronique states her age: "19 years, 8 months, 14 hours and 20 seconds." (A new form, that: *cinémathématiques-vérité.*) Or take the scene in which Guillaume and Véronique hurl words at each other "to talk as if words were sounds and matter"—which, incidentally, they always are in Godard's films. There ensues, approximately, the following duologue:

> Au bord de la rivière . . .
> Vert et bleu . . .
> Tendresse . . .
> Un peu de désespoir . . .
> Après-demain . . .
> Peut-être . . .
> Un film de Nicholas . . . Ray . . .
> Rouge-gorge . . .
> Rock . . . and roll . . .
> Et cétera . . .

There are also, needless to say, the "in" references to *Johnny Guitar*, Jacques Rivette, and a tirade by Guillaume in which he tries to demonstrate, by means of rather halting sophistries, that Méliès was really the first documentarist and Lumière the first cinematic storyteller—as if that reversal could be made convincing, and as if, in any case, it mattered.

All this is punctuated by dozens of still photographs of everyone who is mentioned—or not even mentioned—from Bakunin to Rosa Luxemburg, from Sartre to Aragon, from Malraux to (I think) Mayakovsky, from Malcolm X to Belmondo. And over and over again there are maxims and slogans littering the screen, often coming on bit by scrambled bit for greater illegibility, and frequently in dizzying competition with the narration or dialogue. It is worse than double pneumonia: double logorrhea, or a kind of iconologomachy simultaneously assaulting the eye and the ear. And, as usual, the ceaseless dropping of sophomoric aphorisms: "What is a word?—A truth that remains silent." "Art is not the reflection of reality, but the realness of that reflection." And so on.

Finally, a kind of skeleton plot emerges from the closet dramatics. The cell decides to assassinate the Russian Minister of Culture who is currently the guest of the University of Nanterre. They draw lots—using one of the Chairman's sayings and an eeny-meeny-miny-Mao—and the last word falls on Véronique. Kirilov is disgruntled at not being allowed to carry out the murder, and kills himself in what looks like a fit of pique. Henri protests against terrorist methods, is declared a revisionist, and must henceforth eat his breakfast and monologize into the camera from another part of the apartment. Also, it would seem, Yvonne no longer sleeps with him.

Véronique now has a long ride on the suburban train with Francis Jeanson, who here takes the place of Brice Parain in *My Life to Live.* Jeanson, a professor of philosophy and editor, had to go into exile during the Algerian war, when he was condemned in absentia for support of the Rebels' terrorist tactics. Véronique advocates bombs and assassinations to close what she calls *"les universités fantoches"* (the puppet universities), and demands emulation of the Red Guards' strong-arm tactics. Jeanson patiently tries to point out the obvious: that the kids have no plans for the aftermath of terrorism, that there are no substitute universities that could take over, that the situation in contemporary France does not compare with the Algerian war situation and that terrorism today would win no sympathizers. Véronique barely listens and talks mostly at cross purposes. The scene goes on forever, registering every station stop; except for a few closeups, the camera holds the same two-shot with well-nigh Warholian doggedness. Jeanson's arguments do not prevail, and, in any case, Godard himself is not for them, as Stanley Kauffmann and Pauline Kael have both shown, though with differing evaluations.

Next, Véronique and a male friend drive up in front of what I take to be the University Guest House where the Russian minister is staying. His name is Mikhail Sholokhov, and if he is really meant to be that middle-brow writer who hounded Pasternak, Sinyavsky, and Daniel, he almost deserves to get plugged. Véronique walks in and, off-camera, bumps him off. As she jumps into the leisurely getaway car, she realizes she got the wrong room number and guy. *"Merde!"* she mutters, and goes back to get the right one. Presently she emerges on the balcony and signals that it's all taken care of. She and her crony drive off unmolested. Here, as always when dealing with violence, Godard is totally masturbatory. There is not a shred of reality in any of this: no detonations, no people around, no police, no remorse, no aftereffects of any kind.

There follow some peculiar and wholly disjointed scenes, the strangest of which (twice repeated) has Guillaume in period costume in an opera house or theater, walking along the railing from box to box, and spouting at the similarly costumed and confused spectators in the boxes something I could not make any sense of. (The dishonest critics who write about this and other films by Godard as if they were perfectly lucid, never mention such scenes.) At last, the daughter of the regular tenants arrives in the apartment and deplores the mess. We hear the off-screen voice of Véronique announcing that, as she went back to school, she grasped that what she had taken for a great step forward was, in fact, only the first timid step of a very long march. So much for the murder of two men, one wholly innocent; and so much for this film, artistically and morally imbecile.

La Chinoise is even more unreal, disconnected, pretentious, and insignificant than that; the moment you transpose into words and summarize, you impose an order and meaning the original fragments lack. Godard either cannot or will not tell a story; either way it comes to the same thing. This is not the place to argue the point, but let me at least state that I firmly believe that a full-length film needs a plot, however complex, simplified, or unconventional it may be. But Godard has been quoted as saying, "For me, the movie is what is shot, just as the day is what is lived." This is a piece of double idiocy: first, life and art cannot be equated; secondly, what is shot is indeed the movie, but can we leave aside the question of whether it is a good movie? Godard's slapdash, improvised method covers the screen with the requisite ninety minutes of film, but what is it, since it is not a story?

The two standard defenses of Godard's self-indulgence are (a) that he is a blender of story and documentary, of *cinéma* and *vérité;* and (b) that he is a cinematic essayist. Aside from the fact that these explanations are mutually contradictory, neither of them holds up individually. To begin with the first, I used to have a professor at Harvard who was widely known as a scholar and gentleman—that is, the scholars considered him a gentleman, and the gentlemen a scholar. The fact that the scholars did not consider him a scholar, nor the gentlemen a gentleman, did not matter; his reputation was made by the simple device of having a foot in both doors. Thus documentarists seem willing to concede that Godard turns out interesting fictions; and fictionists allow that he may be telling it as it really is. On these complementary misunderstandings and disclaimers, Godard thrives. In this light, the sequence in which Guillaume argues that Méliès was really a documentarist and Lumière a fictionist takes on added pathos.

Even genuine *cinéma-vérité* has rightly been questioned as to its documentary validity; how much more spurious, then, is the pseudo *cinéma-vérité* in which Godard, in one way or another, puts the "improvisations" into his actors' mouths. It might be objected that *The Battle of Algiers,* for instance, is also a staged documentary, and a fine, valid film. True, but it is a re-creation of historical facts; what Godard re-creates is a social pseudofact—his notion of how a country girl who went from bourgeois housework to bourgeois prostitution, and thence to Maoist housework and prostitution, would respond to questioning about her background and opinions. If this were incorporated in an honest fiction film, it would be both truer and less true than life; in any case, it would be honest. To make something look like on-the-spot reporting when, in fact, it is fiction (and not very good fiction at that) is dishonest. Above all, it is neither fact nor fiction.

As for Godard's so-called fictions, what are they? Relationships are not even clearly indicated in *La Chinoise*, let alone developed. The nearest thing to a glimpse of Véronique's and Guillamue's relation is a joint reading session at which the boy questions the girl's ability to do two things simultaneously. So she puts on a record of romantic piano music and, at the same time, informs him that she no longer loves him. It turns out that he was aware of both the music and his dismissal. There, she tells him, he has done two things at once. Richard Roud, in his preposterous Godard monograph, takes this scene at face value, as the end of an affair. Actually, it is just a piece of rather nasty Godardian hi-jinks; not at all a genuine action, let alone two at once. The "plot" of *La Chinoise* is made up of such bits. No doubt, someone will argue that that is sufficient plot: the adequate representation of the lives of youthful activists or hippies. But would stringing together a number of incidents reported in the *East Village Other* constitute a story?

What is patently lacking in Godard is a point of view, a vision, or just a strongly held opinion. (I discount such modish affectations as "Maosim is in, so let's make a film about Maoism, more or less endorsing it.") Now, many writers and critics have sensibly protested against the simplistic attribution to the author of a character's opinions. Nevertheless, it is clear that a good novelist's sympathies can be located (I am not speaking of the wretched *nouveau roman*): one can tell whose side Mann, Proust, Kafka, Joyce, Beckett, Genet, are on—to say nothing of earlier masters, no matter how naturalistic, objective, or marmoreal they were. What makes these writers more complex than others is that they can see good even in the characters they are against, bad even in the ones with whom they identify themselves. But one can reconstruct their moral universe from their works.*

In Godard, too, the good and the bad are mixed; unfortunately, they are downright scrambled, and it is not even clear which is which. Though I am convinced that Godard is wholly for the kids (in which case Jeanson becomes merely the voice of yesterday's radical sadly hardened into dreary "common sense"), it is possible to argue that he is condemning them (in which case Jeanson becomes the basis of sweet reasonableness), or that he is making gentle fun of them but still prefers their youthful intransigence to Jeanson's middle-aged middle-of-the-

---

*The same arguments can be made in behalf of great filmmakers like Fellini, Antonioni, Bergman.

road position. Now, I submit that it may even be possible for a story-teller to be uncommitted to any side, though I doubt it. An essayist, however (and thus I refute the second argument for the defense), must have a point of view: in the essay it is point of view that assumes the role of plot in the story. One of the chief distinctions between the essay and journalistic chitchat is precisely point of view, be that something as simple as love of nature, sympathy for old age, or belief in God. If Arnold had not had a preference between them, *Culture and Anarchy* could not have been written; if Eliot had not had a feeling for both of them, there could have been no "Tradition and the Individual Talent."

Much has been made of Godard's coining the phrase "The children of Marx and Coca-Cola," and having made a "film-essay" about them, *Masculine Feminine,* to which *La Chinoise* is considered a sequel of sorts. But what does that phrase mean? That the world is dominated by the ideologies, cultures, and politics of Russia and the United States? If we didn't know that already, what *do* we know? In *La Chinoise,* the division becomes tripartite, with Red China triumphantly —or is it triumphantly?—added. But what, in either "essay," does Godard tell us, or merely clarify, or just try to illuminate? His sup-posedly ambivalent attitude toward these kids, swooned about as something new and wonderful by Miss Kael, is at least as old as the gangster movies; was present again, in all its wonderful wishy-washi-ness, in our films about rebellious youth (*e.g., The Wild One, Rebel Without a Cause*); and comes to us now, without benefit of Godard, from every corner of the map.

There are other kinds of admiration. Andrew Sarris extols *La Chinoise* for, apparently, no more cogent reasons than the alleged visual allusions in it to old Lubitsch and Murnau movies, and its being "more than Godard's valentine to youth . . . also his valedictory." Godard, needless to say, cannot bid youth adieu, for youth or, more exactly, childishness is all he has got. He cannot make a movie about grown-ups: his one try, *Contempt* (which, moreover, was imposed on him), was perhaps his most resounding failure. *The Married Woman* and *Alphaville* cannot be called films about adults: the child-wife and the invulnerable supersleuth are infantile figures.

"A satire that loves its targets more than it loves anything else," Miss Kael miscalls *La Chinoise.* Clearly, a satire that loves its targets cannot cut them up, and a noncutting knife is not a knife, just as an essay that does not essay or assay is not an essay.

The acting in *La Chinoise* is paltry stuff. The new Mme Godard, Anne Wiazemsky, exhibits, as Véronique, the same lack of talent as in her first film, Bresson's *Balthazar.* It is hard to say whether that lopsided face is a plucked chicken's or a skinned rabbit's; it is, in any case, absolutely sexless and endowed with only one, not so much all-purpose as no-purpose, expression. Jean-Pierre Léaud, the New Wave hippie *par excellence,* is equally ungifted and unprepossessing. As Guillaume, he combines plebeian inconsequentialness with pushy pipsqueakery. He, too, has one basic look, a kind of hairy, wise-guy hungriness, underlined by a tuneless, wizened voice. No less repellent is the Kirilov of Lex de Bruijn, a sullen nonentity distinguished only by his monstrous butchery of the French language. He has a curious way of pronouncing *l'art* as *l'aïl* (garlic), a fortuitious but not altogether inept description of Godard's endeavor.

Here a parenthesis. It is interesting to note the *nouvelle vague's* predilection for casting someone in their films who will rape hell out of the lovely French language. Thus we had Jean Seberg, Anna Karina, Jack Palance, Fritz Lang, Eddie Constantine, Akim Tamirov, László Szabó, and de Bruijn in Godard's films; Eiji Okada, Giorgio Albertazzi, and, to a much lesser degree, Ingrid Thulin in Resnais's; Oskar Werner in Truffaut's. There are thick accents also in the films of Chabrol (*The Cousins, Leda*), Malle (*The Lovers*), Eric Rohmer (*Sign of the Lion*), and so on. On the surface, this might appear to be prankish antichauvinism or even genuine yearning for internationalism; but I think that something deeper is at work here: hatred of language, the desire to desecrate the word.

The other two principals are acceptable. Michel Sémeniako is pleasant as Henri, with his somewhat bruised equanimity; and Juliet Berto is at least ingenuous and toothsome as Yvonne. Nevertheless, in her on-camera monologue, her continual fiddling with her hair or face (whether or not it is intentional, whether or not it is forced on her by Godard) manages to be intensely irritating.

The point about Godard, ultimately, is that he is always beside the point. Let me illustrate that on three levels. First, in his details. In the reveille scene, Henri and Yvonne, who are lovers, are seen sleeping in a double bed. Guillaume sleeps in a chair, with his feet on the radiator. Where his girl, Véronique, or Kirilov sleeps is not shown at all. Now, it is wholly improbable that Guillaume would spend a summer sleeping in a chair; and what about those other two? There are no visible "sleeping possibilities" (as the German word has it) in the apartment. This is because the apartment used was that of the director Antoine Bourseiller, who had just been hired to run the theater in Aix-en-Provence. The one double bed was enough for Bourseiller, but not for the characters in the film, or for our being able to see their true *modus vivendi.* But Godard is sublimely indifferent to such simple, homely truths.

Take the next level, the intellectual one. Godardians have assured me that a key to the film is the parable told by Guillaume. The ancient Egyptians, believing their language to be divinely inspired, locked up some infants in a room away from all human contact. After fifteen years, they let them out, expecting them to speak perfect God-given Egyptian. Instead, the children were bleating. It was then noticed that the room overlooked a sheepfold. From this we are supposed to deduce that it is the world they live in that makes Maoists of our youth. Well, kids may grow into goats, or even sheep—but Maoists? As the atmosphere around them became daily more stodgily bourgeois and restrictive, the French students finally revolted. That, however, was reaction against one's environment—the exact opposite of what obtains in Godard's parable.

Now for the third level, that of social and political relevance. On this subject, I urge you to read Stanley Kauffmann (*The New Republic,* April 27, 1968). I cite only his conclusion: "Either *La Chinoise* is fundamentally serious or it is an inconsequential divertissement on a serious theme. If the latter, it is irresponsible; if the former, it is glib." In the very issue of the *New York Times* (April 4, 1968) in which Godard's latest bit of *chinoiserie* was glowingly reviewed, there appeared a news story with the caption "Leftist Students Win Concession at University in Suburb of Paris." This was the beginning of the student revolt, which originated precisely at Véronique's University of Nanterre, and which, to Godard's admirers, proves that their idol possesses, beyond his cinematic genius, uncanny prophetic powers. When Godard made *La Chinoise,* student discontent was already brewing; still, it was observant of him to take serious note of it. As for the details of his prophecy, they proved no more accurate than the vaticinations of other popular seers from Nostradamus to Jeane Dixon. There were to be no political assassinations, certainly no attacks on Russian dignitaries; yet in other ways the students's revolt assumed much greater dimensions than Godard predicted. If Pauline Kael wishes to consider this as being ahead of the headlines, she may do so; I call it being beside the point.

But what does all this matter when our debased criticism is ready to approve Godard's seven-league-booted self-indulgence every step of the way? Miss Kael proclaims Godard's "genius" to the middle brows in the *New Yorker;* preaching to the high brows, Susan Sontag declares: "*Les Carabiniers* is the only [Godard] film in which death is arbitrary while it fits, because the whole film is arbitrary." (Quoted by Herbert Lottman, *The Columbia University Forum,* Spring 1968) Aside from the splendor of the diction—"death is arbitrary while it fits"; will it become germane when it ceases to fit?—consider the profundity of the

thought. It means nothing less than that you can justify the nonsensicalness of a part by the nonsensicalness of the whole, and, no doubt, vice
versa. In an era in which Miss Sontag can pass for an eminent critic,
Godard should certainly pass for a great artist.

The very proof of his importance, said Andrew Sarris to me at the
end of a radio debate, is the amount of time we spent on him. But that
only proves that there are different kinds of importance. Godard is
insignificant as an artist, but highly significant as a disease.

Spring, 1968

P.S. (July 1970): When I wrote this article, student unrest in France
had not yet gone beyond its initial phase. I have, therefore, slightly
updated the piece. Whoever suspects my hindsight of being better than
my sight is invited to consult the original version, "Bull in the China
Shop," in the Spring 1968 issue of *Film Heritage.* He will find that I
have made no substantial change because none was necessary. My
review of *La Chinoise* in *The New Leader* (May 6, 1968) was essentially
a briefer version of the *Film Heritage* article. It did, however, contain
a paragraph worth reprinting here: "When Godard can't have intertitles, he has his pseudoaction . . . surrounded by slogans and inscriptions
of all kinds on posters, blackboards, or directly on the walls. Whenever
possible, the narration or dialogue clashes with these inscriptions or
titles. The result is rather as if one of those heinous TV commercials,
where the mythical superiority of a product over all its identical com-
petitors is simultaneously written and shouted at you (so that mere
blindness of deafness should be no excuse for not buying it), suddenly
went schizophrenic and assaulted your unbelieving eyes and ears with
berserkly divergent messages. Your enjoyment of *La Chinoise* will
depend entirely on how partial you are to organized schizophrenia."

BENJAMIN

At the end of *Benjamin* there is a note reading, "Benjamin *est une oeuvre
de pure imagination."* Those responsible for—or, better, guilty of—this
film lack the least inkling of "pure," to say nothing of "imagination."
Benjamin is a marathon tease, an uninterrupted series of interrupted
coitions, meant to keep us in suspense about which one of a slew of
budding or overripe beauties will first bed the seventeen-year-old

protagonist. To make the costumes and repartee saucier, the feebleminded plot is couched, or bedded, in the eighteenth century, permitting deeper *décolletage* and profounder epigrams. Yet Nina Companeez, the scenarist, gets no closer to Chamfort and Rivarol than to St. Thomas Aquinas, and the director, Michel Deville, is no better than any other eighteenth-century filmmaker.

With the décolletés, to be sure, the film does considerably better; it becomes a veritable nipplorama. Among the young ladies, Anna Gaël is an absolute stunner, and a few others are worth a lip-smacking or two. But caught in the painful pseudosophistication of *Benjamin,* they all prove dangerous acquaintances. And as the young protagonist, Pierre Clémenti merely reaffirms the blood ties between cuteness and atrociousness.

One thing must be said, however, for this deplorable film. It has a splendid cinematographer in Ghislain Cloquet, who is inventively assisted by Claude Pignot's art direction and Rita Bayance's costumes. We get large areas—fabrics, walls, foliage—in strong solid colors instead of the usual fussy patterns. This creates a posterlike effect, with sizable chunks of one or two striking colors leaping out of an equally brilliant but contrasting solid-color background. *Benjamin* is like a gorgeously wrapped and beribboned Christmas package containing an empty box, and, as such, emblematic of the present state of French culture.

April, 1968

LES BICHES

The one purveyor of pretentious tripe who can almost hold his own against Godard is Claude Chabrol, who gave Godard his first real break. Credited with fathering the New Wave, Chabrol hit his stride with his initial film, *Le beau Serge,* and the rest was downhill. Whereas Godard takes all human knowledge and endeavor for his province, Chabrol's satrapy is the depth of the human soul, which he sounds without the slightest regard for psychology but with a voracious zeal for perversion, for whose logic he shows equal disregard. A film by Chabrol is like a game of chess where, at Chabrol's whim, a pawn can get knighted, and a bishop can carry on like a raving queen.

It may well be that, pretentious as he is, Chabrol would call his realm Evil and refer to it as Cosmic, which is to say Elemental, Arbitrary,

Unsoundable. In fact, it is a nasty, junior-grade sadism his characters practice on one another, usually consisting of leeringly rubbing in some kind of advantage (sexual, intellectual, financial) over someone less privileged, who may suffer humiliation in abject submission or bite back like a rabid underdog. There are some variations in the pattern, but the gratuitous bitchiness is always there—the more unmotivated, the more Metaphysical, Significant, and Profound.

Les Biches, on whose script Chabrol collaborated with his favorite scenarist, Paul Gégauff (he can be seen playing the piano in Godard's *Weekend,* and please shoot the piano player), is as stupid, ugly, and mean-spirited a film as you can find this side of Godard and that side of Losey, without even the perquisites those other two may offer. In *Les Biches,* a rich, idle young woman, Frédérique, picks up a pretty girl named Why, which makes her the eponymous heroine of Chabrol's world. Why earns a precarious—and totally implausible—living by drawing chalk pictures on the sidewalks of Paris. Frédérique seduces her, and whisks her off to the lush villa in St.-Tropez, where she already maintains a pair of semicretinous and presumably pederastic males who apparently serve as jesters but do not really amuse anyone.

St.-Tropez is dull in winter, and Chabrol makes it even duller by not being able to convey the rhythms and patterns of hibernation. The relationship of the two women remains unexamined, except that we know Frédérique dominates and Why occasionally sulks; the latter, in a rather ambiguous speech, declares herself a virgin. At a boring party for the locals, Why meets Paul, an architect, who talks and behaves like a satyr under sedation. His humorlessly snotty dialogue and sultry lower lip prove irresistible to Why, who falls an easy prey. Frédérique resents the competition and promptly takes over Paul herself. Why *seems* to be suffering, but in a Chabrol film it is hard to tell anguish from mild dyspepsia.

After a trip to Paris, Paul and Frédérique settle down at her villa. The two trolls have been dismissed, and Why becomes the servant-victim of the lovers, both of whom have had and rejected her. Her attitude is slavish adoration mixed with sporadic arrogance and petty sabotage. When the lovers carry on in bed, Why watches through the keyhole and has sympathetic orgasms. Or they all three get drunk together, and Frédérique's black-stockinged foot toys with Paul's face under Why's nose. (Roughly one-half of Stéphane Audran's performance as Frédérique consists of wiggling her toes.) When the lovers go off to Paris again, Why follows Frédérique to her town apartment, passionately exhorts her, is rebuffed, and stabs her with her own poisoned dagger. Whereupon Why puts on the dead woman's clothes, lies on her bed, impersonates her on the phone with Paul, whom she summons to her side. As Paul is about to enter, the film ends—as evasively and phonily as it progressed.

Even out of this unpromising material something could be made, if Chabrol had a feeling for people, places, and continuity. But his people are only mean little puppets jolted hither and yon by a mean little puppeteer. Thus when Frédérique torments her in various humiliating ways, Why accepts it calmly; but when Frédérique writes her an honest letter explaining where things stand, Why sets out to murder her. It is never made clear what anyone sees in anyone else, why loyalties or affections or desires (or whatever it is that these personages have) change in the way they do, and what the various relations involve or even imply.

The backgrounds are always glamorously tony and caught by Jean Rabier in varieties of soft focus aspiring to the conditions of pastel. There are interminable tracking shots of one or two heads in closeup floating against a dreamy landscape to the accompaniment of Debussyesque music. In the interiors, the emphasis has shifted somewhat from the baroquely overdecorated, as in *The Cousins, Leda,* and *Landru;* or the atmospheric and picturesque, as in *Les bonnes Femmes* and *The Third Lover.* They now strive to be symbolic, with expanses of empty wall space interrupted by isolated, flashy objects: a crazy drawing by Why showing a doe (*biche,* a term also applied to young girls) in the womb of another doe weeping tears of blood; a pair of toy radiometers by Frédérique and Paul's bed; an odd *objet* above Why's bed that looks like a stylized alembic or retort in which a red fluid is brewing; a poisoned dagger mounted above a large caption, "POISONED DAGGER"; and so on.

The dialogue is commensurate. One of the male clowns says of the other's painting, "It's shit; and, furthermore, everything is shit!" Just before the killing, Frédérique says, "You horrify me. You disgust me. Your love disgusts me." Whereupon Why comments, *"Alors salut, la vieille!"* ("Then cheerio, old girl!") and does her in.

But worst of all is the pacing. Episode drifts into episode, movement is haphazard and not followed through, random violence is expected to create tension. What we need is not shown, what we don't need is, often at fatuous length. The acting maunders along with the film. As Why, Jacqueline Sassard (the girl in *Accident*) once again looks cow-eyed and lymphatic as she mopes and pouts through her part. Stéphane

Audran (Mme Chabrol—which explains a thing or two, though not everything) combines the vacuous, far-off gaze of a blind explorer with a surly, pinched delivery of lines as if they were shoes several sizes too small. Jean-Louis Trintignant looks into the camera with the morose solicitude of a dandy counting his gray hairs in the mirror, and only in the drunk scene does he allow his well-starched expression to get ever so slightly rumpled. The women look interchangeable (interchangeability being a favorite Chabrolian theme), and you can almost see tubes attached to the heads of all the characters, through which the meaning has been sucked out of them and Chabrol pumped in.

December, 1968

LA CHAMADE

An old-fashioned Gallic pill with some "now" sugarcoating is Alain Cavalier's *La Chamade,* the film he and Françoise Sagan adapted from the latter's novel of the same name. Sagan is rather like an old wound that seems to have cicatrized until her next opus appears, and we once again feel the same pain in the neck or arse. *"C'est toujours la même odeur ici,"* someone says in *La Chamade,* which the subtitle renders as "It always smells good here," though with reference to Sagan a more literal translation would be preferable.

The story concerns Charles, the super-rich middle-aged businessman, who lives with Lucile, the gorgeous young butterfly, and is so understanding that he virtually pushes her into the arms of impecunious young Antoine, the lover of a rich widow and employed as a publisher's reader. Poverty in Mlle Sagan always means modest yet tasteful surroundings, such as Antoine's cozy, book-lined *garçonnière* overlooking the back of the Elysée Palace. But Charles is nevertheless somewhat upset when Lucile, having drunk herself into a sun-baked stupor at St.-Tropez out of sheer yearning for Antoine, finally announces that she is leaving his palatial mansion in Neuilly for the said tastefully modest surroundings. The old cook, to be sure, knows better; she predicts Mademoiselle will come back.

It is very idyllic in Antoine's nook all summer long while Antoine doesn't have to work. But when, in the fall, he does, Lucile still enjoys waiting for and looking after him, and even reads some of the books he brings back from the publisher's. Of course, she also makes love divinely. But for Antoine, callow youth that he is, this isn't enough; he wants her to do useful work. So he finds her a job as a file clerk with a newspaper, which seems absurd when she could so easily be fashion editor of *Marie-Claire* or *Elle:* after all, it is Catherine Deneuve who enacts—or, rather, wears the clothes of—the part. In almost no time, Lucile quits the grubby job, takes it easy, and sells her jewels to make Antoine believe that she is still gainfully employed. When he finds out the awful truth, he gives her one medium-hard slap. But love conquers all—even a little white deception and a medium-hard slap—and everything might still be salvaged.

Alas, Lucile becomes pregnant. (Nowadays, that bespeaks a certain backwardness, so perhaps she couldn't have made fashion editor at *Elle.*) Antoine wants the baby and marriage, but one look at the outside of the ultramodern apartment house they then would have to live in —no old-world charm whatever!—and Lucile opts for an abortion. Magnanimously, Antoine consents, but can provide only an inexpensive local abortionist. Now this is where money really makes a difference; Charles, apprised, supplies Lucile with a stylish and safe operation in a Swiss clinic. However, it is hard on an impecunious lover's pride to have his baby aborted in style at a pecunious ex-lover's expense. The relationship is hurt to the quick. One evening, when Antoine has to confer with some of his authors, he deposits Lucile at a cinema showing *Hour of the Wolf.* Quite rightly, Lucile sneaks away to accept an invitation from Charles to a high-society musicale.

Though the Bergman film contains some Mozart music, what is that compared to a Mozart sonata performed live in a salon full of chic people? During the recital, Lucile sips champagne while Charles, with exquisite connoisseurship, whispers in her ear something about "the same little phrase—those four notes that obsessed Mozart all his life." Although that seems to describe Sagan's art more accurately than Mozart's, Lucile is so happy to be reimmersed in all this moneyed graciousness that she spends the night with Charles. Toward dawn, she makes one more trip to her love den, touches the sleeping Antoine ever so lightly, follows his pinned-up instructions to turn down the stove, and, fighting back her tears, sets the breakfast table for him. She goes down to her neighborhood bistro, phones Antoine, and, repressing further tears, tells him it's all over. As day breaks over Paris, Lucile resolutely trudges back toward luxury and Charles.

Once again, Mlle Sagan has demonstrated her profound, her incomparable knowledge of the human heart's darkest recesses. The film is directed and photographed with exquisite elegance, and contains, aside from the above plot, the requisite number of decadent minor characters, expensively furnished interiors, Yves St.-Laurent clothes, and high-priced cars.

September, 1969

LA FEMME INFIDÈLE

Claude Chabrol has long been one of my most execrated filmmakers, so that I am no less amazed at the genuine virtues of his *La Femme Infidèle* than I would be if the calendar that my cleaners will, any day now, stick under my door were hand-painted by Pablo Picasso. It is once again a triangle, in which a somewhat mousy upper-bourgeois husband kills the jovially caddish lover of his languid, supercilious, but not unmaternal wife. He disposes of the body meticulously but not without some comic difficulties, and ends up by regaining his wife's love for this deed of passionate devotion just as, ironically, the police come to get him.

The story could not be more trivial, and the fact that Chabrol (who this time wrote the screenplay without assistance from the dreadful Paul Gégauff) does not even bother to tell you how the case was cracked or what its outcome will be, reduces the plot to yet greater meagerness. But Chabrol succeeds in making his fairly standard characters interesting in their minor quirks, the slightly raveled texture of their lives, the urbane banalities they bandy about, which seem somehow to debouch on malfeasance and crime.

Most absorbing, however, are their silences. They are often grindingly long, yet they provide spaces that we can furnish with our own surmises. This, of course, requires excellence in the actors, and Michel Bouquet, as the husband, and Maurice Ronet, as the lover, have it to spare. Stéphane Audran (Mme Chabrol) is merely polished, but she fits her role by sheer snottiness and a face and figure that disturbingly flirt with both beauty and ugliness, never settling down with either. Most of the supporting parts are also well handled, and only an overeager secretary's sham sexiness is given the customary Chabrol comic-strip treatment. For the rest, he has directed with assurance, indeed finesse, restraining even that ostentatious interior decorator who lurks in his indecorous interior.

The one decidedly poor thing about *La Femme Infidèle* is Jean Rabier's photography. The colors (and I doubt that it is merely a matter of the particular print) are so pale and deliquescent in the exteriors that you expect them to start running into one another. The interiors are better; they are, however, unattractive for different reasons, such as the vast stretches of mauve wall in the married couple's bedroom. But, in contradistinction to other Chabrol films, this one has a very effective musical score by Pierre Jansen, modernistic in an unobtrusive way, and scored, I believe, mostly for cello and piano, and sometimes for piano solo. Even when the music becomes highly dramatic, the sparseness of melody and Spartan instrumentation keep it from turning hammy.

But let us get to the principal virtues of the film: its ability to tell a great deal through suggestion, and its evocative blending of the ordinary and the extraordinary. The crazy or monstrous is shown as impinging on the everyday occurrences, coloring and distorting them, yet unable finally to vitiate something basic, enduring, and brave about human life. We open with a family scene: Charles, Hélène, their son Michel, and Charles's mother sitting at a garden table and looking at old photographs. We learn much about them both as a group and as individuals through overtones and implications, and the way Hélène's infidelity is hinted at to the audience while remaining hidden from Charles is simple and effective.

By slow, casual stages we find out what is lacking in this marriage, but also what modest strengths it does have. Charles's love is not virile enough for Hélène, yet it is full of touching solicitude, which she duly appreciates. Michel is a real kid—not too attractive, bright but not clever, and a trifle spindly as one somehow expects the child of a much older father to be. Alcohol, TV, nightclubs, are shown as somewhat pathetic substitutes for passion; even the fussily overdecorated sub-urban home is not without its pathos. Still, there is that marvelous civility between the spouses: rather formal, as one finds it in the French upper middle class, but comforting in its very ceremoniousness.

Then, gradually and believably, we are shown Charles's awakening suspicions. Michel Bouquet is a remarkable actor; he can exude the nervous overconcernedness of an aging and insecure huband for a young and remote wife, he can pour the sweat of anxiety into a look or intonation without losing his worthiness and likableness in our eyes. There is something quietly manly even about his weakness, and the childish pitifulness in his worried gaze is never allowed to become ludicrous or mawkish. Best of all, he can suggest a fanaticism that would stop at nothing and also a pervasive gentleness. Out of belea-guered love, this man could do insane things; mostly, though, he is no different from the rest of us, except perhaps nicer.

Stéphane Audran, as Hélène, floats through it all like a bored but not discontented fish in an affluent aquarium. Roger Greenspun, in the

Times, was prompted to write: "She controls a sense of social parody so sustained that her simple 'Bonjour' becomes a major critique of French language and civilization." One would like to know, if that is true, what Greenspun's idea of a *minor* critique of French language and civilization might be—the novelistic work of Marcel Proust, perhaps. The fact is that she does have a cloudily abstracted stare that may well stem from myopia, and a languidly husky way of speaking that may easily be caused by adenoids. Yet the two things produce in us a fascinated exasperation, a yen to shake her by the shoulders, drown her in a magnum of Arpège, or just rape her on the nearest bearskin rug. But the French language and civilization would, in any case, remain inviolate.

Eventually Victor, the lover, enters the scene, and he is brilliantly portrayed by that extraordinary actor, Maurice Ronet. It is ineffably sad that the handsome Ronet should have gone physically to seed, but his acting is as good as ever, or better. He makes the lover into a refreshing combination of a moderately wealthy, callous playboy-dilettante and a good provider for his divorced wife and fond father to their two children. In a boudoir scene with Hélène, he is a superb mixture of courtesy and thickskinnedness, attentiveness and unromantic casualness. He looks after all her bodily and some of her emotional needs, leaving her spiritual ones cavalierly alone.

The best scene of the film, and one as good of its kind as you are likely to get, is the confrontation between husband and lover. Here dialogue, pacing, camera movement, and acting merge into an experience that shuttles between humor and horror, relentlessly exploring the no-man's-land between comic absurdity and stupefying pain. Victor tries to be sophisticatedly amicable but manages repeatedly to put his foot in Charles's entrails; Charles tries to be worldy and nonchalant while agony hangs out of his eyes. Finally, it is the ridiculous that proves hardest to bear: a giant Zippo lighter Charles gave Hélène for their third anniversary now graces Victor's bedside table. When the husband and lover speculate about why Hélène passed it on to him, Victor suggests that maybe she just likes to have it around.

That inoffensive, conciliatory remark is most hurtful of all: does Victor consider Hélène, whom Charles worships, just someone to have around? Does Hélène think of herself as more around Victor than around Charles, so that a favorite knicknack must migrate to an adulterous bedside? Incensed to the point of insanity, Charles picks up a little reproduction of an Egyptian head (a Nefertiti, I think) that strangely resembles Hélène's, and clubs Victor to death.

The last part of the film concerns the effect of this murder on the couple and their child, how the police start closing in (though their methods are left vague), how Hélène discovers what happened and takes it as the supreme token of love. When Charles is led away, he may have lost his life, but he has gained his wife's love. "I love you," says Charles, his look intensifying the weak words ad infinitum. "I love you," says Hélène, kissing his palm. "I love you like a madman," he says and goes to meet the policemen. And that is what the film is about: an otherwise ordinary man's madness, *real* madness, in his love.

There is an unusual scene in which little Michel accuses his parents of being stark mad, and the boy himself has a faintly sickly, neurotic cast about him while remaining a believable enough boy in Stéphane Di Napoli's intelligently uncute performance. Chabrol knows how to handle his actors. Thus he realizes, at least unconsciously, that his wife is not much of an actress, and he stages the scene in which Hélène believes her lover has betrayed her (though he has merely been killed) for maximum efficacy without the prerequisite of genuine histrionic ability. Hélène slowly reclines on her opulent bed, her feet remaining stiffly on the floor; she lies gravely composed like some latter-day *gisant* and, with an interval between them, emits two grisly little groans. Then the camera moves in for a closeup to catch a last, stricken moan.

Throughout the film, the camera does excellent things; it moves around quite ebulliently but, in contrast to previous Chabrol movies, its trips seem necessary or at least pleasurable rather than merely ostentatious. There are bravura moments. Thus when, having returned from the murder, Charles finds his wife in the midst of a kiddies' party on the front lawn. He has gone inside the darkening house and watches through the window as Hélène approaches. The camera closes in on the taut, anxious back of his head, while Hélène's approach is seen distantly, out of focus. The music sounds more and more frantic; the blurred Hélène keeps coming nearer and nearer—the next frame should bring her into focus. But it doesn't. Instead, the music breaks off in sour cacophony like a record running down, and the image on the screen fades away. Even the greatest love gift, murder, cannot bring these spouses together.

Another time it is Hélène at the window, uneasily awaiting her husband's return after her first encounter with the police. We get a lateral wipe that spreads across the screen from left to right, catching as it progresses the vertical staves of the window frame. This corresponds to Charles's car pulling up to the curb from left to right, so that the optical effect taking place inside the house and involving Hélène repeats an actual movement outside the house and involving Charles. Here the suggestion is one of husband and wife united at least in their shared guilt and anxiety.

I do not wish to exalt the film beyond its due. It is intended as a minor work, and resolutely minor it remains. Moreover, Chabrol is, as usual, overstressing his notion of the encroachments of the bizarre on everyday life. So there is an obnoxious drunk or madman at a bistro counter grotesquely repeating everything that is said; in a posh nightclub, an unknown beauty suddenly and sinisterly reaches over to light Charles's cigarette—later, an inebriated man sits down in her seat and insults Charles for no reason; a police inspector is continuously and preposterously playing with his nose while his colleague does all the questioning. When Charles first comes home fully aware that he is being cuckolded, the camera lingers on a large African antelope mask hanging on the wall and displaying huge horns. Nevertheless, *La Femme Infidèle* tends to be subtle and searching, and also accurate—as when Charles is delighted during his impromptu visit to his rival to be offered some bourbon and to consume, for once, the booze reserved for his wife; or when, having a terrible time getting the dead body out of the trunk of his car, Charles, rattled as he is, still takes his jacket off carefully and methodically folds if before resuming his agonizing task.

December, 1969

THE SICILIAN CLAN

It is interesting to contrast Truffaut's *Mississippi Mermaid* with Henri Verneuil's *The Sicilian Clan.* Verneuil is one of those slick, competent, routine directors of whom the French cinema over the years has produced a harvest second only to Hollywood's. If the *auteur* theory had been evolved by Americans instead of Frenchmen, the grass would, of course, have seemed greener in Billancourt than in Burbank. What sublime *auteurs* could then have been made out of Verneuil, Decoin, Marc Allegret, and a host of others; indeed, now that *auteur*ism has spread to America, certain French and French-based mediocrities like Abel Gance and Max Ophüls have been elevated to *auteur* status. Still, I doubt that Ophüls, despite his certifiable mediocrity, would have entered the Pantheon, had he not turned out a certain number of Hollywood films, which is almost *de rigueur* for canonization. Anyway, Verneuil is monstrously competent without a scintilla of genius. *The Sicilian Clan* is nowhere near up to his best, but still has that smooth purposiveness Truffaut's film lacks. Yet *The Sicilian Clan* is much more boring to watch.

It concerns another one of those superheists brilliantly carried out despite overwhelming odds as well as a few unpredictable monkey wrenches tossed in by chance—only to be undone retroactively by a piddling utterance from the mouth of a babe. It has all been done better before, and the final showdown between the dignified old mafioso, played by Jean Gabin, and the trigger-happy punk, outlined by Alain Delon, has no excitement whatever: it is the final and visible trickling out of what was always, even if lively, a shallow stream. Gabin is an imposing white whale of an old man, all bags and pouches under his snowy locks, but with blue eyes that still could stop a bullet in its tracks. And since this film invites petty speculation, let me raise the question whether any filmed eyes, however meltingly or mysteriously black, could ever compete in hauntingness with the blue ones of a Gabin, Brando, or Peter O'Toole? I speak of male eyes; women's seem to function differently on screen. To this blueness, Henri Decaé's impeccable color photography contributes handsomely.

The film has other assets, such as the fine supporting performance by Lino Ventura as one of those dogged detectives who are always accorded one humanizing trait—in this case, a running battle with cigarettes, which the inspector proves unable to give up. The gag is put to good albeit fairly standard use. There is also a most engaging score by that gifted and versatile film composer, Ennio Morricone. The only absolute liability, in fact, is Irina Demick. When she was Darryl Zanuck's special protégée, no further question was necessary; now that Zanuck's attention has moved on, one must emphatically ask why Miss Demick remains.

The final interest of this pair of films lies in the different approaches to the thriller by the old pro and the young New Waver, the *nouvelle vague* having arisen precisely in opposition to the Verneuils and their ilk. Quite obviously to anyone but himself, Truffaut is not content to let plot predominate—to permit imitation of Hitchcock, which is not much different from Verneuilism, to maintain the upper hand. Instead, a Renoirian side asserts itself; *Mermaid,* in fact, is dedicated to Renoir and begins with an awkwardly dragged in quotation from his *La Marseillaise.* The chief Renoirian characteristic, a loving involvement with people, is very much present in Truffaut's film and makes it the worthier failure of the two.

April, 1970

SYMPATHY FOR THE DEVIL

There is no sense of humor whatever in Jean-Luc Godard's latest abomination, *1 + 1,* also known as *Sympathy for the Devil.* I suppose that what is so truly dreadful about Godard is that even his jokes—for he makes them, occasionally—are utterly mirthless, chillingly excogitated, mean. But if his fun is the lipless laughter of the skull, his indignation, which makes up most of his filmic content these days, is the rattling of dry bones. *Sympathy for the Devil* is not, however, the dance of death for bourgeois society Godard would have it be, nor the scourge of black revolutionaries whose dilatoriness it is meant to sting into action. It is merely the jiggling of Halloween paper-cutout skeletons, the sound and fury of an idiot who cannot even tell a tale.

Although the film was made in England, it is meant, one presumes, to comment on the American situation. The leitmotif is a session with the Rolling Stones, who are seen recording their song, *Sympathy for the Devil.* We are obliged to watch these five scruffy types plinking and plunking away, and hear Mick Jagger repeat the same lyric over and over again. Even if the stuff were bearable to begin with, it would not be so the bumpteenth time around. Relentlessly, in recurrent scene after scene, Godard rubs our eyes and ears and, above all, our noses in the mess.

Joseph Morgenstern, in *Newsweek,* calls this "a grand metaphor for growth." If, in its finished version, the Stones's song were *Wozzeck,* or Strauss's *Four Last Songs,* or the ceiling of the Sistine Chapel, I could see using its evolution as a persuasive metaphor for something—artistic growth, most likely, not universal growth. But that the piddling over a tenth-rate piece of pop music, photographed in the most languorously repetitive way, should become a metaphor for anything but the debauched values of our time, strikes me as absurd.

There we sit hungry for bread, and Godard gives us Stones. Alternating with this, he provides us with bits of political-philosophical comic strips that are even more appalling. He shows us a bunch of black militants encamped in an automobile graveyard, where they mostly read aloud from various pamphlets and books while guns are being passed around; or else, three abducted white girls in white nightgowns are being pawed on camera, or, off-camera, raped, buggered, and shot to the reading of Eldridge Cleaver's descriptions of his lust for white girls. (You may ask how I know about the buggery; the posture and state of the bleeding corpses reveal it.) At other times, one Negro will endlessly be reading an inflammatory text to another black, who slowly repeats it to his taperecorder. Thus we get the benefit of hearing it all in duplicate. Still another time, two black girl reporters interview one of these revolutionaries, and are given long, possibly improvised, answers redolent with bellicose platitudes.

My favorite sequence is the one where guns are being hurled from left to right of the screen, going from hand to hand, until they reach the anchor man, who neatly piles them on the bodies of two blood-smeared white girls (the cadavers still have their nightgowns on—lest the important ideas involved be degraded to mere flesh and blood; blood, to be sure, is all right, but flesh would be demeaning). When the girls are completely covered with guns, he starts removing the guns and tossing them from right to left across the screen, where they again go flying from hand to hand of picturesquely stationed blacks amid automobile corpses, while off-screen, we hear a random fusillade. We have here, presumably, another grand metaphor for the pettifogging aspects of this as yet inadequate revolution.

It is all indescribably uncinematic and boring. And as if this were not enough, Godard keeps introducing his homely and untalented wife, Anne Wiazemsky, in a number of preposterous scenes, as a character called Eve Democracy. Eve is either being interviewed for the benefit of a film within a film that is being shot; or getting shot literally in the end, in a filmed-within-filmed black uprising. In between, we see her scrawling Godardian quasi-clever political *jeux d'esprit* on everything from the plate glass of the London Hilton, where she is staying, to bridges, billboards, parked cars, and any other surface that will stand still long enough to be smeared with a sophomoric slogan.

The interview scene is particularly insufferable. A callow youth with a microphone pursues the picturesquely gotten-up Miss Wiazemsky all over a woodsy landscape, among trees and around bushes, while pitching elaborately neo-Marxist questions at her—questions couched in sentences of Proustian length, to which the answer is either Yes or No. While weaving in and out of the shrubbery, Eve Democracy ponders these grave posers she is pelted with, and, after three or four seconds of profound meditation, disburses her oracular answers. Meanwhile the cameraman in the film scrambles about, cables are jiggled around, the interviewer (who is also the film-within-the-film's director) flips the pages of his notebook, and the whole thing adds up to a splendid tribute to conjugal love: since Mme Godard, alias Mlle Wiazemsky, alias Eve Democracy, is obviously too inept to improvise answers, these elaborate Yes-or-No questions had to be specially prefabricated in her husband's uxoriously solicitous brain. It is *cinéma-vérité* at two removes from *vérité*, and heaven only knows how many from *cinéma*.

In between the black militant, Eve Democracy, and Rolling Stone sequences, we are treated to those famous Godard titles, captions fraught with punning and anagrammatic wisdom. This time around, the lettering on the screen is illegible, and the word games farfetched and unfunny. (For example, "Sight anD Sound," meaning that England's favorite film-buff magazine equals Students for a Democratic Society. Even if that were true, it would still be a pitiful attempt at verbal wit.) It is a case of three-dimensional dementia: verbal, cinematic, and ideological.

The *Daily Texan* has reported some of Godard's statements to the students of the University of Texas. Maître Godard has been touring the country with one of his latest masterpieces, *See You at Mao* or *British Sounds,* and after each screening he answers student questions. Here are some of his utterances:

"We are making a political film, in a political way. That may mean stop making a movie. . . . People don't need images. None are self-evident. . . . The movie is an ideological product. It's still 100 per cent controlled by imperialists. Hollywood is just a branch in ideology of the CIA. Imperialism has produced images, but almost no sound. . . . We need to produce few images and lots of sounds, which have been suppressed. We need to change the ideology that makes the Bank of America possible. . . . When I understood that money is the ruling force, like Marx said, I turned into a revolutionary." His films, Godard added, serve as blackboards. "They tell other revolutionary groups how it's coming, what to do, what not to do."

This is all very touching, but why should it have to be judged as cinema? And why should Godard expect it to move or persuade anyone not already in his camp? Why is it not being distributed as leaflets, pamphlets, or blackboards? Why shouldn't sane film critics, as the *New Statesman*'s John Coleman did, walk out on it in disgust? Why should ordinary filmgoers be expected to pay money for it? Why should well-paid bourgeois film reviewers, like the *New York Times*'s Vincent Canby and Roger Greenspun, *both* publish Pantherish raves about it? And why should *Newsweek*'s Morgenstern write "the informing idea is sheer genius"? Some genius, I guess, is so sheer, it is positively threadbare.

May, 1970

9

Young Directors

SOME OF the young directors whose works are discussed here are not all that young, but they are new to us and do represent a more enterprisingly youthful kind of filmmaking. Many of them, however, are literally young, and since they come from such diverse countries as Canada and Israel, Sweden and Hungary, America and Czechoslovakia, it stands to reason that they are representative of what is happening in the new, young cinema. There are underground filmmakers here (Robert Downey) and recent graduates of film schools (Jiří Menzel, Dan Wolman); directors fresh from television (Michael Ritchie, Robert Altman) and others who have made quite a few films already (Elio Petri); men who have come from swinging London to hip Hollywood (Michael Sarne, Peter Yates), others who have since gone the other way (John Cassavetes), and some who have just stayed in one or the other place—England, after all, has its Pinewood. There are men of very solid talent (Jaromil Jireš, Zbyněk Brynych, Robert Enrico), others with just about none (Michael Sarne, Dan Wolman), and still others who may have genius (Jan Troell, Miklós Jancsó, Marco Bellocchio). What, if anything, do they have in common?

The one distinctly encouraging resemblance among most of these filmmakers is their willingness to be both experimenters and traditionalists, to try new techniques without overthrowing venerable and still workable modes. Another quite heartening common denominator is the international look of all these films. You cannot say of Kenneth Loach, for example (questions of talent aside), that he is typically English in his approach; you will find in *Poor Cow* as much Hollywood and Godard as you will England and Elstree. Though Robert Enrico is French, his sympathy for people both young and old, his eye for odd types one stumbles across during nocturnal wanderings through the city, his sense of life changing from ludicrous to tragic between systole and diastole seem very much related to certain Italian masters like Fellini, Monicelli, Olmi, and make *Zita* more of an Italian film than a French one—felicitously, considering what today's French films are like.

To be sure, the most international element in many of these films is not a happy one: the Godardian influence. But, be it said to the credit of many young filmmakers, they make use of Godard as freely and idiosyncratically as he made use of the Monogram pictures and other Hollywood trash served up to him by Henri Langlois at the Cinémathèque Française. Thus Němec's *Diamonds of the Night* may in some ways resemble *Les Carabiniers,* but how much more humanly it indicts the inhumanity of war. Bellocchio's missing, or misleading, establishing shots may stem from Godard, but how much more wittily and suggestively he uses the device. Jancsó's non sequiturs, like the episode of the Red nurses being made to dance for the Whites and then being sent back unmolested (in *The Red and the White*), may also have its analogues in Godard; but it is only weird, not preposterous.

The young European filmmaker, when he can raise the requisite backing, is clearly luckier than his American counterpart. I have just learned how much guff the scenarist of *Downhill Racer* had to take from Paramount, to what extent the script had to be softened and watered down. Such interference, though on its way out, is still very frequent, and it is the younger and less established director who gets the worst bullying. Of course, he may operate independently, like Robert Downey with *Putney Swope,* and be impeded just as much by his own lack of discipline. Sometimes a first film may succeed under the American system just because the experienced technicians virtually direct it for the fledgling director—as may well have been the case with *Pretty Poison.* This may be one reason for successful first works without follow-up. Or it may be that a country just isn't geared to the production of feature films—as is the case with Canada, for reasons that I cannot quite fathom—and so a promising first feature like *Isabel* leads to nothing. On the other hand, in Europe, the individual talent can do wonders, as when Jan Troell writes, directs, photographs, and edits his film *Here Is Your Life,* and it comes out a work of unquestionable art—except that the American distributor chops fifty-seven minutes out of it! A minor tragedy, but nothing compared to the major one of Czechoslovakia, where resurgent Stalinism swallows up, along with personal freedom, great cinematic achievement and even greater expectations.

A risky art, film, where the young artist is beset at every step by monsters and pitfalls more dreadful than those that await the knight errant on his quest. But once he has made his film, a lively international audience approaches it with sympathetic voraciousness, and, whereas there was only one Holy Grail, there are now more awards and prizes than you can shake a clapper at.

FESTIVAL OF CZECHOSLOVAK FILM: PART I

Kenneth Tynan has remarked that, for whatever reason, all exciting theatrical aggregations are Left-oriented. The reasons (as Tynan must know perfectly well) are fairly obvious. Theater tends to become enthralling when it is youthful, when it possesses a solidarity transcending individual needs to shine, and when it is fired with some sort of humanitarian zeal, usually one of protest against prevailing inertia. These conditions, evidently, are much more likely to be met by some form of radicalism than by conservatism or reaction; besides, youth is almost by definition radical, and woe betide should it be otherwise. Similar principles obtain in filmmaking, at least in countries where it is a group activity in which young people can band together, and not the prerogative of a senescent commercial empire or the refuge of untrained and undisciplined drifters.

What particularly inspires and invigorates an artistic movement is a new-found freedom; a political thaw, however incomplete, following upon years of war, dictatorship, and political repression. This condition is, of course, beneficial to all the arts, but especially so to those of youth, and youth, nowadays, turns with a rapturous predilection to film. Accordingly, we have seen an extraordinary flowering of the Polish film, now already spent; there are healthy signs of a coming efflorescence in Hungary and Yugoslavia; and in one country, Czechoslovakia, the film renaissance is in full, heady progress. But until just now, we in this country have not been vouchsafed a fair sampling of it.

The films that made America aware of what has been called "the Czech film miracle" were, perhaps predictably, less than first-rate:

Kadár and Klos's *The Shop on Main Street* and Miloš Forman's *Loves of a Blonde*. We have been shown films as good by Weiss, Passer, and Brynych, but they did not catch on; neither did Forman's earlier *Black Peter*, more imaginative though it was than his *Blonde*. Nevertheless, we should be grateful to those ice-breaking films that, in all likelihood, made possible the present Festival of New Czechoslovak Cinema, jointly sponsored by the Film Department of Lincoln Center and the Museum of Modern Art.

Out of the twelve films shown, one seems to me a masterpiece, four are very fine indeed, one is above average, and four are not without their moments. I would consider dead failures only a silly, but at least harmless, musical, *Lady of the Trolley Tracks,* and the favorite of the Festival directors, Amos Vogel and Willard Van Dyke, *Daisies.* This is a rank weed of the Godard-Warhol variety, to which Jaroslav Kučera's often stunning and sometimes only clever photography proves a peripheral and adscititious blessing. There was also distinguished work among the short subjects, both live action and cartoon, often by the same directors and cinematographers who made the features. Here the most remarkable were Evald Schorm's *Reflections,* about life and death in a hospital; Ivan Passer's *A Boring Afternoon,* about social conflicts and changing values as seen from the point of view of an uncomprehending bartender; and, best of all, a Boccaccian puppet film by the master puppeteer Jiří Trnka, *Archangel Gabriel,* one of the very few short subjects I dare unhesitatingly pronounce a work of lasting art.

What specific influences contribute to this large, luminous, sudden constellation of filmmakers? There is FAMU, the Czech film school, which gives fledgling *cinéastes* years of expert guidance, artistic freedom, and financial security. There are the excellent facilities of Prague's Barrandov Studio, increasingly made use of even by foreign productions. But there is also posthumous pollination by the work of great Czech artists in other fields. Kafka has been mentioned both by Amos Vogel and Bosley Crowther, though on the evidence of these films his influence is slight, showing up in *Hotel for Strangers,* disastrously, and in *Diamonds of the Night,* erratically. More important, I think, are the novels and plays by Jaroslav Hašek and Karel Čapek, with their bittersweet, ironic love of man; and that strange blend of surrealism, humanism, and Communism that produced the poetry of Vítěslav Nezval and Jiří Wolker. Personally, I would like to think also that an echo of the great composer Leoš Janáček has enriched these films in which, as in Janáček's music, the half-grotesque, half-plaintive melodies and rhythms of Czech speech are transubstantiated into the texture and character of an art.

Jiří Menzel's *Closely Watched Trains* is a film where everything works, including that most dangerous of devices, the shift, at the last moment, from comedy to tragedy. This *pièce de résistance* of the Festival is a comic view of Czech resistance to the Nazis in which a bumbling youth tragicomically comes of age in sex and war. A dispatcher trainee at a puny railroad station, he has troubles with his work that stem from greater troubles with lovemaking, which terrifies him. The figures that surround him, notably the ambitious but inept stationmaster and a fly-specked Don Juan of a train dispatcher, are, like himself, drawn with a humor so sweeping that it would hurtle into satire or caricature were it not for the intense joviality and humaneness that inform it. Tenderness mitigates the farcical, a certain seriousness gives an edge to the laughter, and a lyricism in the photography and editing poeticizes the foolishness.

Few things lend themselves more readily to photographic exaggeration than trains, but their use here is judiciously sparse and visually lovely—they function, in fact, as a kind of wipe between sequences of the plot, and their sound is a *ritornello* in the music of daily life. Menzel and his cinematographer, Jaromir Šofr, have achieved some of the most moving effects by the use of the camera unaided by anything except, perhaps, lighting and set design. The main devices are highly imaginative framing of the actors and eloquent use of the extreme closeup.

Thus, for example, the shy hero is frequently shown very near the edge of the frame, or being marshaled toward it, so that his quality of timorous onlooker is conveyed by the composition. The camera often avidly closes in on an object; here, as in most of these Czech films, a suit that is being tried on, a rubber stamp, a pair of glasses, an old phonograph, can produce an enormous visual and emotional impact. Things are charged with an immanent glory that has nothing to do with materialism or fetishism; rather, it bespeaks a profoundly affectionate reverence for the artifacts that have become our companions in living.

Menzel's actors perform with uncanny expertise. They, like almost all these Czech actors, know not only how to be larger than life when necessary but also how to be smaller. They have a way of rendering the trifling and irrelevant even pettier and more piddling than it is, extracting from it all the comedy or horror. Though not a single part, however short, is done less than expertly, Josef Somr, as the philandering dispatcher, is a veritable bastion of absurd fatuity yet full of feckless geniality as well; if Czechoslovakia does not have an Oscar or Otakar, one should promptly be created for Somr. There is something so spontaneous, unconcerned, and complete about such a performance that it affects our entire sensorium—finger tips, nostrils, and palate no less than eyes and ears.

I wish I had more space to expatiate about this superb film (I have not even mentioned as yet the fine screenplay by Bohumil Hrabal), but let me at least say a final word about Menzel, who also appears as an accomplished comic actor in this and several other films of the series. As a director, he reminds me most of Ermanno Olmi and, through Olmi, of their common master, Fellini. But there is also in him a visual and textural elegance that suggests Bergman and Antonioni. None of these influences, if such they be, is obtrusive. The best thing about *Closely Watched Trains* is that it impresses one as unique, indebted ultimately only to its individual genius.

Scarcely less outstanding is *The Fifth Horseman Is Fear,* an intelligent and forceful examination of people under the Nazi terror, done as much through images and the use of sound and music as is humanly, or cinematically, possible. The protagonist is an elderly Jewish doctor, now forbidden to practice; a chance event propels him to rise, however recalcitrantly, from pariahdom to heroism. Even though the film ends tragically, Dr. Braun reasserts his dignity in death, and the sad ending becomes almost a happy one.

Zbyněk Brynych's film is remarkable not only for its sympathetic probing of the hero, unsurpassably played by Miroslav Macháček, but also for its imaginative and hallucinatory re-creation of a cross section of people as they react to a wanted man's hiding out in their building, their untidy private lives meshing with their behavior in the emergency. The tension of a razzia is built up with superlative, cool understatement, and the terror is all the more chilling for being scaled down and, as it were, humanized. Moreover—and this must make such films particularly exciting on home ground—the implication that such terror is not limited to German manufacture is palpable throughout.

But the greatest triumphs of this film are the photography of Jan Kališ and the mood of increasing horror of a diffuse, universalized sort that the director is able to convey. There are vignettes of a woman turned suicidal dope fiend, of a nightclub for patrons desperately dancing, drinking, doping themselves up under the sword that hangs over their heads, of life in a Jewish insane asylum; these owe much more to Dante than to Kafka. If the film errs in any way, it is in underlining too hard at times, in striving too much for expressionist effects. An episode in an army brothel, with Jewish girls pressed into service, is rather too sensationalistic and was added later for the American market. But the photography yields miracle after miracle—just the way the spiral staircase is shot, or the pathos wrung from the protagonist's spectacles is worthy of a critical study—and everything from wildly varied background music to the skill of the bit players blends into a whole as artistic as it is devastating.

I was particularly struck by the opening sequence, showing a synagogue converted into a warehouse for confiscated Jewish property. While harsh voices are loudly sorting out banned books, the hero, who, like other Jews, is in charge of outfitting the despoilers with desired articles, wanders through this awful kingdom of furniture, roomful after roomful of a single item like clocks or radios. Each object is neatly labeled with the name of someone already dead or in a death camp—each object is a cenotaph. The wide screen fills up with these ghostly things that, bizarrely agglomerate, assume nightmare configurations. Braun traverses the chambers of this necropolis until he collapses on top of one of an army of large, black, batlike pianos. One of these is being tuned: while we see a stop-shot of Braun crumpled over a piano, a triadic progression of notes climbs higher with ghoulish insistence. Despair could not become more archetypal.

No less engrossing, though in a much lighter vein, is *Nobody Laughs Last,* in which an art instructor and critic who shrinks from confronting people with unpleasant judgments tells a white lie about the work of a dogged but untalented middle-aged aspirant to art historianship. A set of hilarious yet sinister consequences results. In the end, the hero, a man neither good nor bad but at least gifted and unconventional in his ways, is dragged down by the pathetic nonentity he carelessly encouraged and ends by losing both a good job and a delightful mistress.

Hynek Bočan has made his film into an affecting serio-comic tale in which various elements neatly prop up one another—the excellent script by himself and Pavel Juráček, a sprightly score, evocative sets, understated but pungent cinematography by Jan Němeček, and a flawless cast, led by Jan Kačer, the Czech Mastroianni, as the critic, and Štěpánka Řeháková, as his moody, sensuous, childlike mistress. But he has done more: in any number of quietly puncturing ways Bočan pokes fun at existing social conditions in the Socialist Republic, and at the tyranny of the inferior majority over the more talented individual.

What makes *Nobody Laughs Last* especially interesting for me is that it falls into the middle of the thematic scale; it is neither irresponsible froth nor portentous drama or melodrama. That middle area is as yet scarcely explored by films (particularly in this country); again, the problem here is largely esthetic and intellectual—can you imagine a serious American film whose hero would be an art critic? And there is more: the love affair in the film is thoroughly everyday—the lovers are neither blissful, nor consumed with ennui, nor locked in vicious combat. They are rather mismated, mildly deadlocked, and moderately amused. They are real. And the film abounds in wit, delicacy, and a kind of intelligent melancholy.

Let me switch now to the bottom of the barrel, *Daisies,* by Věra Chytilová, a one-time fashion model and never director. Amos Vogel has called this a "splendiferous masterpiece," and Willard Van Dyke told me that if the Czech government had stuck by its refusal to release this film for export, there would have been no Festival. As it happens, for the wrong reasons no doubt, the government was right.

Daisies concerns two teeniest-brained teenyboppers who decide that the world is rotten and so will they be. We are now taken on a round of escapades, disconnected, silly, and essentially uneventful, in which these cretinous beatniks cavort in a manner derived from the dregs of silent comedy, Godard, and Warhol (who has nothing but dregs). Not only is all this uproariously unfunny, it is also unconscionably dragged out. The amateur actresses are, furthermore, supremely untalented and reasonably unattractive, and the whole thing is further embellished with surrealist touches *à la* Hans Richter, himself a considerable purveyor of dregs.

What makes this film particularly distasteful is its idiot yearning for Western beatnikdom, its slobbering (and, I suspect, lesbian) adulation of its ghastly heroines. Then, to get it past government censorship, it must be supplied with the limpest cop-out: the wholly amoral girls are suddenly afflicted at being ignored by members of the working class, and a chandelier that changes into an atom bomb (the dreariest cliché of underground cinema) drops on them for good measure. The feeble pretense that this emulation of what is worst in the West can be made to conform to what is worst in the East succeeds only in making *Daisies* heir to the worst of both possible worlds.

I shall go on about this Festival. But I want to stress two points here and now. The first is that the subtitles are consistently execrable in all these films: they miss the flavor and finesse of the dialogue; they translate into appalling English—a man, for example, refers to his mistress as "little besom"; and they leave about a quarter of what is said untranslated.

The second is my admiration for the courage and ability of most of these filmmakers to convey a good deal of implicit and explicit social and political criticsm. In *The First Cry,* Jaromil Jireš's charming film, there is an all-important line that the subtitles fail to translate. A film critic is dictating a review of an unspecified Antonioniesque film. His mind wanders and he dictates: "The film is remarkably outspoken for a work made in a Socialist . . . er . . . capitalist country." That is a brave touch, and these films are replete with such bravery.

July, 1967

FESTIVAL OF CZECHOSLOVAK FILM: PART II

Memory plays odd tricks on film criticism. Since my last article on the Czech Festival I have seen some of the films again and have thus discovered, for example, that the protagonist of *The Fifth Horseman Is Fear* does not, in the scene I described, slump over one of the accumulated pianos. The camera merely freezes him alongside one of them, and the black-garbed man and the black instrument merge into yet another, centaurlike monster in a world of monstrosities. And the objects confiscated from the Jews were not tagged with names but with numbers, which made them no less into cenotaphs but into still more awful, bureaucratically dehumanized ones.

Even odder, alas, are the tricks of film distribution. Two of the very best of these Czech films have not found an American outlet: neither *Nobody Laughs Last* nor *The First Cry* is to get commercial distribution here. The blame may rest principally with our audiences. These films are unsensational—no great stars, sex, or violence in either of them— and our canny distributors figure them for financial losers, which they well might be. I see no easy solution to this problem, except some kind of government or foundation subsidy, and that seems regrettably remote at this stage.

Jaromil Jireš's *The First Cry* is about a young married couple having their first baby. While she is at the hospital, before, during, and after giving birth, he is either going about his work as a TV repairman, or telephoning the hospital, or just trying to—telephones are busy, out of order, or remain unanswered. Both of them have new experiences: she meets sympathetic or indifferent hospital personnel and fellow patients, and, finally, gives birth; he encounters unusual situations in the places where he goes to fix television sets. Both of them, though separately, reminisce about their shared past: their meeting, living together, tiffs, and marriage. They are so joyously attuned to each other that these flashbacks seem to be complementary phases in the functioning of a single memory; indeed, the young couple conduct an imaginary dialogue that overarches time and space. She has a fairly difficult birth; he gets entangled with various cynics, a seductress, schoolchildren, and a bout of ludicrous fisticuffs. But through it all their memories and imaginary conversations reconstruct a courtship, affair, and marriage that have the exact savor of youth and an exuberance that will not be encumbered.

Jireš handles the flashbacks and shifting point of view with utmost ease and spontaneity, and Jaroslav Kučera's photography goes from one miraculous shot to the next as if there were no such thing as using the camera in a merely utilitarian way for even a moment; and where brilliance is so natural and consistent, there is no self-conscious artiness. For example, in one scene, the boy and girl frolic through a poplar grove, the leafy spires bolt upright under a lucent sky. Nearing parturition and apprehensive, the girl sees the poplars at crazy angles, blinding light beating through their branches. As she is being wheeled to the delivery room, the slanting trees change in a vision into weird, cancerous-looking fungi hanging threateningly close to her upturned face.

When the hero is silently rushing to the hospital at night, his face is seen mostly in silhouette hurtling past glaring shop windows. From this, the camera cuts to the hospital for a closeup of his baby: it is firmly held, bathed in light, and bawling. Then back to the darkened contours of the father's face now seen against a gliding streetcar window. The newborn girl has become the luminous, loud, indignant center of the universe, the father merely a soundless shadow speeding toward it.

A particularly moving scene has the young expectant father looking through his family photograph album while he sits in his twilit apartment, the unwatched television set flickering erratically. The photographs evoke, with foreshortened tenderness, generations in swaddling clothes, wedding finery, old-age black, in peace and in war. There are wedding pictures of different periods, and with each an off-screen male voice gently urges a bride to hold herself straight, and each time a new female voice intones the old lament, "I can't. My skirt is so tight." There are droll pictures of a grandfather involved with an already antediluvian behemoth of a World War I dirigible.

But most affecting of all is a picture postcard from our hero's father in World War II, showing a dour seacoast. The young man turns the card around; the postage stamp bears the face of Hitler. "Dear Věra," says a kindly, somewhat ghostified voice, speaking from a work camp, "it is not so bad here. Remember how I used to yearn for a glimpse of the sea? Now I would gladly exchange it for your bathroom. But I should be home soon now. Kisses to you and Slávek, Dad." At this point on the soundtrack there is the ghastly hoot of a dive bomber, cut off in mid-flight by the son's censoring memory. But we know that the father is dead. Then, once more, the voice: "Kisses to you and Slávek, Dad." And we know also that the father is not wholly dead: his lovingkindness has been handed down.

Bits of overheard dialogue, an all but overlooked gesture or glance, and a minor character betrays his absurd or tragic existence; the movement of crowds in the street to the sound accompaniment of a heartbeat; a silly little cactus at an expectant mother's bedside and the story of its provenance; incongruous situations—words or objects from the past that recur in a new light casting richer implications; the texture of life down to its least blemish, to the very pores through which it breathes. The dialogue of Aškenázy and Jireš, the cinematography of Kučera, Jireš's lovingly expansive yet incisive direction, the unerring performances from the leads to the half-submerged faces in the background, the sparse but intelligent music of Jan Klusák—these make *The First Cry* a sturdy, unsyrupy, constantly inventive film about that most dangerous of subjects, young love. There is ironic social comment as well as headlong romance in it, surreal imagination yet never a sense of unreality. It breaks my heart that you may never see this film. I rage at being able only to write about it, not to screen it for you.

Whereas *The First Cry* is a perfect minor work, Jan Němec's *Diamonds of the Night* is a flawed major achievement. Two boys escape from a train taking them to a Nazi death camp. They run through forests and rain, across swamps and rock slides. Days pass; they hunger and chew roots; their feet can barely keep up. There is almost no dialogue. The relation between the boys changes. The older one, who traded his last morsel for the other one's boots on the train, was the leader; now, ironically, his booted feet have grown more debilitated than those of the younger, who gradually assumes leadership. The younger boy's visions and fantasies are interwoven with the events of the film. Sometimes they are mere images of horror, as of ants devouring him. Sometimes they are fantasies of homecoming, safety, but seen in a slightly distorted, incongruous form, and so more disquieting than sustaining. At other times, they are true dream transformations of reality, almost inscrutable, yet with that strange pseudologic of dreams in which the absurd becomes meaningful through its obsessive detail, emotional urgency, and stubborn recurrences.

The youths, starved and exhausted, are forced to ask for food from a Sudeten German peasant woman. She gives it to them but subsequently betrays them. A bunch of old men (the younger ones are all away) form a preposterous posse: enfeebled, apoplectic, almost cretinous dodderers, hardly able to prop up some of their number, they manage, almost accidentally, to capture the dog-tired boys. They keep them, starving, against the wall of a banquet hall, while the grotesquely rejuvenated hunters eat and carouse, sing and dance in their triumph. It is not clear what happens to the boys in the end: are they shot by the oldsters, turned over to the military authorities, or allowed to escape—temporarily?

The film is dense and, at times, impenetrable. There may be a little too much running through woods and underbrush, though here, too, Jaroslav Kučera produces a spate of photographic splendors. The dews of the nocturnal forest catching stray moon beams and the faces of the boys glistening with determination in the soul-devouring darkness— these are diamonds of the night glimpsed in what seem to be not so much nervous tracking shots as consecutive flashes of genius. I assume that Kučera used very fast film and natural light to achieve some of his superb effects; often, especially in the visions, he uses overexposure to excellent purpose.

A few scenes are as powerful as anything ever filmed. For one, the younger boy's vision of killing the peasant woman, repeated over and over even while she is cutting off thick, sensuous slices of bread for him. Both of them are terrified, and the way in which the act of charity is interlarded with the fantasy of fear-maddened killing penetrates not only to the fundamental horror of war but even to the very ambiguity at the heart of being. More powerful yet in its ultra-Bruegelian manner is the macabre orgy of the almost visibly decomposing graybeards. They sing foolish German songs about St. Peter in heaven as they stuff and stupefy themselves and dance about precariously before the young healthy boys whom they starve and will deliver to their deaths. This scene is such a head-on collision of outrageous comedy with absolute gruesomeness that whatever sense there may be in life falls apart before our stunned eyes. Nevertheless, Němec's *Diamonds of the Night* is an elegy for, or, better yet, a muted ode to man's courage.

August, 1967

CHINA IS NEAR

"Poets ought to be strangled," wrote the disgruntled Lady Bulwer-Lytton from Italy, "for all the lies they have told of this country." Marco Bellocchio, the twenty-eight-year-old filmmaker, whose second film is *China Is Near,* may be a poet in his handling of the camera, but he certainly tells no rhapsodic travel-poster lies. The Italy he conjures up is not a tourist attraction—at best, a rather sinister circus. No character in this pithy, impudent, cynical little film is sympathetic or sympathetically viewed; though everyone is given the benefit of tolerant, amused understanding, and is made, in accord with Nietzsche's famous motto, human, all too human. To carry off such a sophisticated blend of acrid irony and bittersweet farce is a considerable achievement, even if the squeamish may be fazed by Bellocchio, that uncommon kind of cultural watchdog whose bite is worse than his bark.

The small-town Italian milieu has never been treated in this tone before. Here we do not have the clinical penetrancy of Antonioni, the slightly melancholy euphoria of Fellini, the cheery sentimentalizing of the later De Sica, or the social protest of the earlier. We find neither the intensive humanity of Olmi, De Seta, Monicelli; nor the irrepressible satire of Germi, Risi, Salce; nor yet the radical commitment of De Santis or Rosi. And, surprisingly for one so young, there is none of that attitudinizing self-importance found in, say, Bertolucci. No, Bellocchio is his own man, and while he has learned a thing or two from Godard, he has already surpassed his master.

China Is Near (the title makes sense only in Italian, in which *La Cina è vicina* is a neat political jingle) is the story of poor but ambitious lovers in the little town of Imola near Bologna. Carlo is the bookkeeper of the local Socialist party; Giovanna is secretary to the town's rich political dabbler, Vittorio. Then there is Elena, Vittorio's energetic and emancipated sister, who not only looks after this aristocratic family's fortunes, but also finds time for a voracious sex life that excludes marriage—no one is going to get her money! Lastly, there is Camillo, Elena's and Vittorio's teen-age brother, a nasty little seminarian who has organized a Maoist cell comprising himself and two surly, reluctant followers, and who uses his Maoism in equal measure to frustrate his brother's political chances and to satisfy his own nascent dictatorial and sexual appetites.

When Carlo discovers that the Socialist party is bypassing him as candidate for councilman in order to run the more prestigious but pretentious and inept Vittorio (not a "professor," as most reviewers have claimed, but a high school teacher; *professore*, in Italian, has quite a low threshold), he becomes the rich nincompoop's campaign manager, and, almost simultaneously, Elena's lover. Giovanna, ditched by Carlo, promptly becomes the mistress of Vittorio, whose ludicrous advances she had been spurning. Carlo and Giovanna then collaborate, like a provincial Valmont and Merteuil, to trap their aristocratic lovers into marriage, giving rise to some outrageous intrigues caustically filmed. At one point Vittorio and Elena attend a perfectly dreadful performance of Verdi's *Macbeth,* and they are, indeed, themselves in the clutches of a small-time latter-day Macbeth and Lady Macbeth.

As in his first film, *I pugni in tasca* (*Fist in His Pocket*), Bellocchio starts with his aggressively *in medias res* approach. We are plunged into several typical episodes from the lives of the principal characters without the faintest notion of who or what they are, or how they are related to one another. The gradual revelations are thus all the more eagerly stalked by the spectator—unless it is he, in fact, who is being ambushed by them.

Vittorio, for example, is first revealed sitting in some sort of cubicle, looking up plaintively and exclaiming, "Lord, Lord, why hast thou forsaken me?" Next he opens a door, and we see that he has been sitting on a toilet. He closes the door and rushes away, and we discover that the commode is contained in a bizarre masterpiece of baroque cabinetwork. With lightning speed, and chiefly in visual terms, three points are made: Vittorio is the sort of histrionic fool who blames his constipation on God; he is a nervous Nellie, which accounts both for his oppilation and his darting about; he lives in a luxury that ill accords with his puniness. But this is not something one fully comprehends while it is happening; it either dawns on one as a delayed reaction later on, or one savors it on viewing the film a second time, as one very nearly must.

Consider the elaborate mastery of the scene in which Carlo foils Elena's attempt at abortion. Carlo must save the baby, so that Elena will have to marry him for its sake. One desperate scheme to thwart Elena via her younger brother has failed; now Carlo seeks out his former parish priest, discovered playing games with a bunch of children who make an ass of him. "I knew you would come back to us someday!" the silly young priest rejoices, unaware of the ruthlessly selfish motives that have brought Carlo back to the shabby neighborhood he grew up in. From this irony, we cut to the doctor's staircase and office door to see Carlo forcing his and the priest's way in.

I wish I had the shooting script before me, so I could reproduce the series of quick cuts and hectic snatches of dialogue that follow: Elena looking exasperated on the operating table; the nurse answering Carlo's threatening question about whether anything has been done yet with the idiot tone she doubtless uses on patients who want to know whether it will hurt—"Noh . . . Noooh!"; the priest going down on his knees to thank God. The doctor now hypocritically thanks the priest, "It was my Road to Damascus!" (rendered palely in the subtitles as "You saved me!"), and promises a large donation to the parish poor, while Carlo wheels on him and demands a refund of the abortion fee. The doctor first denies having received any money, then hastily makes out a check, which Carlo pockets with the warning that he'll keep an eye on the doctor until Elena is safely delivered.

All this is punctuated with shots of Elena spread out upon the table like a stormy evening against the sky: she has been truly delivered— into Carlo's hands. The swift pacing of the scene and the counterpointing of obtuseness with nastiness, of corruption with impotent fury, make for one of those genuine sardonic epiphanies, in which our laughter is, as it were, lined with dismay.

Little escapes the playful claws of Bellocchio's wit: higher and lower orders, Marxism and Maoism, youth and age, religion and politics, clergy and officialdom—all are grist for a camera that grinds fast, yet exceeding small. A particularly effective device of Bellocchio's is to cut off an incident right after the climax and dispense with the denouement; not only does this accelerate the pace almost to the point of silent-screen comedy, it also creates an aura of amorality. Actions, however gross or destructive, have no visible consequences. Carry this a little farther, and what have you got? Godard. But Bellocchio always remains within the pale of the artistically possible: he practices foreshortening rather than total dislocation.

The acting is cogently balanced by the director. Thus the aristocrats all have a certain derailed flamboyance, whereas the plebeian arrivistes go about their tasks with tight-lipped, matter-of-fact purposiveness that is more chilling than comic. Glauco Mauri's Vittorio is the staggering embodiment of just about every folly catalogued by Erasmus, while remaining recognizably the fellow man and brother of every *hypocrite spectateur*. As his sister, Elda Tattoli (who collaborated with Bellocchio on the script) conveys precisely that romantic but also very modern state lapidarily defined by Carducci as *"un tedio che duri infinito."* From this ennui that lasts forever, lust alone can arouse her, only to submerge her in yet more bottomless boredom. Miss Tattoli's face, ageless and commanding, projects an eternity of tedium and contempt. The others are equally adept at their work, and Daniela Surina communicates with particular authority how Giovanna's feelings freeze into deadpan ambitiousness.

The subtitles are, as usual, inadequate both in quantity and quality. There is a scene in which Vittorio and Elena are cataloguing the precious and musty tomes of the family library: he reads out the titles and she records them. *A History of China* (how different a China from the one in the film's title!) is followed by a *Chemistry for Ladies* (would that it could keep them from becoming pregnant!); and this, in turn, by a *Concilio di Pistoia* in ten volumes. In the subtitles, the Council of Pistoia becomes, by way of fractured Italian, "The Assembly of Guns." I dare say the subtitulist must know the difference between Pistoia and *pistola,* and between the two meanings of "assembly," but cannot trust the audience. Still, this sort of thing won't do, except perhaps in verse translations by Ezra Pound.

Ennio Morricone's score has the right asperity, and Tonino delli Colli's black-and-white photography improves with each film. After the lushness of his work in *Mandragola,* delli Colli has, in *The Hawks and the Sparrows* and now here, arrived at a splendid flexibility of tones that can be misty or sharp, melancholy or biting, as desired. He may well become the worthy successor of the late, and sorely missed, Gianni di Venanzo. *China Is Near* has been justly compared by Stanley Kauffmann to Goldoni and by Andrew Sarris to Stendhal. Ultimately, though, it is *sui generis* in its harshness that is yet comic, in its rapidity that remains just encompassable, and in its sarcasm that is nevertheless hearty.

March, 1968

POOR COW

Poor Cow, directed by Kenneth Loach and adapted by him and Nell Dunn from her novel, is a lesson from Godard, poorly learned. This is the story of a pretty young London proletarian, married to one burglar and in love with another. Both land in jail. While she waits for her lover's long sentence to be over, to keep her appetites satisfied and to provide for her baby whom she loves, she sinks lower and lower on the socio-sexual scale; but the film, unlike the book, stops short of having her turn into a streetwalker. Loach has adopted many Godardian devices, such as deliberately jerky progression, improvisations, intertitles, long takes of intimate tête-à-têtes, and, above all, sudden switches from haphazard storytelling to quasi-documentary exploration of a milieu.

Whereas Godard's sublime indifference to logic intermittently succeeds in producing a dadaist nightmare, Loach's sedulously literal-minded transcription of the same strategies results in a naturalism gone schizophrenic. Nonetheless, there are two or three good sequences, and the film is further abetted by authenticity of acting and ambience. Carol White, as the heroine, is not bad at all though a shade too respectable, and Terence Stamp is excellent as her lover. Yet from the very outset, when the pop singer Donovan intones one of the self-consciously pseudopopular lyrics by the high brow poet Christopher Logue, we know that we are in bad hands. *Poor Cow* flits uneasily from portentousness to down-to-earthness, as pseudopoetic and pseudonäive as one of Chagall's flying bovines.

March, 1968

WE STILL KILL THE OLD WAY

We Still Kill the Old Way is based on a novel by Leonardo Sciascia just published here as *A Man's Blessing*; in Italy, both book and film are called *A ciascuno il suo,* which means "to each his own," and may be a secret reference to American habits of titling. Directed by Elio Petri in an uncompromisingly, and sometimes irritatingly, up-to-date style, this is no typical Mafia film *à la* Pietro Germi or Alberto Lattuada. This is a zoomingly streamlined representation of smooth, ruthless corruption, in which the glamorous and finally rewarded lovers are, in fact, archcriminals, and the one honest man is hopelessly outsmarted to the point where his integrity and intelligence emerge as supreme, suicidal folly.

Petri, as he has shown in *The Tenth Victim* and in his part of *High Infidelity,* is an adroit director, whose skill, unfortunately, tends to lapse into pointless prestidigitation. Here, for instance, he uses shots of hands, anybody's hands, as a leitmotif; they are made more bewildering by extreme closeups and flash pans. One wonders what is meant: the Black Hand (i.e., Mafia)? The hand is quicker than the eye? All human mischief stems from hands poking around? No interpretation holds up. Nevertheless, this is a more exciting and at the same time more believable film than most of its kind. When have you last seen a hero unable to strike a single blow in his defense before the villains close in on him?

Murder is made neither tragic nor comic here, only shabby and routine. The acting is persuasive, with shambling good and suavely dissembling evil expertly embodied by Gian Maria Volontè on the one hand, and Gabriele Ferzetti and a skillfully dubbed Irene Papas on the other. The color photography is often striking, notably in a closing sequence of malevolent, surreal beauty.*

March, 1968

ISABEL

Isabel is a ghost story from Canada, in which Geneviève Bujold is delightful; the Gaspé peninsula, in Georges Dufaux's exciting color photography, picturesque to a fault; and the nature, Quebec townfolk, and goose-pimple scenes, under Paul Almond's direction, apt and artistic. Ice has been melting in many a film about the North yearning for spring, but never with such understated jubilance and in such emotionally charged extreme closeups as here. But, alas, Almond's writing goes pretentious: from straight ghost story, toward the end and without warning, we get an ultra-Jamesian turn of the script, and, like the heroine's father and brother in the Gaspé Bay, the film drowns in a squall of bogus depth psychology.

There you have it: film after film goes bad on us trying to be more or less or other than it was cut out to be. I am all for finding the new, but not at the cost of making hash of the old and dependable. Unless what all this means is that the old can no longer be depended on.

August, 1968

ZITA

A small, intimate film about ordinary people, yet with subtle implications, Robert Enrico's *Zita* is a gem of purest ray serene—well, let's except one or two impure rays. Enrico, who made the extraordinary

---

*Volontè, by the way, is to be seen also in *The Violent Four*, a competent crime film by Carlo Lizzani, whose *Hunchback of Rome* had left me cold. What makes Lizzani's new film memorable is Volontè in the role of the jolly psychopath who heads the gang of bank robbers. He is superb throughout, but his acting in the last reels and his hysterical laughter on which the film closes will haunt me long after I have forgotten all else about this work.

In the Midst of Life (seen here, unfortunately, only piecemeal, episode by episode) and some excellent shorts, subsequently turned to commercial adventure films. With *Zita,* based on a story by his wife, Lucienne Hémon, he returns to delicately personal themes resonant with understated universality.

Annie, a young student living with her mother, is unable to bear the fact that her beloved Aunt Zita is dying in the next room; she escapes into a big night on the town. Her father (Zita's brother) was Spanish and died in the civil war; now the whole Spanish, paternal side of her family is becoming extinct. During her nocturnal adventures, encouraged by the sage family doctor and friend (a charmingly and unsentimentally drawn figure acted to perfection by Paul Crauchet—antiseptic, acerbic, yet ruefully human), Annie meets up with all kinds of men. Each of these, down to a truckdriver who gives her a lift, contributes more than a vignette. They are all individuals with some special forte they hold out to Annie, who learns from them whether she accepts or refuses.

One man is a sardonic young Negro activist who nevertheless keeps his cool; another is a handsome farmer from the South of France whose beribboned prize ram escapes and leads them all a merry chase through nocturnal Paris; still another is a young double bass player and sports car enthusiast who finally becomes her first lover. There are other people and incidents, such as a near-rape by a bunch of hippified hoodlums, and much riding about in various vehicles, which however is never boring as in Godard and Lelouch.

In one exquisite scene, Annie sits in the police station with a Spanish refugee who has been brought in for killing a cat he meant to eat to keep from starving. Annie first tried to protect the cat, then she tried to defend the Spaniard against the cops; now he sits in that cage where the Paris police put their pick-ups and she sits just outside it. He speaks no French and she very little Spanish, yet she attempts to tell him about her father who could blow up bridges; finally she is talking in French just to herself to keep her courage up. When Annie alone is released, she has a splendid outburst against the police. The dialogue, as always, is free of platitudes and literate.

The climactic scene is both brilliant and on the verge of soupiness. Annie takes her bass player to the suburban house in which she grew up under Aunt Zita's care. We know that Zita lies in another house, dying. But here she is, alive and bustling about, and Annie (without changing appearances) is both the child she was and Simon's girl friend showing him around the house. They rub shoulders with Aunt Zita, and the past and present merge. Such is Enrico's artistry that the scene functions joyously as reality even though we know that it is fantasy.

The editing here is masterly: there is a sequence in which Annie goes up the stairs to what used to be her room, and the simple ascent of a stairway becomes, through brilliance of photography and montage, both a thrilling exploration of unknown territories and a sentimental return to the *vert paradis* of childhood. The imagined seduction scene is a mite gooey; but the real sexual initiation, later on in Simon's apartment, has thus been provided with an effective foil. The latter scene is fresh, tactful, and savory.

When Annie gets home, she finds that Zita has died, but mother and doctor are there to offer quiet support. She insists on going in to see her aunt, whose agony was so unwatchable. Now that Zita is dead, Annie has a vision of herself as a child once again playing in Zita's garden as the camera fairly rapidly pulls away. Zita suddenly turns a corner around a hedge, and the skipping little girl's figure continues its dwindling alone—right into the final fadeout. This, again, might be sticky, but it is handled with a winning lightness and purity.

Zita is greatly helped by François Roubeix's discreetly penetrating music, often just a Spanish guitar solo. Even more outstanding is the color camera work of Jean Boffety, who, by a slight change in lighting, can make the same room exude vastly different hues and emotions. Boffety's colors may not quite match the sheer loveliness of a *Red Desert* or *Elvira Madigan,* but they have a flexibility and variety that would be hard to equal.

The performances are all good, crowned by Joanna Shimkus's Annie. Miss Shimkus, besides improving from film to film, has an incomparable basic warmth and simple naturalness. Her Annie is child and girl by turns or both at once, and zigzags into ripeness before our eyes. Her infinitely various face—tomboyish from some angles, flawlessly beautiful from others—helps; but, ultimately, it is her unself-conscious, unhistrionic acting that lends Enrico's fine film its final glory.

September, 1968

BULLITT

I am not overfond of crime pictures, but *Bullitt* strikes me as a good one, and the most watchable movie in some time. By "watchable" I mean something that steadily holds your interest, nourishes your eye, and does not insult your brain. I mean performers and scenery that are sightly, dialogue that can hold its own against rice crispies, and a plot that has a working minimum of plausibility. *Bullitt* meets all these requirements handsomely.

San Francisco, made to look ludicrous in *Petulia,* here reasserts itself as one of the world's most photogenic cities, and William A. Fraker has color-photographed it with tasteful understatement, though he excels with interiors where such materials as wood become almost preternaturally substantial. The acting is appealing, not the least so because of the large number of new or newish faces. Most impressive among the newer comers are Don Gordon, who plays the eponymous detective lieutenant's sidekick with a loyal doggedness that always remains just this side of stolidity, and Jacqueline Bisset, who brings to the stock part of the hero's girl friend, complete with embarrassingly noble platitudes, an insuperable loveliness and intelligence. This young actress from England is the best thing to have hit Hollywood in many a paper moon. Only Robert Vaughn makes a scheming politician a bit too obvious, but then so do our politicians.

The two chief assets of *Bullitt,* however, are its star and director. Steve McQueen is just about the only young Hollywood actor with incontrovertible charisma. He is a kind of earthy Cary Grant, but you can find in him succulent bits of Gable, Cooper, and Spencer Tracy as well—besides what is uniquely his own. McQueen improves with every picture, and has by now perfected his charmingly paradoxical gift for making extroversion look like something very introverted and profound. He turns Lieutenant Bullitt, a fairly sketchy and schematic figure, into something fully rounded, by inconspicuously pouring his own humanity into the crevices of the script.

Equally valuable is the British director Peter Yates. His two climactic chases are stupendous yet believable, and he is no less good with low-key passages that merely establish character or mood; in all these, Yates displays sensitivity to details and a fundamental affection for the grainy texture of life.

November, 1968

PRETTY POISON

Pretty Poison is a fine, imperfect, absorbing first film by Noel Black. It is the story of a very bright but disturbed young man released from a house of correction who gets a job in a small New England town. He falls in love with a cherubic highschool drum majorette, and, partly through his infatuation with what proves to be a psychopath, partly through the imbecile hypocrisy of our society, and partly through misplaced magnanimity, ends disastrously. Despite the rather different ages of the characters, this is a kind of *Lolita,* with the childlikeness of the girl perhaps overstressed by her licking her lips during the performance of crimes. The aphrodisiac effect of murder on her is likewise hit a trifle too hard.

The last part of the film, in which melodrama refuses to grow into tragedy, seems a bit hurried, a bit undernourished. But the film has high directorial style, an efficient script by Lorenzo Semple, Jr., atmospheric camera work by David Quaid, and apt performances by Anthony Perkins and Tuesday Weld. Rush to see *Pretty Poison:* it has the taste of bitter truth, which once again is proving poison at the box office.

December, 1968

FACES

A deserving film, though ultimately disappointing, is *Faces* by John Cassavetes. Made on a shoestring over several years, mostly around the Cassavetes's or friends' houses, and always ducking the unions with their deadening demands, *Faces* is quite an accomplishment despite its obvious flaws. Its story line is simple: a middle-aged husband and wife disguise their boredom with inane jokes and hollow laughter; but, disgruntled, the husband spends a night with a sympathetic call girl (some other businessmen and another lady of the night add grim local color); the wife goes to a nightspot with other neglected wives, and they pick up a somewhat over-age hippie whom they take back to the wife's house. She ends up in bed with him and, in the morning, attempts suicide. The hippie saves her, only to escape hurriedly as the husband returns. Husband and wife again face each other and their emptiness, this time without laughter.

Out of this fairly arid and fairly trite material, Cassavetes has fashioned a film that contains a good deal of aridity and triteness. The number of bad jokes that are told in the house that is not a home and in the home that is not a home is legion; and the forced laughter that accompanies them sounds as if the characters were being *literally* tickled to death. We are to understand that these are the cachinnations of the damned, but we would get the point without having our heads stuck in a loudspeaker chock full of canned laughter. Indeed, the first half of the film is heavy going because of the relentless cataloguing of triviality. We are told that there was a written script, yet the film tends to look and sound like actors' improvisations. Even that laughter could be explained as a gap-filler until one thinks of what to say next. At best, Cassavetes may have committed a lot of Method exercises to paper and film.

Once the wives and the hippie take over, *Faces* does generate excitement and that brash, tawdry pathos that is so germane to southern California, and not wholly unrelated to the rest of our world. This is due in good measure to the acting. Seymour Cassel as the hippie who is beginning to go to seed and is all the more out for good times—but who is also a decent enough chap at heart—is exactly right. I don't know how much of it is acting and how much type casting, but whatever Cassel does has the clumsy charm of a fat baby disporting itself in its crib.

Better yet is Lynn Carlin as the wife. Miss Carlin is (or, I hope, *was*) a secretary in real life who never acted before. What she does here surpasses anything that all except two or three of our very best actresses could do, and they could not improve on it. Not since the heyday of Italian neorealism have we seen such unacted acting, such *living* on the screen. Miss Carlin's suicidal frenzy and postsuicidal hysteria and exhaustion arouse enough pity and terror to satisfy the strictest Aristotelian. It is the kind of performance that makes me feel utterly indebted to the performer; were she to pop up before me and ask me for my purse or my honor, I could not refuse.

Faces is marred by a foolish introductory gimmick—in a prologue, the film itself is presented as a publicity film being screened for the husband and his business associates—and by its grainy, excessively hand-held camera work that makes you wonder whether the images perhaps weren't shot on film at all but directly on some kind of specially treated shoestring. In addition, John Marley as the husband and Gena Rowlands as the call girl are only just passable. Nevertheless, this is (along with *Rachel, Rachel, Bullitt, Pretty Poison,* and *Greetings*) one of a small handful of American films released in recent times that can be viewed by adult audiences without blanching.

February, 1969

JOANNA

If you want your unadult movies unadulterated, I doubt that you could do better (or worse) than *Joanna.* It is another trashy piece about the glories of mod London, made even trashier by the fact of taking itself seriously. Joanna, a rich, feckless cutie from the provinces, comes to London to study art. Before you can say Mick Jagger, she is cutting classes, sleeping around, absorbing hedonistic commonplaces from a pompous young German art instructor, and even worse epicurean platitudes from a rich young playboy-lord, who is slowly dying of a disease he gallantly hides until the end. Unfortunately, he is not nearly so secretive about his philosophy, which gushes from him in faded epigrams that come straight out of mothballs, if indeed they aren't the mothballs themselves. Needless to say, they are all variations on the theme of living life to the hilt; and in this film, believe me, the hilt is a phallic symbol.

Lord Peter dies with a lordly, understated pathos, but meanwhile Joanna has found true love with his madcap Negro mistress's brother, a gorgeous and sophisticated young African who owns a nightclub and has, apparently, possessed every nubile girl in London, i.e., roughly nine-tenths of the population, but, naturally, falls deeply in love with Joanna. Everything would be fine, except that some villainous underworld connections beat him up, whereupon he gallantly kills one of them only to be sent unchivalrously to jail for a lengthy stretch.

Joanna, remembering some of Lord Peter's more exquisite maxims, goes back home to bear her lover's child and, presumably, wait for the happy reunion—though she makes some mention of returning to London and who knows what peripeties that may bring. As her train pulls out of the station, the entire cast of the film sees her off with a song and a dance—a delightfully Brechtian alienation-effect that would surely turn Brecht's stomach. Joanna is played by Genevieve Waite, a piece of fluff with a thinnish sound piped into it (for all our advances in electronics, automata have not yet acquired fully human voices), and sliding whichever way the ground underneath inclines.

As her ebony lover, Calvin Lockhart is like beautiful; as her lordly but moribund mentor, Donald Sutherland is nauseating: Toad of Toad Hall's conception of Oscar Wilde. Walter Lassally has photographed in fantabulous color, especially a super-Noldeish North African sunset that is just super. Michael Sarne, the young director who is Miss Waite's former lover and present Pygmalion (orders do reverse themselves!), has directed with chic fragmentation and all the artistry of a manicurist who applies a different shade of polish to each artificial nail. It's all absolutely groovy and perfectly ghastly.

February, 1969

HERE IS YOUR LIFE

Here Is Your Life is the first film of Jan Troell, a young Swede who was once Bo Widerberg's cameraman and whose second film has since gone on to win the grand prize in Berlin. Troell photographed, edited, directed, and co-scripted it from an autobiographical novel by Eyvind Johnson, one of Sweden's leading novelists. (His tetralogy, *The Story of Olof,* of which this is a part, should, along with its two or three sequels, be translated into English.) The film is shown here in a version that (as Stanley Kauffmann pointed out) has fifty-seven minutes cut— presumably because it was running too long—yet this is a gemlike work combining true humanity and that high technical skill that humane, good-natured films so infrequently have.

Here Is Your Life spans the years of World War I, during which young Olof muddles through into maturity, starting out as a boy worker in a sawmill of the stark North, and gradually working himself down to the South through a multiplicity of odd jobs, but clearly headed for a literary career. We follow his encounters with loneliness, death, love, Marx, and culture. If you think this is typical or predictable, you are only very superficially right. Troell, like Johnson, has infused it all with keen specific observation bursting with truth; the direction and photography are always at that exact point where life and art meet, and from which any veering in one direction would spell drab naturalism; in the other, arty cleverness.

There is one color sequence in this soberly black-and-white film, and that is a revelation. Never was color used so sparingly, Spartanly, awesomely, to suggest that even to the eyes of memory (this is a memory sequence) the past can be both lovely and unbearably tragic. Olof's adventures are funny and serious, private and universal, and Troell always gives you the exact feel of an experience or setting, from what is most exhilarating about it down to what is most painful. Poetry and squalor go hand in hand and form, together, a wonderfully visual, palpable poetic prose. Some of Sweden's most famous actors appear in small parts, but even the least-known perform with great exactness and dignity; *Here Is Your Life,* like the works of Olmi, is a necessary film. It is proof of its power that I felt, and still feel, those missing fifty-seven minutes hurt me like an amputated limb of my very own.

February, 1969

THE RED AND THE WHITE

A strangely unrealized film is Miklós Jancsó's *The Red and the White*. As in this promising Hungarian director's previous film, *The Round-up*, there is much intensely filmic talent in evidence, but, even more than in the first film, the import, as distinct from the impact, is negligible. There he was attacking inhuman police methods, and though the ostensible villains were the Rightists of long ago, it had to be clear even to the worst (or, at least, second-worst) clods that the target was equally the leftist police state of today.

In *The Red and the White* we are shown some of the fighting in the aftermath of the Russian Revolution, during which a certain monastery is seized now by White, now by Red, conquerors, the latter reinforced by a Hungarian volunteer regiment. The victors of the day proceed to massacre the losers; and though the Whites are shown as rather more reprehensible than the Reds, the Reds are pretty sanguinary, too. And though the Reds are more heroic and humane, the Whites also have their decent moments. But there are rotters everywhere, and horror is rampant; the point is that it takes two sides to tango into hell.

Now this may be news in Iron Curtain countries, and undoubtedly takes uncommon courage to express there, but it does not, in itself, make a good film. What we get here is a great deal of seesawing brutality, a large number of characters insufficiently developed to involve us, and a good many loose ends and improbabilities. The same defects were present in *The Round-up*, and I wonder to what extent the fault is that of Gyula Hernádi, Jancsó's collaborator on all scripts, and to what extent Jancsó's own. Nonetheless, the basic texture of this film is superbly right: dry, sharp, harrowing without any fancy effects or histrionics. Things happen in a straightforward, acerbic manner, and the mere posture of a man when he is being executed tells more than a mess of dialogue in a lesser film.

Noteworthy, above all, are the camera setups and movements. With his extremely able cinematographer, Tamás Somló, the director has devised some unusually fine compositions in long and extreme long shots, and the camera movements reach the ultimate in suggestive mobility—any more, and we would become unpleasantly conscious of them. In an interview in the Hungarian periodical *Filmvilág*, Jancsó mentions that for two of his other films he switched to another cameramen, János Kende, whose reliance on natural light has given the camera a 360-degree mobility over Somló's 180. How the fluidity and ubiquitousness of Somló's camera could be improved upon I have yet to see.

The acting by a Russo-Hungarian cast is generally satisfactory, although it hardly gets a chance to be more than poignant faces forcefully displaying themselves. Jancsó may, to be sure, have scored a first by getting Soviet actresses to undress for the camera, but the shots are all from the rear, so that in the race for the crotch we are still well ahead of the Russians.

April, 1969

PUTNEY SWOPE

Putney Swope is a movie with which the underground filmmaker Robert Downey comes up for air, but neither the air nor Downey does much for the other. It concerns an ad agency that falls into the hands of black militants—minimal militants, though, less engaged in putting up a fight than in putting the honkies on. There is some wild humor here, mostly one-liners. Yet from a fairly consistently funny start, *Putney Swope* goes on to a middle so shaky as to make you seasick just watching it, and to a dreary ending that isn't really an ending and really is dreary.

September, 1969

DOWNHILL RACER

A film of understated, lower-case virtues is *Downhill Racer*. It is of a genre that I usually have little love for, the big sports competition story, with the ruthlessness of the game serving as a frame for the tale of the tough competitor-protagonist who finally makes it big, or, in an alternative schema, gets foully framed, though innocent. In this case, the sport is more elegant: Olympic skiing in glittering European locations—Swiss, French, Austrian—and the hero, David Chappellet, is neither a Galahad-like greenhorn nor a hardened professional out for the money, but something in between.

This in-betweenness is both good and bad. Chappellet is a rube from Idaho Springs, Colorado; the very town is a happy choice: Colorado aspiring to the Pierian Springs or Sun Valleys of Idaho! But he is not a very nice rube: he is out to win, come hell or icy slopes. Yet he is doing it for fame rather than money, for some self-serving notion of gamesmanship rather than pure greed. There was a chance here to create a truly interesting complex character—complex, that is, within his simplicity—but James Salter, the scenarist, has seized only one-half of the opportunity. I have not read the Oakley Hill novel from which the film was made, but a glance at the book tells me that Salter has wrought enormous changes. The best thing he has done, bespeaking the professional novelist in him, is to have made the dialogue not just clipped and tough but also artistically telling. The people here speak a kind of Hemingway of the slopes, which, however, does not lapse into parody.

Though Salter has done well with his Alpine chitchat and the minor skiers, especially with the strong, decent, inarticulate coach of the American team, who—here comes the switch—is not very bright underneath, some characters remain unduly shadowy. Carole Stahl, the fascinating, shallow, sexy camp-follower, who likes to make the winners tumble into her bed; and Machet, her somewhat shady boss, a ski manufacturer whose mistress she may or may not be—these characters are not seen fully and enlighteningly. A curious thing, when you consider that Salter, in his other films and fiction, specializes in European characters and settings. Most damaging of all, is the fact that the hero, despite good little touches, remains an ultimate blank.

To some extent, though, Salter redeems himself with his home folk: David's drugstore-cowgirl girl friend, and his taciturn hayseed father, both convincing mixtures of pettiness and forthrightness, materialism and outspokenness. They are horrible in their provincialism, yet imbued with a directness and soundness the Europeans lack—a Jamesian motif, as it were. And they are revealed with a swiftness and economy that avoids seeming rigged up. The pair provide some justification for Chappellet's need to claw his way out of his milieu, and, at the same time, make for a poetic justice running through the film. The world is full of champions, observes the skeptical father, harshly but not untruthfully; and if David uses his small-town girl friend for quick soulless sex, he is repaid in kind by the cosmopolitan but fickle Carole. Whereas Carol Carle is perfect as the gum-chewer from Colorado, Camilla Sparv is inept as the international playgirl—her very German is inexcusable, even from a Swiss, which she is supposed to be. Still worse is her performance, typical of a high-fashion model turned actress: zero in all departments except clothes-horsing around.

No matter; there is enough else to enjoy in *Downhill Racer.* There is the first-rate action photography, capturing Olympic champions burning up some of Europe's most photogenic slopes. Much of this color cinematography was done from skis chasing after the champions at 60 m.p.h. And the beauty of it is that in this film, for the first time, it does not just look easy and graceful, but graceful and grueling. Michael Ritchie has directed these sequences skillfully, with the right proportion of cutting, crosscutting, and tracking. There is something peculiar about the opening sequence, though, which smacks of front-office interference and does not make very good sense. Distracting, too, is the dreary music, but in later action sequences it luckily leaves the skiers alone, to do their work unserenaded.

The dialogue among skiers, their camaraderie and rivalries, are, I repeat, well managed, and so, too, are scenes in which the coach, persuasively played by the dependable Gene Hackman, struggles to convince American business interests to subsidize this amateur sport despite the un-American fact that it is neither baseball nor football. More could have been done with this, too, but one is grateful for what there is of it. Robert Redford, who had to fight hard to get this film produced at all, deserves more credit for that than for his performance, which is good but not up to his best. Still, the role has its severe limitations, and Redford, at any rate, is one of the most valuable young players of our cinema, in international as well as national competition. Moreover, Michael Ritchie makes one of the most auspicious directorial debuts in many a snowy season. *Downhill Racer* does not get beyond the level of competent, intelligent entertainment, but of how many recent American films can one say even that much?

December, 1969

M*A*S*H

A thoroughly enjoyable, unpretentious film, on the other hand, is *M*A*S*H*—but because the spelling of its title falls flat on its asterisks, it will be hereinafter referred to as *MASH*. The title is an abbreviation of Mobile Army Surgical Hospital, and there is an *objet-trouvé* humor in that baleful anagram which is in official use. Indeed, it is almost as if the tone of the movie had been derived from it, for the film is full of something that falls just short of gallows humor, and might perhaps be termed scalpel humor. The action takes place in such a hospital during the Korean war—a second-class war, and, we are led to believe, a second-class hospital, too, at least as far as the prevailing discipline is concerned.

The film, in the tradition of those service comedies of which, for no particular reason, *Mr. Roberts* seems to have become the archetype, deals with the adventures of three surgeon-captains: a Southern cracker, a Yankee eccentric, and an ethnically less defined practical joker. Actually, all three of them are jokers; in fact, the dramatis personae can be divided into jokers and patsies, though with a certain upward mobility, so that the commanding officer and a nurse major rise in the end (not quite convincingly) from patsydom to jokerhood.

The humor derives basically from two circumstances. One is the unending influx of badly wounded, bleeding soldiers, a veritable red sea seeping through bandages, its waves parting only before jokes—wisecracks of any kind to keep oneself from cracking up. The other circumstance is the absolute need of the army for trained surgeons, who know that they are irreplaceable and permit themselves the most outrageous behavior off and even on duty.

In a sense, then, *MASH* is almost an edifying movie, celebrating as it does the resourcefulness and resilience of the mind, which, by an almost inhuman sense of humor if need be, protects itself and survives whole. And, for all their shenanigans, these surgeons and nurses try to do their best by the patients.

Though the operations and gore are not dwelt on unduly in the film, some people may find the red refrain disturbing. On the other hand, the comment of a youth who came out of the theater exulting that, because he did not have to avert his eyes, he felt he could go to medical school, seemed to me a trifle overoptimistic. Be that as it may, without the bloody scenes there would be no movie.

Robert Altman, a director who comes from television, has directed the film at a good comic-revue clip; the gags are almost never lingered over (except that one potentially amusing pseudosuicide scene is allowed to drag on), and things are permitted to register on us without any leering, churning, or pushing. Ring Lardner Jr.'s script, based on an obscure novel, is urbane in its approach to GI humor, which is broad and corny; and the mixture of suavity and Rabelaisianness pays off handsomely. What makes *MASH* a landmark, however, is that it is the first Hollywood film to be openly and uncompromisingly against religion. The two biggest fools in the movie are the proper, devout, obtuse major, well played by Robert Duvall, who is eventually driven berserk; and the silly chaplain, a joke from beginning to end, restrainedly acted by René Auberjonois. But all the performances are funny, and, what is especially gratifying, relaxedly so.

Donald Sutherland, as the prime farceur of the three surgical musketeers, is a curious actor. When this young Canadian plays an Englishman or aristocrat, with the appalling accent he then affects—as in
Joanna, Interlude, Start the Revolution Without Me—he is absolutely
awful. When he is playing an American, with some kind of Western
Hemisphere accent—as in *The Dirty Dozen* or *MASH*—he is very
funny and just fine. Elliott Gould is also good, but a certain dopiness
that is his basic comic resource, useful in other parts, does not work
so well here. Tom Skeritt does a neat job of the Southerner, without
turning on any excess charm.

There are weaknesses in the film. The odious nurse, Major "Hot
Lips," brilliantly played by Sally Kellerman, turns from a horrid
female into a regular guy, as, in the end, does Roger Bowen's doltish
CO—again, no fault of the actor. In fact, the whole picture becomes
a little too cute, too desperately calculating, and, finally, old hat and
trivial. Thus a four-letter word has to be brought in for comic effect
during a funny, but not all that funny, football game, and though the
device proves startling, in scriptwriting, unlike in athletics, there is no
great glory in becoming a four-letter-man.

If the film peters out, it is at least rounded off, though not recouped,
by a charming device at the end. I recommend *MASH* to those who
can enjoy it without expecting a political satire or devastating antiwar
black comedy. The film is no more antiwar than it is anti-surgery, but
it is rich in irreverent laughs that will echo loudly from both cliff walls
that constitute the generation gap.

February, 1970

THE DREAMER

Israel's official entry at Cannes this year was *The Dreamer,* and, significantly, its producer, director, and cinematographer, three Sabras in
their twenties, all graduated from the N.Y.U. film school. The movie
is typical film-school stuff: boring, pretentious, arty, self-conscious,
self-righteous, and false. Students *should* learn through such mistakes,
but the public might profitably be spared them.

We are presented with a home for the aged where a young man, Eli,
is employed as a handyman, maundering about calf-eyed and uttering
no more than a few pregnant platitudes. He draws quite proficient
academic sketches of the inmates, especially of the eloquent face of an

old woman, Rachel, with whom he has a deep involvement that remains unprobed by the filmmakers. When an attractive young girl, equally inexplicably, falls for and seduces him, he remains the same calf-eyed, taciturn oaf. And when old Rachel starts sulking about his new relationship, he promptly and incredibly drops it.

Something could perhaps be made of this if either Eli or Rachel, and preferably both, were given some depth, and if their relationship extended beyond his sketching her and their going shopping together. Thus when Rachel talks about the old country and her memories of war, one hopes for something visually and verbally poignant. Instead, she utters a few unmoving commonplaces (representing the author-director, Dan Wolman, just as much as the speaker) and is photographed in the most obvious closeups. We are asked to understand that Eli is some deeply sensitive, visionary being, in short, The Artist; but all we get is a sullen, liquid-eyed bore. The girl's parents, who are supposed to typify bourgeois crudity, seem perfectly right to consider him a halfwit.

Berta Litvina squeezes some good moments out of the stereotyped part of Rachel; the others are, or come across as, amateurs. Paul Glickman's color photography runs amuck with such perennial favorites as gnarled old faces, poetic meadows traversed by young lovers, and naked bodies revolving in sexual ecstasy. The direction, like the screenplay, lacks a sense of rhythm, to say nothing of shape and substance. When Wolman tries to introduce racy details or juicy minor characters, they emerge as perfect clichés or gratuitous grotesques. And Gershon Kingsley's score settles on the film like saccharin on dust.

June, 1970

10

Is Hollywood Going Contemporary?

HOLLYWOOD, AS most of us know, is not a place but a state of mindlessness. Jacques Demy comes to Los Angeles from France and makes a film, *The Model Shop,* that out-Hollywoods Hollywood; M.G.M. goes to Africa and makes *The Comedians,* a film that turns the Gold Coast into our West Coast. Anyone can make a Hollywood film anywhere, provided he comes equipped with enough native bad taste, has money to burn, and has soaked up a sufficient number of other Hollywood films. Some, to be sure, can do it better than others; but some of the most typical specimens were made neither by nor in Hollywood—as, for example, *Interlude, Charlie Bubbles,* and one or two other items in this section.

Recently, however, Hollywood has become shaky—I mean the real Hollywood, out there on the West Coast that can no longer be turned into a Gold Coast. I shall not rehearse here the well-known facts of how the industry started dying from being too bulky, toothless, and dated—just like all those other saurians of a few aeons ago. But this particular Mesozoan tries to fight extinction and decides to get with it: if everyone else goes Paleocene, it, too, will cease to be Cretacious. And so there are films coming out of the new or streamlined old studios—or from abroad, for Hollywood invests heavily in foreign productions— that look swinging, with-it, and "now." And indeed, a *Thomas Crown Affair* or *The Arrangement* displays a specious kind of authenticity: it talks tough, goes through the motions of sex, dips its toes into the sea of troubles that surrounds us.

But, somehow, it all comes out hollow and wooden—or Hollywooden—try as it may. There are exceptions, of course; but the creaky giant is collapsing and, like King Kong (an African made in Hollywood) and Godzilla (a Hollywoodite made in Japan), dying. Still, it will live forever in the hearts of buffs and heads of *auteur* critics.

THE COMEDIANS

In *The Comedians,* the second-rate novelist Graham Greene is abetted by the second-rate scenarist of the same name, and the potentially electrifying story of love and death in dictator-ridden Haiti comes to standard melodrama gussied up with mumblings about "lost Faith." Surely there is enough religious and literary bad faith in Greene to qualify him as our era's number one unfrocked Proust. Add to this Peter Glenville's politely effete direction with the camera, for greater safety, mounted on a snail's back, and performances—well, these deserve to be preserved in alcohol and exhibited alongside of two-headed calves and dogs that would not come unstuck.

Elizabeth Taylor plays a German woman with what, when she remembers it, is a bastard French accent. Perhaps she thought of herself as hailing from Alsace-Lorraine, and indeed she is portly enough for her head to come from one province and her rump from the other. The one fortunate thing about the accent is that it keeps her voice from its ascent into that falsetto fit only for canine hearing; the rest of her performance, however, is much the same as ever: happiness is baby burbling over its lollypop; unhappiness, baby having tantrums over being deprived of its sucker. Opposite her, Richard Burton repeats his most inexpensive performance—almost a tic—which consists of playing everything from sensual fulfillment to metaphysical anguish with a lemon in his mouth and this time the lemon is as big as *The Comedians.*

Various black and white actors give black-and-white performances, among which only two stand out: Peter Ustinov is quietly touching as a South American diplomat unhappily in love with his wife; and Roscoe Lee Brown is gleamingly dapper and convincingly Haitian as a political go-between. Perhaps the one instructive thing about *The Comedians* is its photography. Henri Decaé has achieved, in films like *The Lovers* and *The 400 Blows,* some of the most exaltedly lyrical effects the camera can aspire to; yet here his color cinematography is strictly routine. Which goes to show that not only can a brilliant photographer sometimes work wonders for a floundering director (think of a film like *My Sister, My Love*) but that, also, a flat-eyed director can devitalize a gifted photographer.

December, 1967

CHARLIE BUBBLES

Albert Finney makes his directorial debut in *Charlie Bubbles,* and he proves less than inspired. What is worse, he also stars: Finney the director places what is left over of himself in front of the camera; the result is a split personality that seems to benefit neither half, and least of all the film.

Another trouble lies with Shelagh Delaney's script. Miss Delaney is being vaguely autobiographical again, which is fine, but she is also being autobiographical about something that did not quite happen to her and that she does not really succeed in imagining. The first part of the film is an extended binge on which Charlie, a Manchester lad turned London literary lion, goes with a pal of similar description— only this one not quite so big a hit and, apparently as a result, not quite so corroded with the dry rot of success. After the binge, there is the prolonged sobering-up at Charlie's sumptuous London house; whereupon we follow Charlie on one of his rare trips to Manchester to see his divorced wife and small son. The wife, of course, is tough and real and unspoiled by it all; the precocious son is slightly spoiled but, of course, real and innocent and full of the instinctive wisdom of childhood.

The whole thing is a pullulating anthill of pseudosophisticated prejudices: the successful writers at the club, beset by agents, lawyers, and such; at home, bullied by their hired help; stepping outside, and promptly beleaguered by predatory friends or nosy strangers. Above all, the film shows no true understanding of the successful writer's life. Miss Delaney's success was, it seems, of too short a duration for her to find out, and what she imagines is not much different from Steigian dreams of glory, only here the glory is made infantilely sour rather than infantilely sweet. Nevertheless, Miss Delaney has an ear or two for dialogue, and the scene, for instance, in which an airman on leave cadges a ride with Charlie and his secretary and proceeds to monologize ("Do you still work, Sir, or do you just do the writing? . . . I can

relate a story very well, but I can't get it down on paper. I have the
brains, but I haven't got the education.") is acutely observed, as well
as abrasively directed. Alan Lake's airman, too, is the apogee of guile-
less obnoxiousness.

There are other nice touches. Lottie, Charlie's wife, has dialogue of
a somewhat jaded earthiness with real resonance and sting to it; about
her home-baked bread, just praised by Charlie, she remarks, "All the
ingredients are very pure; there are no chemicals at all in that muck
you're eating." And Charlie says of her, "Lottie doesn't get up much
before Sunday on a Saturday." Such verbal felicities apart, the script
has little to offer. When Delaney and Finney hit on a good gimmick,
such as the multiple-screen closed-circuit television that enables Charlie
to survey the activities in all parts of his house, they milk it shamelessly,
both anecdotally and photographically. But what is finally defeating is
the sense of unearned disenchantment that hovers over several of the
characters, a kind of offensive defensiveness that is either a hopeless
stereotype or else requires closer and fresher examination than it is
accorded here.

The supreme deadweight in the picture is Liza Minnelli, Judy Gar-
land's daughter, whose screen debut proves easily the most inauspi-
cious since Turhan Bey's. Miss Minnelli is so untalented and homely,
and so blithely unaware of it all, that her performance must rate high
on the list of any collector of unconscious camp. Moreover, her role
—a gushy American would-be writer, part secretary, part mistress to
Charlie—is so awkward and extraneous that one suspects it was written
in for Miss Minnelli.

On the other hand, the film has an apt performance by Billie White-
law as Lottie, and a smashing one by Colin Blakely as Charlie's literary
drinking partner. The color photography by Peter Suschitsky is cleverly understated, and Mischa Donat's score is an acerbic distortion of
saccharine melodies that does what the film merely aspires to. *Charlie
Bubbles* ends with the hero seeing a balloon (the Jules Verne, not the
kiddy kind) outside his wife's window one morning, getting into it, and
taking off. I take this to be a piece of symbolism; what it symbolizes
is that Finney and Delaney couldn't think of a better ending for their
trifling film.

March, 1968

BYE, BYE, BRAVERMAN

Bye, Bye, Braverman is based on Wallace Markfield's *To an Early Grave,* which I haven't read and, after seeing the film, probably never will. There is little to recommend Sidney Lumet's heavy-handed—or, rather, heavy-hearted—satire: satire that tries to be devastating without having the courage to be satire. Boris Kaufman has some very nice helicopter and automobile shots of a car ride to Brooklyn, and there are two accomplished performances by Joseph Wiseman and Sorrell Booke. But these are more than vitiated by a poor script, unsure direction, unbearably coy music, and some execrable acting. George Segal, Jack Warden, Zohra Lampert, Jessica Walter, and Alan King deserve to be awarded jointly the Tin Griffin of the Perth Amboy Festival.

A currently much disputed question in Hollywood, I am told, is whether the film is anti-Semitic. This may indeed be the only question that can be raised concerning the opus. In defense of *Braverman* it has been put forward that everyone in it and on it is Jewish. Which reminds me of my answer to a young woman's charge that a certain English drama critic must be a latent homosexual because of his constant ferreting out of supposed inversion in the plays he reviews. "Not necessarily," I said; "for example, not all anti-Semites are Jews."

March, 1968

2001: A SPACE ODYSSEY

A regrettable failure, though not a total one, is Stanley Kubrick's *2001: A Space Odyssey.* This long film, five years and ten million dollars in the making, is fascinating when it concentrates on apes or machines (though there is too much of this, too) and dreadful when dealing with the in-between: human beings. Absolute dreadfulness, however, is reserved for the metaphysical, the (gasp!) Divine, which appears in the form of a large slab that mysteriously materializes whenever mankind is about to launch on a stage of higher development. Looking like a Mies van der Rohe version of one-half of the Tables of the Law, this Pentalogue has no writing on it, but can emit a mystagogic buzz.

The Slab appears first to a bunch of prehistoric apes. These men in ape costumes are so convincing and terrifying that by comparison the ones in *Planet of the Apes* (a set of costumes—and film—I quite enjoyed) are pussycats. They behave perfectly brutishly to some friendly tapirs, and fight over territorial rights with a neighboring bunch of apes as if they had read their Ardrey and Konrad Lorenz, which they probably have. Things go badly with them until the Slab appears, whereupon one of them thinks of using a bone as an offensive weapon and, behold, they slay the leader of their rival apes. After he is thoroughly dead, one of the victors hits him once more viciously, which is a nice human touch, and sets the stage for the next stage of history.

A triumphant ape hurls a bone into the air; by a clever matching shot, it becomes a space ship circling (somewhat interminably, but twenty minutes are about to be cut from the film) a space station to the tune of *The Blue Danube.* The music throughout is eclectic to the point of ecumenicity: when it isn't Johann Strauss, it's Richard, and Beethoven and Khachaturian also get their licks in.

The section begins with a Dr. Floyd stopping off at a space Hilton (trade names are often, and no doubt remuneratively, made use of) on a secret mission to the Moon. We get some mildly amusing scenes involving space stewardesses (they can walk upside down, as in an Ingmar Bergman film), space food (it's all liquid and only the picture on the container tells you what you're imbibing), and space toilets (where were you when it hit weightlessness?). At the Hilton there is some dull verbal fencing with quasi-friendly Russians, and Dr. Floyd has a dull (Bell) telephone conversation with his daughter on Earth. When he gets to Moon Station Clavius, he conducts a dull briefing session about why quarantine has been imposed on Clavius.

We realize now that the dullness, as well as the commonplaces and evasions, must be satire. Kubrick and his co-scenarist, Arthur C. Clarke, must be trying to ridicule the naïveté, disingenuousness, and benighted bureaucracy of creatures who handle all that mighty heavenly hardware. Apparently, though, one is allowed to be truly satirical in Hollywood only on a low-budget film such as *Dr. Strangelove;* when millions are at stake, we don't gamble on an art form Americans do not understand. So the satire throughout is tepid and halfhearted, and tends to look like quite unintentional stupidity.

Anyway, the Slab has been discovered on the Moon! It is emitting signals *ad astra,* to be specific, toward Jupiter. So the next and main section of the film shows us an expedition to that planet in an interplanetary spacecraft, a hydrocephalic electronic caterpillar the length of an average street. It carries several astronauts in sarcophaguses in a state of hibernation, two others who conduct the craft, and a supercomputer called Hal 9000, of the famous 9000 series that can do everything except go wrong.

Here the point is to show the astronauts as completely efficient
chines in mind and body, and Hal as a solicitous, omniscient den
other, patronizing, quite pompous, and, as it turns out, eager to assert
superiority. In other words, men have become computerized and
nputers humanized, with bad consequences for both. Unfortu-
ely, neither of them is an interesting enough species to keep us
erested in their ensuing struggle for supremacy and survival.

I won't go into the details of this astral agon, but let me say that one
ronaut finally makes it to Jupiter, or the fourth dimension, or what-
er it is that is represented by fifteen minutes (at any rate, it feels like
mauvais quart d'heure) of fancy yet not quite fancy enough trick
otography. Oh, I forgot to tell you: we saw the Slab precede him
ther! Some very odd things then happen in the Beverly Hills–Louis
VI apartment the astronaut ends up in: he discovers himself there,
, older, and, as the Slab appears, dying and being reborn as a kind
Buck Rogersy Superbaby, a new and presumably better species.
tually, there's no presumably about it: after the ones we have spent
film's two and three-quarter hours with, any species would be an
provement. The Slab, of course, is never explained, leaving *2001*,
all its lively visual and mechanical spectacle, a kind of space-*Spar-
us* and, more pretentious still, a shaggy God story.

May, 1968

BOOM!

om! is more of a mystery than a horror, though it is that, too. Why
uld anyone have wanted to make a film out of a Tennessee Williams
y that dropped dead twice on Broadway besides falling flat in San
ncisco? Why cast Elizabeth Taylor as a dying old bitch (any other
d, yes), Burton as a delicate young man in his twenties, the dwarf
chael Dunn as a giant bodyguard, and the pretty Joanna Shimkus if
u are going to shoot her as unflatteringly as possible lest she steal the
's thunder, or Noël Coward at all?

The once delightful Coward is now a mincing senior citizen of
prechaunia, still aiming for rapid-fire repartee with one foot in his
usoleum and the other in his overdentured mouth. Joseph Losey, the
ector, strains desperately to inject a note of art, but keeps missing
vein, if this dressmaker's dummy of a film can be said to have one.
e single remarkable thing here is the luxurious villa Richard Mac-
nald designed for the top of a Corsican cliff. Though made out of

paper and held together with spittle, it is the most gorgeous piece of neo-Renaissance Moroccan ever dreamed of. It's more than a *palazzo;* it's a whole camp unto itself.

July, 1968

INTERLUDE; THE THOMAS CROWN AFFAIR

Now take *Interlude,* the initial effort of a young Britisher, Kevin Billington and an updated remake of *Intermezzo,* that happy Hollywood remake of a Swedish film, in which the lesser Bergman (Ingrid) rose to stardom. It's about a sweet young thing's ultimately hopeless love for a great conductor; the maiden and the married maestro is an infallible tear-jerker, complete with that highly satisfying Freudian symbol, the baton. The movies constantly sprout these constant nymphs; I recall offhand Elisabeth Bergner, Katharine Hepburn, Susan Peters, and Joan Fontaine yearning to make beautiful music with the man who elicits it so beautifully. But this script by Leo Langley and Hugh Leonard is utter balderdash, wallowing in a stream of platitudes and unredeemed by any directorial invention—even the borrowed plumage was already moth-eaten.

Where the film falls down completely is in the casting and acting. If Oskar Werner ever was a heartthrob (as he certainly *was* an actor), he is now an aging Bill Buckley: the same faded blond boyishness, rabbity smile, paranoid stare, and curious vocal gymnastics. Werner carefully pitches every utterance an octave higher or lower than appropriate; this, coupled with his Teutonic accent and somehow adventitious intensity, makes for a mannered, anaphrodisiac performance.

The two women are no better. Barbara Ferris as the sweet young thing is neither very sweet nor very young, and certainly not very attractive. As the aristocratic, suffering wife, Virginia Maskell looks halfway between Virginia Woolf and a horse. Besides, both women are afflicted with hairdos out to sabotage their faces. And Gerry Fisher's color photography—or is it just a bad print?—makes England's green-swards look like layers of bluish-green roach powder. I kept watching the audience; not an eye was moist.

Equally unsatisfactory is Norman Jewison's *The Thomas Crown Affair.* This slick film uses plot devices like a fancy bank robbery and technical devices like a vastly subdivided screen with multiple images repeating, augmenting, or clashing with one another; but underneath all that it is only interested in one thing. It wants to exploit a luxurious Boston millionaire setting, against which a sexy, bank-robbing nabob is hounded by a beautiful, beddable insurance detective. First comes the affair, then the love; and all the time the gorgeous sleuth is trying (especially in bed) to get the goods on her plush lover. The situation is piquant, the *mise en scène* lavish (though not always in the best taste: Faye Dunaway's gowns, coiffures, and, above all, hats become progressively more insufferable), and Steve McQueen has undeniable charm, even if rather more of the Beverly Hills than the Beacon Hill variety.

The problem is that in order to milk the lushness of the emotional embroglio—love versus duty, or lust versus successful insurance detective's bonus, or cat and mouse with the roles and sexes continually reversed—all plausibility, to say nothing of construction, is abandoned. Any supposedly intricate situation that could be resolved as simply as having a small tape recorder hidden in one of Miss Dunaway's excess bits of clothing while McQueen charmingly (and repeatedly) confesses his guilt, lacks that minimum of credibility without which a film of suspense becomes a film of self-indulgence.

August, 1968

THE CHARGE OF THE LIGHT BRIGADE

As superproductions go, *The Charge of the Light Brigade* is preferable to some. Tony Richardson resembles our leading cultural superproduction-maker, Franco Zeffirelli, in more ways than I care to mention, except that he is more derivative. Nevertheless, he has conjured up here, with help from others, some remarkably faithful period atmosphere, so that even what has drawn most criticism—the cartoon sequences and the emphasis on glaring social contrasts—is truly Victorian, and worthy of corresponding passages in Dickens. For once, Richardson succeeds in eliciting fine performances that resist the pull toward caricature; John Gielgud as Raglan and Trevor Howard as Cardigan are particularly persuasive. David Watkin's color photography knows exactly how to coddle or jolt the eye, and the marvelous background music of John Addison often surpasses the foreground.

All the same, despite excellent bits, *The Charge of the Light Brigade* is not a satisfying film. For one thing, the story—or whatever one should call the haphazard incidents serving as pedestal to the Crimean episodes—is insignificant and uncompelling. For another, Charles Wood's dialogue verges on the unfortunate hyperboles of military stupidity he piled up in *How I Won the War;* here, moreover, the surreally imbecile dialogue uncomfortably clashes with the visual *verismo.* Most importantly, the final section of the film is impossible to follow; in fact, considering the lucid book on which it is largely based, it is almost as inexcusably muddled as the British commanders at Bala-clava. Richardson was trying to say something about unduly heroic liberals being no less at fault than the finky old fogeys, but the intention gets lost in the battle scenes whose turmoil is partly splendid and partly a mistake.

Two further complaints. It is regrettable to have both leading ladies in such a dashing film seemingly vie with each other for this year's Homeliness Award, just as it is misguided to entrust the gallantly swashbuckling lead to David Hemmings, who, besides being a medi-ocre actor, looks in long shots like something out of *Planet of the Apes.* A more serious grievance concerns the exhibiting of the film: I doubt that so vacillating a product should be turned into a road show; but for such prices the public is at least entitled to a larger screen than that of the Fine Arts Theatre, and a projectionist who will not add his own vacillations to those of the film.

November, 1968

NEGATIVES; PAPER LION

Precious little that is positive can be said about *Negatives,* a spurious and pretentious film co-scripted from his own novel by Peter Everett, directed by the allegedly promising newcomer Peter Medak, and enacted by Glenda Jackson, Diane Cilento, and Peter McEnery. De-spite the large input of Peters, a potentially interesting idea peters out before it has half begun.

Theo, a young antiques dealer of dubious virility, and Vivien, a young girl of shady background, achieve a precarious but working relationship through a set of sexual games in which he is Crippen the murderer, and she the women in his life. Along comes an older woman and more sinister games mistress, Reingard, a German photographer, who seems to be equally attracted to both our sandbox perversionists.

She sets them to playing weirder games that result in disaster for the pair as she flits off toward further evil.

This plot would have possibilities, if only psyches were explored more deeply, if the people had some human dimensions to them, and if the dialogue were not so stilted. The novel was written entirely in the present tense, which gave it an unpleasantly show-offy quality. The film substitutes nervousness and fancy editing for analysis and true originality.

The acting is awkward: Glenda Jackson, the compelling Corday of *Marat/Sade,* is a lumpish drab of a Vivien; the usually sparkling Miss Cilento is equally unconvincing as a German and as a pervert, and Peter McEnery is too surly and stolid as Theo. But Ken Hodges's photography puts unnatural colors to suggestive use, and Basil Kirchin's sentimental, almost morbidly insinuating score has the proper corrupt charm. The film, however, always gives us too much or too little, and never involves us with its people whose pathology cannot achieve pathos.

From papier-mâché to plain *Paper Lion.* Since I find neither football nor the apparently puckish golems who play it of the slightest interest, I cannot judge either the thrill- or authenticity-value of the film. But I can say that Alan Alda, though a charming and gifted actor, lacks the blue-bloodedness that is the *sine qua non* for playing Plimpton and getting the full contrast out of the situation. I can well believe that George edits *The Paris Review* in his shower, but hearing him assign an essay on Hegel to the next issue of that essayless publication sets up a credibility gap bigger and much less sexy than the gap between Lauren Hutton's, the fetching leading lady's, two front teeth. But perhaps this is a hidden clue to the interpretation of the film. If journalism is the thesis, football is the antithesis, and *Paper Lion* is synthetic.

November, 1968

RACHEL, RACHEL

There are still some nice small movies left, our stars be thanked, even in America. The stars in the case of *Rachel, Rachel* are Paul Newman, who proves himself an adroit director with this his maiden effort, and his wife, Joanne Woodward, as always a matchless portrayer of the effortful maiden.

Rachel is a thirty-five-year--old schoolmarm who, at the exact middle of her life, finds herself in the *selva oscura* of a boring provincial town, without love and exploited by a dreary mother. She drifts from one fruitless experience to another: masturbation, religious revivals, a fellow teacher's lesbian advances, a prosperous undertaker's lifeless attentions, frustrated attempts at mother love toward her pupils and ghastly daughter love toward an exasperating mother. At last a man comes along, takes her and leaves her pregnant; the pregnancy comforts her until it, too, turns out to be no more than an operable tumor. Finally she goes off, with her mother trailing along, to a new job in Oregon; perhaps Horace Greeley's advice holds good for a not-so-young woman as well.

The stuff is plainly that of women's magazines and women's pictures. But with a difference: it is more real, more restrained, more literate. If it is a woman's picture, it is the new woman's, and Stewart Stern's screenplay, based on a novel by Margaret Laurence, has not only the ring of authenticity but also the gift of modulating tones with considerable finesse. True, the film tends to verge on dullness, but something always saves it. Often it is Miss Woodward: she is one of those rare actresses who can put a basic lack of charm to good advantage by playing it off against a certain pathos which, coming from someone so rough-and-tumble, becomes moving rather than coy.

The supporting parts are ably handled, with Kate Harrington outstanding as the usurping yet pitiable mother. Only Estelle Parsons is a bore, giving the same bovinely giddy performance she now dispenses in every part on stage or screen. Gayne Rescher's color photography is poor, but Jerome Moross's score has a nice American folk quality, even if it is a bit of a steal from his own music for that delicious stage musical, *The Golden Apple,* of which someone could make a smashing film.

NOTE: I have since learned that Newman turned over an enormous mess of footage to the editor, Dede Allen, and that it was that lady, repeating her wonder-working for *Bonnie and Clyde,* who turned *Rachel, Rachel* into the adequate thing it is.

November, 1968

THE GIRL ON A MOTORCYCLE; THE FIXER

If Chabrol's *Les Biches* is like a pornographic film with the porno parts carefully excised and the pre- and postcoital tiresomeness left in, *The Girl on a Motorcycle,* released roughly simultaneously, does deliver some sex—otherwise it is almost as bad a film. Based on the novel *The Motorcycle* by André Pieyre de Mandiargues, a Goncourt Prize-winning pornographer (but a genteel, scholarly, avuncular pornographer of the old school), it turns a quaint, queasy little fiction into a blaring, attitudinizing film.

The novel concerns Rebecca, a young girl married to Raymond, a decent, dull Swiss who teaches in an Alsatian school. But she first became the mistress, under bizarre circumstances, of Daniel, a dominant middle-aged intellectual, who is librarian at the University of Heidelberg. As a wedding present, her lover gave Rebecca a huge black Harley-Davidson (to motorcycles what Baldwin is to pianos, and fifty times as loud) on which she shuttles between her connubial bed and her lover's brutal caresses. During one such predawn to early-morning ride from her small Alsatian town to Heidelberg, she recapitulates in her mind the stages of her affair with Daniel.

As their sexual encounters become progressively more sadomasochistic (though they remain within bounds as well as bonds), Daniel initiates Rebecca in varieties of more or less esoteric lore, and teaches her to ride a motorcycle to boot. There are arcane symbolisms based on the names and nationalities of the characters, and the book is a curious mixture of minute topographical descriptions, motorcycle data, philosophizing, and moderately kinky sex. Throughout, the motorcycle is represented as a great phallic beast, the symbolic extension, or erection, of the lover, sometimes even transcending and superseding him. At the end of the ride during which the reminiscing occurs, Rebecca, on the outskirts of Heidelberg, dies in a highly symbolic crash.

The script, by Ronald Duncan, an effete religious verse dramatist, and Gillian Freeman, a swinging sociological novelist (she wrote the scenario of *The Leather Boys* from her own book) is a reduction—as well as a detumescence—of the plot. The book, moreover, is full of wild metaphors: the motorcycle has "a distinguished drunkard's cough"; "the rubber of the tires on which she was riding was a kind of artgum; she was in the grip of a craving to erase." The film translates this into mod oversimplifications: "A twist of the throttle and I obliterate this muck and turn myself on"; "Rebellion is the only thing that keeps you alive." Or take this, all part of the film heroine's voice-over *monologue intérieur:* "I was an adulterous teenage bride. . . . Why did I marry him? Was it because I was a masochist? . . . You're a sadist, my darling, a magnificent sadist BASTARD!!!" And so on. Here Mrs. Freeman's researches for her recent and shallow book about the pornographic press, *The Undergrowth of Literature,* must have been enormously helpful.

More damaging—insofar as the diminution of something already minuscule can be viewed as damaging—is the lessening of the sexual images. Where the lover in the novel whips the tied-up girl with a bunch of roses, here a vase full of roses serves merely to hide the lover's pudenda during a cuddly nude scene. Where the lover in the novel tells the girl he undresses that he is flaying her like a rabbit, here he informs her (and this must be the contribution of Ronald Duncan, the mystic author of *This Way to the Tomb*), "Your toes are like tombstones."

Indeed, the grave-robberish script digs up such decomposing tropes as "all of us are like lemmings on our way to the cemetery," where the book says "she would always be no more than an object in transit," epitomizing Rebecca's adulterous bike rides. But the clearest indications of the comedown in tone is that in the novel Daniel buys from Rebecca's bookseller father works by Swedenborg and Dom Bernard de Montfaucon; in the film, Teilhard de Chardin and Robert Ardrey!

Poor as it is, the film has one superb asset: its cinematography. Jack Cardiff (remember the beach scene in his *Sons and Lovers?*) both photographed and directed, and as will happen when those two jobs are done by the same person—one thinks of *A Man and a Woman*—the cinematography gets the starring role. There are some shabby effects in *The Girl on a Motorcycle,* especially when solarization dilutes the wilder sex scenes into psychedelic semiabstractions, but much of the photography is beautiful enough to justify seeing the film, just as a great performance might. The extreme long shots of the girl on the motorbike riding into the dawn along Rhenish forests, I shall keep remembering with a shudder of reverence. Marvelous, too, are shots of the black-leather, mechanized centaur against sleepy towns or soaringly sculptured bridges that leave even the antimotor viewer spellbound by the machine's *beauté du diable* as it striates the works of man and nature.

Though Alain Delon is not the mature, masterful Daniel, he has a handsome, set face; Marianne Faithfull is bedecked with fine equipment from bosom to pubes, and has the right kind of mauled yet unquenchable innocence. Acting does not enter into the picture. Her demise, when like a man shot from a cannon she zooms through an oncoming car's windshield, is surely one of the finest visual exit lines on film.

The Fixer is another adaptation that failed. I am told that Malamud's novel is far from what it might be, but I am sure that the film is considerably farther. John Frankenheimer's direction has skill in scenes like the initial pogrom, but lacks distinction in the subtler passages. Dalton Trumbo's lackluster screenplay pullulates with Jewishisms ("Luck I was always short of ... A hero I'm not ... Wise I never was," etc.), and the accents as well as the acting are a hodgepodge of everything from Central London to Central Casting.

Alan Bates gives a creditable performance as a Cockneyfied Jew, and tries to infuse the unrelieved suffering exacted from the protagonist with as much variety as can be squeezed from pain. If he lets his head revolve and his eyes rove a trifle overmuch, who can blame him for casting about for a way out of the fix or *Fixer* he is in. His bare posterior, known to us from *Georgy Girl* and *King of Hearts,* makes another timely appearance here, thus becoming one of the most exposed arses in cinematic annals. Dirk Bogarde, as the sympathetic investigating magistrate, gives an altogether intelligent, incisive, and charming performance, and any film that offers Bogarde a chance to display his talent merits some attention. The other supporting work ranges from the out-and-out ham of Hugh Griffith and Georgia Brown to the much more kosher performances of Ian Holm and William Hutt, with a unifying principle conspicuously absent.

Two people deserve special credit for the fine looks of the film, though all the visual aspects are commendably managed. One is the Hungarian art director Béla Zeichán, who helped Frankenheimer come up with interiors and exteriors (the latter in Hungary) that far better films might envy; the other is Marcel Grignon, who has photographed it all in rich, mellow, yet understated colors—as if a dark violet veil had been cast over the opulence. Maurice Jarre's score is not so good as what he has composed for small European films, but better than what he usually turns out for large Hollywood-sponsored ones. The extensive use of a solo string instrument is particularly effective.

December, 1968

GOODBYE, COLUMBUS

Social comment of a sort is provided also in *Goodbye, Columbus,* Larry Peerce's incompetent film version of Philip Roth's novella. Incompetent and vulgar, to be exact. On the one hand, the already sufficiently horrid, petty-bourgeois, parvenu, Jewish milieu of the story is underlined and overstressed in its horridness to the n-th degree; on the other hand, Neil and Brenda's affair is suffused with color so glowing, framed by surroundings so pastoral, that, at the very least, it seems intended to sell Doeskin toilet tissues on TV.

For all its attitudes of daring, the film boggles at any number of things. The various characterizing references to Mary McCarthy are omitted as, presumably, too literate for the average viewer. Omitted as too disturbing for the viewer are things like Neil's and Brenda's anti-Semitism; thus the bit on the telephone, when Brenda asks Neil how she will recognize him at the Boston station (" 'I'll be disguised as an orthodox Jew.' 'Me, too,' she said.") is cut from Arnold Shulman's allegedly ever-so-faithful script. It is a curious phenomenon that so-called courageous films are almost always made by bunglers, cowards, or phonies, or all three in one.

Emblematic is the treatment of Harriet, Brenda's sister-in-law. Whereas in the story she is just like Brenda, only bosomier; in the film, she is a horsy, ungainly creature. Whereas in the story her conversation is subtly unnerving with its dignified banality; in the film, she merely chortles and acts equine.

Even the very point of the story, Brenda's deliberate abandoning of the diaphragm where her mother will find it, gets fudged over and submerged in near incomprehensibility. Not made clear is the ghastly sense of guilt and belonging that subverts Brenda's seeming emancipation: the horror of the family that has not released her from its tentacles, and of her own weakness in not being able to extricate herself. The fact that the hotel in Boston is made into some sinister dive instead of the standard Sheraton it should have been; that Brenda is shown from the beginning of the last scene outraged and angry, as if some Higher Morality were propelling her; that Father and Mother Patimkin's letters are not reproduced in their disheartening entirety—all suggest a belated moral awakening rather than a surrender to dehumanizing conventionality.

Peerce's direction is steadily obvious, sometimes pseudopoetic, often coy. The sex scenes in particular become one big cute giggle, though here Richard Benjamin's otherwise more than adequate Neil is also to blame. A typical Peerce touch is the opening shot of the film in which a pretty girl emerging from the country club's swimming pool loses the top of her bikini—what has this to do with the *nouveau riche* ambience and theme of the film? Again, a hammy rear-view closeup of Neil's and Brenda's profiles nuzzling each other luminously in the narrow gap between the two dark backs of their beach chairs is actually repeated, lest we miss its cleverness. And so on, leapfrogging from blatancy to blatancy. But Peerce is fortunate in most of his performers, especially in Jack Klugman as Patimkin; and in his discovery, Ali McGraw, he has a very lucky find: an ex-model who, unlike most ex-models, actually is an actress.

Miss McGraw, and for this Peerce may deserve some directorial credit, gives a delicately balanced performance, her Brenda emerging tough and unfeeling at times, tomboyish and silly at others, considerably yet not repellently narcissistic all along. There is inchoate feeling and vestigial thought, and also, at the right moments, something touching and pitiable. It is a graceful, nicely shaded piece of acting, enhanced by the fact that it comes from a young woman not merely lovely, but actually gifted with a kind of thinking man's loveliness. The updating of the movie, and such things as turning Brenda into a Cliffie of the late sixties when she is clearly a Wellesleyite of the fifties, are unfortunate —they frequently dull Roth's sharpness of observation; but Ali McGraw exudes a pervasive authenticity that almost puts everything back into focus.

April, 1969

THANK YOU ALL VERY MUCH

Thank You All Very Much, based on a novel by Margaret Drabble, is the latest Sandy Dennis film, and would that it were the last! The penultimate one, *A Cold Day in the Park,* made in British Columbia, was about as pretentious, loathsome, and stupid as a film can get; this one, made in Britain, is none of those things—it is careful, inconsequential, and plodding. But a Sandy Dennis picture is always in a category by itself: an excuse for displaying the persona of Sandy Dennis, which is inexcusable. Having come to the end of the road with her early phase, the totem-pole school of acting (one horrible face on top of another), Miss Dennis now affects the minimalist mode: an all-purpose budding sensitivity arrested in mid-development.

Through most of the picture Miss Dennis sports the expression of a fly trying to be stoical about having been caught in amber, but there are muted undercurrents of the old tics, twitches, and congested sinuses. In addition, at judiciously spaced intervals all stops are pulled from the vocal cords and facial muscles and, once again, the art of the tremolo and the palpitating lip storms the very heavens. Thank you very much, but no thanks.

September, 1969

THE ARRANGEMENT

In Elia Kazan's *The Arrangement* all possible cinematic clevernesses—usually yesterday's—are dragged out in an endless parade, perfect for tying up the traffic of ideas, to illustrate a senseless and banal story that reels from platitude to platitude. The film was adapted by Kazan from his own dime novel, and, exactly as at the dime store, everything in the film has gone up to two-bit goods. Thus we start with a pretentious montage of brief shots meant to epitomize Eddie Anderson's, the ad-man-hero's, life—and if we aren't shown at least twenty fancy gadgets at work (some in extreme closeup), we aren't shown one.

The main problem is that Kazan is not enough of an artist or thinker to convey just what this supposed greatness of Eddie's, which has somehow been prostituted, consists of. Florence, Eddie's tearful wife, laments: "You could have been—*what* you could have been! . . ." and, significantly, she has to leave it at an aposiopesis. Even his brilliant ad campaigns don't strike one as particularly dazzling; beyond that, his mistress, Gwen, apparently finds him terrific in bed. But man does not live by bed alone: what is this talent of Eddie's that it is death to hide? He speaks in the same clichés as the rest of the characters, and when he splits into two selves on the screen, he merely becomes a double stereotype. Eddie is, in fact, a nonentity, and neither Kazan nor Kirk Douglas, who plays him mediocrely, can turn his dying interest in making money, his dying marriage, his dying love affair, his dying father, his dying will to live into matters deserving our serious concern.

To be sure, there is enough plot here—and incessant rapid cross-cutting makes a long film seem positively interminable—to see your average soap opera through a season; and not only is it presented with condign triteness, it is also full of that relentless flashiness that typifies Kazan's direction. Thus it is not enough to shoot Eddie's and Gwen's lovemaking reflected in a pool, a computer panel, a plate-glass window; there has to be even a shot in which Eddie watches his mistress through not only a glass door but also, superimposed, her lavender spectacles, which he holds at a dramatic distance from his eyes. There are nude love scenes with Gwen on a beach (with the anatomy exposure indecently calipered for an R rather than X rating) which later appear as snapshots that Florence tears up and throws at Eddie's feet. Eddie looks down, and lo! like a tapeworm, each snapshot fragment, on a divided screen, comes to life writhing with mutilated but unquenchable dalliance. Perhaps the most irritatingly hammy Kazan trick is to follow every high-angle with a low-angle shot, or vice versa, the schematism of which is as jarring as the predictability is boring.

Kazan is not only vulgar in his effects ("forthright," wrote Dwight Macdonald, "the way a butcher is forthright when he slaps down a steak for the customer's inspection"), he also steals them from all over. From the New Wave he takes the *hommage* to a favorite director, and has the gall to insert a clip from his own wretched film, *America America;* from *Hamlet* (among other sources) he takes the conceit of a visible imaginary presence with whom one character converses to the bewilderment of others; from *Persona* he takes the arc lamp made suddenly visible inside the projector—but whereas in Bergman this means something, in Kazan it is a purely gratuitous piece of pilfering; from *Le Bonheur* he takes the device of a man's copulations with two women shown so that at first you cannot tell which one he is currently in bed with; from Fellini (if not from *Lady in the Dark*) he purloins an adult protagonist watching himself as a child, and even reenacting, in his adult body, scenes from his childhood; and so on.

It is all particularly heavy-handed when it reaches for symbols—as when the hero, refusing to return to his job, watches a TV documentary in which wild dogs devour an antelope alive. Not only is this dragged out unconscionably, it is also intercut with the coming of his employers to reclaim him, and, on top of that, reiterated at a crucial point in the film. Kazan, moreover, cannot make human relationships come alive: we never understand what Eddie sees in Gwen, or Florence in Eddie. And Eddie's relations with his father, which are supposed to be shattering, are sagging, elongated commonplaces—compare the terseness and penetrancy with which a similar relation is portrayed in *Downhill Racer.* Add to this the final cop-out: the whole tangled and seemingly insoluble situation resolves itself handily to everyone's satisfaction. What, then, was all the fuss about?

The color photography by Robert Surtees is suitably unsubtle—note especially a night beach scene with garishly clashing pink, yellow, and indigo; and an autumn lawn breaking out with an impetigo of blatant orange leaves. David Amram's score translates Eddie's Americanized Greek origins into tea-shop bouzouki, and is as plodding as they come. Among the performers, Faye Dunaway and Hume Cronyn at least convey some authentic flavor. But *The Arrangement* is as dead as a flower arrangement in an undertaker's parlor. It is the kind of filmmaking against which a far-out horror like *Futz* arises in fanatical reaction, leaving the public only the choice of being done in by the poison or the counterpoison.

November, 1969

CATCH-22

I am going to be brief about the superproduction of *Catch-22* because I am one of those illiterates who did not read the novel, having found its humor, on the whole, not my canteen of tea. But I have skimmed it, and I can tell that Mike Nichols's conception and Buck Henry's screenplay, though ostensibly faithful to the book, have really tried to turn its absurdities into a kind of superabsurdism; that a work essentially related to *Dr. Strangelove,* and perhaps rather less radical than that film, has been forced into the Richard Lester (*How I Won the War; The Bed Sitting Room*) mold. In other words, exaggeration has been re-exaggerated, the satirically distorted turned into the swinging surreal, and the black humor of the fifties upgraded into the psychedelic humor of the late sixties and seventies.

As a result of this hyping up, a figure like Milo Minderbinder, rather than being just the ultimate caricature of free enterprise gone hogwild, becomes a cartoon version of the American dictator of the seventies. Or when Nately's whore does her stabbing disguised as a GI, in fatigues, her identity impenetrable to anyone not intimate with the novel, this is considered great fun—the obscurer, the more with-it and better.

The scene in which Yossarian is struggling in the water toward a raft has, as executed here, no visible purpose except to display Paula Prentiss naked, her beaver gleaming even blacker against an artfully whitened background. Or we get a swift, modish survey of the horrors of nocturnal Rome (read: the World) as Yossarian staggers from observing instant fellatio in one doorway to a masturbating faggot in the next, from tots rolling a drunk on one street to a drayman viciously flogging a fallen white horse on the next. We race from sex to satire to Significance at breakneck speed, and what is jettisoned is the novel's hallmark: its dogged, doggy worrying of every funnybone it can clamp its teeth on.

Still, a new and different style would not be necessarily bad, if only it did not, as here, inevitably clash with what survives of the old. Moreover, absurdism on film is devilishly hard to carry off, because, unlike the stage picture, the screen image perforce packs in a lot of direct, visual reality, and thrusts upon the absurdist filmmaker the opposite of Brecht's alienation effect, a reality effect. Nichols combats this by making the fantasies and the story blend indistinguishably, by using certain incidents as recurrent yet mutually contradictory refrains, by dislocating the narrative sequence, and by fast cutting. But all this does not so much create a style as recapitulate most of the styles now in vogue, and it does create, at least for someone not familiar with Heller's novel, mysteries too thick to penetrate.

This is too bad, because Nichols clearly has real talent in several areas, although his greatest deficiency—an underlying lack of ballsiness, seriousness, perhaps even humanity—repeatedly trips him up. Here he has carried off a number of scenes with considerable wit, and others with a nice sense of visual shock effect. He has even managed a few quiet moments aptly: the penultimate scene, with Yossarian, Danby, and Tappman each debating from a different hospital bed, and the static camera taking it all in from above; or the scene in a greenish corridor where Yossarian hesitates before breaking the bad news to the dead Nately's whore. And with the help of his versatile cinematographer, David Watkin, Nichols has made everything look sun-bleached, dust-bitten, and, above all, heat-wavy, so that a squadron of rickety bombers taking off seems to swim jerkily through the liquefying air.

The actors have a way of getting lost in the script or in the directing, and many of them look so similar or are seen so briefly that they certainly lose you. Alan Arkin's Yossarian, though intermittently effective, reminds me of too many other Arkin performances, and needlessly deintellectualizes the character. Orson Welles's General Dreedle is bloated and vacuous enough to float right into Macy's Thanksgiving parade; Buck Henry, the scenarist, packs more corn into Lieutenant Colonel Korn than a force-fed goose could survive; and Bob Newhart turns Major Major into a minor disaster. The others will more or less do. What is most wrong with *Catch-22,* though, is that it tries to look so dedicatedly different that it turns difference into another kind of predictability.

June, 1970

11

Musicals

OUTSTANDING MOVIE musicals are few and far between; no more than a midget handful. I suppose that the main problem here is that the Hollywood musical always conceives of itself as the last bastion of nostalgia, lavishness, and family picture-making. In the finished product, this comes out as unendurably syrupy sentimentality, ostentatious display of soulless opulence, and a naïveté bordering on imbecility. Two of the six musicals discussed here have value, but even they are not free of the weaknesses that beset the genre. One, *Paint Your Wagon,* tries to be sexually daring, but its polyandrous and homosexual elements are treated with such guileful blandness that they get lost in the musical's conformity to the three generic clichés. The basic unadventurousness is further evidenced by the fact that all six films are either adaptations of stage hits or musical remakes of successful nonmusical films. Where are the original screen musicals?

CAMELOT

To start at the bottom, take *Camelot:* three hours of unrelieved glossiness, meticulous inanity, desperate and charmless striving for charm. This film is the Platonic idea of boredom, roughly comparable to reading a three-volume novel in a language of which one knows only the alphabet. The alphabet of *Camelot* is one big fat soulless closeup after one big fat pseudomedieval interior or big fat Disneyland exterior—all together they spell shrdlu. The opening nocturnal shot of Arthur in a huge black cape, as he faces away from the camera toward a darling storybook castle, makes us think Dracula will finally meet Disney. But no such luck. The film is not even an elephant; only a flea under intense magnification. An already feeble stage musical is here given the Joshua Logan deep-freeze direction, the Alfred Newman calliope orchestrations, set design in which trees are made of glass, acting in which people are wrapped in cellophane that is never removed.

But it is opulent. All the horses wear $6,000 suits of armor; this is helpful in that it enables us to distinguish them from Vanessa Redgrave, who has never been shot to look so equine before. Richard Harris keeps us constantly wondering: will he, in the next sequence, wear his Richard Burton face or his Marlon Brando one? There are other games that people condemned to watch *Camelot* can play—such as guessing who in the cast will pronounce "joust" in the preferred manner, rhyming with "must," and who in the infra dig way, rhyming with "oust." Arthur does the former, Guinevere the latter; clearly such a marriage of unequal minds could not have lasted.

December, 1967

OLIVER!

Oliver! is a nice, big movie musical about which it is hard to say anything of special interest to the reader or even to oneself. Lionel Bart had applied his verbal and musical emollients to *Oliver Twist* and, with the help of some good performances and splendid sets by Sean Kenny, concocted a pleasant, unabrasive, and undisturbing stage musical. The screen version expands the show—not back toward Dickens, but forward to greater make-believe and more sumptuous foolery.

The tunes continue to be sporadically ingratiating, the lyrics as spotty as a leopard with measles, the dances by Onna White less than imaginative but more than amiable. Once again there is an inspired set designer, John Box, who has created a many-hued, Mayhewish London that is real enough without being too real, and where all kinds of cavortings—choreographic, melodramatic, or just cornball—can feel at home. Most of the performances are at least appropriate, and Ron Moody's Fagin is as definitive as a Bart-time Fagin can be. The children all do well, though Mark Lester's Oliver seems at times a trifle too pale. Oliver Reed is a somewhat lackadaisical and overrefined Bill Sikes, and Shani Wallis is lumpish and insipid as Nancy, which is too bad.

The most brilliant piece of casting has Sikes's dog enacted by a pit-bull terrier, with various cicatrices painted on in sheer redundancy. For a pit-bull terrier is easily the creepiest looking dog in existence, and whatever menace Oliver Reed may lack, that albino rat-faced, salamander-legged canine readily supplies.

There is, further, the color cinematography of Oswald Morris, one of the screen's devoted and complete artists. Morris has done more for cinematography and, being unflashy, received fewer hosannahs than anyone I could name. How much he contributed to films like *Lolita, The Hill,* and *The Taming of the Shrew,* we could properly estimate only if we could see these films without his camera work. And *Oliver!* is directed by Carol Reed, who did handsomely by it, even though this potent director of suspense films is hardly in his element here. Still, even the musical numbers are shot with a briskness and verve characteristic of Reed. The only false note is Bill Sikes's dead body swinging back and forth on a rope—that is more in keeping with films like *Odd Man Out* and *The Third Man* than with this benign extravaganza.

Unlike Zeffirelli's *Romeo and Juliet,* to which you may take children but not adults, *Oliver!* is suitable for everyone, at the very least for being the liveliest illustration of Dickens since Phiz, and providing in Ron Moody a truly fizzy Fagin. The film is not only zestfully atmospheric, it is also marvelously Moody.

December, 1968

PAINT YOUR WAGON; GOODBYE, MR. CHIPS

Two big musicals based on old materials but refurbished to suit our ostensibly more sophisticated times bid for our attention. First there is *Paint Your Wagon,* from the old Lerner-Loewe stage musical, remembered for its bad book and pleasant songs. In their egalitarian way, the filmmakers have scrapped most of the bad book and quite a few of the pleasant songs. For the cast-off songs they have substituted new ones with music by André Previn that strikes the ear as stimulatingly as sheet music an eye that cannot read notes. These tuneless tunes flow into one another like a river bent on disproving Heraclitus's dictum that you cannot bathe in the same water twice. And on the old songs, Nelson Riddle's orchestrations do their leveling worst.

As for the new plot, it is the contrivance of Paddy Chayefsky, and has Lee Marvin and Clint Eastwood as loving partners in a gold claim in rowdy Tent City, where men are men and women don't exist. At least not until the day a Mormon arrives with two wives and is persuaded to sell one off by auction. The highest bidder, with his partner's money, is hard-brawling, hard-guzzling Lee Marvin, who marries Jean Seberg, the surplus spouse, in a quaintly *ad hoc* ceremony. The wedding night would be no better than a rape if Miss Seberg did not make an impassioned and civilizing speech just after Marvin has torn as much clothing off her as is consistent with showing no more than one-eighth of an inch of aureola. Thereupon the wedding night proceeds amicably, though with Eastwood no longer sharing his partner's tent.

While Marvin is off waylaying a cargo of French whores destined for Sonora and rerouting it to Tent City (so they won't all hanker after Jean), Eastwood and Miss Seberg fall in love, and there is nothing for it, after a little roughhouse between the partners, but to start a polyandrous ménage. This provides a welcome change for Miss Seberg from all that polygyny. She is a real little homemaker, and gets her husbands to build the first log cabin in Tent City for her to play house-and-a-half in. This architectural model, the gold, and the French whores bringing in customers from all over, soon enable Tent City to become big, bustling, sinful No Name City.

In due time, the wicked town meets a fate worthy of Sodom and Gomorrah. Marvin and his cronies have been digging secret tunnels under each house to recover the gold dust seeping through floorboards. One fine Sunday, when the whole town is watching circus games instead of praying in church, every last building collapses from Marvin's undermining. So, too, the connubial threesome collapses after a set of unhilarious *contretemps.* Marvin's wanderlust drives him on to new bonanzas, while Eastwood and Miss Seberg settle down to farming and a morally uplifting ending, which nets the film the relatively permissive rating of M—recommended for mature audiences.

Realizing, no doubt, that mature audiences wouldn't know what to make of this film, Paramount has contested the rating and is demanding a G—general, i.e., family-audience classification. *Paint Your Wagon* should certainly delight the entire family, especially if it comes equipped with more than one parent of either sex. Indeed, the film's message, if taken to heart, may prove an effective means of combating the rising divorce rate. For similarly high moral reasons, I presume, Joshua Logan's direction does not include a single love scene—not even a kiss—between Jean and either spouse, concentrating instead on the true male tenderness between Marvin and Eastwood.

If you add to this that none of the stars can sing—a minor obstacle Marvin and Eastwood surmount by the use of *Sprechstimme,* and Seberg by getting herself dubbed by someone else (the wiser solution, on the whole)—and that the climax with all those funnily crumbling houses would hardly elicit a smile from anyone but a professional demolition worker, you wonder why Paramount spent anywhere from eighteen to twenty-four million dollars on this venture. Of course, if there are enough misguided souls around to make the company recoup its invest- ment, we shall have our answer. Meanwhile we can definitely learn one thing from the film: Miss Seberg has a much larger bosom than has hitherto been evidenced—unless it, too, is part of the trick engineering that built collapsible No Name City.

The other, even less musical, musical, is a remake of *Goodbye, Mr. Chips,* which should have stuck to tearjerking instead of dabbling in tunejerking. The music and lyrics by Leslie Bricusse conquer new depths of ineptitude, and having these nonsongs done mostly in voice- over as interior monologues adds preteniousness to their basic awful- ness.

James Hilton's novel and its charming original movie version have been updated in Terence Rattigan's script, but before the cognoscenti get too rapturous about the original version's superior quality and credibility, they should be reminded that it also had Greer Garson. Not that Petula Clark, homely and bow-legged, is much of an actress, yet she is at least a straightforward, unmannered human being. And Rattigan is the right scenarist for this sort of bittersweet entertainment exuding civilized sentimentality.

What justifies the film, besides Oswald Morris's supremely tactful color photography, and some quite palatable supporting performances, particularly Michael Redgrave's headmaster and Sian Phillips's scarlet lady of the theater, is Peter O'Toole's Chips. Modeling himself in part after Redgrave (not a bad choice here), O'Toole makes Chips as gauche as he is lovable, as archaic as he is intelligent. But he uses conflicting traits as adeptly as a modern painter does clashing colors to create unexpected cohesions. And O'Toole's talent has a fortuitous ally in his face, which manages to look at all ages (the makeup, by the way, is not the best) like a British public-school boy's face: crisp, limpid, and impervious to wear and tear. Best of all, O'Toole's Chips is dignified even when he is ludicrous.

Herbert Ross directed this supreme pizzicato for heartstrings, and aside from the fact that doing the musical sequences for *Funny Girl* and choreographing *Doctor Dolittle* were scant preparation for this large- scale directorial debut, he is altogether an odd choice for the job. For Ross is famous as the choreographer of such dazzlingly perverse ballets

as *Caprichos*, *The Maids*, and *Tristan*, a far cry from this monument to
naïve innocence. That he did such a creditable, even if occasionally
flawed, job is a lovely surprise. I must confess that *Goodbye, Mr. Chips*
moved me to tears. But I must also confess that I attended the Leys
School in Cambridge, the subject of Hilton's novel, and that I was one
of those new boys who at the start of every Michaelmas term tramped
up Trumpington Road to have tea with the kindly old retired master
who was the model for Chips. So I may not be an unbiased judge.

November, 1969

HELLO, DOLLY!

Hello, Dolly! is a multimillion-dollar musical superbore, which, along
with *Paint Your Wagon*, seems to have killed off the genre of the huge,
extravagant movie musical. You may join in the celebration of its
demise if you do not yourself expire somewhere around the second or
third hour of *Dolly*. A word of praise should go to the production
design of John De Cuir, whose sets manage to be cheerful as well as
lavish, but a second word of praise to anyone or anything would be
excessive. As a number of reviews pointed out, downgrading the age
of Dolly Levi to where it would fit twenty-seven-year-old Barbra
Streisand makes, even with the corresponding rejuvenation of other
characters, hash of what small impact the tale might have. What has not
been stressed sufficiently is the repulsiveness of the star.

Pauline Kael has raved about Miss Streisand in the *New Yorker*, and
has voted for her as the best actress of the past year. This, I think,
would be impossible if Miss Streisand did not look so pronouncedly
ugly. I suspect that the success of this performer, not untalented but
not exceptional either, hinges on the number of homely women who
can identify themselves with her. Not the way one identifies with, say,
Sophia Loren, wishing and hoping that one looked even vaguely as
good as she; but the way one identifies oneself with Streisand, confident that one looks every bit as bad as she, and look to what pinnacles
she has ascended! She even gets the leading man.

A full-face closeup of Miss Streisand is a truly terrifying experience:
as the camera moves in tighter and tighter, you know how Edmund
Hillary must have felt, and there is no Tenzing Norkay to catch you
if you slip, or just reel backward in horror. As for the star's acting,
Machiavelli observed in a letter: "I think that just as nature has given

everyone a different face, so she has given to all a different intelligence and imagination, and each acts according to this personality." Miss Streisand, perhaps because she lacks intelligence and imagination, is obliged to act according to her face—aggressively, smugly, and with a masturbatory delight in herself.

January, 1970

ON A CLEAR DAY YOU CAN SEE FOREVER

On a Clear Day You Can See Forever is not really obscene, except insofar as it foists upon us Barbra Streisand in a dual role, with accents that are exaggeratedly Yiddishy in one part and Britishy in the other, and with eighteenth-century costumes and wigs that make her look like everything from the Grand Turk to Fanny Brice as Octavian during the presentation of the rose. There is even a duet sung by two separate but equally obnoxious Barbras. More than by the heroine's ability to make flowers grow miraculously, I was struck by the sprouting of Barbra's ego, which starts as a single giant cactus and ends as a one-woman rain forest.

What is it about America that takes a repellent, egomaniacal female impersonator—whose ostensible gift is belting or shrilling out songs, but whose real one is making love to herself on stage, screen, and TV —so readily to its collective bosom? I believe that it is a collective inferiority complex, an overwhelming sense of anonymous submersion in an egoless mass society, from which the Giant Masturbator sticks out in what appears to be heroic defiance. Outrageous is confused with courageous; vulgarity becomes the incarnation of the people's dream (let us not forget that the word comes from *vulgus*, people), and shamelessness the overcoming of our natural national timidity. I also believe that any pronounced member of a minority group—Negro, Jewish, Indian—who basks in its real or presumed characteristics, captures not only the benevolence of that group but also much guilt-induced applause from the oppressive majority.

As for the film itself, it is the complete ruination of what little merit there was in the stage version. The plot has been made more ridiculous, important story elements have been cut out (originally intended as a road show, the film has been whittled down awkwardly for continuous showings), and pointless extra characters have been added (the gifted Jack Nicholson in a no-account part). In addition, the doctor's rival for

Melinda's love (Robert Tentrees) has been reduced to a reject among dressmaker's dummies, an artfully unhappy ending has been faked in for greater "maturity," and Herbert Ross's dances (not his best, but still, a musical must have dancing) have been left out completely. In the process of wanton cutting, one of Burton Lane's best tunes, "The S. S. Bernard Cohn," was thrown overboard, and what was worst all along, Alan Jay Lerner's book, was given greater prominence. The sundry changes Lerner made for the screenplay are not so much rewriting as rewronging.

Yet perhaps the saddest thing about the film is Yves Montand in his first English-singing role. Montand was once a singer but never a linguist, and he performs here as one who has forgotten singing and not yet learned English. Vincente Minnelli, the *auteur* critics to the contrary notwithstanding, was always a mediocre director with some flair for tear-jerking, as in *The Clock;* his alleged talent for directing film musicals never registered on me. In the present case, only one musical number, "Come Back to Me," can be said to come off, but only at the cost of desperate trickery. Thus, to put Dr. Chabot not into his office but on top of the Pan Am building when he is trying to will Daisy back to his experiments and his arms, means preferring visual flashiness to emotional validity. As for the film's last hope, the legendary Cecil Beaton's costumes, I can only quote an actor friend: "Even poor Cecil was asleep at the swatch."

After seeing *On a Clear Day,* I went back to listening to Barbara Harris's renditions of the songs in the original-cast album. Suddenly there was feeling for the words, sensitivity to the character singing them, and no attempt to shatter icebergs, break glasses, or pierce eardrums. After Barbara, what is missing from Barbra is not only an a, but also everything from b to z.

June, 1970

12

Pseudo-Art

THE FILMS in this category of "pseudo-art" are a particularly obnoxious bunch: they are not merely trash, they are trash posturing as art. Sometimes they are derived from respectable sources, as in the case of *The Wanderer,* but transmogrified by the director; more often they derive from questionable novels or plays, themselves pretentious, and now further bloated for the screen. Or they may be originals: some hack's notion of what constitutes art, for which the screen provides the most suitable means of overinflation and undercerebration.

What is most regrettable here is that nowadays pretentiousness succeeds better than any other vice and most virtues. In an inflationary age of increased culture-mongering, when college diplomas, for example, are hardly worth the paper they are printed on, when minimal art enjoys maximal adulation, it is only natural for trashy movies no longer to try to out-trash one another, but to strike ever more grandly hollow attitudes of artiness. This is a state unhealthier than any that went before: trash appealed to the audience's illiteracy, plain and simple, and left art alone to fend for itself—which it is well equipped to do. Arty trash, however, garishly masquerades as art, and the undiscerning or untrained eye cannot tell the transvestite from the real thing—to the benefit of the impostor and the detriment of both art and the public.

And this is where the inadequacy of the reviewers comes most depressingly to the fore. For every one of these films that fails, like *Hard Contract* or *Candy,* there are several that succeed, like *Accident, Midnight Cowboy, The Lion in Winter,* and many others one could name by just glancing at today's newspaper. For such successes, the public must bear the ultimate responsibility, and the filmmakers the initial one. But in between there is that middle brow middleman the reviewer, whose middling performances may add up to a major threat. To be sure, not all the movies in this category are equally bad, and not all of them have been equally praised—some, in fact, have not been praised at all. But by juxtaposing the more obvious drivel with the less obvious, and with items that have some merits even among their demerits, I hope to give a clearer picture of the nature and scope of pretentiousness, which it is our duty to ferret out and expose.

ACCIDENT

It is Harold Pinter's misfortune to be an unusually clever child. At a time when the whole English-language theater is in one of its periodic stages of infancy, and the nursery is full of goody-goody toddlers, bawling brats, and burbling tykes, Pinter is just plain precocious. He has cunning, impudence, and wit way beyond his years, so what matter if his psyche is that of a baby? He is cosseted, rewarded, bowed down to, well beyond his deserts and ability to cope. If this child grows up at all, he will turn out bad.

These pediatric remarks are prompted by *Accident*, but they apply with roughly equal relevance to almost any film or play of Pinter's. This former and, occasionally, present actor has worked out a three-part program for himself. (1) Use dialogue with cryptic laconism; make it mostly commonplaces but surround these with an indefinable, lurking, omnipresent nastiness and have the most banal utterance bulge with an ill-concealed threat. (2) Stick in as many ugly jokes and befogging ambiguities as possible; even a sophomoric jape in a tart sauce of ambivalence strikes the gullible palate as *haute cuisine*. (3) When asked about your work, keep smilingly silent, or practice every form of put-down or put-on you can muster. (Being an actor helps.) You will thus shroud yourself in a tantalizing mystery and be a sort of intellectual Greta Garbo. With a measure of talent and mastery of this trio of tricks, you become the Kierkegaard of the kindergarten.

Accident concerns the rivalry of two Oxford dons, Stephen and Charley. Both have nice wives and children, but Stephen, the philosopher, is forty and worried about it. Charley, the archaeologist, is also a novelist and television personality, a brash *arriviste* whom the scrupulous Stephen envies. Stephen has a pupil, William, a young aristocrat in love with another pupil, Anna, an Austrian princess. Stephen has a discreet hankering for this moody girl, but assumes that she is involved with William. During an interminable Sunday get-together at Stephen's (the best scene in the film; as the day meanders into drunken night the undercurrents of animosity become more pronounced) it emerges that Stephen is going up to London to see Charley's BBC producer about appearing on Charley's show, and that Rosalind, Stephen's wife, will be off to granny's to have her third baby.

In London, Stephen is callously slighted by the assistant producer (a cameo part played raffishly by Pinter himself) and consoles himself by briefly renewing an old affair with Francesca, his provost's daughter and now a London career woman. On returning to his house he finds Charley and Anna carrying on; it seems they have been lovers for quite some time. There is another scene bursting with barely suppressed hostilities: Charley reads out loud a letter his wife has written Stephen, begging him to induce her husband to return to her. Stephen gives Charley a key to his house and leaves; first he goes to see the two wronged wives, Charley's and his own (the time sequence is muddied here), then on to a house party at William's aristocratic mansion, where a brutal version of indoor rugby on marble floors is played by the young male guests while the ladies watch; here the hostility between William and Stephen becomes manifest.

Later, at a genteel cricket game where we are treated in turn to the hostility between William and Charley, Anna informs Stephen that she is marrying William (no reason given) and asks Stephen to convey this to Charley and report his reaction to her. None of this takes place. Instead, William and Anna drive over to Stephen's late at night after a party: William wants Stephen's advice about something. He and Anna have been drinking; they crash right outside Stephen's house. (This is actually the beginning of the movie: the foregoing synopsis is a huge flashback.) William is killed and Stephen hides the dazed Anna; he tells the preternaturally incompetent police William was alone in the car. He then makes advances to Anna, who, at first, resists; when Stephen guesses that she was driving, she finds it safer to submit, however rancorously.

Stephen sneaks Anna back into her dormitory at dawn. Afterward he and Charley meet in her room; she is packing and about to fly back home. The bewildered Charley tries to remonstrate with Anna and also with Stephen: why should the girl who loves him and whom he craves leave just because William is dead? Stephen, quietly gloating, tells him that she was to have married William; Charley even has an inkling that Stephen and the girl may be in cahoots—how, otherwise, could she have known about the accident so early? Anna leaves and Stephen returns to his tutoring and family life, but the noise of the accident is repeated balefully on the sound track: it will haunt these people forever.

I have dwelt so long on the seamily inconsequential plot precisely because it is on seaminess and pseudoconsequence that Pinter and his director, Joseph Losey, thrive. Let me give a typical example, As the principals lounge around Stephen's lawn that Sunday afternoon, Charley complains of terrible flies while William denies their being around. "They're Sicilian horseflies," says Charley, swatting one, "from Corsica." What is the exact meaning of Sicilian horseflies from Corsica? It is just such points in Pinter's plays that have been learnedly scrutinized and stormily debated for years. In a rare moment of communicativeness, Losey revealed (usually he wraps the mantle of obscurity as tightly about himself as Pinter does) that the line stems from Pinter's coming for a script conference to Corsica, where he was vacationing, and where, apparently, Sicilian horseflies also come for a vacation— or for the vacationers. What is the existential significance of these Sicilian stingers amid Oxonian vespers? Consult next year's film journals for the metaphysical explication.

The simple but by no means convincing plot (it is full of such improbabilities as Anna's leaving the party with William on the fatal night going totally unnoticed) must now be Pinterized. The first step is to siphon out the maximum amount of meaningful dialogue, leaving about four-fifths of the film pregnant silence hovering ominously over the remaining fifth of speech. That fifth must, next, be reduced to commonplaces, banalities, echolalia, all in the interest of a greater sense of dislocation, solipsism, alienation. For instance, when Stephen meets Francesca again: "It's been ten years.—It can't be. Can't be!— Must be.—It is.—You don't look a day older.—Oh, really, I'm ten years older." Or, when Stephen next sees her father, the provost: "I saw Francesca when I was in London.—???—Your daughter.—Ah! How is she?—She sends you her love.—Thank you. Please give her mine when you see her again.—Oh, I don't know when I'll see her again." From this sort of thing we learn that *(a)* people are lost in self-absorption; *(b)* they do not communicate, or else only in half-truths, lies, trivialities; *(c)* meaning has gone out of human utterance; and *(d)* it's all just one non-utterance after another, and that's life—in a Pinter opus, at any rate.

But this somnambulism has to be further enhanced. Rosalind puts on a dressing gown. "What are you doing?" asks her husband. "Putting on a dressing gown," she replies. People in the film keep asking other people who are making beds or packing their bags what they are doing; others, who are doing their garden, declare, "I'm doing the garden." This can have numerous profound significances: people have nothing to say, or only the obvious, or cannot accept the obvious or the evidence of their senses. You may object that this writing reeks with platitudes. Ah, but the platitudes reek with profundity.

The next step is to infuse the whole thing with an all-permeating nastiness. Charley is a brute in don's clothing; Anna, who hardly ever speaks and then only in grunts or barks, exudes a menacing apathy; Rosalind, tormented by jealousy, shuttles between provoking taciturnity and needling sarcasm; even the gentle William becomes violently hostile during the vicious rugby game complacently watched by old men and maliciously savored by women of all ages, including scarcely nubile girls. Stephen, the most sympathetic character, commits perfunctory adultery with Francesca and brutally domineering adultery with Anna. During the latter he is interrupted by an imperious ring of the telephone: his wife is giving birth, she may be in danger. The hell with it: he wants Anna and must have her, out of revenge on her, on Charley, on growing old. And those characters who are not shown as competitive, spiteful, vindictive, are either callous, like the BBC producer, or silly and ineffectual, like the Oxford faculty.

The deadliest venom is reserved for the women, however. Anna and Rosalind are instinctive rivals and enemies, yet they can take a friendly walk together as if nothing were amiss. Francesca may seem to be an easy-going, sexually obliging woman, yet after sex with Stephen she is smoking furiously in bed, while Stephen's feet under the sheet vainly seek hers, stiffly outstretched and unyielding. If William, who adores Anna, wants to take a walk with her, she is too tired; but let Stephen say the next minute that he is off on one, and she promptly accompanies him—this fish, after all, still needs hooking. And when, for no other apparent reason except to spite Charley, Anna decides to marry William, she wishes Stephen to bring the bad news to the loser and report back on the reaction—for tripled sadistic delight. And Laura, Charley's wife and the gentlest of women, is shown as the prototypical dumb victim, who is, as it were, asking for everything she gets.

Not without some justification, the question of repressed homosexuality has been raised in connection with the work of Pinter and Losey, both joint and separate. What is deleterious to an artist is not the nature of his sexuality but the stratagems into which repression drives him. At a combination press conference and symposium, Losey praised a questioner who wondered whether the usual dominating, predatory female in Losey's films (the heroine of *Eva* is archetypal here) had not, in

Accident, become a man, Charley. I don't want to become Freudian
about the implications of Anna's gratuitous bitchiness, or about the
meaning of two or three closely related men sharing her or even
promoting the others' involvements with her. But I strongly feel that
there is an unexplored murkiness here that does not complement the
willed obscurities but only aggravates them and further confuses the
issue.

There is a scene in which Stephen tells his pregnant wife about
Charley's affair with Anna. Rosalind has an atypical outburst and covers Charley with abuse, obviously venting her rage at Stephen's
guessed infidelity in this indirect way. Like certain other psychological
details in the film, this is well observed, but one has the unhappy
impression that Pinter and Losey have much less insight into their own
indirect or generalized hostility. And, in the case of Losey, whose
sympathies are with the Left (he was blacklisted in Hollywood), the
matter is complicated by a social animus against the upper class. Thus
in *The Servant* the noxious machinations of the protagonist against his
aristocratic employer seem to be in part justified by class warfare. Or
are they to be explained as an incipient homosexual dominance of the
servant over his master, which is, in turn, part of the basic rivalry in
a power-mad society? Similar confusions pullulate in *Accident.* The
critical spirit is willing, but the mind boggles.

After the process of Pinterization comes Loseyfying. The director
decks out the picture with all kinds of arty gimmicks, such as, for
example, a series of pointless zoomings out. We get a closeup of the
sun, and zoom out to Stephen walking. Soon after, Rosalind is watching the others at tennis, from which we zoom out to the players. This
is followed in short order by a closeup of bottles on a lawn from which
we zoom out to the various principals and the children scattered on the
grass. There are diverse angle shots, some good, some studied; there
is the whole Francesca episode done in voice-over (action and off-
screen dialogue deliberately unsynchronized) for no cogent reason;
and there is Stephen's visit to his wife intercut with his calling on Laura
for purposes of comparison that would be as palpable without the
pyrotechnics.

There are also scenes of deliberate obfuscation, such as the Sunday
sleep-in at Stephen's when Charley, Anna, and William stay over, and
mysterious female feet float along the darkened staircase—to whose
room?—which is followed by a curious boudoir scene between Stephen and Rosalind in which not only the motivations but the entire
situation is purposely kept dark. When Stephen comes home from
London to find Charley *in flagrante* with a woman, several tricks are

used to keep the audience in suspense about whether it is Anna or Rosalind. There, again, the point may be the untenable one that all women are interchangeably untrustworthy.

Interchangeably untrustworthy, certainly, are Pinter and Losey, so that it is hard to say, for instance, which one of them conceived of panning to gargoyles in an Oxford cloister while Stephen tells William that "all aristocrats were made to be killed." Why gargoyles? Does this mean that aristocrats are medieval and obsolete? That they are monsters yet fascinating? Or that they are water spouts? Now there's ambiguity for you to ponder. And what about the end of the film, when the symbolic accident is heard on the sound track: the family dog is seen madly racing toward the front gate—is there perhaps another real accident, after all? Losey explains that the dog was supposed to go into the house, but chose to run off in the opposite direction. Indeed! The dog could have been made to perform properly in a retake, or the footage of his misguided race could have been cut rather than lovingly dwelt on. But here was another irrelevant, misleading, and therefore irresistible ambiguity. Not content with putting us on, Pinter and Losey must also put on the dog.

It must, however, be added that there is wit in the film, as in a senior commonroom scene, as well as good color photography by Gerry Fisher. Oxford and environs look seductively alluring, and there are laudable performances by Dirk Bogarde, Vivien Merchant, Stanley Baker, and Alexander Knox. Delphine Seyrig is wasted on the non-part of Francesca, but Ann Firbank somehow manages to squeeze a pathetic radiance out of her brief moment as the neglected Laura. As the young aristocrats, Michael York and Jacqueline Sassard are hopeless ciphers, possibly abetted in this by the director, but plainly supplying a good deal of native insufficiency. It is interesting to note that almost all the shirts worn by the dons in the film have a pattern of squares; clearly even Beatrice Dawson, the costumer, is a perfect Pinterite symbolist.

June, 1967

HOW I WON THE WAR

It is with an unhappy feeling that I must declare *How I Won the War,* which won the suffrage of some of my favorite critics, pretentious tomfoolery. Richard Lester, the director, is a clever fellow, in the best

and worst senses of that expression, and the two—as this film shows—
are as far apart as A and B. Not long ago Lester told an interviewer,
"We wanted to do the war, really do it." Now he says—rather un-
courageously—that what he intended was a take-off on previous war
films. That strikes me as a pitiful cop-out where what was clearly
intended was the reduction of war to the ridiculous as conceived by
the Absurdists.

But the depths of the ridiculous run the dual risk of not being funny
at all while offering no substitute for funniness. The film follows a
hopeless squad of infantrymen led by an inept grammar-school boy of
a lieutenant from basic training through the African campaign—where
they are delegated to build an "advance cricket pitch" behind enemy
lines—to France and Germany. All except the asinine eager-beaver
lieutenant and the pseudo-psycho case end up killed. Everyone in the
British army and in any of three other ones glimpsed is either an idiot
or a coward, often both, and not infrequently a crook as well.

The one exception may be the tough corporal played by Lee Mon-
tague, but he is so much a cliché of the tough sergeant that most
reviews actually referred to him as a sergeant. Nor is he that much of
an exception; when the horn of an army truck jams, he punishes the
vehicle as if it were a live creature by ramming his bayonet into its
grille. This gag is, like many others, too precious to Lester to be used
only once; later on, the gung-ho cavalry colonel is shooting disabled
tanks with his revolver "to put the poor wounded horses out of their
misery."

The failure is plain: where everybody is a moron or scoundrel, there
is no contest, no drama, nothing. Remove Gulliver from Lilliput, and
there is no issue, no novel. Take Candide out of his story, and there
is no story. One Caliban contributes to making *The Tempest* a masterpiece; all Calibans—or all Stephanos and Trinculos, as in Lester's film
—and you have gibberish. But, Lester's champions will say, this is
cinema of the absurd. Well, then, look at Theater of the Absurd. To
begin with, theater can be consistently unreal in its *mise en scène;* in film,
at any rate in this film, it is in front of real deserts, real tanks, and real
machine guns killing in veristic style that the absurdity is placed, and
the jokes stick in the craw.

Lester does not understand the Theater of the Absurd in any event.
He seems unaware that the Absurdist characters are often likable and
even, in their way, noble. In their dustbins or holes in the ground,
among accumulations of furniture or growing numbers of rhinoce-
roses, some of them uphold humane values and are worthy of empathy,
if not sympathy. Lester's characters—and he has tended in this direc-

tion all along—are mere props, while the props and gags become the *dramatis personae*. This has been hailed as his superb originality; in fact, it is just an amalgam of TV commercials (in which Lester got his training), vaudeville or silent-screen comedy, and Godard. (Godard's idiocy is at least his own; Lester's reeks of its sources.) The concoction is then plunked in the middle of a serious situation, as it is not in vaudeville or TV commercials—and "significant innovation" is in full swing.

Let us take a typical example. A soldier in the desert has both his legs blown off; agonizingly, he contemplates his bleeding stumps when, out of nowhere, his wife comes running to him over the dunes. To his whimper, "It hurts, Flo!" she replies, "Go run them under the cold tap, luv!" This has been reviewed as the wounded man's infinitely touching fantasy, and its presentation "a little triumph of the imagination." Characteristically, no one quotes the wife's preceding line. Squatting beside her mangled husband, she rattles on in a fulsome BBC voice, "It is impossible to tell all the touching and heroic stories we . . ." until her husband's moan interrupts her.

Clearly this woman (or her eidolon—it scarcely matters which) is an imbecile and a hypocrite who spouts pious platitudes when not telling her legless, moribund spouse to go run his bleeding stumps under the cold tap—a sick joke of the first water. The aim is to reduce everybody to worm's size—battle front and home front are equally affronted. It might, of course, be contended that Lester is indicting the human race itself; but for a task of that size he has neither the mind nor the artistry.

Lester's notion of the absurd is mere vaudeville. Thus he has his staff officers avidly swapping bubblegum pictures of the war when not babbling about cricket and such. The lieutenant keeps falling off landing crafts, into the sand head first (ostrich, get it?), under rollers that flatten him (but he bounces back—this is the Absurd, you see), on to hand grenades that are about to kill his men but prove duds and make his gesture look foolish. The men are perfect bunglers who can do nothing except shoot down their own planes and take a German stronghold by marching in whistling the theme song from *The Bridge on the River Kwai.*

When a road roller is being dragged across the desert, the unit's water supply is kept inside. John Lennon, who plays a soldier no more cretinous than the rest, empties out the water to make the roller lighter. He then faces his irate comrades with a defiantly shouted explanation which he repeats several times. The repetition is meant, I presume, to lift the scene out of the realm of the comic (in which, alas, it never was) into the higher one of the Absurd. Like so many of the film's unfunny laughs and shallow depths, it is only embarrassing.

There is so much straining for comedy and significance that one wonders how Lester and his scenarist Charles Wood (also responsible for the feeble screenplay of *The Knack* and the dismal one of *Help!*) escaped without herniotomies. Most objectionable, however, are the pretentious effects. The "comic" skirmishes are translated onto the historic plane—a member of the squad is first seen dying in full color in an episode of the plot; promptly he repeats his death in a newsreel-like re-creation of a major battlefield, Dunkirk or Dieppe, each filmed in different monochrome. Thereupon a ghostly soldier from the monochrome sequence, painted from top to toe in the appropriate color—green, pink, yellow—joins the squad, looking like something out of Disney but terribly portentous.

Again, the ground of an argument is continually shifted. A ridiculous harangue delivered by the colonel in a dugout ends on the stage of an empty theater; a squad member who won't fight locks himself into a truck which, in the next shot, becomes a prison or hospital room. These are the devices of Lester's previous films, particularly *A Funny Thing Happened on the Way to the Forum,* flatly and unthinkingly transferred where they do not belong. Here they emerge as grandiose, *recherché* effects that will be lost on the run-of-the-mill viewer; whereas the enlightened one neither needs nor wants to have his nose rubbed in obvious editorializing.

Finally, and importantly, there is a question of taste. Granted that anyone wishing to make mincemeat of war would prefer to pick not some obscure border incident but a righteous crusade like World War II—a war to end war in which God, as is known, was on our side— a scene like the following still remains highly questionable. While the captured lieutenant awaits interrogation by the Nazis, he is leaning against a freight car. Suddenly a hand appears from a chink in the boxcar's door above the hero's head. It wriggles about, cannot escape, and promptly vanishes. In its ineffectualness and irrelevance, the gesture is meant to be grotesque. So much for those six million Jews.

Humor can be of all colors, and there is no reason why Lester, having tried green, pink, and yellow, shouldn't have a go at black. But, first, it has to be really humor, and, second, it must have the courage of its convictions—it must go to such lengths as to make considerations of taste seem trivial. Thus the comic horror of the death of Marlowe's Edward II, a bugger killed by impalement through the behind, is black humor so outrageous and at the same time so meaningful as to make squeamishness appear petty. Lester's gimmick is furtive and pointless, and therefore offensive.

The film has, to be sure, a few genuinely comic moments, especially when the splendid Michael Hordern as the fanatical colonel is on screen. Other actors, like Michael Crawford as the lieutenant, work hard to little effect; still others, like Jack MacGowran as a stand-up comic who walks through the war in baggy pants, does unfunny comic turns, and bosses the top brass around, are more oafish than their parts. And John Lennon remains a cipher throughout.

A frequent complaint about *How I Won the War* is that much of the dialogue, either because it is British service slang or because it is given a mumbled, slovenly reading, is incomprehensible. I have no quarrel with the parts I didn't understand; it's the other ones that I minded. Lester has said (before he started copping out), "I have tried to give . . . a picture of what war actually is." All we get, I am afraid, is a picture of what Lester actually is.

January, 1968

PETULIA

There are times when the film critic's lot, never to be envied much, is not to be envied at all. Having already reviewed the superb *The Fifth Horseman Is Fear* and the provocative *Fist in His Pocket* when they were seen here at festivals, what am I left with?

Well, there is *Petulia,* Richard Lester's first film with an American setting. This is a clever movie, the first commercial adaptation here of Resnais's technique of fragmentation, with flashbacks, flash-forwards, and just plain flash-aways; with the quick, fidgety pace we think of as peculiarly of our time. But it is also a soulless, arbitrary, attitudinizing piece of claptrap, for all its occasional twitchings into an undeniably funny grimace.

Petulia had anywhere upward of two strikes against it for being based on a book by John Haase, another of whose potboilers, *The Fun Couple,* I have had the misfortune to read. Haase, a male Californian Rona Jaffe, is a specialist in rancid archness. And this atmosphere prevails in the film *Petulia,* whose heroine proclaims, enshrines, and zealously cultivates her "kookiness"—a kind of premeditated devil-may-care spontaneity that should turn the most solidly anchored stomachs.

Penelope Gilliatt, in the *New Yorker,* defends this nonsense, along with the hero's implacably smart-aleck superiority, as "two ironic lifestyles devised by the two central characters" to deny the existence of all the pain and injury around them. But that is absurd: how dare these shallow, well-heeled inhabitants of charmingly, exhilaratingly frolicsome San Francisco pretend that life for them is so dreadful only clowns' masks and emotional shell games can make it livable? If there were any indication that these characters are specially sensitive beings unjustly put-upon, all right; but this is either not implied or, worse yet, meant to be taken for granted. The principals are as banal as their supposedly inferior spouses, mistresses, and friends, and we are left to derive our satisfaction from the nervous, attenuated cleverness of the script, editing, and direction. Under the circumstances, all three would have to be a damned sight cleverer and more dependable.

There is a totally unconvincing unhappy ending: Petulia abandons the hard-working surgeon who loves her and whom she seems to love too, and goes back to her homosexual playboyish husband who, in a benign mood, breaks her ribs, and, in a less benign one, beats her to a bloody pulp. This is nonsense, but serves two purposes: it makes the movie more "adult," and the Catholic extremists happy—a bad marriage perpetuated is better than divorce. Accordingly, *Our Sunday Visitor* (which sounds like the title of a film by Stanley Kramer, but is a Catholic publication) has already declared *Petulia* one of the year's ten best.

July, 1968

THE LION IN WINTER

James Goldman's *The Lion in Winter* was the kind of play to delight Walter Kerr: vaguely literate, somewhat historical yet saucily anachronistic, and as stuffed with suburbanly sub-urbane epigrams as a Victorian sofa with horsehair. Henry II of England, Eleanor of Aquitaine, and their three sons, using a French king and princess for pawns, wrangle over succession to the throne, power behind the throne, and disputed territories; this is presented as TV domestic comedy, dilutedly Freudian and Shavian, and concentratedly middle-class Jewish. The film version, from Goldman's own screenplay, sticks closely to the original and suffocatingly in our craw.

The basic device, again, is the epigram, and a medieval royal family doggedly brandishing not broadswords but thin witticisms can be pretty funny—the wrong way. The two most quoted *mots* are, "The year is 1183 and we are all barbarians," and (tossed off after some particularly murderous scheming and counterscheming) "Well, what family doesn't have its ups and downs?" The first is the sort of thing we get in Shaw, Giraudoux, Anouilh, with the difference that the anachronism there is not self-consciously winking at you but is slipped in almost unnoticeably. The second item could come out of any post-Odetsian Jewish comedy, and the joke, if any, derives as much from that as it does from the understatement.

Nevertheless, to the casual glance this might not seem all that different from, say, *Saint Joan* or *Judith*. But, of course, it is. In discreetly modernizing medieval Europeans or ancient Hebrews, Shaw and Giraudoux tried, without violating the spirit of those peoples, to raise their language to literature, and their problems to myths. Goldman, however, lowers the rough-hewn dignity of the Middle Ages to brittle cocktail-party chatter: "He came down from Paris with a mind like Aristotle's and a form like sin. . . . We violated all the commandments like a shot. . . ." Clearly, the dialogue fares no better than the Decalogue.

One gem that produces especially knowing laughter is, "In a world where carpenters are resurrected, everything is possible." Now this is completely alien to the spirit of the twelfth century; but how can the twentieth feed on such dated schoolboy blasphemies? And consider these further examples: "Henry's bed is *his* province," Eleanor declares, "he can people it with sheep for all I care—as I believe on occasion he does." Or this: "ELEANOR: Have you found a way to sell everyone to everybody? PRINCE GEOFFREY: Not yet, mummy, but I'm working on it." Or: "ELEANOR: When can I believe you, Henry? HENRY: Always, even when I lie." If you ran out of peanuts, you might possibly serve this with the martinis, but when it comes marching at you in serried ranks waving pennants inscribed "Literature," "Drama," or "Film" and trying to puncture you like a tin of canned laughter . . . but there I go sounding like James Goldman. Anyway, no thanks.

If I make so much of the bad writing in *The Lion in Winter,* it is because this kind of pseudoliterate hack work seems to be on the upswing—what else is one to conclude after seeing within a short space *Secret Ceremony, Negatives,* and this film, all in that genre of which Ben Hecht's *The Specter of the Rose* remains a supreme example. Goldman's script, moreover, can boast of a multiple echo. Thus Henry's "I am an old man in an empty place" reverberates with two lines from Eliot's "Gerontion," and Eleanor's "The sun was warmer then and we were every day together" comes from Jacques Prévert's *chanson "Les Feuilles mortes": "Le soleil [était] plus brûlant qu'aujourd'hui . . . Nous vivions tous les deux ensemble . . ."* "Sleep and dream of me with croutons" says Henry to one who would devour him; the trouble is that you cannot see the soup from the croutons.

Add to this the weightily inept direction of Anthony Harvey (remembered—would that he were not—for *Dutchman*), which mistakes boom-and-zoom-happy camera histrionics for liveliness and imagination. A typical sequence has Henry rattling up to the battlements of Chinon Castle, only to crumple there as the camera rises and rises to show us the king pitifully small from its eagle's-eye view. Simultaneously, John Barry's abominable score (a kind of Roseland Ballroom version of the *Te Deum,* complete with heavenly choir) soars to a pious crescendo, completing the image of man's puniness, especially when he gets involved in a film like this one.

But, obviously, no one has a feeling of slumming. Katharine Hepburn conveys a profound sense of being immersed in Art perhaps even greater and more shattering than *Guess Who's Coming to Dinner,* and she sheds enough tears to erode the gold plating from a dozen Oscars. With the tears go assorted quavers of the voice and palsied quivers of the chin, and since Miss Hepburn's voice even in carefree moments consists of an ambiguous rasp meant to suggest mischief, her Eleanor emerges a bundle of bravely packed-away miseries bursting at every seam. Yet if there is anything Eleanor of Aquitaine should not be, it is a cross between Willie the Weeper and Smilin' Thru. And there is the problem of playing opposite Peter O'Toole: this king and queen have an unnerving way of looking like King Oedipus and Queen Jocasta.

O'Toole's Henry is all hulking about, stomping around, harrumphing and Laughtoning it up: "tough" mannerisms, "shrewd" mannerisms, "lusty" mannerisms, with nary a characterization to hold them together—though this, needless to say, is equally the fault of the script. The three plotting sons seem to be rivals not so much for the throne of England as for the crown of Stock Performer of the Year. Jane Merrow, as Princess Alais, is considerably less apt and attractive than she was in *The Girl Getters.* Timothy Dalton provides the one performance well worth watching, turning the young French king into a complex, passionately and cunningly dedicated figure.

But I keep coming back to the inanities of the script. They extend from such low-level nonsense as Henry's having his mutinous sons guarded by one solitary soldier when Eleanor and others of their faction are freely roaming the castle, to such advanced absurdities as having the cynical Henry overwhelmed by finding out about a homosexual liaison of an unfavorite son, or going to pieces over the discovery of his wife's long-past escapade with his late father. In terms of neither history nor plot nor character does this make sense—only a rather twisted twist of the plot.

Even the *Times* reviewer, not exactly remarkable for her astuteness, has noted the patent silliness of a much reiterated device: a character will say or do something quite ordinary and inconsequential only to have another proclaim exultantly that *he* has won, because that ordinary and inconsequential thing was just what he wanted the first fellow to say or do. I could add a thing or two about that but won't—lest Goldman declare that this was precisely what he wanted to provoke me into doing.

November, 1968

SECRET CEREMONY

Connoisseurs and would-be connoisseurs of chaos are urged to see *Secret Ceremony,* in which Joseph Losey, George Tabori, and Elizabeth Taylor combine their considerable lacks of talent and good sense to produce a film which, worse than bad, is militantly loathsome. Only a crazy *auteur* theorist (if that is not sheer redundancy) could persist hereafter in respecting Losey—so solidly are the film's flat feet planted on the rock bottom of taste. Basing the movie on a prize-winning story by an Argentinian postal clerk, Losey has come up with the prize specimen of his own genre: a cross between pseudopsychological Grand Guignol and pseudostylish tragicomedy of manners.

We are asked to believe than an insane young heiress (Mia Farrow) finds a whore (Miss Taylor) to be the exact look-alike of her dead mother and that, apparently believing her to be Mom, she installs her in that role in the fabulous, vast Edwardian mansion she inhabits absolutely alone. Pseudomother and twenty-two-year-old backward nymphet enter into a sadomasochistic and paralesbian relationship, with Mom warding off skrikish female relatives and daughter carrying on a taunting quasi-affair (perhaps even consummated—the film makes nothing clear) with her worthless and lecherous stepfather, an Anglified American college professor, for which part Robert Mitchum is ideally unsuited. A kind of love-hate also develops between Mitchum and Miss Taylor, and, aside from three-way sadism, we are treated to various forms of exhibitionism and voyeurism, a demented false pregnancy, suicide and murder. Worst of all, Losey insists on treating this garbage as mystic ritual, a sumptuous moral parable, the unveiling of existential enigmas.

George Tabori, one of our leading pretentious hacks, has written a script exclusively made up of arrogant cutenesses, supposedly daring vulgarisms, and arrant pseudopoetics. Examples: "I couldn't rape a randy elephant. . . . That should be worn on a day when it rains like piss—I was having tea with the Duchess when she used the selfsame expression. . . . Was Daddy Albert a great lover? Was he greater than Daddy Gustav? Was he stupendous, stupendously gentle and also brutal? . . . In the last two months [I've had] a masseuse, two faculty wives, a toney little black lady majoring in political science. . . . She was so proud of her breasts, those fantastic, opulent, mother-of-pearly globes. . . . You bet your shiny arse. . . ." etc., etc.

To all this, Elizabeth Taylor bequeaths every kind of bad acting and a willingness to wallow in swinishness of every sort that looks more and more like a predilection.

November, 1968

THE MAGUS; CANDY

The Magus is a pretentious, heavy-handed adaptation of a likewise pretentious book; those who were able to finish it will have to pronounce it superior or inferior to the film. Some credit should perhaps be given a film from a major studio that dares to be incomprehensible, but the obscurities and ambiguities are more Malaprop than Mallarmé. It takes more to create a successful set of levels of meaning than parading the first edition of Empson's *Seven Types of Ambiguity* for the first time across a colored wide screen.

The Magus concerns a series of odd incidents that occur to a callow English teacher on an Aegean island, incidents that seem at first enacted by a supernatural agency. Then, however, the supernatural is ostensibly rejected, and we are left with three possibilities: the hero was involved in an elaborate scheme by an avant-garde psychiatrist, or in a movie being shot by an unorthodox director, or he made up everything out of his tormented fantasy. And in the end we are again coyly nudged toward the supernatural.

Each hypothesis can be refuted separately, but put them all together and they spell kitsch—unless, that is, you believe in God's working in as mysterious and pretentious ways as this novel and screenplay by John Fowles. *The Magus* tries to make much out of some lines from "Little Gidding" that it quotes: "We shall not cease from exploration/And the end of all our exploring/ Will be to arrive where we started/And know the place for the first time." I knew the place before the film had half started, and consider it not worth exploring.

Guy Green, the director, succeeds in making sententiousness visual as well as aural, and multivalence as fascinating as the multiplication table. Billy Williams's color photography seems always overgrown with a thin film of greenish algae, and John Dankworth's score is banal. Anthony Quinn and Michael Caine are out of place in a film emphasizing (however ineptly) the cerebral and spiritual, and Candice Bergen cannot act. Which leaves us with Anna Karina, and any film in which she can walk off with the acting honors is in serious trouble.

If you know someone you want to start the new year as nauseated as possible, send him to see *Candy.* As an emetic, liquor is dandy, but *Candy* is quicker.

December, 1968

LOLA MONTÈS

A deplorable exhibition is the fuss being made over *Lola Montès,* the last film of the late Max Ophüls, vintage 1955 but only now shown commercially in a more or less uncut version. In 1963, Andrew Sarris called it "the greatest film of all time," and went on to announce his willingness to stake his "critical reputation . . . on this one proposition." By 1969, though he still raved about the movie (a great favorite also of Susan Sontag's, and of all *auteur* theorists here and abroad), he added that "reservations about the . . . coldness of decor now make me drop it down a notch or two from the very summit of greatness." We were not told whether he was simultaneously dropping down his critical reputation a notch or two. As I see it, now and in 1963, *Lola Montès* is a masterpiece for chambermaids, especially of the antebellum, Austro-Hungarian sort, and for all those who share that worthy profession's legacy of dime-store romanticism.

In the introductory remarks to *The Threepenny Opera,* we are told that it is meant to be as lavish as only beggars could conceive it; *Lola Montès* is as lavish as only beggarly intellects could conceive it. It is based on a fictionalized biography by Cécil St.-Laurent, a Prisunic novelist if ever there was one. Collaborating on the script with Ophüls were Annette Wademant and Jaques Natanson, competent enough hacks. The life story of the notorious dancer-courtesan is told in terms of an extended circus metaphor: a ringmaster is putting on a spectacular circus show, whose tableaus are jumping-off points for flashbacks; cracking his whip, he describes Lola as the most dangerous wild beast of all, and, at the end of the film, exhibits her in a cage. This idea, the best in the film, is a steal from Frank Wedekind's *Earth Spirit,* in whose prologue a similarly bedizened and whip-wielding animal trainer steps before the curtain and introduces the heroine, Lulu, as a snake that can embrace a tiger to death.

The film gives us the ultimate baroque overelaboration of the circus, being to that genre what Busby Berkeley's choreographed Grand Central Stations were to the Broadway show numbers they supposedly represented. But the episodes that weave in and out of the circus setting to chronicle the picaresque odyssey of the pseudo-Spanish dancer-adventuress are both superficial and old hat, and tend to be rushed to the point of ludicrousness. Perhaps the best such scene is the first, showing the end of the Lola-Liszt affair, although Will Quadflieg, a decent actor, lacks Lisztian dash. But Georges Auric has cleverly woven Liszt's "Valse d'adieu" into his score, and the scenarists have evoked the parting of jaded sophisticates with reasonable cleverness. Jacques d'Eaubonne's designs for the film are always effective, and Christian Matras's color photography is good for that by now much-surpassed period.

Yet occasional scenarists' raisins and directorial sugar-coating notwithstanding, *Lola Montès* sinks under the combined ballast of banality, sentimentality, and pointlessness. The tough ringmaster is, finally, as mushy as the rest, and we are to believe that Lola loved her bumbling King Ludwig tenderly. In the main masculine roles, Peter Ustinov fails to give the ringmaster meaningful definition, and Anton Walbrook makes the King of Bavaria an avuncular comic monarch out of an Offenbach operetta. Oskar Werner's performance is distinguished only by the rosebud mouth the makeup department bestowed on him. The film's albatross is Martine Carol: a dumpy, putty-faced Lola with just about no acting ability, whom even the clever costumes of Marcel Escoffier cannot make sexier than one of his bustier dummies. When, at the film's finale, rough New Orleans menfolk are allowed to kiss Lola's fabled hands for a dollar, they are overpaying nearly as much as the customers of the Beekman Theater, who are spending three times that amount on the elegantly scented garbage of Max Ophüls.

What of the direction provided by this "Pantheon director," the supreme title an *auteur* critic bestows on one of his top ten or twelve directors? It features, besides enough dolly shots to put the gyrations of the Dolly Sisters to shame, the very devices for which non-*auteurs* like Bourguignon have been damned by the pundits. There is no latticed bedstead, no gauzy curtain, no trapeze artist's net through which the camera does not shoot, no porthole or carriage window through which it does not peep. When King Ludwig requests a needle and thread so that Lola, who cut open her bodice for him, can depart decently, the order is passed on from chamberlain to chamberlain, lackey to lackey, laterally across corridors and reception rooms, vertically down tiered galleries and staircases—a film cliché as old as the hills, or at least as the snow-capped peak in the Paramount trademark.

May, 1969

HARD CONTRACT; THE WANDERER

The United States, too, has a mighty contender in the intellectual obscenity sweepstakes. It is called *Hard Contract* and was written and directed by S. Lee Pogostin, who once wrote a western in verse ("began as a poet and dramatist," says the press release) and was or is (I forget which) a big name in television. *Hard Contract* is like a flat-footed James Bond story that soaked its feet in a hot bath of existentialism. Its hero is the world's *"numero uno"* professional assassin, a natty dresser and conservative voter who has sex only with whores whom, though they seem very nice, he never kisses or lets spend the night with him. As played by James Coburn, he is all white-gold hair and hand-carved ivory teeth brightly flashing while corpses drop mysteriously around him, and he could go on being that if he did not meet Lee Remick on a murder mission to the Costa del Sol.

I can spare you the details of the plot, but I must call your attention to the profound and poetic conversations about God that Miss Remick leads Coburn into, first while sightseeing and later in bed. The gist of them is that God is here one second, gone the next; here again, gone again. During the here-seconds, a heavenly breeze plays with Miss Remick's hair, though not with Coburn's, who probably has it in his contract that during neither murder nor God scenes is a single one of his brushed-gold filaments to be dislodged. That, presumably, is what is meant by a hard contract.

In another between-the-sheets nonplatonic dialogue, the pair calculate the probable proliferation of their heirs. (Miss Remick, you see, has lured Coburn away from whores by, at first, impersonating one; and when, subsequently, Coburn can no longer make it with a professional, he knows he can't stay *"numero uno"* much longer.) Coburn speculates on the exact number of millions of their descendants in X years, all the time using Miss Remick's fingers as an abacus. I kept hoping that as this philosophy in the boudoir reached trillions, which it did, he would have to resort to further and more interesting parts of her anatomy, but no such luck.

We do get later on, though, a disquisition from Burgess Meredith, as Coburn's carefully unidentified boss, delivered in front of Goya's "The Firing Squad" at the Prado, to the effect that murder for profit may be considered immoral, "it is just that in our time it's not *that* immoral." Pogostin's predilection for such elephantine subtleties makes him easily Hollywood's most casual casuist. The dialogue often reaches heights worthy of *The Lion in Winter*, as in "It's a miracle!—There's no such thing as a miracle.—I know; that's what is so miraculous."

Not all pretension nowadays is mixed with sex; some of it is remarkably pure. Take *The Wanderer*, a ferociously literal translation of Alain-Fournier's novel by Jean-Gabriel Albicocco. The filmmaker previously tried his hand disastrously at a free modernization of Balzac's *The Girl with the Golden Eyes;* alas, poor Albicocco is equally unfortunate with literal as with free translation. The film was shot in Marie-Laurencinish hues by the *cinéaste's* father, Quinto Albicocco, and for greater lyricism the image is made to curve away and go fuzzy around the edges, giving the impression that the entire film was shot through an ellipsoid glass paperweight. The acting, mostly by newcomers, is stolid. Especially disturbing is the presence of Brigitte Fossey, the enchanting five-year-old moppet of *Forbidden Games;* now a full-grown mop of twenty-two, she proves unbeautiful and undistinguished, and looks for all the world like Bonita Granville, another gifted film elf who grew into unemployability.

June, 1969

THE LOVES OF ISADORA

Isadora, Karel Reisz's biography of Isadora Duncan, started out as a three-hour film; even as Universal cut one hour out of the movie, it added three words to the title, which became *The Loves of Isadora.* This soupy, old-style title is much more fitting, for we have seen and heard all this before, when Cornel Wilde was chopping up Chopin and Robert Walker walked through Brahms. The script by Melvyn Bragg, Clive Exton, and Margaret Drabble, even disregarding the discontinuity perhaps caused by the cutting, is banal and unsearching. It relies exclusively on Miss Duncan's less than reliable autobiography and on the scarcely more trustworthy biography by Sewell Stokes—and even these have been simplified and flattened out.

A vast body of pungently pertinent literature, including the important revelations of Gordon Craig, has been blithely ignored. Neither Isadora's pursuit of her art, nor her underlying amateurishness, nor her American innocent-abroad quality has been properly explored and evaluated, and her incontinent sexuality has been largely housebroken. True, a little more promiscuity and decadence are to be glimpsed than in the good old days, but, after all, Duluth and Tulsa are no longer quite what they used to be, either.

The film does have a delicious performance by Vanessa Redgrave. She manages the American accent creditably and makes a game stab at the dancing; the dedicated, irresponsible, galloping genius, the selflessness and the selfishness she conveys to a fault. Her gradual aging and dissolution are masterly, staunchly reinforced by Wally Schneiderman's superlative makeup. Costumes, sets, art direction, blend harmoniously, and the color cinematography and editing suffer only mildly from a certain artiness especially noticeable in the tricky dissolves. But the supporting cast is as feeble as the script: Isadora's lovers come out sticks or travesties.

Reisz's direction (again, allowances made for the Draconian cutting) is pedestrian, always tripping up on the light fantastic. Reisz's ineptitude is exemplified by the scene in which Gordon Craig first sees Isadora in the nude. We have already noted that, despite her other endowments, Miss Redgrave has no breasts to speak of. Craig, however, shouts about them: "Maaag-nifff-icent! ! !" Which her performance, on the other hand, is.

June, 1969

Midnight Cowboy seems to be this summer's *The Graduate;* the kids who loved Dustin Hoffman sweet and clean are just as happy to love him dirty and sweet. John Schlesinger's film is better than *The Graduate,* but it, too, suffers from an ultimate cleverness and sentimentality that fall well short of art. Very much as in Schlesinger's *Darling,* we get all the trappings and trimmings of brutal honesty; there is no evident attempt at prettification—there may even be a slight tendency to revel in the squalid—and still, still one does not quite believe what one is seeing.

Everything is calculated for maximum concision, pointedness, and poignancy—everything is so blasted efficient. But art, real art, isn't like that at all. It is full of asperities, rugosities, the inexplicable. It does not get where it wants to go in the manner of a genteel equestrian cantering on a dappled gelding, but as a sleepwalker or high-wire artist making it by a combination of desperate skill and some strange, incalculable providence. *Midnight Cowboy* is just a little too knowing, pert, and pat.

If, like me, you have not read the James Leo Herlihy novel on which the film is based, you may want a short synopsis. Joe Buck, a dumb but lovable and handsome Texas youth, victim of a lonely childhood, leaves his job as a small-town dishwasher, buys himself a fancy cowboy outfit, and takes a bus to fabulous New York, full of rich, frustrated women willing to pay generously for the services of a fine Texas stud.

In New York, Joe's meager savings are soon spirited away by con men and women of all sorts, including "Ratso" Rizzo, a tough little Bronx gutter rat who, pretending to set up Joe with a superpimp, sends him to a crazed religious fanatic. Egged on by absurdities spouted at him by the media, Joe is sucked ever deeper into failure—now with pathetic homosexual customers rather than women. On the verge of starvation, he re-encounters Ratso, whom he threatens to beat up but goodheartedly spares. Ratso, hobbling on his deformed foot and pitiable for all his shrewdness and bluster, invites Joe to his lair in a condemned building, where the two set up a comic-pathetic housekeeping. The city rat teaches the country mouse the art of hustling and making out.

After a series of misadventures, Joe at last seems to be on to some young women (their youth is improbable, but let that pass) willing to subsidize the prowess of this Texas longhorn. But Ratso has been plagued by not only his foot but also a sinister cough; precisely now (another bit of stretched probability) the illness comes to a terrifying head. Ratso refuses to see a doctor. All he wants is to get to his dreamed-of panacea and Eldorado: Florida.

To make this possible, Joe beats up and robs a pitiful aging homosexual who asked him up to his hotel room (where, significantly, no sexual acts were performed!) and gets on a Florida-bound bus with his fever-racked friend. There is hopeful talk now of giving up hustling and getting jobs, but as the bus nears Miami, Joe, like the father in "Erlkönig," is propping up a dead Ratso.

There are in this film more dishonesties than one can easily point to. As Joe rides the bus to New York, for example, images from his childhood and young manhood come rapidly dancing by. We decipher something about a boy entrusted to a well-meaning but neglectful slut of a grandmother; and, later, about a loved and loving girl friend who becomes the victim of a gang rape, goes mad and insanely denounces Joe, whom the gang forced to watch the vicious act and, if I read my subliminal images correctly, buggered as well. Already we are confused: how exactly do these two widely divergent unhappy experiences contribute to pointing Joe toward a career in hustling? It seems to me that a little psychologizing is a dangerous thing; we need either a good deal more of it, or none at all.

Worse yet is the glib exploitation of America the all-purpose bogey as the cause of Joe's downfall: the mass media with their mendacious siren songs; the suspiciousness and lovelessness rampant in the land; the cruel socioeconomic gap between haves and have-nots; the maniacal, dehumanizing pursuit of money and success; etc., etc. But aside from the fact that these are commonplaces and remain so in the film, no matter how gussied up with superficial cleverness, there is no clear demonstration of how the society affects Joe Buck, of how his individual guilt is begotten by the community.

If, indeed, there is any guilt at all. Rather, Joe is shown as the victim of the most prodigious streak of bad luck since Pauline of the Episodic Perils, and the whole film has the quality of *Candide* rewritten in collaboration by the authors of the Grand Guignol and the Bibliothèque rose. Everything misfires for our cowboy: people won't talk to him; or if they talk, it is only to ridicule him; and if they don't ridicule, it is only to bilk him.

He, for his part, is rather spectacularly stupid, and there is some doubt in my mind about how he could have conceived the idea of going to New York to hustle. His jinx inhabits the very objects he touches: the last cup of coffee he can afford has to be ruined by half the catsup bottle accidentally spilling into it, as well as over his pants. And if he succeeds at last in getting picked up by a homosexual, it has to be a student who proves penniless. I would have thought that even the dumbest hustler required payment in advance.

All through the ugliness, Joe manages to remain wondrously innocent. He never seems to get involved in active or passive pederasty— the closest he ever gets to it is submitting to fellatio from that pathetic student in a 42nd Street movie theater. During that act, we see Joe's pained face, and hope that he is saving his soul by thinking beautiful thoughts. One wonders why such an angelic and heterosexual fellow, upon the collapse of his pocketbook and dreams of easy living, does not opt for some kind of homely but honest labor. The "midnight cowboy" we see on the stage in Mart Crowley's *The Boys in the Band* is every bit as good-natured, stupid, and blond as Joe, but neither so pure nor so heroic—and, therefore, believable.

Ratso is a much more convincing character, and though his heart, too, is basically as pure as filtered canal water, at least he chisels and swipes things, bickers and curses. But once we put Ratso and Joe together, doubts arise again. Are we to believe in the tender platonic love of a male whore and his pimp under the cover of brawling and banter? Well, we used to be asked to believe in the female whore with the heart of gold and untapped reserve of love. Did we believe it then? Sometimes, as in the case of Cabiria, who was a kind of halfwit—and not even she would have shared a beautiful experience with her procurer.

Still, it may be unduly captious to reject out of hand the thesis of the film, that such a relationship can and does spring up. The question is how well is it demonstrated, how searchingly and persuasively is it explored? Reasonably well, considering how much of the footage is devoted to other, often only marginally relevant matter. Yet that "considering" is in itself a damaging concession. Thus there is a crazy drug-pop-psychedelic orgy sequence—enlisting the services of some of the gang from Warhol's films and some from the musical *Hair*—that is as slick as it is tangential.

Some of the other atmospheric material is good, however, and almost all of the Joe-Ratso interplay (parts of it, apparently, based on improvisations) is delightful and affecting. This is due in large measure to extremely winning performances by Jon Voight and Dustin Hoffman, the former accomplishing the difficult task of reconciling militant stupidity with charm, the latter able to turn scrounging into a gallant, Robin-Hoodish activity. There may be something a mite schematic about the way acerbic humor and mock rancor are summoned up as screens for the touching devotion between two men, but this device, as sentimental in fact as it is virile in intention, is a hallowed mainstay of American filmmaking and, before that, American fiction.

What is more disturbing about the film is its contrived, manipulative technique, adroit though it may be much of the time. I get the feeling that it is made up entirely of little skits, anecdotes, and blackout sketches, complete with final sight gag or punch line, laid end to end. I am not referring to the fragments of the past that pop up in flash frames or sharply abbreviated sequences, sometimes in deliberately scrambled order. Except for the fact that they make Joe's past unduly arcane, I don't object to them. What does bother me, though, is the patness and didacticism of episode after episode in the present.

Take a typical incident: Joe, new to New York, is walking down Fifth Avenue; suddenly, there is a man sprawled across the sidewalk. Joe is shocked and about to come to his assistance. But the mass of passers-by just walk around the man (dead? in a coma?) as if he were merely a minor nuisance, say, a largish puddle. Astounded, Joe does as the New Yorkers do. At this point we notice a plaque on the building in back of the fallen man: Tiffany & Co.

It is this rubbing in that I find mildly but distinctly offensive. In the final scene, when Ratso dies on the bus just as it is about to reach Miami, his death causes a flurry of indignation among the passengers. But that is not enough: the next shot must have an ancient and repellent female rabidly coating her mouth with lipstick, in preparation for living it up at the Fontainebleau.

Women, by the way, get much the worse deal in this film which, while ostensibly holding up heterosexual values amid the homosexuality, actually exudes a homosexual sensibility, thus increasing its dishonesty. Revealing, in this respect, is the choice of actress for the young woman who gives Joe his first break, the one relatively sympathetic feminine part: Brenda Vaccaro. With the exception of Sandy Dennis, there is no more irritatingly unfeminine actress around these days than Miss Vaccaro, a cube-shaped creature who comes across as a dikey Kewpie doll.

Nevertheless, the film has solid virtues as well. Much of it is very neatly directed; most of it is well acted—except for Miss Vaccaro, Viva and her fellow creeps, and a rather miscast Ruth White as Joe's sexy granny. Adam Holender has kept his color photography nicely within the bounds of the required seediness. The editing is crisp. Landscapes and city-scapes convey spacious or cramped loneliness, clean or dirty clutter. And over all of it, the irrepressible performances of Voight and Hoffman dispense their special grace.

July, 1969

A WALK WITH LOVE AND DEATH

A thoroughly disastrous film is John Huston's *A Walk with Love and Death*. Like Hans Koningsberger's paltry novel on which it is based, the screenplay (by the novelist himself but based on a screen treatment by Dale Wasserman, one of Hollywood's superhacks) is one of those gratuitous exercises in viewing the past with the eyes of the present. This tale of the Hundred Years' War is about as medieval as Erich Maria Remarque, full of enlightened liberalism condescending to the Middle Ages while, in the same breath, drawing significant parallels to our own time.

Though the film has a modicum of authenticity in its *mise en scène*, this is achieved at the expense of keeping everything down to a beggarly minimum, so that a castle seems to have no servants in it, and a peasant rebellion comprises barely enough people for a third-rate tourney. Huston has directed in a bored and lackluster fashion, and his performing of a minor role is deplorably leprechaunish. The ending of the picture is an absolute botch, and there is a perfectly blank, supremely inept performance in the feminine lead by Huston's daughter, Anjelica, who has the face of an exhausted gnu, the voice of an unstrung tennis racket, and a figure of no describable shape.

As for Asaf Dayan, the son of General Moshe Dayan, in the male lead, I suspect that his father could not only act, speak, and think, but even see better.

October, 1969

FUTZ

The bill of fare in *Futz* includes: zoophilia (the hero, Futz, in carnal love with his pig, Amanda), homosexuality, transvestitism, troilism I (man, woman, pig), troilism II (two men and a repugnantly porcine girl, naked, gamboling in the mud), coprophilia (the slaughtering of Amanda before your eyes, the villagers smearing one another with, and wallowing in, the pig's gore), pyromania, masturbation, fetishism, varieties of sadism, sex murder, incest and sacrilege (an idiot and his sexually doting mother repeatedly compared to Christ and the Virgin Mary), voyeurism, exhibitionism (every kind of gratuitous nudity, and particularly a shapeless-bodied and sick-faced Sally Kirkland riding naked on a pig—this scene, like several others, not integrated into the plot, just dragged in for the sheer beauty of it), and various forms of mass copulation. The amazing thing is that out of this pleasant assortment of bestialities, the scenarists, Joseph Stefano and Rochelle Owens, and the Director, Tom O'Horgan, have not been able to create anything more than totally asexual boredom.

Why? Because neither Miss Owens (on whose dreary play this drearier film is based) nor Tom O'Horgan (who, having misdirected the play, mis-misdirected the film) has an ounce of genuine feeling. Miss Owens is a primitive: she writes "poetic" banalities ("lust for animals is like a run in spring rain"), illiterate English ("how can well I go describing on?"), cute, pseudo-folksy patois ("flahfy Amanda ya faymale!"), and flights of fancy that plummet into bathos ("his kneecaps high like the two hemispheres"). But there is worse.

Though the hog-hugger may not be the ideal image for the nonconformist martyr of a conformist society's intolerance (Futz is killed by the villagers), we could accept him as such if only his author could love him. But she laughs at him, patronizes him, even belittles him as a coward: under pressure, he denies his love for Amanda. And Miss Owens and O'Horgan are equally craven. They never come near showing us Futz amorously embracing his sow; so we get the irony of a film that postures as a gallantly shocking provocation of the Establishment actually copping out into mere off-screen grunts. Furthermore, in their hatred of "normal" society, Miss Owens and O'Horgan have made the villagers themselves so flagrantly bestial that it is hard to conceive of them not condoning and joining in the Futzian fun.

O'Horgan, however, is no naïf, or faux-naïf, like Miss Owens; he is an effete, campy, fey sophisticate manqué, who coats her subliteracy with layer upon layer of window-dresser's style. He uses, with meretricious indiscriminateness, every technical device—from negative exposure to solarization, from superimposing monochrome gelatins of two different colors to shooting the film both as a filmed play and as a "realistic" film, and continually shuttling between the two modes. There is grotesque distortion, elaborate foolery with the depth of focus, shifting from color to monochrome; there is rapid cutting almost with single-frame shots; there is Futzing around with the sound track (misplaced oinks) and sets (in a seemingly authentic countryside, a paper moon); there is slow and accelerated motion, and much zooming out from a narrator in closeup to action in long-shot. O'Horgan, who also wrote the abominable pseudo-folk-music score, will dwell on one repeated bar more maniacally than Carl Orff; or he will indulge in cheap parody, as when the words "Nobody knows and the pig won't tell" are set to Tchaikovsky's "None but the lonely heart"—just as in the midst of Dogpatch shenanigans we get a visual parody of Michelangelo's Pietà or the Creation of Adam.

The effect of all this is to kill any erotic involvement we might feel, while not substituting for it anything more intellectually stimulating than gimmickry. The mind is drawn away from Miss Owens's shallowness only to hurtle into the picturesque abyss of O'Horgan's vacuity. Needless to say, there is no such thing as consistency of plot, character, or anything else; the village idiot will speak of Mozart and Shiva, and the untutored Futz will invoke Zeus. It is this adulterous hodgepodge of everything (to use Corbière's phrase) that makes the film an esthetic obscenity as well as an eloquent document of the sickness of its makers.

But Clive Barnes found that "Miss Owens's play presumably has a moral purpose." Personally, I don't know what a presumable moral purpose is; the only possible morals I can derive from the movie *Futz* are that society won't buy a poke in a pig, and that you cannot make a slick farce from a sow's rear.

November, 1969

PERFORMANCE

You do not have to be a drug addict, pederast, sado-masochist, or nitwit to enjoy *Performance,* but being one or more of these things would help. *Performance* is one of that new breed of movies that do not try to win you over by wit, seriousness, humor, plot, characterization, logic, dialogue, or any other such outmoded paraphernalia. Instead, the film is built up—if anything so slapped together can be said to be built—from shocks piled on shocks. Not surprises, which are a time-honored device; not titillations, equally established though somewhat less honorable; and not even shocks in the sense of bouts of honest-to-goodness indignation. Rather, the film progresses by what I imagine a series of electroshocks to be like, but a shock treatment administered not by a therapist but by a misprogrammed computer.

The genre can only be called the Loathsome Film. There have been a good many LFs around in recent years: *Boom!, Secret Ceremony, Candy, End of the Road, Myra Breckinridge, Beyond the Valley of the Dolls, Something for Everyone.* But in *Performance,* made in swinging and swishing London, the LF achieves what may well prove its foulest flowering, the perfection of its technique. If something can be seen long enough for it to take on shape or sense, quickly cut away from it; if anyone speaks meaningfully for more than one sentence at a time, bring on the Moog Synthesizer to turn the sound track into an unsound digestive tract sending out signals of distress; if there is a good-looking person on the screen, either disfigure him with weird makeup, fright wigs, vicious blows administered on camera (James Fox); or get her up in togs that look like the Sargasso Sea and put enough kohl arond her eyes to make them look like kohl mines (Anita Pallenberg); or never show more than one breast, elbow, or foot—or else a jumbled, fuzzy mass of unidentifiable parts—before you cut from her (Ann Sidney) to an automobile.

There is something promiscuous and amoral about the very construction and editing of the film. The first half is a gangster melodrama jazzed up with bizarre visual effects and spiked with homosexuality and sadism; the second half is mostly dropping out and turning on, polymorphous perversity, exchanges of gender and identity, psychedelia and rock music. It is like crossbreeding George Raft and Tiny Tim in a loo of the London tube. But like the scenes in Turner's (Mick Jagger's) pad, almost every sequence is a structural orgy in which disparate and jarring elements are nasty together and beget monsters.

Take the opening sequence: a silvery Rolls-Royce is rolling into town through the nascent dawn, and two roistering naked bodies are rolling over each other in a nocturnal bedroom. The film cuts rapidly back and forth between these two individually meaningless and conjointly inscrutable actions, as if this were some Griffith movie churning to its climax—only there is no climax, except for a histrionically souped-up sexual one, and certainly no Griffith movie. The sound track blares up and is struck dumb (this one they got from Godard, but depredations on all other fashionable filmmakers follow) and periodically erupts into whooshing, swooshing beeps and, yes, bagpipes, though Scotland, like Hecuba, has nothing to do with it. To make things racier, there are suggestions of kinkiness in the sex—a whiff of what might be a riding crop or a garrote—but these are flash frames and we are kept guessing. The filmmakers count on our having a better imagination than theirs (which wouldn't be hard) and on our being stimulated into visualizing perversions unrecorded by the camera or Suetonius.

Now let me skip to a scene in this overmasculine bedroom where James Fox, playing an enforcer for a protection racket—who is apparently known in England as a "performer"—gets beaten up by some vengeful thugs, with one of whom he is implied to have a special relationship. His apartment has already been wrecked and crimson paint has been splashed all over the walls; this is soon to mingle with real blood, making a Suprematist composition worthy of Malevich: red on red. Fox is stripped and flogged, and you get to see enough welts and pain to equip a neo-Romantic movement with *weltschmerz*. On a wall, in paint or blood, a thug has written "POOF" (a jolly British synonym for faggot), and the whipping is to continue until Fox cries uncle—or, in this case, perhaps aunt—by repeating the dictated words, "I am a poof." During the whipping, we get a quick cut to Fox making love to the girl from the opening sequence, and, lest we miss the connection, a thug snarls, "You love that, you little . . ." But before he or Fox could say "poof," Fox has grabbed his gun and makes his chief tormentor, and ancient enemy and lover, cower and grovel for a record length of time until he shoots him in a particularly campy way. At this point we cut, in black and white (the rest of the film is in garish color, unworthy of its co-director and cinematographer, Nick Roeg), to a brief shot of two boys fighting on the school steps; this is the childish but troubled past of the now murderous antagonists—and also a device lifted from Roman Polanski's *Repulsion*.

Next, let us skip to Mick Jagger's townhouse boudoir—oh, yes, there is a semblance of a plot on which these scenes are hung, but it doesn't make sense, anyway—where Anita Pallenberg, lovely but made and gotten up like a groupie that just hit the fan, approaches a canopied bed. Though young, she is already an alumna of at least three LFs (*Barbarella, Candy,* and Marco Ferreri's odious *Dillinger Is Dead*), and she draws the bed curtains with magisterial decadence to reveal two cavorting bodies of four sexes. There is Mi-chèle Breton, who makes the hermaphrodite in *Fellini Satyricon* seem positively monosexual by comparison, and *she* does it all without makeup. And there is the supreme horror of the film, Mick Jagger, whose lack of talent is equaled only by a repulsiveness of epic propor-tions—on those shocking-pink blubber-lips alone a complete *Iliad* and *Odyssey* could be inscribed. Jagger looks so epicene that, in the prevail-ing arty lighting and photography, he is almost indistinguishable from Miss Breton, and though I have forced myself to see this film twice, I still don't know whose nipple Miss Pallenberg proceeds to toy with. After that, they all three fall to it, and none of them knows whose what is which.

Jagger plays a rock star who dropped out and into a *ménage à trois* with these two ladies (who have, on the side, a little ménage of their own), a house full of the most lurid bric-à-brac a studio property department was ever coerced into assembling, and a thriving mush-room culture that these walking myxomycetes feed on between shots of stronger stuff. Fox comes to rent a basement room from the three-some, to hide out from his gang who are out to kill him; the trio, as fascinated by his gun as he is by their fungi, get involved with him in every possible combination. He pretends to be a juggler recovering from a car accident—another kind of "performer," you see?—only to be confronted with yet another, more diabolic, kind of performer, Jagger, who portentously informs him that he has been waiting for him for years.

There ensues a piece of stupid and revoltingly pretentious meta-physical camp. (The film, like another current LF, *Something for Every-one,* is predominantly homosexual in spirit, despite bows to other, more or less exotic, persuasions. The MPAA might consider whether such already existing ratings as G, GP, etc., for the guidance of parents, should not be supplemented by others, like H, S-M, etc., for the guidance of perverts.) We get the fusion and exchange of identities: the hood becomes the hippie and vice versa. Here this indescribably sleazy, self-indulgent, and meretricious film—written and co-directed by one Donald Cammell, whose name does not deserve to live even in igno-miny—dares to plagiarize and subvert one of the most brilliant themes from one of the profoundest films of all time, Ingmar Bergman's *Persona:* the faces of Fox and Jagger melt together and, thenceforth, the two perform toward, against, and into each other.

But, as if this were not enough, *Performance* treats us to collateral transmogrifications, as, for instance, when Jagger changes into the boss of Fox's gang. If you thought him flabbergasting before, he'll jagger-blast you in a three-piece brown business suit, prognathism, sideburns, and hair greasily slicked back over a pinhead. The lips now look like a butcher's nightmare, and the *parlando* song they deliver (it is written by Jagger himself) is a turgid hymn of hate. The photography turns green, the gangsters are suddenly naked and sprawled out, while the camera recedes and recedes in little jump cuts, making one wish one could follow it right out of the movie.

There is more, however. A depraved little girl of, say, nine being groomed, apparently, for Jagger's harem; a fly gratuitously shown dying in extreme closeup; Miss Pallenberg shooting drugs into her behind for a double visual thrill; Miss Breton taking a bath (her first?) in unappetizing detail—even that great writer Jorge Luis Borges is dragged into this cesspool. At one point, Jagger is reading aloud from a Borges story about transferral of identity (and he reads in the same zonked way he speaks all his lines); later, when Fox shoots Jagger—if that is what happens—Jagger's face turns into a portrait of Borges before it is torn open by the bullet into a gash looking like a gaping vagina.

It is all mindless intellectual pretension and pathologically reveled-in gratuitous nastiness, and it means nothing. The filmmakers's sensibilities are so jaded, their senses so atrophied, that I doubt they could even feel the swift kick they so richly deserve. Yet Roger Greenspun concluded his juggling act of a review with the words, "You are in the presence of the ultimate metaphysical comic strip—which is what you've always gone to the movies to see." If that is not what you go to the movies to see, as I don't, you might as well desist.

One final warning. At the 6 P.M. showing of *Performance* on August 10, our nostrils were invaded by a strong odor of vomit. Two days later, friends reported being obliged to breathe through their mouths, so strong was the scent of puke. One wonders whether the Trans-Lux East is never cleaned, or whether *Performance* elicits the identical performance from someone at every showing.

August, 1970

13

The Festival and Awards Game

A CHARACTER in *The Time of Your Life,* speaking most likely for Saroyan himself, remarks: "The thing to do is to have more magazines. Hundreds of them. *Thousands.* Print everything they write so they'll believe they're immortal. That way keep them from going haywire." Though there is a recession in magazines now to the point where not quite everything that is written gets printed, there are enough awards and festivals going for almost everything on celluloid to be recognized and even rewarded. At the Venice Festival you could get until recently a gold or silver lion; at Cannes there is the gold palm; in Berlin, a gold or silver bear; in Locarno, a gold or silver sail; in San Sebastian, a gold or silver shell; in Pulj, Yugoslavia, a gold or silver arena; in Melbourne, a silver boomerang; in Cork, Ireland, St. Finbarr statuettes (material unspecified—presumably cork); and so on, *ad nauseam.* You have to be a rare filmmaker indeed not to get something, somewhere, be it an Oscar or a FIPRESCI prize, or at least a screening out of competition at Cannes, all of which somehow finds its way into your credit sheet and the advertising of your film. It is certainly enough to keep "them" from going haywire; but what will preserve *us?*

For we are deluged at film festivals with movies whose awfulness we could take in our stride if they came at us one by one, but which, *en masse,* knock us out. To be sure, there is one good thing about festivals: they bring together film people from everywhere and they stimulate discussion and general interest in the medium. When they start giving out awards, however, they tend to become more harmful, both in the bad they preconize and the good they ignore. Serious filmmakers, for example, rightly refuse to have their works prejudged by something like the Cannes jury, which is apt to include experts like French film producers and Hollywood movie stars. Politics of every kind enters into prize-giving, and the attendant hoopla and publicity manage to tarnish what little valid prestige the award might have left.

But even festivals that do not give out awards—and the trend is toward these—are dubious blessings. Thus the New York Film Festival has for its director Richard Roud (until recently also the director of the London Festival)—a man for whose taste I would consider "execrable" a flattering term—and the films chosen by him and his permanent panel of judges (*also* chosen by him and including Susan Sontag, Andrew Sarris, and Arthur Knight) reflect his predilections. As a result, the Roudian taste in movies sinisterly infiltrates public and media thinking (I use the word loosely): *these* are the best movies being made anywhere in the world, like them or not. Worse yet, young filmmakers conclude that these are the films they must imitate if they wish to succeed. And, worst of all, Vincent Canby reviews an important film like Ermanno Olmi's *One Fine Day* unfavorably at the festival, and, promptly, the film fails to get public distribution and the rest of the world is denied the chance to see it and make up its own mind.

As for awards, I deal here with the Oscars, with which I am most familiar. Readers will note that in my 1970 article for the *New York Times* ("Oscars: They Shun the Best, Don't They?") I repeat, deliberately, some of the things I wrote in the 1967 *New Leader* piece ("The Oscar Is Wild"). Alas, the Academy Awards do not change for the better, the same grossness continues, and there is no way for a critic not to repeat his imprecations. The time may come when one will get so discouraged by the whole thing that one will construct an all-purpose review of The Awards, and just leave a few blanks for the titles and names that may—or may not—change from year to year.

THE OSCAR IS WILD

At last year's Oscar ceremony, Bob Hope remarked that the Oscar was filmdom's most coveted award because it was given by experts. It is, he said, like praise for a wall not from random passers-by but from bricklayers. But the Oscars are not given out by bricklayers—would that they were! Or by shoe salesmen, dog breeders, or retired sanitation workers—anyone, in fact, except the members of the Motion Picture Academy. The very term falls upon the ear rather as Call Girl College would, not because motion pictures are not to be taken seriously, but because Hollywood isn't.

I am occasionally asked whether I have ever made a movie, or, failing that, worked for, on, or in one—or, at the very least, watched one being shot. Upon my repeated no's, the scraggly filmmaker or filmy teen-ager inevitably asks how, then, can I evaluate movies. The answer is the Oscars. Everyone who votes for them is an expert, and has worked in, around, behind, or under movies; yet the awards, with very few exceptions, stink unto heaven, or however near heaven the Hollywood smog permits.

But to return to Hope's analogy: though bricklayers may know about walls, what do they know about buildings, architecture, art? Oscars are largely a business proposition, adjudged by some of the world's most uneducated, tasteless, and inbred people, as like as not buddies, business partners, bed partners, of the winners. Above all, they are people for whom salability matters: the Oscar-winning film is not only one that will make pots of money after it is chosen, but also one that, usually, has already been raking it in when it was nominated. Still, I suppose, there are honest votes, too—the honest votes of the culturally and mentally underprivileged.

Movies may or may not have been getting better, but they certainly have been getting longer. In keeping with the trend, this year's Oscar ceremonies themselves lasted two and a half hours, and may, in due time, last four, with a fifteen-minute intermission for dinner, taking a walk, or, if one happens to care about film, hanging oneself in despair. This year's two and a half hours were made even bleaker by the fact that the commercials provided no welcome respite. They were for Eastman Kodak, and they kept encouraging people to go out and take snapshots and make movies, when only a moment before or after we were made horribly aware of what it all leads to.

Bob Hope was telling jokes again, cleaner than in past years but also less funny. My mind wandered to the million dollars Hope pays out annually to his gag writers, and I tried to calculate just how many thousands of dollars' worth of wit were being wasted on me every minute. The jokes are mostly in-jokes, which make the on-the-spot audience feel wonderfully important for begetting them, and the far-flung TV viewers wonderfully "in" for getting them. For one night, Hollywood can splash about in the drool of sixty-five million stargazers, feel that it is the Nation; and the Nation, in turn, feels at one with Hollywood. It would be a perfect communion of souls, if only there were any soul in it. Hope did have one funny gag, though. He explained that the clips from the films nominated for best picture would no longer be shown *en bloc* but scattered through the program and separated by commercials, "so that you should know what they'll look like on television." On second thought, that's too true and too sad to be funny.

As in past years, the dreariest part was the jokes exchanged by award-announcing actors between themselves, or in repartee with Hope. These jokes are, as everyone knows, rehearsed, but are supposed to sound spontaneous. This presents the stars with a terrible dilemma: should they rattle off the gags by rote, and appear to be dolts; or pretend to improvise, and appear to be phonies. Most of them try for a middle course—"You know that this isn't impromptu, and I know that you know, but isn't it fun my pretending I can fool you and your enjoying it enough to go along with the pretense?"—but for such an elaborate piece of acting, alas, none of them is a good enough actor.

There is no need to dwell on the garishness of the sets; on the soporific orchestra under the multiple Oscar-winner, Johnny Green; on the actors' toupees, like rain forests of the Amazon; on the actresses' hairdos which, in an age when the most elegant hair is allowed to fall naturally to the shoulders, are veritable stairways to the stars. The gowns were the last—pleonastic and obsolescent—word; Shelley Winters's, for example, not so much a dress as an environment. It all testified to the tinselbound insularity of Hollywood, in which Julie Christie with her "contemporary" look seemed to be not from another city but from another planet. It may be worth adding that the songs competing for the Oscar—not very good to begin with—were suffocated by vulgar production numbers, contorted into not just un- but anti-musical arrangements, and caterwauled by tone-deaf pop singers.

Present, too, were the usual boners: Candy Bergen rushing forward for an award not being granted her; Olivia de Havilland struggling to read out names as though a choir of nightingales had nestled in her throat and managing to sound perfectly incomprehensible; Sidney Poitier trying to impress us with his culture by pronouncing the good English name Vivien Merchant with what he took to be a devilishly French accent; and so on. And there was the usual fatuous fun in all those awards named after deceased Hollywood moguls or character actors, which are given for great humanitarianism and world citizenship to mean-looking geezers with ghastly accents, whose names are known only on Hollywood Boulevard and Flatbush Avenue.

But the real scandal, as always, was the Oscars themselves. True, this year there was no *Sound of Music* winning the supreme accolade; even so, the stage of the Santa Monica Civic Auditorium gave off more nauseating farce in one evening than the Three Stooges in a lifetime. The hallmark of the awards is a mixture of bad taste and intense parochialism and xenophobia. Rare indeed is the gifted foreigner who can snatch an award from the most mediocre domestic contender. For example, in costume design, Danilo Donati's costumes for *The Gospel According to Saint Matthew* had an exhilaratingly tactile, homespun, authentic peasant quality, but also, when needed, an arrogant, barbaric brio. But the Oscar went to Irene Sharaff, whose costumes for *Virginia Woolf* were invisible to all but the Motion Picture Academy's eye. Piero Gherardi provided *Juliet of the Spirits* (never mind the quality of the film) with art direction that transformed gaudiness and tawdriness into a mannerist phantasmagoria, but the Oscar was adjudicated to a piece of American silliness, *Fantastic Voyage*. And so it goes. It is a cheap trick even to have opened the Oscars to international competition and made the awards look ecumenical when the prizes *actually* go to homegrown hacks.

There are exceptions to this. The English are sometimes allowed to squeak by because they speak a language that Hollywood, in its naïveté, takes to be its own. Again, someone like Sophia Loren will be given an Oscar because she has made enough Hollywood movies to be practically one of us. So this year the award for the best original screenplay went to Claude Lelouch for *A Man and a Woman*—a French work but patently Hollywood-influenced and ranging all the way from froth to caramel.

But look at the main awards: the Oscar to the best actress could not be given Anouk Aimée, superb in Lelouch's film; nor to the worthy Ida Kaminska; nor even to one of the Redgrave girls, who, though they did little in *Morgan* and *Georgy Girl* to endear them to me, are still not without talent. No, it had to fall to that pristine untalentedness called Elizabeth Taylor for her impersonation of Little Lulu in *Virginia Woolf*. In the best supporting actress category, Sandy Dennis, who (again in *Virginia Woolf*) offered us the crude and sick substitution of private dementia for the creation of a character, was crowned over Vivien Merchant, whose performance in *Alfie* was delicate, precise, and compelling in its understated suggestiveness.

The best supporting actor turned out to be Walter Matthau, whose work in *The Fortune Cookie* was indeed brashly clever and raffish as the part required; but Robert Shaw, as Henry VIII in *A Man for All Seasons*, went well beyond the requirements of the part, dizzyingly evoking the seething depths of a soul. The award for the best direction went to Fred Zinnemann, whom Hollywood has adopted just as he adopted it, for *A Man for All Seasons,* decent unimaginative work; not to Antonioni, who, even in *Blow-Up,* is a pathfinder and a master.

True, two Oscars went foreign: one to Paul Scofield, and one to *A Man for All Seasons.* But these are, at least, English, and the film about Sir Thomas More is a monument to middle-brow culture, to say nothing of spiritual uplift. (Previously, *A Man for All Seasons* won the first Protestant-Catholic interfaith film award, even though More helped "heretics" to the stake, and himself preferred death to Protestantism —there's more balm in Hollywood than in Gilead for the healing of ancient quarrels.)

Still, Scofield deserved an award for his More, even though Michael Caine's Alfie was an equally flawless performance, and one created for a film, not transposed, like Scofield's, from the stage. And what of Max von Sydow in *Hawaii,* who was not even nominated? Surely a performance that rose out of the endless and simplistic surrounding trash (and in a role neither well-written nor sympathetic) to the heights of complex human grandeur deserves an Oscar and a half. But it is equally sure that the gilded Oscars do not deserve a golden Max.

April, 1967

FIFTH NEW YORK FILM FESTIVAL: GROWING PAINS OR PAINFUL GROWTH?

This year my deadline obliges me not to wait till the end of the New York Film Festival but to write from the thick of it. That is, if so thin a festival can have a thick. Unlike last year, four-fifths of the Fifth Festival proved an exercise in fine futility, having produced only one incontestably superior film—which could already be seen the following day in a regular movie house. Though it may have lacked the excitement of a cocktail-party *primeur,* Gillo Pontecorvo's *The Battle of Algiers* turned out to be an artistic and political experience that eats its way into the toughest consciousness. While occasioning a thorough upheaval in the viewer, it succeeds in concealing not only its art, but even its craft. One thinks one is watching at the very least a spectacular newsreel, if not indeed history itself in the making.

Five years ago, Pontecorvo gave us a routine piece of concentration-camp melodrama, *Kapo,* from which no one could have begun to expect a development into the dark splendors of *The Battle of Algiers.* The film, apparently based on strictly documentary evidence, tells of the always intrepid, sometimes ugly, and finally tragic struggle of the FLN to liberate Algeria. Almost all of the leaders were exterminated or imprisoned, and only several years later did a new organization and renewed uprisings accomplish the liberation.

Pontecorvo's film is remarkable in many ways. First, in that, though heartily on the side of the rebels, it manages to make the French seem human, their leaders almost sympathetic, their techniques of torture iniquitous and repellent, yet, given the circumstances, not incomprehensible. In an impossible situation, the French paratroops conduct their mandatory brutality not without some regret, some immanent sympathy for their victims. Secondly, the rebel leaders are shown almost exclusively as fighters or strategists, without any luxuriating in the pathos of their private lives; even so, the intelligent script and sensitive direction manage to convey well-defined and differentiated personalities and the varied nature of their involvement.

Thirdly, the film is admirable in its balance of cataclysmic violence with conciliatory exhilaration and soft-spoken thoughtfulness. Fourthly, it never becomes slick or over-produced as other pseudodocumentaries, such as *The Four Days of Naples,* have tended to be. Fifthly, it maintains a forthrightness and slight graininess in the photography as in newsreels, but without overdoing it. Its amateur actors, sixthly, are impeccable, though this is something that we have, wrongly, come to take for granted in Italian neo-realism, of which this is a cogent offshoot. The editing, seventhly, is exceedingly canny, always conveying the impact and meaning of a scene, but stopping short of vulgarly journalistic details. Lastly, the crowd scenes have been staged and shot with a verisimilitude that had spectators in other countries (before a headnote to the contrary was appended) convinced they were seeing documentary footage.

And some credit must go to the director, too, for the excellence of the one professional actor in the film, Jean Martin, who plays the paratroop colonel. It is an infinitely rich and complex performance: soldier, showman, thinker, epigrammatist, enlightened martinet, histrion, egotist, human being, this colonel—whatever of him is fact, and whatever Franco Solinas's screenplay—is a character the very best theater can envy.

Immediately after *The Battle of Algiers,* particularly meaningful for the United States today, came *The Feverish Years,* a piece of cinematography inept enough to have been produced in Outer Mongolia, not the artistically fairly awakened Yugoslavia. Dragoslav Lazić's film is an unhappy concert of trite scenario, undistinguished acting, amateurish photography, and unimaginative direction. Lazić and his cohorts have no idea how to achieve a smooth, or even purposively choppy, continuity; the film lurches, sputters, creaks, and stumbles ahead—or, more often, sideways. Lazić, furthermore, is a pushover for fashionable clichés, such as sneaking in a sequence from a Hitchcock film (*The Birds*, of all things) or having the camera pan endlessly in circles *à la* Chabrol; he is also quite unaware of the small, personal touches that create authenticity. He does, however, dwell at length and in extreme, cloddish closeups on people washing or wolfing down their food. Whether because he thinks this joyfully sensuous or because such pleasures are hard to come by in Yugoslavia, I cannot say.

The subtitles, albeit the largest I have ever seen, do not manage, regrettably, to blot out more than a third of the image. But they do succeed in extirpating what little flavor there is in the dialogue; thus, for example, *"Ne seri!"* ("Don't give me that shit!") emerges as "Don't blubber!" The subtitles also contribute the only bit of (inadvertent) fun in the film, when they keep translating "tumor" as "humor"—viz., "If he had a humor, it would be swollen."

Another Yugoslav film, Dušan Makavejev's *An Affair of the Heart* is a much more sophisticated affair: a tragicomic love story salted with lively social comment and peppered with cunning devices to produce Brechtian *Verfremdung*, it is daring as well in its use of total nudity that would be advanced even for a Western country. The writer-director has a sense of humor (not tumor) and he tells his story with neat back-and-forward flashes. The dialogue is racy, full of Serbian four-letter words only sparingly rendered in the subtitles. These are a mite better here, though they still lose the satirical edge: When someone says, "I live like our delegation in a foreign country," they give us, "I live like an ambassador," which misses the political irony. The cast is amiable, and Eva Ras wears her almost non-stop nudity stylishly.

The two German films do little to dispel our image of Germany as a filmic desert. *Yesterday Girl*, by the avant-garde novelist Alexander Kluge, is as involved and desiccated as his fiction. It is based on the story "Anita G." in *Lebensläufe*, which seems to have been written by an absent-minded computer that reads anti-novels on the sly. Although trying to be a little less chaotic, the film retains the spastic quality of the story and much of its carefully fostered formlessness and aimlessness. There are, nevertheless, a few amusingly cynical moments in this chronicle of a petty thief and part-time prostitute, and an episode at a school for police dogs is howlingly funny. Kluge's twin sister, Alexandra, stars, and her face has a kind of precocious know-it-allness that some may find fetching.

The other German entry, Volker Schlöndorff's *Young Törless*, is an earnest but pedestrian transcription of Robert Musil's brilliant first novel. As I wrote in my Afterword to the Signet Classics edition of the book, its purpose is "to show that the world is, at the very least, a double-bottomed box. Whatever solution is found is not the ultimate one: hidden beneath it is another layer of reality or truth, and that may not be the last bottom, either. And that is not all. Upward, heavenward, there is no single roof: the box is also double- or multiple-topped. There is metaphysical truth beyond metaphysical truth just as there is psychic reality within psychic reality." The film version of this story of a gifted boy's coming to terms with life concentrates on the plot outline of sadistic goings-on at an Austrian military school circa 1900. But it omits a large part of the sadopederastic doings and of the deep metaphysical unrest that together rived the hero, Törless—thus the film is like a piano missing both the bass and treble parts of its keyboard, unfit for serious music.

What is substituted is simplistic broadening. Basini, the victim, is tall but slender in the novel, "with slack, indolent movements and effeminate features." In the film, he is a heavy-set bumpkin with a large, pathetic cube for a head. The mathematics teacher, an ordinary young man, is turned into a Peter Lorreish grotesque; whereas the aging whore, Božena, becomes that young charmer, Barbara Steele.

For just one specific example of this much-lauded film's insensitivity, consider the ending. Out of the carriage taking him away forever from the odious school, Törless looks at Božena's window. It was Božena who had once shocked him by suggesting that she and his mother were sisters under the skin. He glances sidelong at his mother, who asks, in the book, "What is it, my child?" Törless gives an evasive answer, followed by the novel's closing sentence: "And, testing, he inhaled the subtle odor rising from his mother's waist." In the film, nothing is done with this olfactory ending that makes the once mysterious mother into a mere woman like the lowly prostitute. Worse yet, his mother addresses the boy as "Törless." No mother would address her son by his last name—could this have been the filmmaker's clumsy attempt at suggesting a coming-of-age?

The acting and direction are routine, and the subtitles, as is their wont, finish off the film. When the pseudophilosophical Beineberg tells Törless that pitying Basini is *"Verschwendung der Lebenskraft"*—the squandering of vital energy—the subtitles reduce this to a mere "waste." The vulgarization of a major work of modern literature becomes complete.

The Swedes, too, were represented with two works. Jonas Cornell's *Puss & Kram (Hugs & Kisses)* is an epigonous piece of cutie-pie New

Wave tomfoolery distinguished only by the fact that Cornell shows off his wife's pubic hair in it (no doubt the eponymous "Puss"), and that it begins with a long monologue that remains untranslated. The initial subtitle given is for the exclamation "John!" which translates "John!"

The other entry, *Elvira Madigan,* is substantially worthier. Made by Bo Widerberg, whose *Raven's End* showed promise, this is a tragic idyll of the Scandinavian *belle époque.* A young aristocratic officer runs off with a beautiful circus tightrope-walker. They share an intense, passion-filled summer despite haunting thoughts of his wife and children; at the end of it, they commit suicide. As an aristocrat and deserter, he cannot, it seems, stoop to menial labor abroad. The plot is hackneyed and unconvincing, and though Widerberg's dialogue strains for freshness, it shows mostly strain.

But there is Jörgen Persson's almost extravagantly beautiful color photography in which things take on deeper, more daring colors than in life. A gray sea is a vast expanse of pitiless steel; a prodigal evening into which the lovers walk is all white and ultramarine; a Copenhagen blue velvet bow fairly darts out of Elvira's cascading blondness that periodically overflows the screen. As that one and only danced-out summer drags its feet into winter, we can feel the temperature of the film's colors dropping, colors that have the Nordic expressionist wildness of Edvard Munch. And there is Widerberg's direction, lively without becoming frantic, lyrical without wallowing in its lyricism.

The acting, too, is commendable, although Thommy Berggren's noble lieutenant seems to have been infected with the plebeian mannerisms of the Actors Studio. The others, however, are fine, notably little Nina Widerberg, all bespectacled gravity and yet a child. As Elvira, seventeen-year-old Pia Degermark is sheer felicity. With her somewhat obstinate, craggy profile she combines tenderly dissolving full-face loveliness, so that from the side she harks back to the Eddas, from the front to Hans Christian Andersen. Not only does she act with disarming unaffectedness, she seems even to have learned to walk a tightrope authoritatively.

Not the least engaging feature of this film is its subdued but unquenchable sensuality, which can forgo spilling over into explicit sexuality. There is no more nudity on display than the briefest glimpse of the beginnings (the French, beautifully, call it *naissance*) of one breast, yet it conveys everything. If only Widerberg's scenario and dialogue could have eschewed triteness, this might have been a film to remember for many a summer. As it stands, it is a much more satisfying version of *Le Bonheur,* which it resembles even down to its Mozart score.

The Polish director, Jerzy Skolimowski, was responsible for (or, more accurately, guilty of) two films. The Festival directors, two years ago, provided us with another Skolimowski diptych of choice loathsomeness; now they have helped history to repeat itself. *Bariera*, made in Poland, is a pretentious, turgid allegory with a mildly provocative opening sequence and ponderous obscurity thereafter. No doubt in today's Poland social criticism is permitted to go about only if heavily veiled, but if under seven times seven veils Salome is a pig, was this dance necessary?

Le Départ, which Skolimowski made in Belgium, is barely better. The facility with which he and his fellow scenarist Andrzej Kostenko could adapt themselves to New Wave clichés is downright indecent. Nevertheless, this banal tale of a young hairdresser who wants to be an auto racer and will stop at no reasonable crime to achieve his goal, has a few witty or dashing moments. But, for the most part, it is routine Godardian slickness; the heroine is militantly unattractive; and, as the hero, Jean-Pierre Léaud proves conclusively that he has long since exhausted his slender acting resources. Krzysztof T. Komeda contributes his usual catchy score (he may prove the true heir of Nino Rota), and the title song, *"Vie de toujours,"* drawn from the main theme, is a worthy successor to the one from *A Man and a Woman*.

It is hard to conceive what Rossellini thought he was doing with *The Rise of Louis XIV*. Even the fact that it was made as a spectacular for French television does not quite justify its singular vapidity and pointlessness. Not only does it break off just as things might become interesting (perhaps further installments were contemplated), it also fails to probe behind the surface of what it does tell, and so makes no social, historical, or artistic contribution. It affects me as a history lesson from a lackadaisical high school teacher who gets steamed up only about a few quaint customs, some bizarre etiquette—which he assumes will tickle the uninvolved palates of his pupils—and for the rest is content to rattle off political and historical facts with unseemly haste.

Rossellini's direction is literal-minded and devoid of emotional or intellectual intensity, and the acting is at best what one might expect from accomplished television hacks. Only Katharina Renn, as Anne of Austria, was a face familiar to me, but not much dearer for that. Jean-Marie Patte seems miscast as Louis; he would have been much better as the protagonist of *The Blob*. Georges Leclerc's cinematography is competent enough, but it is hard to believe that he used the same Eastmancolor which, in *Elvira Madigan*, yields such gorgeously painterly results. The only possible explanation for this film I can excogitate is an apology for the benevolently paternalistic despot, whether his name be Louis XIV or Charles de Gaulle. If that is all Rossellini, the quondam radical, had in mind, he might as well not have discommoded himself with a transalpine journey.

One of the better films in the Fifth Festival's tail was the Hungarian *Father,* by István Szabó. Szabó's previous movie, *Age of Illusions,* augured well for its then twenty-six-year-old maker. It was full of Truffaut, but fertilized rather than fettered by him. In its most memorable scene, the young lovers watch newsreels of recent Hungarian history—war, aftermath, Communism, revolution, counterrevolution —and comment on it all detachedly, or talk about quite other matters, including a friend who escaped to America and is doing nicely there.

In *Father,* the Truffaut technique of creative horseplay reappears. A boy growing up in postwar Budapest invents breakneck daredeviltries his father is supposed to have performed in peace and in war among the partisans. We *hear* about the real father, a decent deceased surgeon, but *see* his fantasy feats, as we also see the boy showing off with and profiting by this dead hero-father. Gradually, the boy grows into a courageous and capable young man who can now bury the fictitious father. There are fetching scenes in the film, though they are not the bravura set-pieces; rather, they are bits like the one in which three grade-school kids grapple with the concept that the father of one of them is an escaped count, and that the son is considered an "enemy of the party." This conversation, splendidly managed by the author-director and the children, presents their incomprehension of political claptrap as charmingly sensible, and heralding the day when humanity may transcend ideology.

Another effective scene has the hero as a young man strenuously swimming across the Danube by way of a singularly valorous *rite de passage.* Almost at his goal, he looks back, only to see the heads of all his male—and female—chums bobbing merrily and casually right behind him. The acting is consistently good, and I particularly liked Dani Erdélyi as the boy: unpathetic and uncute, a child's child.

Peter Whitehead (when will a new British director *not* be a man called Peter?) was represented by a brace of documentaries, *The London Scene,* stuck together back to back, and quite uncomfortable. The first, *Tonite Let's All Make Love in London,* assembles a mosaic of the swinging life, pop and proto-pop: interviews with the famous, glimpses of the obscure. There is everything from Vanessa Redgrave leading a protest group in a North Vietnamese song she sings with quivering authenticity, to Edna O'Brien and Michael Caine pronouncing on the new sexual mores; there are speculations on art and life from the head of the Rolling Stones and a painter who paints on naked girls, turning them into a riot of strolling tones. There are also hauntingly surreal, off-focus slow-motion color shots of a writhing discothèque, but these are dragged out a bit. I don't know whether London is truly so sedulously swinging, and, if so, whether that makes it a pendulum abreast of the time or a hanged man in his death throes, but a mood is captured here, graphically and with unusual variety.

The companion piece, *The Benefit of the Doubt,* proved dreary. It is the filmed record of Peter Brook's production of *US,* the anti-Vietnam war improvisation by the Royal Shakespeare Company, interspersed with actors' comments on their roles. *US* was a lumpish enough affair, but actors pontificating about their work surpass everything in fatuity and dullness. Still, Richard Peaslee's tunes and Adrian Mitchell's lyrics have their moments—but no thanks to anything Whitehead has done in this plodding documentary.

From the London scene to the typical festival scene—for what festival would be complete without at least two films by Godard? Here we had an old one, *Les Carabiniers* (1962), and a new one, *Made in U.S.A.* (1966). My contempt and distaste for Godard are so great that I cannot do justice to them in an omnibus review. I therefore beg the reader's indulgence for referring him to my essay, "Godard and the Godardians" in *Private Screenings,* where I set forth in some detail what is so deleterious and despicable about Godard and his vogue. I hope that those concerned will take the trouble to look up this piece.

Let me say here only that both the above films are vintage Godard, which is to say pretentious nonsense in full bloom. But I cannot resist quoting John Coleman, the film critic of *The New Statesman,* with whom I am in full agreement on this matter: "If anyone else tries to tell me that Godard represents the new intellectual cinema as opposed to the draggy old one (which somehow managed to accommodate creators like Renoir) I shall do a damage. Only a period in thrall to adolescence, in its publicized form a product of commercial astuteness, could so doggily roll over and bark at such permissive nonsense."

Young American filmmaking was represented by John Korty's *Funnyman,* and there is something so amiable about the film and so likable about its maker that I wish I could summon up some praise. It is the story of a comedian acting with San Francisco's "Committee," and shows his tribulations on and off stage as he tries to make money, good, and girls. Peter Bonerz, who really is with "The Committee," has some amusing moments with ad executives, cartoonists, and just himself, but the script, by him and Korty, gets nowhere slow. The resolution—the restorative love of a Good Woman, here in the guise, or guiselessness, of a nude model—is patently naïve, a quality that was also in evidence in Korty's previous film, *Crazy Quilt.* There is no telling whether Korty, for all his talents as a cartoonist and still photographer, has in him the stuff of a cinematographer and filmmaker. By the way, I am getting heartily sick of films that switch from full color to various monochromes—yellow, blue, green, etc.—for no apparent reason except perhaps to save money while still seeming colorful. Wajda, Lelouch, and now Korty have done it, and it doesn't work for any of them.

It did work, to some extent, for Abel Gance, who, however, used single tints with a meaning—say, red for revolutionary slaughter—in a film like *Napoleon* (1923–27), which was shown as part of a Gance retrospective. I saw only a fraction of this four-hour silent Leviathan, which, like all beached whales, has a certain ludicrous pathos. A piece of apocryphal hagiography (incidents based on fact have captions at the bottom of which the abbreviation "Hist." appears—and it appears less and less frequently as the film progresses), it has intermittent spurts of invention, and lusciousness in the *mise en scène.* But Gance—as two other films of his I caught in the Special Events screenings confirm—was essentially a vigorous hack, whose frenetic overindulgence in longitude and multitude is the movie buffs' delight. A good many frames of *Napoleon* might have more aptly borne the caption "Hyst."

Masaki Kobayashi's new film, *Rebellion,* is inferior to his *Harakiri* (itself a flawed though impressive work) but still has much to recommend it. This is yet another movie in which Toshiro Mifune pits his swordsmanship triumphantly against more blades than there are blades of grass, but the final mayhem, as in so many Japanese films and so few westerns, is artistic as well as absurd. And the slow-paced inner struggles that lead up to the cathartic bloodletting are not without a stately beauty of rhythm, a dignity that manages to be as dainty as it is grave. The photography, in and out of doors, is incisive enough to clutch at the heart no less than at the eye.

René Allio may be, as I hear, a good set designer; as a filmmaker, he seems hopeless. *The Shameless Old Lady* was saved by Sylvie; Allio's wife, Malka Ribovska, couldn't save a kitten from drowning, and certainly not a dud like *The Other One.* A play-within-the-film shows a production of *Uncle Vanya,* with such excellent actors as Philippe Noiret and Claude Dauphin, and I kept unsuccessfully trying to will the Chekhov into swallowing up the Allio. *Far from Vietnam,* a collaboration by six filmmakers (one of them, you guessed it, Godard!), is a clumsy piece of agit-prop anti-Americana, but it has its points of interest, viz. Joris Ivens's views of embattled North Vietnam, infected though they were with prettifying distortion. For all my hatred of the

Vietnam war, I do not readily respond to tendentious oversimplification.

Another double bill of documentaries consisted of the Canadian Donald Brittain's *Memorandum,* an often effective reportage about some concentration-camp survivors revisiting their former places of torture; and of *The Lion Hunters,* a truly ghastly film by Jean Rouch. In it, a group of abysmal African hunters, with bone-mangling steel traps and poisoned arrows, hunt down in the most craven and pain-inflicting fashion lions that show intelligence, courage, and nobility far beyond that of the mumbo-jumbo-mumbling fools who inhumanly kill them. Rouch thinks that these black hunters are the dying remnants of an ancient chivalric order; in their program notes, the festival directors call the film an "epic poem." If that be chivalry and epic poetry, the sooner both of them are totally extinct, the better.

I did not see two revivals from the Hollywood of 1929, *Applause* and *Show People;* I leave the unearthing of such neglected non-masterpieces to the Camp followers who so abundantly deserve them. Nor did I see Shirley Clarke's *Portrait of Jason:* 100-minute outpourings of a drug-and-drink-sodden, goaded and taunted Negro male whore strike me not as *cinéma-vérité* (itself banal enough) but as egregious lack of *cinéma-charité.* But I did see Mark Donskoi's platitudinous and archaic tribute to Lenin's mother, *Sons and Mothers.* Its Russian title, *A Mother's Heart,* rightly suggests not Turgenev or Lawrence, but the tear-jerking Eduardo de Amicis. In the Special Showings, I also caught a few documentaries, among which *The Titicut Follies* seemed thought-provoking, and *Warrendale* and *Every Seventh Child* absolutely required viewing.

October–November, 1967

UNMAGNIFICENT SEVENTH

The Seventh New York Film Festival opened with a picture that was not only slick, commercial, typically Hollywood and thus hardly suitable for a festival—let alone a festival opener—it was also something worse: one of the most dishonest films ever made, and, therefore, loathsome. *Bob & Carol & Ted & Alice* (hereinafter called *BCTA,* though *&&&,* or even *$$$,* might be more appropriate) cops out not just at the end but right off the bat, making it a new and more contemptible genre: a cop-in.

BCTA begins, to the sounds of the Hallelujah Chorus, with a young married couple, Bob and Carol, arriving in their fancy sports car at something called The Institute, which is meant to represent Esalen. The Institute nestles in the mountains, and the first sign of it is three typical Hollywood starlets kneeling stark naked on the edge of a plateau and ostensibly sunbathing, but actually setting the tone for the film. They are much too good to be true, and their attitude, preposterous for tanning, suggests some esoteric Indian love ritual. We see other folk in various stages of jolly undress, including a grizzled patriarch in a wooden tub reading the *New York Review of Books*—after the sexual, the intellectual cachet. Or, conversely, the joke may be on those who read that magazine. A laugh for everyone, egghead or boob.

After various shots of bucolic-erotic serendipity, we see Bob and Carol in a group-therapy session. Now group therapy, more than any activity I can think of, brings out ambiguous feelings in the observer. Are these people in search of such things as "a better orgasm," as one weird-looking redhead puts it, to be taken with compassion or derision? A crying girl's false eyelashes begin to come off—is that pathos or travesty? A man introduces himself as "the group leader," and quickly corrects himself, "Well, group leader is too strong a word." Later on, he is weeping along with, and lying virtually on top of, Bob and Carol in one of their semiprivate moments—is he to be viewed as a humane therapist or a ridiculous quack? The scene ends with a human pyramid piled up in a corner, everyone clinging to one another for dear life—is this meant to be touching, inspiring, or imbecile?

You have now guessed what the tone of *BCTA* will be throughout: perfectly uncommitted exploitation of socio-sexual phenomena, sometimes slanting toward the funny, sometimes toward the nasty, but even the slanting always undercut by its polar opposite. You can thus take the film any way you please—as a daring comedy essentially affirming the sexual revolution, or as a daring comedy essentially satirizing the sexual revolution—and, in either case, feel smugly up-to-date laughing at its pusillanimous japes.

So in the next scene we see our documentary filmmaker, Bob, and his Carol dining in a restaurant with their friends: Ted, a young lawyer, and Alice, his wife. How anyone making documentary films can be as rich as Bob is shown to be, or how anyone successfully practicing law can be as generally cloddish as Ted, remains, like so many other questions, blithely unanswered.

Bob and Carol are dressed in dude hippie gear, Ted and Alice in classic Los Angeles expensive. Without going into the whole ludicrous scene, let us examine only a fragment of it. Bob demands to know what

Ted thinks of his long hair. For a while Ted insists that it looks just fine. Bob taunts him on until Ted hesitantly concedes: "I feel it's a little long." "That's *beau*tiful!" Bob bursts out rapturously and goads on: "You think I'm a middle-aged man trying to look young?" At last Ted erupts, "O.K., I think your hair looks ridiculous!" Whereupon both Bob and Carol warble "Oh, that's *beau*tiful!" and similar expressions of ecstasy. In fact, the word "beautiful" and the ejaculations "I love you!" and "I'm so moved!" recur as refrains throughout the film, always with the same sleazy ambivalence. As an expression of legitimate feelings this is, of course, inadequate; as satire, it is too glib and easy.

What is happening? Is Bob applying Institute techniques to get Ted to express genuine emotions, and thus performing a fine therapeutic task? Then why all those jargon-ridden, ridiculous exclamations? Or are we to understand that he is dangerously meddling with Ted and Alice's peaceably conventional values, and provoking trouble both in their marriage and between the two friendly couples? In that case, why are Ted and Alice portrayed as thick squares simply begging to be kicked? In fact, all four of these creatures are made out to be comic zombies of one sort or another; no one is sympathized with and everyone is made ridiculous—sometimes with clever, accurate ridicule, more often with stale comedy turns.

Which leads me to the kind of movie this really is. Larry Tucker, producer and co-author, and Paul Mazurski, co-author and director, are graduates of The Second City cabaret. *BCTA* is really a set of cabaret skits cavalierly pasted together and sometimes inconsistent (Ted and Alice, for example, have one child, yet Ted twice refers to their "kids"). But what pervails consistently is an atmosphere of antipathy toward all four characters, not to mention the minor figures who put in unappetizing marginal appearances.

Now in the cabaret sketch everyone can be absurd or repellent, because what matters is not the people but the joke. We are not in the company of the characters long enough to have to take any of them seriously, except as exemplifying some contemporary lunacy; the important element is the conspiratorial bond between sketch-writer and audience, a chain whose links are laughs. In a full-length work, however, we must sympathize with somebody. Even in such out-and-out satire as *Candide* or *Gulliver's Travels* there is always someone for whom we can feel. In *BCTA* there are only oafs—both before and behind the camera.

Comic bit follows on comic bit. Bob commits adultery and his wife is so enlightened about it that it rather upsets him. Carol proceeds to share the wonderful, moving secret of Bob's peccadillo with Alice and Ted, which upsets the hell out of them. Next, Carol commits her little adultery, and Bob is first furious (double-standard joke), then all too sophisticatedly understanding (single-standard joke). Next, the repressed and henpecked Ted finally commits his little adultery.

Then comes Alice's scene with her psychiatrist, played by a real-life psychoanalyst. This is a funny scene but, again, a dishonest one, getting laughs from a disregard of even minimal verisimilitude (the analyst has never heard of words like "weewee" or "teetee"), from inconsistency of character (the prissy, puritanical Alice runs around in the nude in front of her young son), and from the usual ambivalent presentation (the analyst, though apparently sound and efficient, is extraordinarily unprepossessing and indulges in some peculiar, unprofessional lip-smacking).

For the grand finale, the two couples go off to Vegas for a holiday, and as they are having drinks in one of their two adjoining hotel suites, Alice—yes, Alice!—proposes a bit of wife-swapping. At first there is some embarrassment, but Alice is forthwith declared a *"beau*tiful woman" who sees "where it's at"; it is reiterated on all sides that it would be "purely, purely physical," and that "first we'll have an orgy and then we'll go see Tony Bennett."

Whereupon, instead of each rearranged couple retiring to a separate bedroom, all four orgiasts pile into the same bed—and have no fear, good people, none of the stars exposes an unseemly bit of flesh to the camera (a smidgin of Natalie Wood's arse no longer raises intimations of an "X" rating). Briefly they play footsie under the blanket, and then rue or common sense or the eye on the box office sets in, and they hastily get dressed again. They are off to hear Tony Bennett (a socially condoned obscenity). In the elevator, they still look gloomy and repentant, but as the sound track intones a grand cop-out song about "What the World Needs Now Is Love, Sweet Love," they begin to cheer up.

Now for the super-cop-out. They step onto the plaza in front of the hotel and here, as the ghastly song continues, they become part of one of those Fellinian closing parades (bad enough in Fellini): all kinds of people, young and old, fat and thin, hirsute and glabrous, black, yellow and white, whirl about exchanging loving looks and coming into fraternal bodily contact with one another. The whole world is united in a dance of love and brotherhood, and even the dishonest pretenses to social comment are swept away on tides of simon-pure saccharine. *O tempora! O mores!* O Tucker! O Mazurski!

That the New York Film Festival should have opened with this piece of corrupt drivel is a lasting testimonial to either the cloddishness or the greed of its judges (though one of these, Andrew Sarris, has hastened to dissociate himself from this selection). Most likely it represents the eagerness to start with a film that brings with it an assurance of Hollywood hoopla: glittering stars at the opening-night party and copious press coverage the morning after.

The rest of the Seventh Festival was, for the most part, equally unsatisfactory. Six further films were abysmal, four downright bad, five feeble, one mildly interesting, two worth seeing, two superior achievements, and one (von Stroheim's *Merry Widow*, 1925) unseen by me. Let us get the abysmal ones out of the way first.

Judit Elek's *The Lady from Constantinople* is a piece of Hungarian mock *cinéma-vérité* in which we follow the mild tribulations of an elderly woman who finds it hard to adjust to the Communist society. It is the most pallid of films, trying, apparently, to side with the woman (who, by the way, is not Turkish; the Hungarian title means "Isle on the Mainland") but has to do it with desperate, self-defeating caution. The film rambles by monotonously, and registers on the eye and mind as one vast expanse of gray.

The next horror was *Lions Love,* Agnès Varda's attempt at a more sophisticated version of an Andy Warhol film. For this she used such campy performers as Viva, Warhol's superstar; Jerome Ragni and James Rado, the author-actors of *Hair;* and Shirley Clarke, the avant-garde filmmaker and "personality." Like other *faux-naïf* works, this is a tiresome pursuit of a kind of spontaneity not all that good even when it is spontaneous, and the intermittent moments of fun hardly justify watching the slow leakage of hot air from overinflated human balloons for two unending hours. Particularly distasteful are some fifteen to twenty minutes during which these jackanapes watch Robert Kennedy's life, death, and funeral on TV. They comment on it fatuously, and, as a final insult, the film equates the assassination of Kennedy with the shooting of Andy Warhol. The whole thing is dragged in only to give this epicene hogwash social significance.

An even greater, because more deadly serious, abomination was Marguerite Duras's new film, *Destroy, She Said.* Hitherto the author was content to write bad novels or bad scripts for other directors; here for the second time she combined writing and directing, and the result seems not so much bad doubled as bad cubed.

Two men and two women, in weirdly posed, arbitrary groupings, make endless, arcanely opaque statements past one another. It is supposed to take place in a hotel, but it is obviously someone's country house and backyard. You never see anyone else (though you hear the sounds of a ghost tennis game—*Son of Blow-Up?*), except for the husband of one of the women who shows up at the end of the film to be pounced on by the other four; there is no action, minimal movement, and only that somnambulistic dialogue which, Mlle Duras proudly affirms, is interchangeable. In the end, there is the obligatory Bach fugue, by now indispensable to true avant-garde films, which is heard in a huge crescendo signifying, according to the author, the coming of the Revolution. It could as easily signify the rising birth rate or the devaluation of the franc.

A mess of a different, more pitiful, sort was Walerian Borowczyk's *Goto, Island of Love.* Borowczyk, a Polish refugee living in France, has previously made animated films which, hailed as art, struck me as mostly ghoulishly morbid. *Goto* shows Borowczyk totally unable to tell a story on film, what with ellipses and lacunas and important plot elements to be found only in the program notes. He also uses the most static camera since Marguerite Duras's. The story, in any case, is not worth telling—something about an imaginary island kingdom fraught with tyranny and intrigue, on the level of Pogo's adventures in Kafkaland. The film stars Ligia Branice, alias Mme Borowczyk, who is as untalented as she is unappealing; and Pierre Brasseur, who is a great actor to whom *Goto* shouldn't have happened.

There followed Godard's *Le Gai Savoir,* in which that master's usually well-controlled balance getween inanity and insanity reaches a new perfection, so that it is absolutely impossible to say whether the film is a triumph of imbecility or dementia, though triumph it surely is. The callow Jean-Pierre Léaud, here called Émile Rousseau (get it?), and the puffy-faced Juliet Berto, here dubbed Patricia Lumumba, sit around in artful pitch-blackness blotting out everything except them— and sometimes, though not often enough, even them—and discuss art, politics, life, with Godard's usual, manically misanthropic radicalism posturing as humanitarianism, and much of the time meaning nothing at all.

That is fine, however, because language, it seems, is the root of all evil and must be reinvented. A typical Godardian profundity is that we must not "start from zero," we must "go back to zero." (For Godard, conveniently, the journey couldn't be shorter.) There are, in *Le Gai Savoir,* the customary visual word games, a few staged interviews (one with a babbling youngster and one with a babbling oldster), some shots of posters and other printed matter, one or two dull city-scapes deliberately unrelated to anything. Otherwise it is those two blank faces surrounded by blackness pretentiously gibbering away about the evils of language.

The final horror of the Festival was Pasolini's *Pigpen,* in which two non-stories are intercut. One is medieval, has only one sentence of dialogue (but that repeated thrice), and concerns a young robber-rapist-murderer and his gang who feed on the people they kill. Apprehended at last, they are tied up and left for the dogs to devour. This gives the bandit (played by the repellent Pierre Clémenti) a chance to reiterate his one line, "I slew my father, ate human flesh, and tremble with joy." The other story is contemporary, contains almost nothing but dialogue, and concerns the son of an ex-Nazi and still thriving millionaire. The son (played by the loutish Jean-Pierre Léaud) mouths all sorts of mystical and philosophical claptrap, and resists the advances of a willing girl (played by the new Mme Godard, the repugnant Anne Wiazemsky). It turns out that he has intercourse only with pigs.

There are discussions of business, politics, and war crimes among the elders; there are assertions of neutrality by the protagonist, who will have no truck with his parents but also refuses to join the girl in a protest pissing on the Berlin Wall; and there are some pretty shots of pigs' anuses. If you thought that after *Teorema* there was nowhere for Pasolini to go but up, another one of your cherished notions is hereby shattered.

Moving up the scale from the abysmal films, we come to the merely bad ones. First of these was Robert Bresson's *Une Femme Douce.* Bresson is one of those haunted filmmakers (Buñuel is another) who can turn out a most impressive film when his subject properly interlocks with his manias or fixations. But when the theme refuses to be ruled by the passion, the discrepancy becomes a chasm into which the undertaking irretrievably collapses. Some of Bresson's early films proved suitable vehicles for his brand of paradoxical Christianity (not unrelated to Mauriac's and Graham Greene's), and, even when the subject was ostensibly secular, allowed this ascetic, devious mind to produce something artistic and meaningful.

In *Une Femme Douce,* however, Bresson updates a Dostoevsky story about a woman's loveless marriage to a pawnbroker, with suicide providing the only escape. I have not read the story, "A Gentle Woman," but it is quite obvious that marriage, money-lending, divorce, etc., were not the same in Dostoevsky's Russia as in today's Paris, and that the *données* of the story are unsuited for this kind of modernization. Nor are they any more suited to what Bresson is best at: the single-minded, often fanatical, working out of a scheme or mission (an escape, a vengeance, salvation) to its inexorable conclusion. Perseverance as destiny and Grace, redemption through love or suffering—these things accord ill with a modern, middle-class, urban marriage. And Bresson's viewing that marriage through metaphysical blinkers seems, in the context, capricous rather than dedicated, unbalanced rather than inspired.

A detailed discussion of the film must wait until its release. Let me simply say here that the use of the camera, the treatment of the story, the choice of performers, the handling of symbols, all attest to Bresson's constrictive obsessions and display a view of life that I find medieval, arid, and just as impoverishing as the mode of existence it attacks. It is noteworthy that this esthetically and morally questionable film should have elicited the most rapturous praise in the *New York Times* from Roger Greenspun, whose *auteur*-happy reviews manage to be a blot on that paper's critical scutcheon even though it is by now all blot and no scutcheon.

Boy is a film that tries to use Western avant-garde modes of obliquity in telling a rather humdrum tale of petty larceny in contemporary Japan. Unfortunately, the director, Nagisa Oshima, has nothing much to say about his characters. The film tells of a partly disabled war veteran who teaches his wife and young son how to pretend they have been hit by passing cars and collect hefty sums for not going to the police. Though there are vague attempts at examining how these activities affect the psyches involved, and their relation to one another, the film stays close to the surface, and the surface is far from interesting.

Nevertheless, one scene remains visually haunting: two small boys squatting in front of a snowman in an otherwise empty, flat, snowy landscape. The color film's way of rendering this essentially monochromatic subject matter, combined with the starkness of the widescreen composition, makes for an impact comparable to that of certain modern paintings where the figure is pushed as far as it will go toward abstraction. But this is insufficient to redeem a hollow film.

Susan Sontag, besides being a Festival judge, was represented by her first film, *Duet for Cannibals.* Suspicions of nepotism are, I think, unfounded, for the film is fully bad enough to have made it to the Festival on its own merit. It was shot in Sweden with a Swedish cast, except for Adriana Asti, the Italian actress who, ever since *Before the Revolution,* has been a great favorite with female critics like the Misses Kael and Sontag, and with practically nobody else.

The plot—for there is one—concerns a student couple. Tomas and Ingrid, living together in nonmarital bliss until Tomas goes to work for Bauer, a German Communist leader living in activist exile in Stockholm. It soon becomes apparent that he needs the youth less as a secretary than as a companion for his extremely, shall we say, peculiar wife, Francesca, whom he apparently can no longer satisfy. Tomas is

finally drawn or shoved into an affair with Francesca, who, along with
Bauer, behaves ever more oddly and inconsistently. At last, Ingrid is
also summoned to the Bauers', and a multivalent *ménage à quatre* ensues
(even lesbianism is hinted at, but whenever the film sidles up to it, there
is prompt backtracking), in which Albee-esque humiliation of the
young couple is the Bauers' main objective. Tomas and Ingrid finally
escape, pursued by the Bauers' jeering laughter.

There is a good deal of political and sexual chitchat in *Duet,* and, as
in so many avant-garde movies, the tape recorder becomes one of the
characters. There is also, as in Godard, much reading from books, here
specifically from *The Divine Comedy.* Tomas reads it to the Italian
Francesca in Swedish, and she recites back at him in Italian, thus
affording Miss Asti a chance to dazzle us with her Tuscan—the "vulgar
tongue" as Dante and his contemporaries called it, no doubt foreseeing
displays of this kind.

The Sontag script is a derivative hodgepodge, and cannot even claim
to lose anything in the subtitles, since they are the author's original.
Nor has she done better as director. There are the obligatory Godard
camera movements, the Bresson shots, the Antonioni scene (Francesca
and Ingrid exchanging wigs and personalities before a mirror), even a
device out of Olmi's *The Fiancés* (placing a character within a landscape
that is actually painted on a wall), and all that heap of lifting it takes
to make film a forum. There is no original contribution I can detect,
but I must concede that, although three of the Festival's films contained
vomiting scenes, the one in *Duet for Cannibals* was by far the creepiest.

In an interview with the *Times,* Miss Sontag has declared that "Dostoevsky's personal problems would get in the way of being a film
director." *Duet for Cannibals* may not be worth much as film, but at
least it proves that Miss Sontag has no personal problems.

The Deserter and the Nomads is the second film by the Slovak *cinéaste*
Juro Jakubisko, and though it is more mad than bad, it is also quite bad.
It deals with disheartening incidents from the Slovak past (Austro-
Hungarian tyranny), recent past (Russian tyranny), and future (Ar-
mageddon), all involving war and death. It is desperately naïve—there
are more shot people picturesquely rolling down hillsides than in a
whole kindergarten playing Cowboys and Indians; sedulously arty—
one murderous shoot-up takes place among a flock of geese that get it
bloodily in the neck; and magniloquently metaphysical—the character
Death finally revolts against God in the customary upward-aimed
soliloquies accompanied by profuse eyeball-rolling. All this is photographed by Jakubisko himself with many a fine pretentious and amateurish effect, but also with a sort of insane conviction in the urgency

of the message that makes it almost as touching as it is exasperating. Regretfully, I must include among the feeble films (my next category) Ingmar Bergman's *The Ritual*. It was made for television and has that preponderance of medium and close shots, as well as sparseness of *mise en scène*, that marks TV films and makes them appear agoraphobic on the large screen. Worse than that, this is one of those cases where Bergman indulges his private anxieties and symbolism to the extent of losing the ordinary viewer and excluding even the exegete. Although there are typically lovely performances from Gunnar Björnstrand and Ingrid Thulin, and Bergman brings back to his repertory company the splendid Anders Ek, absent since *The Seventh Seal*, this is a brittle, talky film, lacking the visual impact of Bergman's fully achieved works. It is chiefly distinguished by the fact that verbal description of sexual intercourse reaches previously unheard explicitness. Which makes *The Ritual*, if it was actually broadcast, a landmark not for Bergman, but for Swedish television.

I was present at the world premiere in Paris of Max Ophüls's *La Ronde* (1950), a film that drags on and on by what feels like geometric progression, and was roundly booed at that Palais de Chaillot gala event. I do hope that I joined in the booing (though I can't remember for sure), because, as its Festival revival confirmed, this is yet another example of Ophüls's trivial and nerveless filmmaking. A play as intimate as Schnitzler's sequence of ten duologues, *Reigen*, does not, for all its brilliance, belong on the screen. The scenes, each of them a prologue and epilogue to a seduction, thrive on the snugness with which the proscenium arch frames their filigree foibles and follies. The film was to be remade fourteen years later by Roger Vadim, with his customary vulgarity; the Ophüls version is not vulgar, merely the director's usual sentimental confection. Schnitzler's basic tough-mindedness is lost amid all that fun and froth.

Ophüls tried to find a unifying image to tie together this sexual round-dance, and came up with a carrousel operated by a master of ceremonies in top hat and tails. It is not in itself a bad metaphor (the printed play uses a set of dashes to indicate intercourse), but it is coy and somewhat sugary, with its suggestions of the Prater, Gay Vienna, and the rest—an atmosphere reinforced by the banal music of Oscar Straus and Joë Hajos. (The mood of the play is both more realistic and more acerbic.) As the ringmaster, Anton Walbrook gives his usual faintly stilted and wooden performance, further disadvantaged by not having Schnitzler to write the lines.

Ophüls does not get very good work from the majority of his famed actors. Isa Miranda is a disaster as the primadonna, and her thick Italian accent hopelessly smudges her already poorly delivered speeches. Odette Joyeux is much too old for the sweet young thing, and Barrault gives one of his most cramped and humorless performances as the playwright. Particularly pitiful is the mishandling of that exquisite actor, Gérard Philipe, whom Ophüls turns into the semicretinous Count Bobby of the Viennese jokes, rather than into the typical Royal and Imperial officer Schnitzler created. But the *auteur*-critics, who with characteristic lack of taste (taste does not need such surrogates as auteurism) worship Ophüls, pronounce *La Ronde* a masterpiece. I urge you to read the play (if possible, in German), see the film, and put an end to auteurism.

Another Festival revival was Victor Sjöstrom's *He Who Gets Slapped* (1924), from Leonid Andreyev's foolishly tear-jerking play. Sjöstrom, now remembered mostly for his portrayal of Professor Borg in *Wild Strawberries,* was an important early Swedish filmmaker, but neither in Sweden nor in Hollywood a great director. For all its grandiose trick photography—rather heavy-handed and obvious—the film is the standard commercial product of Hollywood, where Sjöstrom was active for a while. Lon Chaney, John Gilbert, and Norma Shearer give unmemorable performances, Miss Shearer even erasing my memories of her as a very attractive woman.

The most controversial in this group of feeble films was Eric Rohmer's *Ma Nuit chez Maud.* Rohmer is yet another *Cahiers* critic turned Old Wave director, and what I have seen of his previous work (*The Sign of the Lion,* and one segment of a group effort, *Paris as Seen by . . .*) filled me with a great lack of expectation, which *Maud* fully justified. The film is set in Clermont-Ferrand, Pascal's birthplace and the French equivalent of Dubuque. The young engineer hero is a good, fallible practicing Catholic, who spots a blonde at Mass and starts pursuing her. Meanwhile he runs into an old classmate, a Marxist-atheist professor, who takes him to dinner at the house of Maud, his off-and-on mistress.

Maud is a doctor, divorcée, and freethinker, a lively and attractive brunette. The dinner provides the occasion for a long debate on the relative merits of Catholic abstinence and Marxist indulgence in carnal joys, a discussion rather too academic for cinema, and too sophomoric for philosophy. Pascal is quoted and analyzed in ways that fail to ignite either verbally or visually, but that masochists and auteurists may find entrancing. As for me, the eternal chatter of these infinite vacuums frightens me.

With the complicity of her ex-lover and a snowstorm, Maud keeps the engineer overnight, but neither her charms nor her charmingly teasing provocations can get him to make love to her—until, at dawn, he becomes most eager, only to find her no longer in the mood. Soon thereafter, the engineer accosts his blonde, makes a date with her, and spends an even more platonic night in an empty room of her hostel. Though to anyone less than blind or benighted she would seem much less desirable than Maud, our hero woos and wins the blonde by taking her to early Mass: the early worshiper gets the bird in marriage. This in spite of the fact that Maud makes yet a few tentative maneuvers in the engineer's direction. In an ironic epilogue we are told by the now remarried Maud what we guessed long since: that the blonde is the ex-mistress of Maud's ex-husband.

As *scènes de la vie de province,* this is more boring than what it depicts. The hero's dilemma, if such it be, is treated lackadaisically, and nothing compels us to get involved, either emotionally or intellectually, in the excellence or unwisdom of the protagonist's choice. If the film is meant as an existential inquiry, why all that coincidence and anecdotal cuteness; if as a story, why so denuded of incident? Françoise Fabian is first-rate as Maud, but Jean-Louis Trintignant is bloodless in a part in which he is clearly unhappy. *Ma Nuit chez Maud* is number three of a series entitled *Six Moral Tales,* so we can look forward to five more.

Another feeble but at least unpretentious film was the Senegalese Ousmane Sembène's *Mandabi.* In it, an illiterate loafer and scrounger tries to cash a money order and comes up against all the chicaneries of capitalist bureaucracy as well as ordinary human profiteering, until he ends up losing not only the money order (most of which was not meant for him in the first place) but also, it would seem, his and his two wives' house. All this would be bearable in its diluted Mark Twainish or O. Henryish way, if the end did not erupt with a full-fledged Communist harangue to the little people to unite in political action against the capitalist system. At that point the severe improbabilities of the foregoing plot cease to look like harmless exaggerations, and become instead politically loaded dice. Sembène is a clever strategist, though: he has used for the basis of his film a story by Léopold Sédar Senghor, the President of Senegal, and was thus able to raise the capital for his radical propaganda movie.

A mildly interesting item was *The Epic That Never Was,* a British TV documentary that pieces together Alexander Korda's ill-fated attempt to produce a colossal film out of Robert Graves's marvelous historical novel, *I, Claudius.* This unfinished superspectacular—with Charles Laughton, Merle Oberon, Flora Robson, Emlyn Williams, Robert Newton—is shown here in the fragments that were filmed, along with reminiscences of the survivors (from 1937, date of the film, to 1965, date of the documentary) explaining what sank the titanic venture. Some of it is amusing, though Dirk Bogarde makes an insufferably self-conscious narrator, and it is instructive at least in showing what a vulgar phony the original director was: Josef von Sternberg, the darling of all good *auteur*-critics.

Three of the Seventh Festival's films fell into the "worth seeing" category. The first of these was Jaromil Jireš's *The Joke*, about which I will write when it is released. So, too, about René Allio's *Pierre & Paul.* Already released is the third in this category, *Oh! What a Lovely War*—an essentially bad film, yet worth seeing for certain ancillary reasons.

It is now fashionable to say that Richard Attenborough's film version of Joan Littlewood's musical revue misses the bite of the original. At the time of the show's Broadway appearance, I wrote in the *Hudson Review:* "... what might have been mordant as a taut, ten-minute revue sketch cannot begin to make sense as a mellow evening's entertainment. . . . However appalling the casualty figures running along the electrical band may be, in the end we can no longer respond keenly to the one-dimensional satire (particularly when combined with sentimentality about the little man), and more and more we find ourselves responding to the foolish ballads rather than to the flagging bite." This is even truer of the film.

The movie *Oh! What a Lovely War* is a sedulous kind of fun that keeps lapsing into dread earnest, but must always stop short of letting anyone bite the dust. Whereas the show was a collection of skits and song-and-dance numbers, the film (the adaptation, by the way, is credited to no one) tries for something grander, which is to say, easier: it invents a rudimentary plot, tracing a quasi-eponymous Smith family's involvement in World War I. We still get world politics as a parlor game on Brighton Pier, the Army and the War as a carnival show, the General Staff as a bunch of infantile intriguers sometimes literally leapfrogging over one another; but we also get realistic scenes of trench warfare, field hospitals, railway stations with trains disgorging the wounded, and so on.

Through all this we are invited to follow the fortunes of the large, emblematic Smith family—its fighting men, its waiting and working women, its bemused or blissfully uncomprehending children. Bertie Smith is a subaltern officer, the others are noncoms and enlisted men, and through them we see life at the front in a curiously ambivalent way: much of the simulated horror of war, but no on-screen deaths; a good deal of antiheroics but also quite a bit of heroics. And, of course, the swinish cowardice and incompetence of upper-class generals and the noncombatant rich (all perfect bloody rotters), and the bloody marvelous decency of the common soldier, whether English or German. And the songs, delightful in their cajoling and cocky ways, but, overorchestrated in the film, are less satire than things to be stirred by.

There are sentimental and bombastic scenes—enemies fraternizing in no-man's-land on Christmas Day, nurses intoning the-pity-of-it-all soliloquies; and there is army humor of every sort, some of it even funny. There is a refreshing touch of anticlericalism in a front-line church service scene, and there are some good tear-jerking effects. Three scenes are gripping: a pacifist speech by the suffragette Emmeline Pankhurst, splendidly delivered by Vanessa Redgrave; a final helicopter shot of a rolling emerald plain studded with numberless dazzling white crosses, which, say what you will, is a heartbreakingly magnificent sight; and one funny and frightful sequence at a patriotic vaudeville show that ends with a chanteuse (brilliantly played by Maggie Smith) recruiting gullible civilians by the dozen. The staging of that scene, including one brief closeup in which the soubrette suddenly looks like a painted image of death, is comic and pathetic and pointed —if only the whole film were more like it!

Oh! What a Lovely War is ultimately a naïve, sentimental, populist affair, using many (too many) clever devices yet making the same old simplistic statements. There are those three good scenes and one or two others almost as good; there is very respectable color photography by Gerry Turpin; and there are the music and the performances. This is also one of those films awash with stars and near-stars, and there is many a commanding cameo performance, as well as excellent work by newcomers. Some of the veterans disappoint—Gielgud, John Mills, Kenneth More; others, like Olivier, Richardson, Redgrave, Robert Flemyng, do not miss a trick. Of the younger generation, Joe Melia, as the M.C., has the best part, but all are fine. A misguided film, flounderingly directed by a superb actor, with some fringe benefits.

The two genuinely worthy films of the festival were Ermanno Olmi's *One Fine Day,** which I'll review on its release, and Bo Widerberg's *Ådalen '31,* already showing. Widerberg's *Elvira Madigan* was a ravishingly beautiful film with a scenario that was barely mediocre, except for its strong last scene. *Ådalen '31* uses the same device of telling a depressing story based on facts in exquisite surroundings photographed

*August 1970: This remarkable film has still not been released. The reason? A remarkably wrongheaded and illiterate negative review from Vincent Canby in the *New York Times,* enough to frighten Janus Films, which owns the rights.

(by the same Jörgen Persson) in colors that sing out from the screen. Except that here the contrast works because it is more than a lyrical-pathetic setting for a sob story: natural beauty becomes an eloquent reproach to the unnatural injustices in man's life.

Sweden, 1931, the small northern town of Ådalen. We are in the heart of that long-awaited, short-lived north-country summer. Everything would be lovely if the workers in the sawmills were not on strike—not even for a raise, only against a proposed wage cut. There is hunger skulking about, but also a spirit of true comradeship. One worker in particular seems to be the mainstay of this quiet, dignified strike. He is the father of the youthful hero, Kjell, who is conducting an innocent affair with Anna, the daughter of one of the mill owners. They and their young chums lead reasonably normal lives while the grownups plot and counterplot.

Scabs are brought in but are beaten down by the strikers. Just as Anna is hustled off by her mother to Stockholm to have an abortion, the bosses call in the army. There is a bloody confrontation. Kjell's father, the very man who always counseled reason, is killed; so are the hero's best friend and three other people. Anna's father tries to apologize for the abortion to the enraged Kjell. Kjell's brave mother and her children begin to adjust to their loss. As a result of the Ådalen affair, Sweden goes Socialist but, as an ironic closing note states, true Socialism has still not prevailed.

That is a crude outline. There are scenes of charming humor (Kjell's friend trying to seduce girls by means of hypnotism) and of sharp insight (a drunken army officer being thrown out by the mill owners following the massacre accuses them of washing their hands of the army after it has done their dirty work). But mostly there are compassionate scenes of family and community living under stress, and plain, amiable vignettes of everyday incidents. Widerberg, who once again wrote his own script, has a warm regard for people that only rarely goes soft, and a mirthful eye for human absurdities that never lapses into the voyeuristic. There is something of the child about him, with all that entails of naïveté and oversimplification, but also of purity and unfettered fancy.

In its view of politics and tragedy, the film is less than profound or even sophisticated. But we do get a buoyant feeling for nature—the way flowers and greenery are always there between clashing men; for humble tasks—the way washing windows together brings the grieving family back into the routine of living; for innocent young lovers—the way Kjell's and Anna's affair is neither patronized nor prettified. A scene may be effectively improvised—as when Kjell's father argues

with the young roughnecks among the strikers, or when the boy's little
brother (played by Widerberg's son) is allowed to be a genuine child
on screen. Other scenes, like those surrounding the massacre, are carefully staged and composed, yet they too, preserve the element of
unpredictability and surprise, as if the actors never knew what would
happen next, or what hit them.

Fine, too, are Widerberg's period sense, previously demonstrated in
such films as *Raven's End* and *Elvira Madigan,* and his judicious, inventive camera placements—study, for example, Anna's and her mother's
drive to the station through the strife-torn town. The director gets
delightful and humane performances from both professionals and amateurs in his cast, from adults and children alike. He edits his film with
a deceptive leisureliness inside which excitement and pathos slowly
ripen to burst forth like horse chestnuts from their husks.

While *Ådalen '31* seems to me only halfway up Widerberg's ascent
to cinematic importance, it is not a film to be dismissed lightly. The
name of Auguste Renoir is often invoked in it, and Widerberg is a sort
of filmic Renoir: not the Renoir of the sugary salon paintings, but the
artist who took chances—who told Vollard that "there's not a single
process, no matter how insignificant, which can be reasonably made
into a formula."

But the Festival also, for one of its sideshows, dredged up the *oeuvre*
of Renoir *fils,* the filmmaker Jean Renoir, rapturously extolled by
auteur-critics everywhere, and, indeed, by normal critics as well. We
were treated to an exhaustive Renoir retrospective, which proved one
of my saddest and most mysterious movie-going experiences. Sad because these Renoir films, or those I could sit through, emerged, with
one or two exceptions, trivial, banal, sentimental, and mindless, and
composed the portrait of a vastly overrated *petit-maître:* a plodding,
simple-minded, stagy director, a man with an infantile vision and wobbly style, capable of perpetrating such atrocities as *Nana* (1926) and
The Little Match Girl (1928) in his early period, and such doddering
fooolishnesses as *French Cancan* (1955) and *Le Testament du Docteur
Cordelier* (1961) in his late.

The mystery is how, in his middle period, Renoir was able to make
two or three respectable films, and, above all, that masterpiece, *The
Rules of the Game* (1939). I understand his stumbling on partial success
in *Le Crime de Monsieur Lange* with the help of Jacques Prévert's dialogue and Jules Berry's sparkling performance, or in *The Grand Illusion*
with the help of a brilliant set of actors: Gabin, Fresnay, von Stroheim,
and Dalio. But how in that same middle period a man could make
turkeys like *La Marseillaise* and *Diary of a Chambermaid* and the won-

drous *La Règle du jeu,* only the *auteur*-critics can explain, and their explanations are less clear than what they explicate.

October, 1969

OSCARS: THEY SHUN THE BEST, DON'T THEY?

The 1969 Oscar nominations are out and look, at first glance, like an improvement over past years. But, upon slightly closer scrutiny, what might be called the Third Law of Thermodynamics becomes manifest: *plus ça change, plus c'est la même chose,* or, in English, there are no changes, only changes rung on the old tunes.

If the Oscars, the annual awards of the Motion Picture Academy, were taken simply as an excuse for Bob Hope to crack his occasionally funny jokes, and for the denizens of Hollywood to show off their expensively tacky gowns and toupees, there might be nothing seriously objectionable about the event. The unfortunate thing is that in some, admittedly shrinking, circles, these awards are still believed to have something to do with artistic merit. Despite the disappointment and disgust many of them have been eliciting—when not resulting in mere raucous laughter—the notion persists that there is a connection between the Oscars and achievement, though perhaps invisible to the naked eye.

Well, in some cases there is. But before we get down to particulars, let us consider the principles involved. At one Oscar ceremony, Bob Hope observed that the Oscar was filmdom's most valued award because it is given by experts. It is, he declared, like praise for a wall from bricklayers, not from random passers-by. The analogy, unfortunately, does not hold. For though bricklayers may know about walls, what do they know about buildings, architecture, art? The membership of the Motion Picture Academy consists of every kind of technician and film personnel imaginable, and, frankly, a sound mixer's or grip's notion of what constitutes a good screenplay is about as relevant as a veterinarian's or, for that matter, a bricklayer's.

If we believe that the spiritual health of a society is as important as its physical health—and I do so believe—we can say that art is a major national resource, like food or good hospitals. And to reward and encourage good art—by subsidy, intelligent criticism, Oscar awards, and any other means—is precisely to further the country's spiritual health. Now who, I ask, should perform an operation: the surgeon and his assistants, or a Hospital Academy, consisting of several hundred or thousand hospital workers, including orderlies and receptionists, kitchen staff and ambulance drivers? The membership of the Academy may be qualified to adjudicate such awards as Best Sound, perhaps even Best Special Visual Effects, but beyond mere technique its competence does not extend.

Still, it might be objected, an operation means active participation, whereas giving awards is an act of passive evaluation. Nevertheless, award-giving presupposes artistic, intellectual, and cultural training and background comparable to the skill and study involved in becoming a surgeon. Consider the very name of this award-giving body: The Academy of Motion Picture Arts and Sciences. It sounds as fulsome and pretentious as, say, The Academy of Call Girl Arts and Sciences. Not because movies are not to be taken seriously, but because the Hollywood industry isn't. Thus, until fairly recently, Oscars were given only to Hollywood products. This was rather as if General Motors were to give automotive awards, and the only contenders for the Golden Glosscar were G.M. products—not even Chrysler and Ford, let alone anything foreign. Parochial, chauvinistic, and just plain stupid as this was, it was at least inadvertently honest. Then along came the Best Foreign Language Film category; Hollywood-sponsored British films became eligible in the Best Picture category (no doubt on the pleasant but overoptimistic notion that the same language was spoken in London as in Los Angeles); and, very recently, actors and actresses in foreign-language films have been up for awards.

This was truly dishonest. For the awards began to take on an air of sincere ecumenicalism above xenophobic discrimination, but, in fact, did not give foreign achievements anywhere near the chance given home-grown ones. Thus the foreign film that would get nominated was almost invariably the one that aspired to and aped Hollywood standards—a typical example being Claude Lelouch's *A Man and a Woman*, a slick item with all the Hollywood ingredients, down to a shamelessly ear-caressing theme song. When, in 1967, Ingmar Bergman's *Persona* appeared—in my opinion, the most important film of the decade—it was not even noticed by Hollywood (or, for that matter, by the New York Film Critics' Circle, though it did win the award of the National Society of Film Critics).*

*July 1970: It has since been pointed out to me that one foreign-language film is submitted by the country of its origin—but that hardly changes matters: every submitting country picks that film which it considers most to Hollywood's taste. And the MPAA nominating board then narrows down the field to five, making sure that anything too much above Hollywood's head does not get a crack at an Oscar.

Among the current five Best Foreign Language Film nominees, we find *The Battle on the Neretva,* a Yugoslav war film of huge dimensions and even huger banality. Significantly, it has had no official showings in New York, where it would have fared less well than on the Coast. What gets this dinosaur into the running, while a cold shoulder is given to such subtle, mature films as Ivan Passer's *Intimate Lighting* and Claude Chabrol's *La Femme Infidèle?* There is the fact that one of the Industry's shakiest members, Commonwealth United, sank enough money into *Neretva* to make the company's survival at least partly dependent on the film's success. One can imagine the lobbying and brainwashing that must have been conducted in behalf of *The Battle on the Neretva.* Also in its Oscar favor is that the film contains every cliché of the Hollywood war movie as hypostatized in the forties, to which you may add guest appearances by Yul Brynner and Orson Welles.

The main trouble with the Oscars is, of course, that an award of artistic significance cannot be adjudged by a large, unwieldy, semianonymous and influenceable body of *any kind*—any more than a court case can be tried by a panel of several hundred or thousand judges. Whatever their competence or even honesty, an award-giving jury of, say, three to twelve members can be kept track of, sufficiently surveyed by the press and public to be forced to behave. Not protected by anonymity, they cannot be so readily wined and dined by the better-heeled and informed contenders; or, being few and known, they can be equally wined and dined by all. And they can, at least in theory, be appointed on a basis of relevant qualifications.

What are the 1969 choices? In the Best Picture category, there is the surprising inclusion of a foreign-language film, *Z,* a contender also in the Best Foreign Language Film category—which is rather like running for office on both the Republican and the Democratic tickets. Why this fervor for *Z,* even though—or, perhaps more accurately, despite the fact that—it is a good film? It is, for one thing, a picture that has already won so many honors that one can vote for it without having to see it, just by toting up its awards. It has had, moreover, a fair share of two-page advertisements with commendations from figures prominent in such seemingly divergent fields as show business and politics. Best of all, *Z* is a politically conscious film, enthusiasm for whose liberal, indeed leftist, orientation comes cheap, since it so clearly takes place in another country, and, besides, its subversive hero is dead. Dead, along with his followers, both in the film and in Greek history, on which the movie is modeled. It is easy to be self-righteous about dead, foreign radicals, especially if, except by their fascist enemies, they are never called Communists, and, with one exception, look clean-cut and wear neckties. Significantly, when a film addresses itself to similar problems in our own beloved country, as does the uneven, in some ways severely flawed, in other ways brilliant and, for America, highly innovative *Medium Cool,* it not only does not get nominated in this category but also manages to get overlooked in all others.

Also competing for Best Picture and with nine further nominations (more than any other movie this year), is *Anne of the Thousand Days,* the quintessential work of art for people who haven't the foggiest notion of what art is. Based on a simplistic, lifeless play by Maxwell Anderson, it has been turned into a large but not so lavish spectacle; a royal love story that has little love in it, less psychological insight, and absolutely no language—either cinematic or English. But this sluggish dullard of a film conforms to Hollywood's and, for all I know, Dubuque's idea of a grand, historic document in which regal, larger-than-life-size dummies bestride the screen with pachydermous portentousness, their mouths full of spine-chilling platitudes. In a similar vein, the flattened-out, oversimplified, and uncinematic film version of a deserving stage play, *A Man for All Seasons,* won the Best Film Oscar for 1966, and the hoked-up filmization of an already insufferably coy and phony play, *The Lion in Winter,* almost won it for 1968.

Next in the field of contenders is *Butch Cassidy and the Sundance Kid,* a poor man's *Bonnie and Clyde,* or, perhaps, some other pauper's *The Wild Bunch.* What in *Bonnie* was real innovation for America (even if patently derived from the French New Wave); what in *Bunch* was a genuine vision, however romanticized, of a real time and place and problem, and smelled of humanity; this, in *Butch,* becomes a mere exercise in smart-alecky device-mongering, chock-full of out-of-place and out-of-period one-upmanship, a battle of wits at a freshman smoker.

We go up a step or two with the next nominee, *Midnight Cowboy.* This is your typical social-significance film, somewhat less wholesome and inspirational than the sermons in stone of Stanley Kramer, whose mendacious and sanctimonious drivel, *Guess Who's Coming to Dinner?,* was a recent runner-up for the Best Film. (By now, fatuity fallout is measured in microkramers: a dose of more than eleven microkramers is usually lethal.) *Midnight Cowboy* boasts the latest variation on the whore with the heart of gold, the male hustler with the golden heart; it displays homosexuals who really aren't queer at all, pathetic victims of an Evil Society who simply had no choice but to become pimps and prostitutes, and offers hope for the lost soul's redemption through the death of his lost-soulmate. There is a good deal of clever filmmaking here and first-class acting, but my Kramer counter was clicking ominously throughout. In art, you learn to live with truths; in a *Midnight Cowboy,* you are offered the alleged clean, soft underbelly of a hard, dirty truth, and nudged to shed unearned tears over it.

We descend now to the bottom for the fifth item on the list, *Hello, Dolly!* a vacuous, unwieldy, overproduced musical, with not a tune, dance step, or joke (to say nothing of plot device) in it to indicate which century it was made in. The set design is clever and abundant, and there is one filmic idea at work during the title sequence. But after the credits, everything is debit. Miscast in the lead is Barbra Streisand, last year's Oscar-winner and Hollywood's new star-child, who, unlike other children, should be heard, not seen. But she is clearly the darling of the hordes of homely women who have no trouble identifying themselves with her in full face, and feeling superior to her in profile.

Most interesting about this list is the conspicuous absence from it of *They Shoot Horses, Don't They?* Although *Horses* has received, even from the benighted Motion Picture Academy, nine nominations, including those for best director, actress, supporting actress and actor, its not making the field of five best pictures is easily explicable. It is an *honestly* downbeat film and one that can be construed as anti-American by good Birchers, and it certainly shows an aspect of American life, past but not necessarily irrelevant to the present, in all its unappetizing yet thought-provoking truth. Though the film fails in its attempt to turn drama into tragedy, it is clearly one that *by the contest's own criteria* should have been among the nominees. Similar injustices—indeed idiocies—could be demonstrated in all other categories, but my space, like your time, is limited.

To the extent that the Oscars faithfully mirror the Industry mentality, and to the extent that pleasure and interest in them wanes, there is hope. At a recent meeting of the National Society of Film Critics with Jack Valenti, head of the Motion Picture Association, Mr. Valenti asked us whether we thought that, "from the Industry's point of view," the rating system should be scrapped. My own answer was: "No, the ratings are fine. Scrap the Industry."

March, 1970

14

Critical Matters

THE CAMERA, as we find out sooner or later, photographs the photographer. Criticism of other critics may, similarly, tell us more about the person writing it than about the critics or criticism he discusses. I hope that the four following pieces do tell something about their subjects. But I am not averse to their telling something about my critical standards as well. I tried to state these in the introduction to the book; in the subsequent pieces, I *tried* to apply them to various films and filmmakers, and here, finally, I apply them to other writers about film. Perhaps my praise of some will only call attention to my own shortcomings; perhaps my dispraise of others will seem unjust and fall back on my own head. Criticism is a boomerang: it may hit its mark or come back and hit the thrower in the face. Either way, I suspect, it performs a useful service.

AN ILLUSTRATED HISTORY OF THE HORROR FILM

The horror film has something for everybody. It is the lowbrow's delight, the middlebrow's camp, the highbrow's trash. It is also, judging from this labor of love, Carlos Clarens's passion, and it is hard to tell a man that his love is a horror—even if the fact that the genre has little to do with art is demonstratable by simple statistics.

When you consider how little of the enormous body of horror fiction has artistic merit—and, further, how few films of any kind are works of art—the likelihood of there being a sufficient number of horror films for serious critical analysis is nil. That does not, of course, preclude an examination of the horror film from the vantage points of the psychologist, sociologist, cultural historian, among others. Yet Mr. Clarens, despite nods in those directions, prefers to second his blurb writer and call himself the one thing irrelevant here: a critic. In point of fact, he is a buff writing for fellow buffs.

Readers have begun to distinguish between film critics and reviewers; it is now time they started differentiating also between critics and buffs. A buff is an addict; and addiction is almost always formed by drugs and gadgets, of both of which the movies partake. They are, moreover, inexpensive, easily available, and go down, like gruel, without effort. Consequently, though other art forms have their devotees, it is only movies that have true-blue buffs.

Although a buff is by definition omnivorous and insatiable, movie buffs, whether or not they pose as critics, do have standards. These are, in fact, quite elaborate, but, like the ritual of other cults, not open to critical scrutiny. To movie buffs, for example, such resourceful craftsmen as Griffith, Stroheim, and Sternberg are divine artists, even though they may hardly if ever have produced a work of art; likewise, horror films are a serious and important cinematic genre. I would say that not one of the sundry "masterpieces" Mr. Clarens discusses is a work of art.

For all that, his *Illustrated History of the Horror Film* is not uninteresting. First of all, it is a well-researched work, including some seventy pages of filmography, and detailed histories of anything—even, say, the beetroot—cannot but dig up some lively incidents. Furthermore, the author has tried to combine his awe-inspiring, horror-filmic erudition with some awareness of cultural and social issues, and he has justly stretched his concept of the horror film to include such related genres as the adventure thriller and the science-fiction film, when these contain elements of dread. And inasmuch as Mr. Clarens gives us a fair number of plot summaries, we do get some idea of changing (and recurring) fashions in *frissons*.

On the debit side, Clarens writes—perhaps from chronic exposure to terror—an extremely shaky English. (There are errors so crude and, on pp. 76–77, a paragraph so thoroughly garbled by the compositor that I should have thought the most nodding editors and copy editors would have woken up screaming. For a style, he has something that should scarcely suffice outside the scenarios of horror films. For instance:

"Taken in their original contexts . . . the movies of Val Lewton stand out as chamber music against the seedy bombast of the claw-and-fang epics of the day. Brief, precisely constructed, and neatly executed, they continue to generate an effective secret music of their own. Lewton, swimming against the current, could not hope to turn the tide; he was a modest, lone virtuoso in a period which thrived on marching songs, maudlin themes, and the worn-out misteriosi of a genre already too tired to pick up its coffin and go." Small wonder that Lewton, playing chamber music single-handed while swimming against the current (whose tide he, apparently, could have changed only by swimming with it—in which case, why bother?) generated a "secret" music, presumably the underwater burbling of a drowning fiddler. And though I know a marching song when I hear one, and can even recognize a maudlin theme, what kind of music, I wonder, is a worn-out misterioso?

Equally secret as his music are Mr. Clarens's criteria: why are some werewolf films "classics" and others "seedy bombast" on "maudlin themes"? How does one determine which vampires are to stay, and which are to pick up their coffins and go? Even more disturbing is Clarens's schizoid attitude toward his material, which he often patronizes at the same time that he reveres it. Thus *Dr. Jekyll and Mr. Hyde* is "essentially a penny dreadful (but a superb one)"; *The Incredible Shrinking Man* "has become a sort of classic in a remarkably short time"; Bela Lugosi's acting is "a kind of corn-ball, demented poetry," and so on.

As in all writing by buffs, the vague, prestige-conferring words "poetic," "lyrical," and "myth" are made free with; a poisoned rose becomes "a truly poetic detail"; Flash Gordon and Buck Rogers contain "a good deal of poetic imagination"; the old horror films revived on TV "now emerged as myths, more powerful than ever before"; Godard's *Alphaville* proves to be "S-P, science poetry."

If only instead of this muck, Mr. Clarens had taken up relevant problems, some of which he purblindly brushes against—such as the difference between horror and terror, the connection between horror films and sexual perversion, the anti-intellectualism of the horror film! Why is science fiction sexless (if it is)? Why does horror go uncensored in one country, only to be slashed in another? Why is Japan, the very country hit by atom bombs, the biggest producer of film holocausts?

Instead, we have to make do with such nuggets as the fact that Lon Chaney's sacrifices for his art included thin wires that made his eyes bulge painfully, and a bridge of bestial teeth he could endure only for very short times; that sales gimmicks for horror films extended to prints in bilious green, "the color of fear," and electrically wired theater "hotseats"; that Hammer Studios used to make three versions of their product: milder for England, more horrible for the United States, most horrible for Japan.

But, as Mr. Clarens characteristically puts it, "real horror is a fragile, glass-boned thing," and it may be that these ponderous pages of text are too heavy a coffin lid for the delicate subject to lift. The illustrations, profuse and telling, may speak louder, or at any rate shriller, than the thousands of words. The truth about the horror film is, or ought to be, that from viewers may spring buffs, from reviewers only rebuffs.

May, 1967

JAMES AGEE

We have all written a great deal about James Agee because we admire him as a critic and love him as a human being. I have no wish to repeat what others and I have said before, but there remains one question that may not have been fully answered by any of us: what made Agee into such an exceptional film critic? It was, I think—besides his humanity, sensitivity, scrupulousness, and literary gifts, which have been duly noted—the multiplicity of his interests. Agee was so good a film critic because he was not only a film critic.

Of the four or five Americans today who may be worthy of the honorable title of film critic (the rest being reviewers, hacks, or both), there are perhaps two or three whose interests, aptitudes, and background can be called diversified. The simple point is that whereas we are all agreed that film is a total art form, incorporating every one of the others, we see nothing wrong about film critics remaining ignorant of all but film. Do we encounter these ladies and gentlemen at art exhibitions, concerts, operas, museums, the theater, the ballet, and such? Do we have evidence even that they have read much of anything?

Agee, however, had a decent education and, more importantly, manifold artistic concerns. The fact that he was a poet and novelist of distinction helped, of course. But so, undoubtedly, did his love of music. The veneration in which he held Mozart, for one, could not but give him a sense of discipline, an awareness of timing, balances, variations within an order—all that makes for controlled creativity which is true genius. It is not "film culture" that the film critic, like the filmmaker, is so desperately in need of today, but just plain culture.

September, 1967

WHAT NOWADAYS PASSES FOR FILM CRITICISM

Film criticism is suddenly booming. Turn your back on the bookstore shelf labeled "Film," and a cluster of new volumes will have crept up on you. Not just books about film, but actual, or at least alleged, film criticism. Upon examination, the critics prove to be either poorly disguised movie buffs like, for example, Raymond Durgnat, with his starry-eyed woolgathering in *Films and Feelings;* or earnest but pedestrian academics like most of the contributors to the anthology *Man and the Movies;* or a cross between the two—academics trying to make like swingers or vice versa—like, most recently, Huss and Silverstein in *The Film Experience.*

One of the latest addenda to the groaning film shelves is a series of monographs with the collective title "Cinema World," published under the auspices of the British Film Institute, or, more precisely, its magazine, *Sight and Sound.* The latter's editors also edit this series. The first three well-printed and amply illustrated volumes to appear are a *Godard*, a *Losey*, and a *Visconti.* If one knew *Sight and Sound*—its modish, cliquish, and, I am afraid, buffish orientation—one's expectations were likely to have been modest. In the event, modesty is hardly enough; what is called for is abandonment of all hope.

Well, not quite. The volume on Joseph Losey has some merit because it is not an attempt at criticism at all, but a long interview with the director of *The Servant* and *Accident.* Tom Milne, the interviewer, manages to set the tone of the series right at the outset of the book. He speaks of Losey's "lucidity" and adds, "Looking 'lucid' up in *Chambers' Dictionary*, I find, as it happens, an enchanting definition of *Accident* itself. . . ." Only in a very effete ambience do dictionary definitions appear "enchanting"; but precious and fey is what "Cinema World" is. Thus Milne describes *Accident* as the "ideal film"; yet, quite aside from what one may think of that movie, no vigorous and responsible critic can ever pronounce a work of art ideal—that would take it out of the realm of human fallibility into some Platonic heaven inhabited chiefly by the exquisite souls from *Sight and Sound.*

Once Losey takes over, however, things become mildly interesting. Thus, speaking of precisely the sort of admirers that write for film magazines, Losey remarks that their "passionate advocacy" became "a handicap . . . the films were valued, and I was valued, for what seemed to me the wrong reasons. Also, as so often happens with the young and the fanatical, there was the stigma . . . of the clique, of the cult. This put a great many serious people off, and I think that this was right."

Losey has many harrowing tales to tell about "the whole battle of getting films done—and it *is* a battle all the time"—everything from executive stupidity to political persecution. And one gets a sense of the sheer hard work of it: "On *Accident* we went through seventeen prints before I would accept one."

The stories about Losey's Hollywood career are truly chilling: how, for example, a glade had to be expensively built in the studio to avoid location shooting, which alone, and cheaply, could have yielded the desired effect. Or, more frightening, how a wretched, rabble-rousing script, *I Married a Communist,* was offered to various directors as a test: if they turned it down, it proved they were Communists. We also learn things about Losey's intentions—that his main theme is an attack on hypocrisy; and about his mode of work—for example, why and how the voice-over sequence in *Accident* was filmed and why, in his opinion, it doesn't quite work.

Losey's own view of himself seems, in fact, a good deal sounder than that of his admirers, and he deplores both his being pigeonholed as a specialist in violence and the absurd zeal with which symbols are read into everything he does. Unfortunately, the interviewer is no good at following points through to their ultimate clarification, so that when Losey comes out with the suggestive statement that film is both the most abstract and the most realistic art form, no elaboration and elucidation follows.

Geoffrey Nowell-Smith's *Visconti* is an almost totally useless book. It is shot through with sophomoric structuralist and *auteur*-theory notions that produce swaggering phrases but shed no light. For example, we are told that conventional notions like "truth to reality" or "profundity of insight" are irrelevant to a master like Visconti, and that the "criteria can only be the structures revealed in each film and the way these can be related to each other in the total context of the author's work." In other words, Visconti is above standards other than those set by himself; "external criteria," as Nowell-Smith tells us, are invalid, and dismal films like *White Nights* and *Sandra* are to be judged according to how they fit into the Visconti canon, the "total context" of Visconti's work. They fit only too well, alas.

But what can we expect from a critic whose thinking and expression are as fuzzy as Nowell-Smith's? Concerning *White Nights,* we read: "Natural locations are entirely eliminated, and the whole film was shot on a carefully constructed studio set, whose only concession to realism was that it is modelled on Livorno and not St. Petersburg." Since the film is based on Dostoevsky's famous novella, I can't imagine why *not* modeling the set on St. Petersburg should be a concession to realism.

Moreover, the sets for the film, with the possible exception of some rather factitious fog, were entirely naturalistic, so, again, the statement makes no sense. Further, the author says that "the characters emerge from the background and play out their roles against it," which makes the film "theatrical." The characters may indeed emerge from the fog, but that is at least as cinematic as it is theatrical; and what can *any* characters in *any* film play out their roles against except the background?

Because he knows that Visconti has staged many operas, Nowell-Smith makes the equally inept claim that a film like *La terra trema* is "operatic." He explains: "The action unfolds slowly, in a series of tableaux, with its choruses, solos and duets." What this really means is that the film is static and lumbering: obviously there must be tableaus, i.e., images, in any film, just as there will be group scenes (choruses) and sequences involving one or two persons (solos and duets). No more convincingly, Nowell-Smith interprets the "amazingly crude" effects, "the obtrusive camera work," and the "heavy chiaroscuro" in *Sandra* as being "Baroque," and proceeds to one skimpy and simplistic paragraph about mannerist painting. But he does not demonstrate the supposed analogy, or explain why if something is crude, obtrusive, and heavy a reference to baroque should exculpate it.

But Nowell-Smith is not even in control of the language: there is frequent confusion of tenses, moods, and numbers. He is guilty of barbarisms such as "irreal," and he will start a sentence with "But nor." This is shocking from the Director of Italian Studies at Sheffield University, and one can hope only that his Italian is better than his English. Certainly his French won't do: *carosse* is emasculated into the feminine gender. Even Italian facts get garbled: Cesare Pavese is said to have written his thesis on Melville, though he actually wrote it on Whitman.

The key to Visconti's sensibility—particularly apparent in *Senso* and *The Leopard*—is not "theatrical," "operatic," or "baroque," but homosexual froufrou which may, to some extent, subsume the other three. But Nowell-Smith carefully ignores the homosexual subplot of *Rocco and His Brothers,* and invents lame sophistries to justify the casting of the delicate Alain Delon as the peasant Rocco. In a similarly misguided attempt to whitewash his subject, the author never tells us that the reason for *Ossessione*'s not being shown abroad is that Visconti pirated the James Cain novel on which it is based. It should be no surprise, then, that the grand conclusion to which this book huffs and puffs is that Visconti's films "reveal the world in a particular guise . . . how it can be perceived and experienced by a particular individual at a particular time." That, apparently, makes them "works of art." We have all heard of *sancta simplicitas;* this would seem to be its profane counterpart.

Godard by Richard Roud, film critic of *The Guardian* and director of the London and New York Film Festivals (and thus a major arbiter of international film taste), is a book so frilly, pretentious, ill-written, and foolish that I can see no reason for taking up any more of our time with it. At best, one can laugh at it as at a C-grade Hollywood horror movie laying claims to metaphysical significance; if you light upon it at a bookstore, open it at random and get a few chuckles. And an idea of what, nowadays, passes for film criticism.

May, 1968

LET US NOW PRAISE DWIGHT MACDONALD

True film critics in Amerca can be numbered on the fingers of one hand. That is why Dwight Macdonald's decision, at the end of 1966, to stop writing film criticism was as great a loss as that of a finger— to a one-handed man.

Macdonald's chief virtues as a film critic were, are (I cannot speak of him in the past) three. First, the breadth of his vision: his film writings are in glorious Critic-Scope. Unlike the critic of fine arts, dance, or music who can, because of the relative abstraction of his subject, function in solipsistic absorption with the technique of his art (though he, too, would benefit from widening his horizon), the film critic must be immersed in every known discipline as well as in that great indiscipline which is life. For film is an eclectic, ecumenical art, made up of just about everything and eager to make just about everything of itself. To know the other arts, sciences, social sciences, technology, languages, etc. is all grist for the film critic's mill—as it was, consciously or unconsciously, for the filmmaker's. Macdonald is an educated man, interested in almost all things and knowledgeable about many; especially handy is his proficiency in literature, politics and mass culture. It is impossible to read a page of his without feeling in the presence of a man who possesses varied information and disposes of it with a liberality untainted by ostentation.

Which brings me to the second virtue: his style, or, perhaps more properly, his tone. For Macdonald does not have what is usually thought of as style: his is not a particularly cadenced prose, nor is it folksy, jeweled, hieratic, or whatever else is commonly labeled "style." Rather, it is sensibly, easefully, firmly, and sometimes devastatingly, straightforward. This does not mean that it is (though it can be) chatty; it is natural. Of the moral ambivalence in the film *Morgan!,* he writes: "But we give in too easily to the 'buts,' there are always 'buts' around, at some point one must draw a line and say but me no buts, this is this and that is that." The beauty of the sentence is in all those casual commas, all that informal parataxis that miraculously doesn't turn choppy, the hardheaded speed of a movement that hypotaxis would merely have slowed down and blunted. There is a leanness and sprightliness in this writing at least as hard to achieve as the most formal elegance.

Above all, there is a tone. The tone of a civilized man talking to his peers, who sometimes are a bit obdurate in their misapprehensions but usually are right up there with him, capable of understanding if only they are addressed with clarity, civility, and common sense. There is no haranguing, and certainly no hectoring; when Macdonald says of James Agee "that he accomplished as much as he did despite his heroic efforts to fail by all twentieth-century-American standards of success is evidence of his genius," some very big statements are made in the most concise and convivial manner. Of Hugh Griffith as Squire Western in *Tom Jones,* Macdonald says: "It is hard to think of a role for which Mr. Griffith would not be Too Much, with his piercing glare, his insanely dominant nose, his beetling brows and cavernous mouth, his overripe Welsh diction. Perhaps God." The point is made with worldly self-assurance, wit but not bitchiness, a decent amount of poetic-painterliness (note the picturesque interplay of "beetling" and "cavernous") but stopping short of "fine writing," a sternness tempered by good humor.

That leads us to Macdonald's third major virtue, his sense of humor. It is impossible to read something so precarious as film criticism— which is obliged to have truck with movies that nobody in his right mind would want to see—unless it is informed by wit. This is where Macdonald triumphs. Though his wit can be as sharp as anyone's (in *Eclipse* "we have Alain Delon making a decorative hole in the movie"; "Joseph Losey [is] a versatile director who commands a wide range of styles for wrecking a movie"), he excels at humor, jollity, making his point with good clean fun. If the difference between wit and humor is that between a blade that cuts to the quick and a boot to the rear that sends the recipient flying, Macdonald, adept in both, prefers the latter, as in the following: "the good bad movie is a lively authentic and, in its modest way, quite respectable product Hollywood used to make in the thirties and forties before it succumbed to the ravages of Culture, like a primitive tribe coming into contact with civilization and exchanging its simple folkways for Mother Hubbards, pidgin English and syphilis."

The publication of *Dwight Macdonald on Movies* (Prentice-Hall, $9.95), a collection of film criticism spanning four decades, is almost a compensation for the fact that Macdonald gave up his monthly *Esquire* film column in 1966, explaining, "one finds that as the years go by one has already reviewed, under another title, almost every new film one sees." Several objections can be raised against this compilation. The inclusion of a lengthy history of the Russian film in the thirties, though skillful and cogent, is no longer justified by consuming interest, particularly since the survey falls midway between useful information and detailed scholarship. Some early material, as well as some later ephemera, fugitive to the point of flightiness, could have done without being reprinted. Occasionally but quite significantly Macdonald has changed his mind on a film or director; he is always content to indicate this in a footnote, although a goodly postscript or even a new essay would have been more to the purpose. And removing the pieces from chronological order and rearranging them according to topics (usually films from the same country or by the same filmmaker) brings certain repetitions or inconsistencies, which might have passed unnoticed, to the fore.

Indeed there are some words and tropes that Macdonald overworks. "Soggy," "raffish," and "jaunty" pop up a little too often; a scene from *Juliet of the Spirits*, the entire *8½*, Antonioni *in toto*—all manage to remind him of Veronese. "When a modern critic hears the word 'beauty,' he releases the safety catch on his fountain pen," Macdonald cracks, alluding to the infamous Nazi remark; and again: "when a good bureaucrat hears [the words 'creative cinema'] he reaches for his fountain pen." Too much of a good thing. Purists will deplore Macdonald's occasional linguistic and grammatical lapses: "whom she has reason to believe has shacked up," the definition of "centripetal" as "flying out from the center," "irreality," "imbecilic," "thusly," and a few others; they might also regret his misspellings of foreign names (Afinogeniev for Afinogenov, Reifenstahl for Riefenstahl, Michael McLaimmor for Micheál MacLiammóir) and his cavalier indifference to French accent marks. In these matters the poor copyediting and proofreading of his publisher, Prentice-Hall, are an added burden.

But these are minor nuisances—no worse than the toll stations on a scenic highway. And what vistas Macdonald opens before us! His book is not only distinguished film criticism, it is also social criticism and sociology of a high order, and is superb as a nosography of the American mass mentality. Moreover, large parts of it can be read purely as humorous writing of an unusually sustained quality: the section on Biblical spectaculars, for instance (*Ben Hur:* "Watching it was like waiting at a railroad crossing while an interminable freight train lumbers past, often stopping completely for a while"; *King of Kings:* "The responsibility for the crucifixion is again displaced from the Jews to the Romans, who are again made the fall goys"), deserves a place in any Anthology of American Humor. Yet the most valuable contribution may be to esthetics, and not just film esthetics but the universal esthetics of art.

There are insights of the foremost importance into, among other things, the way in which realism carried to extremes becomes itself a form of stylization; the fallacy of making films out of "lots of Big Moments, but no small ones"; the error of having movie characters analyzing their situations rather than exemplifying them; the dangers of overstressing "personal expression" in art at the expense of "impersonal fabrication"; and so on. Here is part of one such insight, which applies equally to fiction, drama, and film: "It has often been observed that women don't enjoy pornography because their eroticism is more emotional and less sensual than men's, but I haven't seen it noted that precisely because of this difference the woman's novel performs for female readers the same humble task of erotic titillation that pornography does for men. If the pornographic hero is a sexual athlete, the heroine of the woman's novel is an athlete of the emotions whose feats of feeling are described in lubricious detail, while the males are reduced to objects of sentimental lust no more individualized as human beings than are the stripped beauties, of whom one learns nothing beyond their anatomy, who satisfy the physical lusts of the males in pornographic fiction. Because for some reason sentimental orgies are not considered immoral in our culture, the woman's novel has always circulated freely, without interference from the police, though it could be argued that its debauchery of sentiment is more damaging to morality than are the pornographer's boldest fantasies." And Macdonald proceeds to argue it, brilliantly, concerning *The Pumpkin Eater.*

There are other good things about *Dwight Macdonald on Movies.* The comments on actors, though sometimes (as on Brando and Loren) too harsh, are often telling: Jean-Pierre Cassel's "insectlike precision," Paul Newman's "one expression an agonized grimace as of wood trying to smile," Audrey Hepburn as "not an actress" but "a model, with her stiff meager body and her blank face full of Good Bone

Structure." (That "full of" is priceless.) He is equally good at dealing with other film critics, often remarkably generously, and his reviews of books and articles by Richard Schickel, Andrew Sarris, Donald Richie, John Russell Taylor, and, especially, Pauline Kael constitute a brief practical course in film criticism. Sometimes—though surprisingly rarely—I find myself disagreeing with Macdonald's judgments; surely he overrates films like *8½, Last Year at Marienbad, The Gunfighter, Trouble in Paradise, Birth of a Nation,* while underrating *I Vitelloni, Eclipse, Sundays and Cybèle,* and some of Bergman's pictures. But this is unimportant and, at any rate, not subject to objective proof. What is of paramount importance, however, is his austere championing of art in the teeth of various forms of encroachment: commercialism, kitsch, camp, film buffery, and faddism.

And something else. Consider this passage from his "Forenotes" in which he evaluates his career as a film critic: "I can't even claim credit for Bosley Crowther's retirement as the *Times* movie critic. He was pretty old—sixty-two, my age." The second sentence, with its sudden switch from wit to seriousness, its terse unpathetic pathos, its dying fall, is sheer art. That is what the best criticism must be; what Macdonald's criticism so frequently is.

October, 1969

Index